Yusei Matsui

Part of my purpose in creating this series was to repay my debt to *Jump* for presenting me to the world. Some big series had just finished in *Jump*, so I thought it would be great if I provided more motivation for people to buy *Jump*.

Intent is one thing, but I tend to disregard profits and was prepared to be in the red if the series ended early. Luckily, that didn't happen, so I'm truly thankful.

Above all, I'm happy that there's no need to worry, because series by young authors are hitting it big in *Jump* one after another.

Yusei Matsui was born on the last day of January in Saitama Prefecture, Japan. He has been drawing manga since elementary school. Some of his favorite manga series are *Bobobo-bo Bo-bobo*, *JoJo's Bizarre Adventure*, and *Ultimate Muscle*. Matsui learned his trade working as an assistant to manga artist Yoshio Sawai, creator of *Bobobo-bo Bo-bobo*. In 2005, Matsui debuted his original manga *Neuro: Supernatural Detective* in *Weekly Shonen Jump*. In 2007, *Neuro* was adapted into an anime. His next series, *Assassination Classroom*, captured imaginations worldwide and was adapted to anime, video games, and film. In 2021, *The Elusive Samurai* began serialization in *Weekly Shonen Jump*.

THE ELUSIVE SAMURAI
VOLUME 3
SHONEN JUMP Edition

Story and Art by
Yusei Matsui

Translation & English Adaptation **John Werry**

Touch-Up Art & Lettering **John Hunt**

Designer **Jimmy Presler**

Editor **Mike Montesa**

NIGEJOZU NO WAKAGIMI © 2021 by Yusei Matsui
All rights reserved.
First published in Japan in 2021 by SHUEISHA Inc., Tokyo.
English translation rights arranged by SHUEISHA Inc.

The stories, characters, and incidents mentioned
in this publication are entirely fictional.

No portion of this book may be reproduced or transmitted in
any form or by any means without written permission from the
copyright holders.

Printed in Canada

Published by VIZ Media, LLC
P.O. Box 77010
San Francisco, CA 94107

10 9 8 7 6 5 4 3 2 1
First printing, November 2022

PARENTAL ADVISORY
THE ELUSIVE SAMURAI is rated T for Teen and is
recommended for ages 13 and up. This volume
contains realistic and fantasy violence.

viz.com

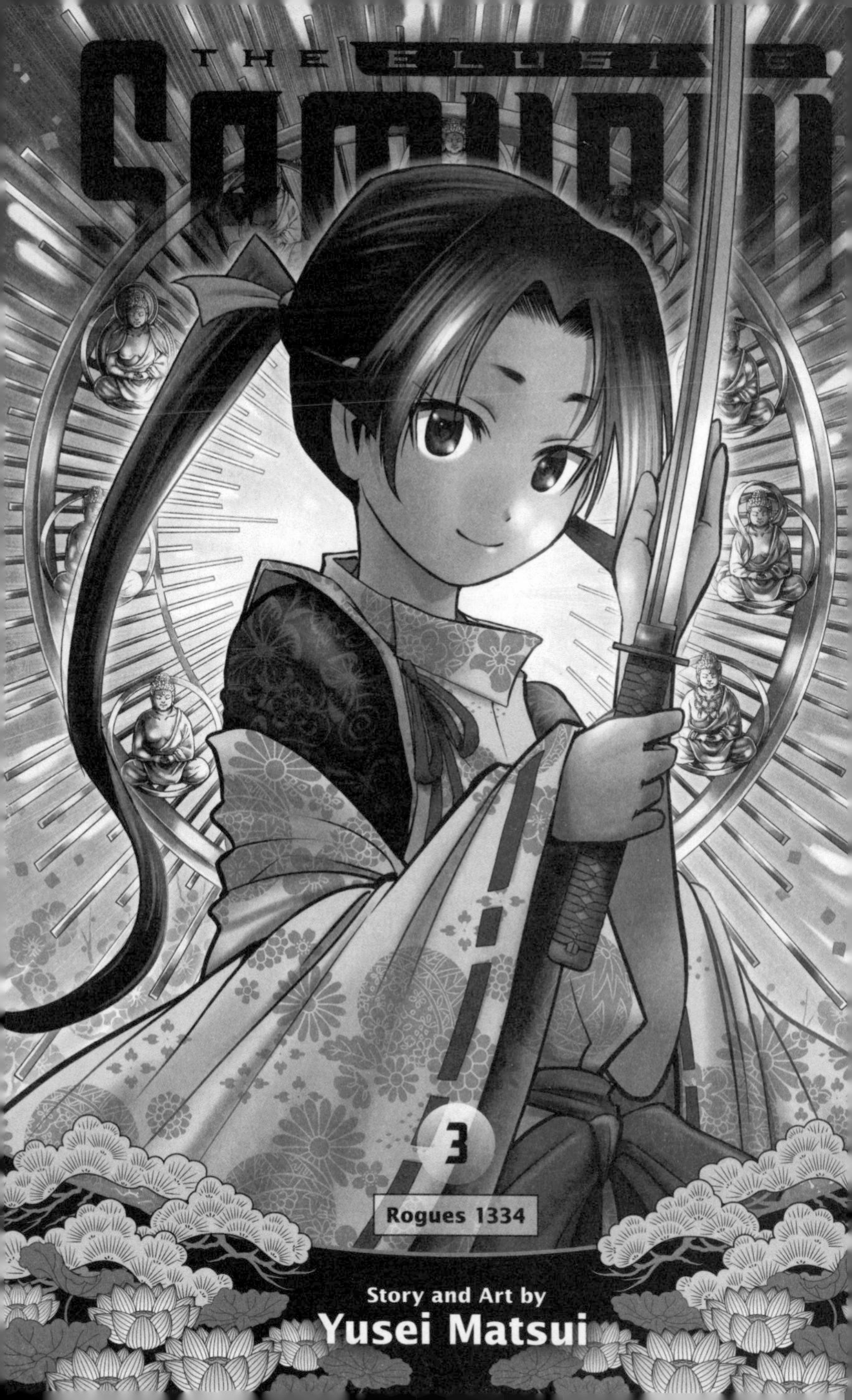
THE ELUSIVE
SAMURAI
3
Rogues 1334
Story and Art by
Yusei Matsui

CHARACTERS

THE ELUSIVE WARRIORS

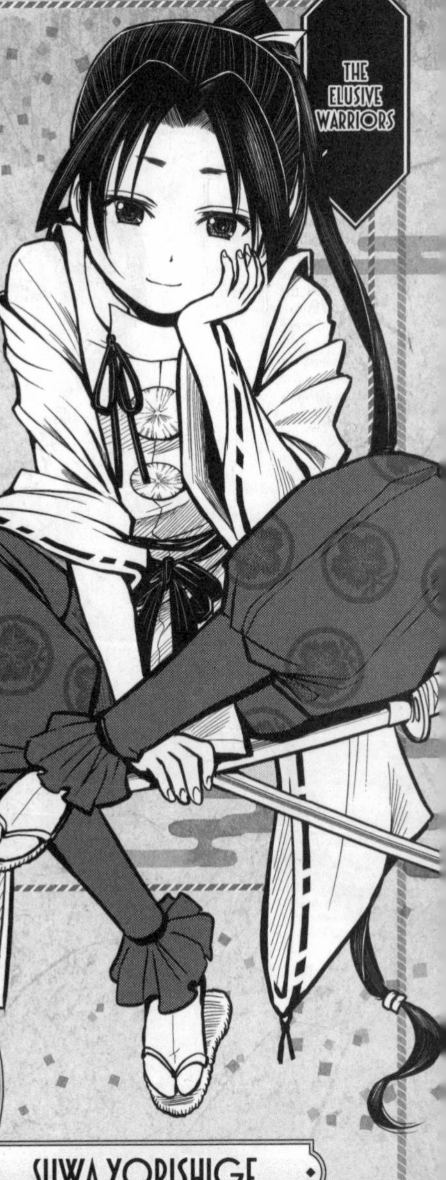

HOJO TOKIYUKI

A boy in the Hojo clan who expected to inherit the rule of the Kamakura shogunate. He excels at fleeing and is now gathering strength at Suwa Grand Shrine so he can use that skill in his efforts to reclaim the throne.

LOYAL RETAINERS

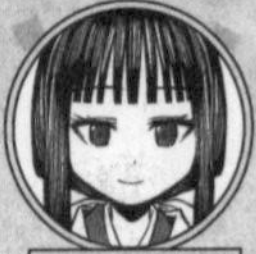

SHIZUKU

A dependable girl who handles affairs throughout the household.

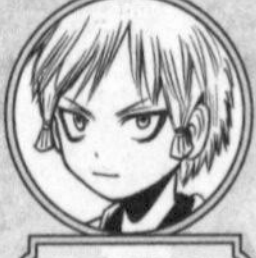

KOJIRO

A boy whose swordsmanship is outstanding for his age.

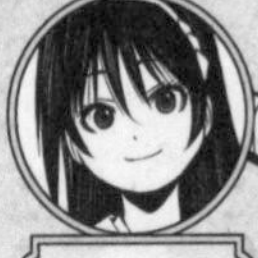

AYAKO

A cheerful and pleasant girl with incredible physical strength.

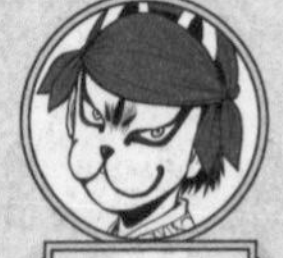

KAZAMA GENBA

A boy skilled at deception and covert activities. He's obsessed with money and tends to be crude.

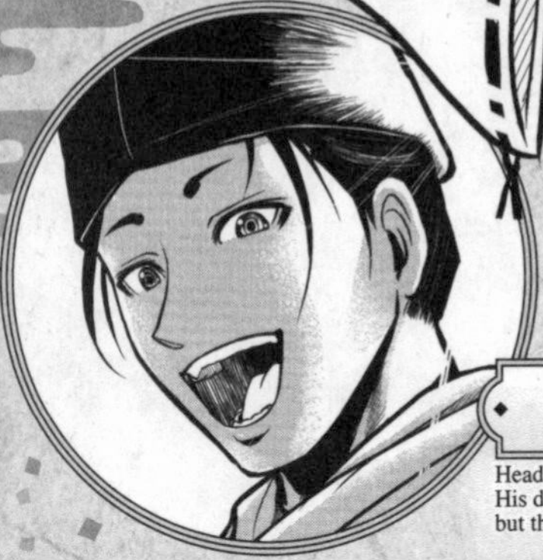

SUWA YORISHIGE

Head of Suwa Grand Shrine in Shinano Province. His divine power allows him to see the future, but the future he sees is...blurry?

THE STO[redacted]

Hojo Tokiyuki was heir to the Kamakura shogunate, but due to Ashikaga Takauji's sudden rebellion, Tokiyuki lost his home. Suwa Yorishige is sheltering him in Shinano, but Ogasawara Sadamune is using the authority of the emperor in an attempt to steal Suwa's territory. Then Tokiyuki and Genba sneak into Sadamune's compound and thwart his plans. A few months later, the Elusive Warriors go on a reconnaissance mission near the northern border of Suwa, where they confront a youth wielding two blades...

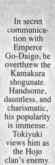

ASHIKAGA TAKAUJI

In secret communication with Emperor Go-Daigo, he overthrew the Kamakura shogunate. Handsome, dauntless, and charismatic, his popularity is immense. Tokiyuki views him as the Hojo clan's enemy.

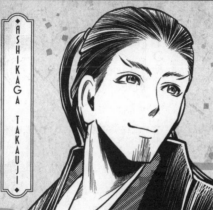

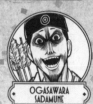

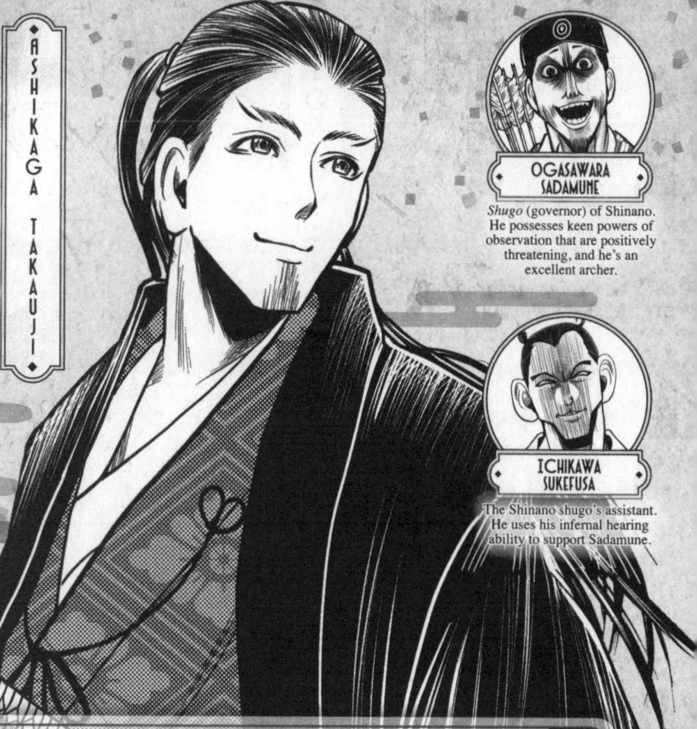

OGASAWARA SADAMUNE

Shugo (governor) of Shinano. He possesses keen powers of observation that are positively threatening, and he's an excellent archer.

ICHIKAWA SUKEFUSA

The Shinano shugo's assistant. He uses his infernal hearing ability to support Sadamune.

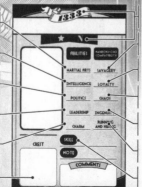

GUIDE TO STATS

1333
ABILITIES
NANBOKU-CHO COMPATIBILITY
MARTIAL ARTS
SAVAGERY
INTELLIGENCE
LOYALTY
POLITICS
CHAOS
LEADERSHIP
INGENUITY
CHARM
RUNNING AND HIDING
CREST
SKILL
NOTE
COMMENTS

- Individual combat strength, including swordsmanship, archery, and horsemanship
- Overall ability, including knowledge, quick thinking, and strategy
- Mastery of internal affairs, scheming, and power struggles
- Ability to coordinate political entities and allied military forces
- Ability to attract others
- Family crest, clothing pattern, etc.
- Character's importance in that year
- Ability to fight and survive in violent times
- Attribute providing strength when needed
- Ability to adapt to changing circumstances
- Inventiveness and will to create a new world
- Adaptability to a time when much happens in secret
- Characteristic skill

THE ELUSIVE SAMURAI

3

CONTENTS

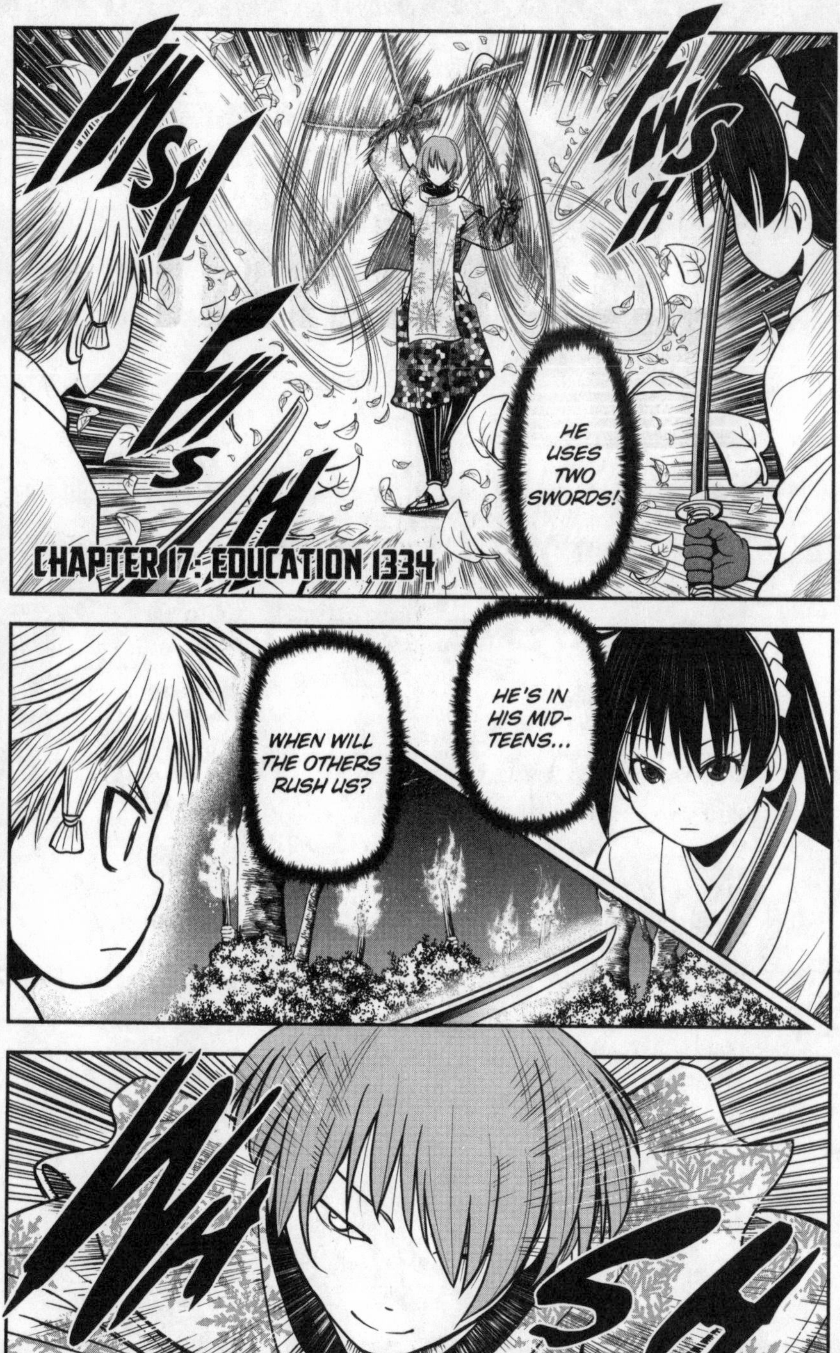
FWSH
FWSH
FWSH
HE USES TWO SWORDS!
CHAPTER 17: EDUCATION 1334
HE'S IN HIS MID-TEENS...
WHEN WILL THE OTHERS RUSH US?
WHSH

CHAPTER 17: EDUCATION 1334

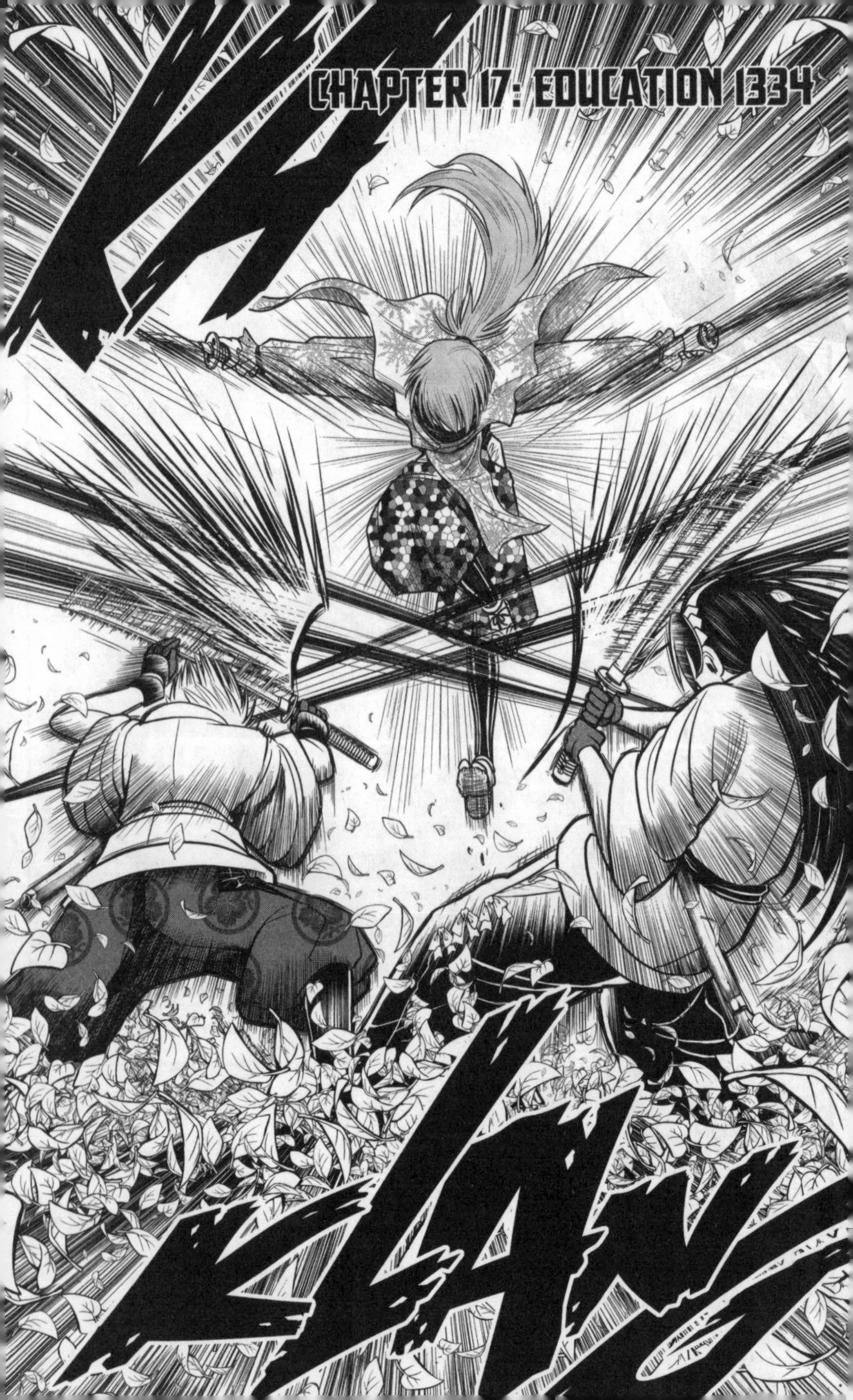

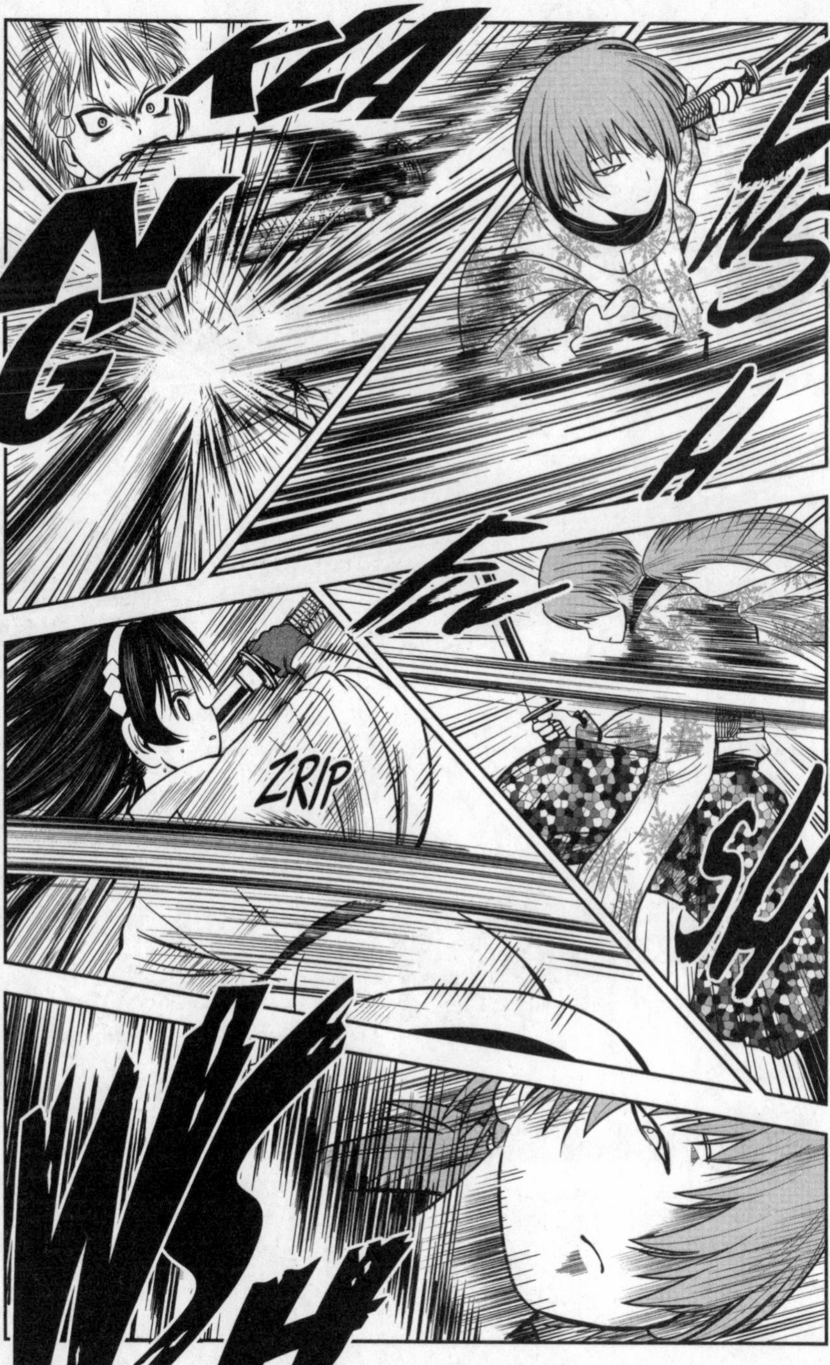
KZANG
ZRIP

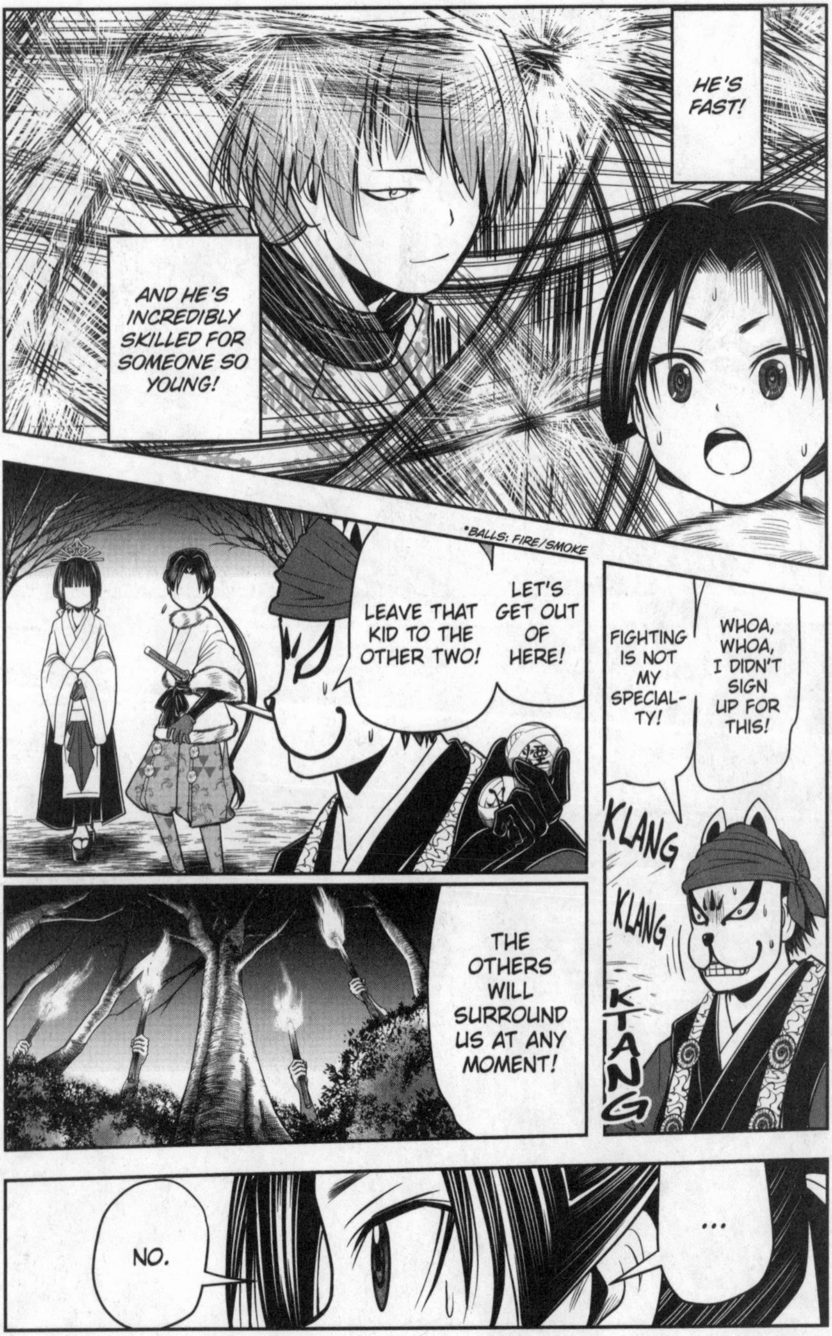
HE'S FAST!
AND HE'S INCREDIBLY SKILLED FOR SOMEONE SO YOUNG!
WHOA, WHOA, I DIDN'T SIGN UP FOR THIS!
FIGHTING IS NOT MY SPECIAL-TY!
KLANG
KLANG
KTANG
*BALLS: FIRE/SMOKE
LET'S GET OUT OF HERE!
LEAVE THAT KID TO THE OTHER TWO!
THE OTHERS WILL SURROUND US AT ANY MOMENT!
...
NO.

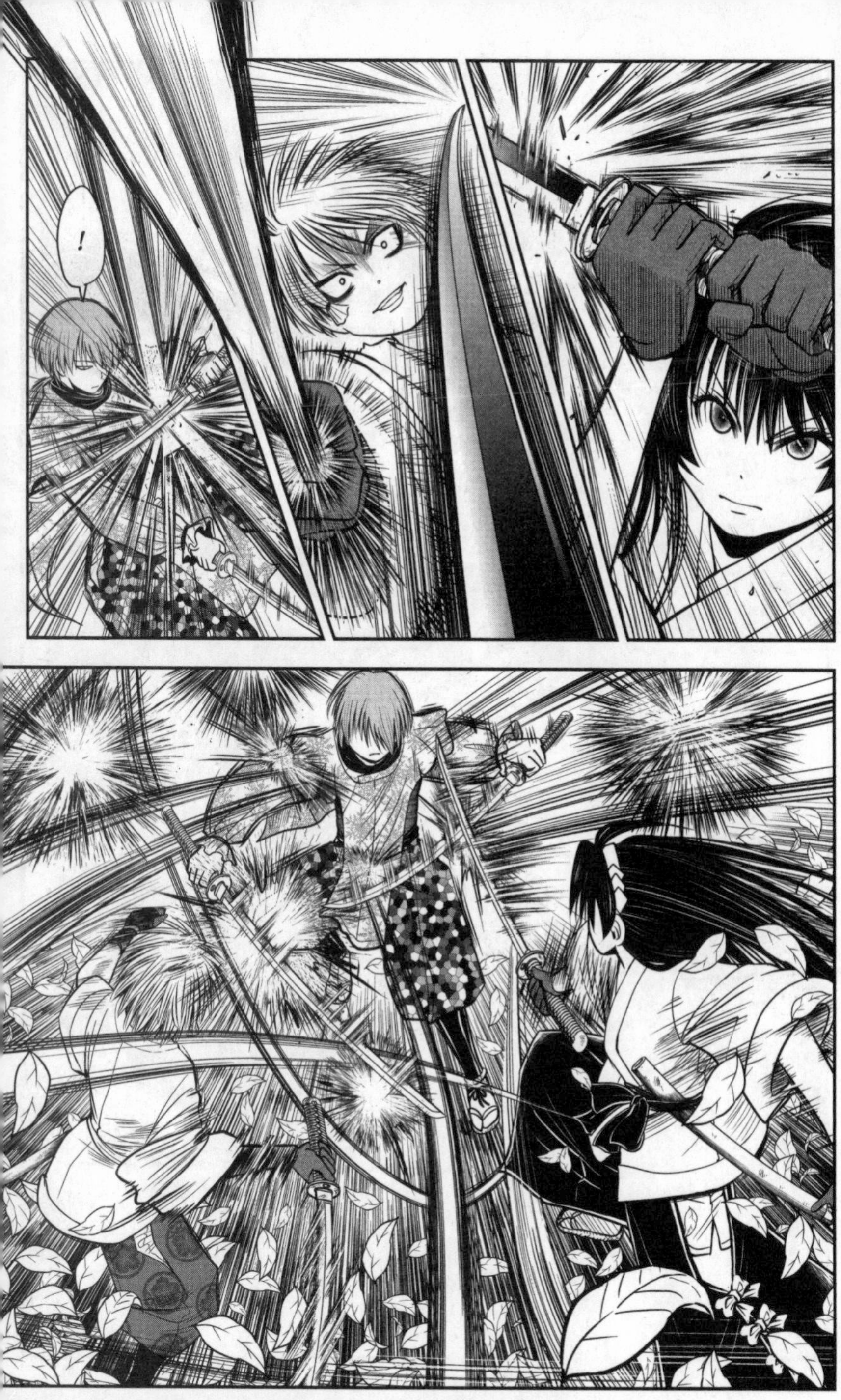
!

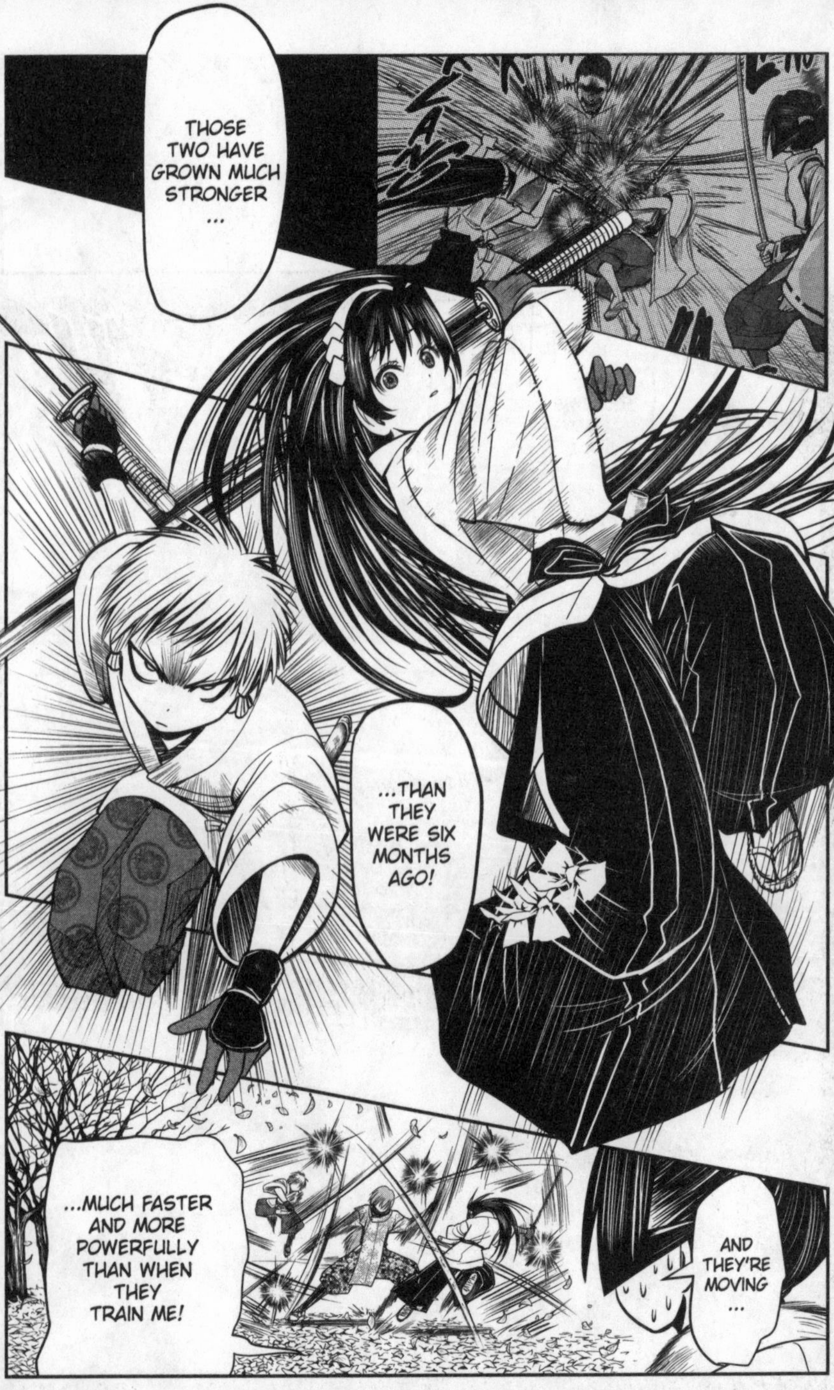
THOSE TWO HAVE GROWN MUCH STRONGER ...
...THAN THEY WERE SIX MONTHS AGO!
AND THEY'RE MOVING ...
...MUCH FASTER AND MORE POWERFULLY THAN WHEN THEY TRAIN ME!

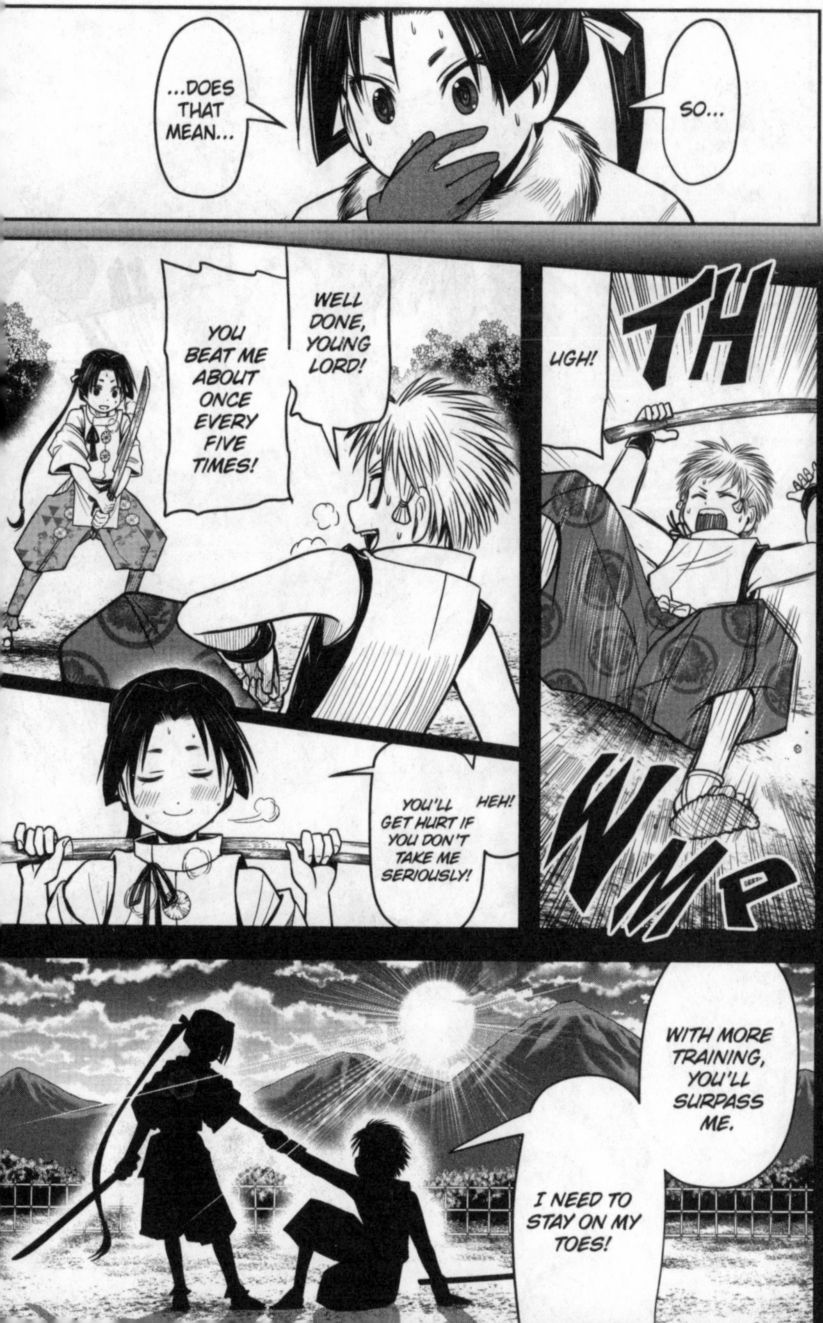
SO...
...DOES THAT MEAN...
TH
UGH!
WMP
WELL DONE, YOUNG LORD!
YOU BEAT ME ABOUT ONCE EVERY FIVE TIMES!
HEH!
YOU'LL GET HURT IF YOU DON'T TAKE ME SERIOUSLY!
WITH MORE TRAINING, YOU'LL SURPASS ME.
I NEED TO STAY ON MY TOES!

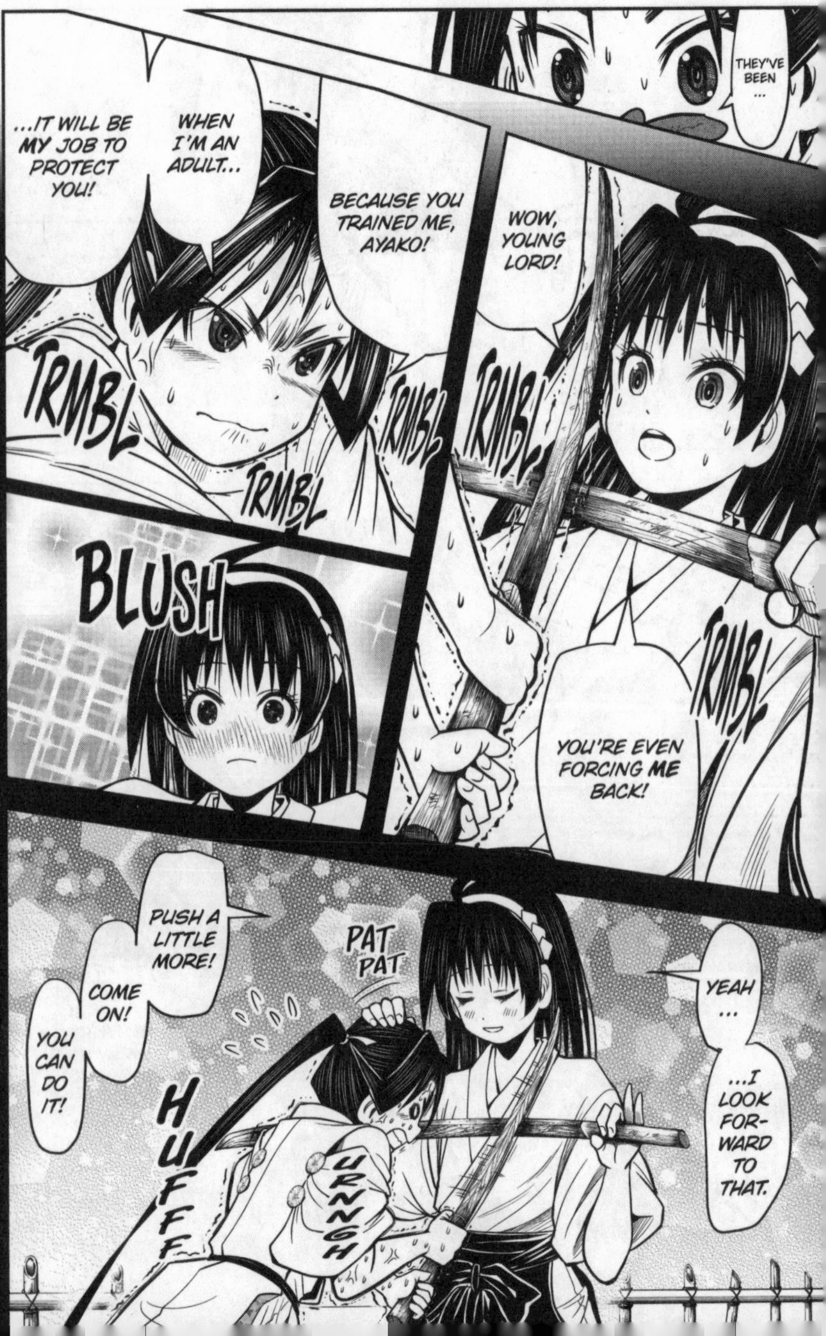
THEY'VE BEEN ...
WOW, YOUNG LORD!
TRMBL
TRMBL
YOU'RE EVEN FORCING ME BACK!
BECAUSE YOU TRAINED ME, AYAKO!
WHEN I'M AN ADULT...
...IT WILL BE MY JOB TO PROTECT YOU!
TRMBL
TRMBL
TRMBL
BLUSH
YEAH ...
...I LOOK FOR-WARD TO THAT.
PAT PAT
PUSH A LITTLE MORE!
COME ON!
YOU CAN DO IT!
URNNGH
HUFFF

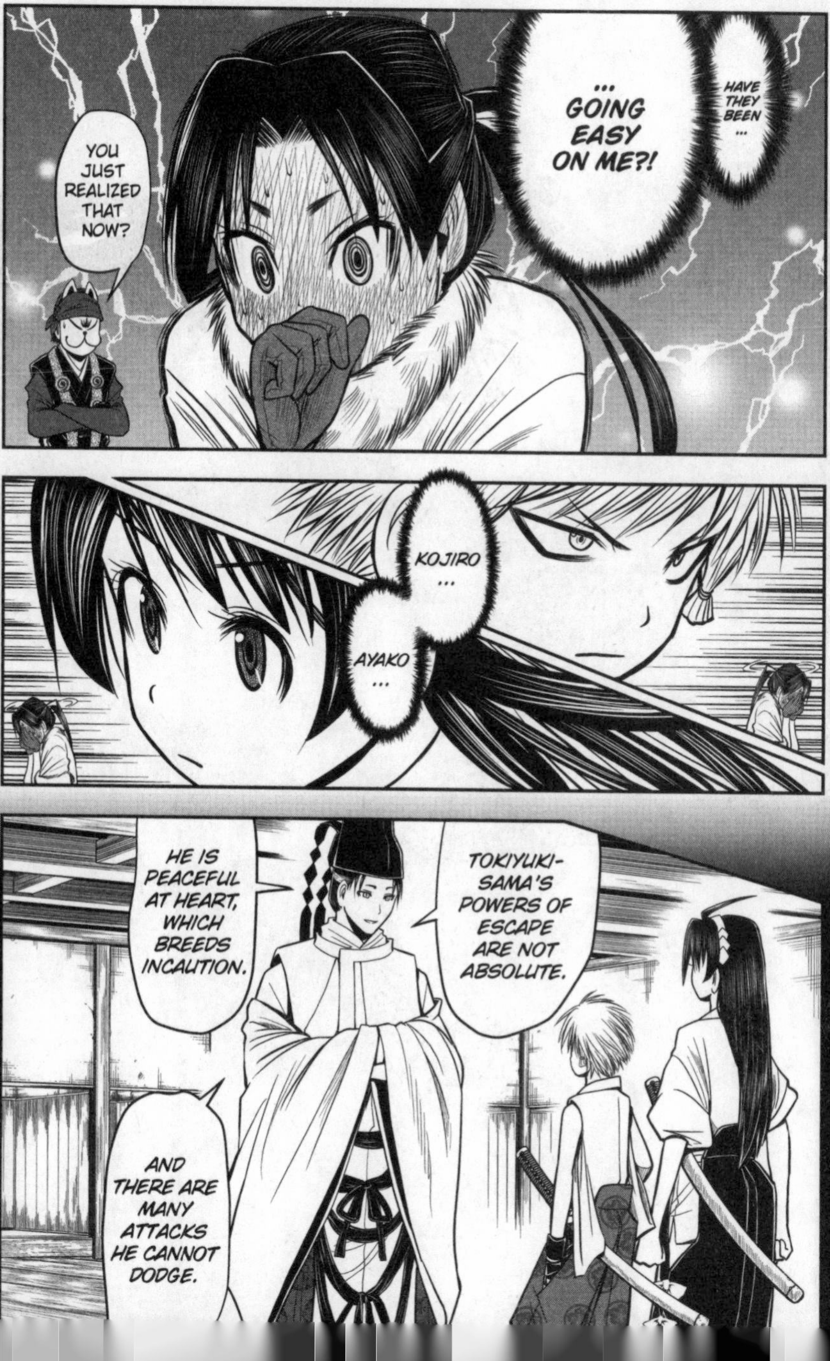
HAVE THEY BEEN ...
... GOING EASY ON ME?!
YOU JUST REALIZED THAT NOW?
KOJIRO ...
AYAKO ...
TOKIYUKI-SAMA'S POWERS OF ESCAPE ARE NOT ABSOLUTE.
HE IS PEACEFUL AT HEART, WHICH BREEDS INCAUTION.
AND THERE ARE MANY ATTACKS HE CANNOT DODGE.

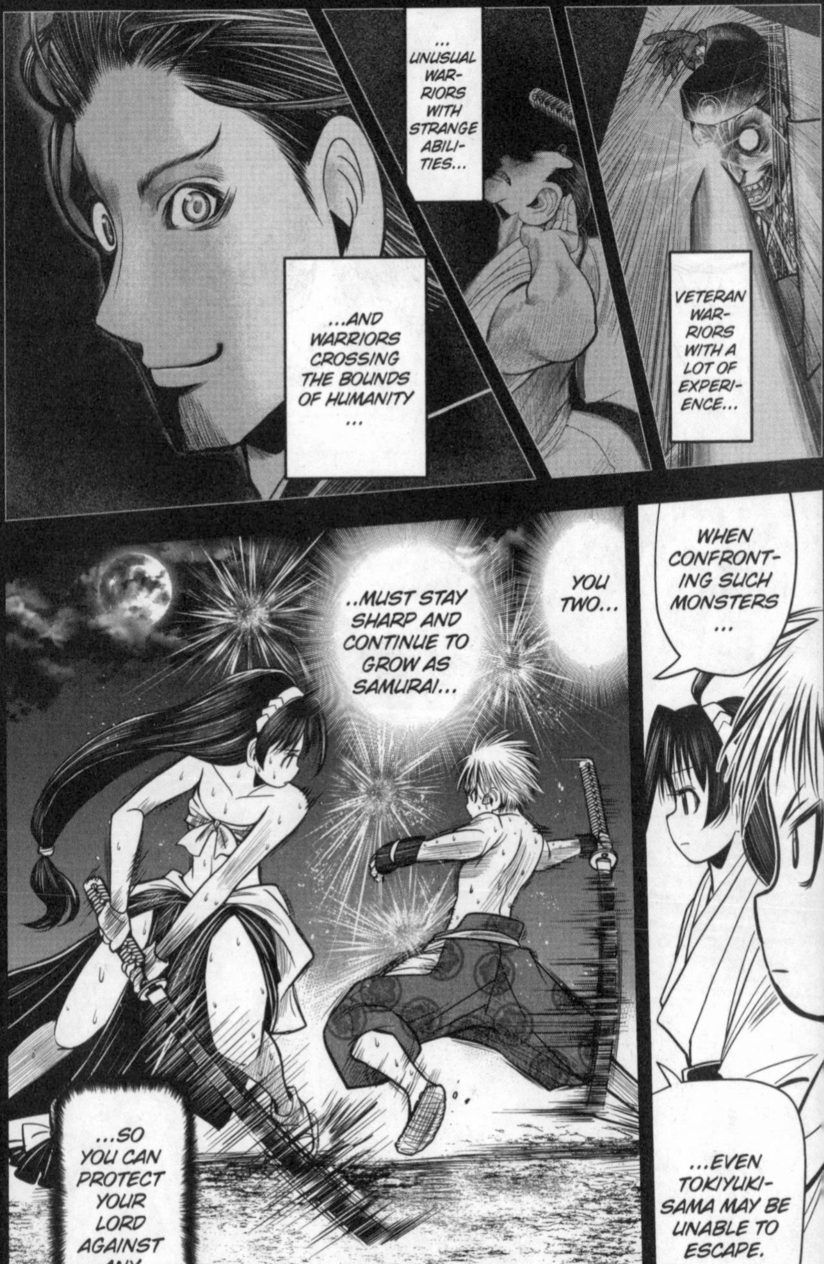
VETERAN WARRIORS WITH A LOT OF EXPERIENCE...
...UNUSUAL WARRIORS WITH STRANGE ABILITIES...
...AND WARRIORS CROSSING THE BOUNDS OF HUMANITY...
WHEN CONFRONTING SUCH MONSTERS...
...EVEN TOKIYUKI-SAMA MAY BE UNABLE TO ESCAPE.
YOU TWO...
..MUST STAY SHARP AND CONTINUE TO GROW AS SAMURAI...
...SO YOU CAN PROTECT YOUR LORD AGAINST ANY ENEMY.

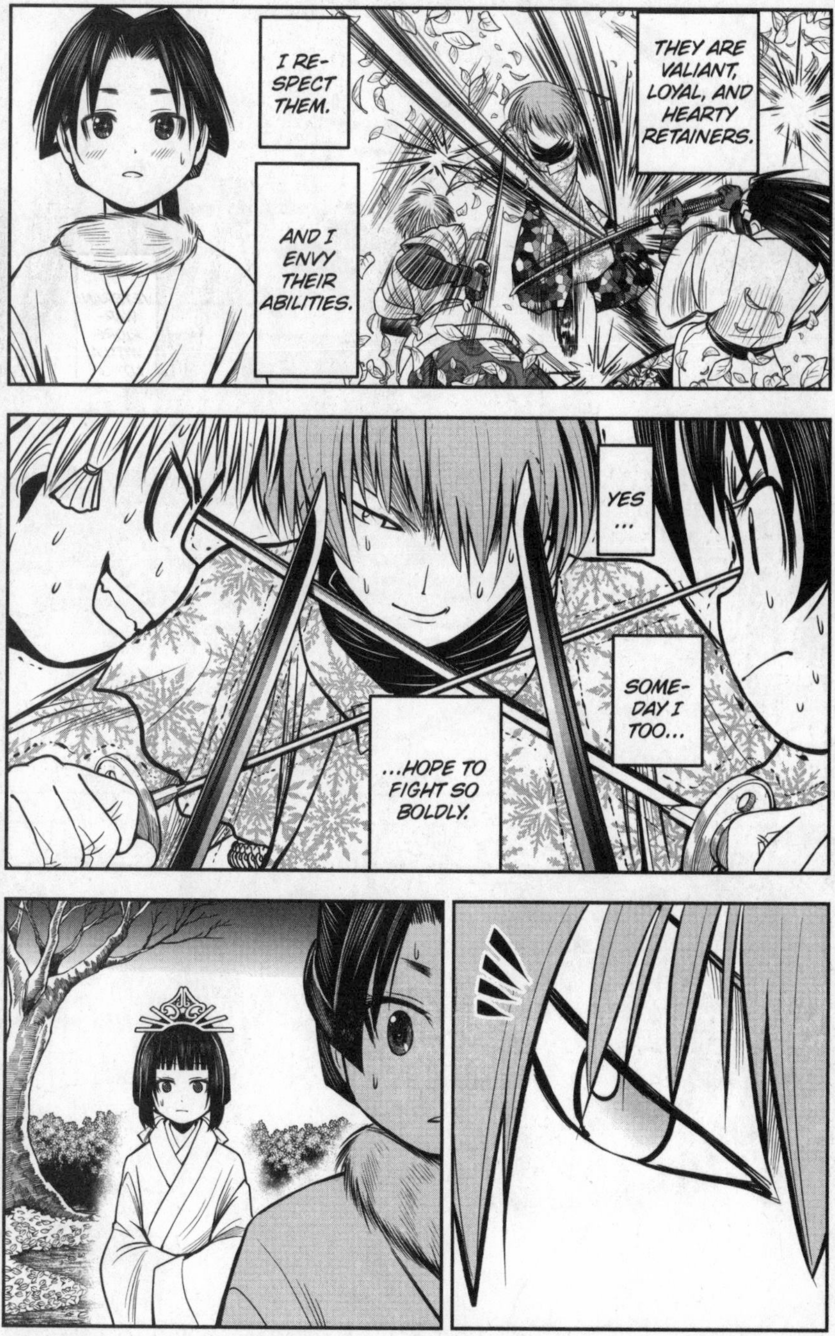
THEY ARE VALIANT, LOYAL, AND HEARTY RETAINERS.
I RE-SPECT THEM.
AND I ENVY THEIR ABILITIES.
YES...
SOME-DAY I TOO...
...HOPE TO FIGHT SO BOLDLY.

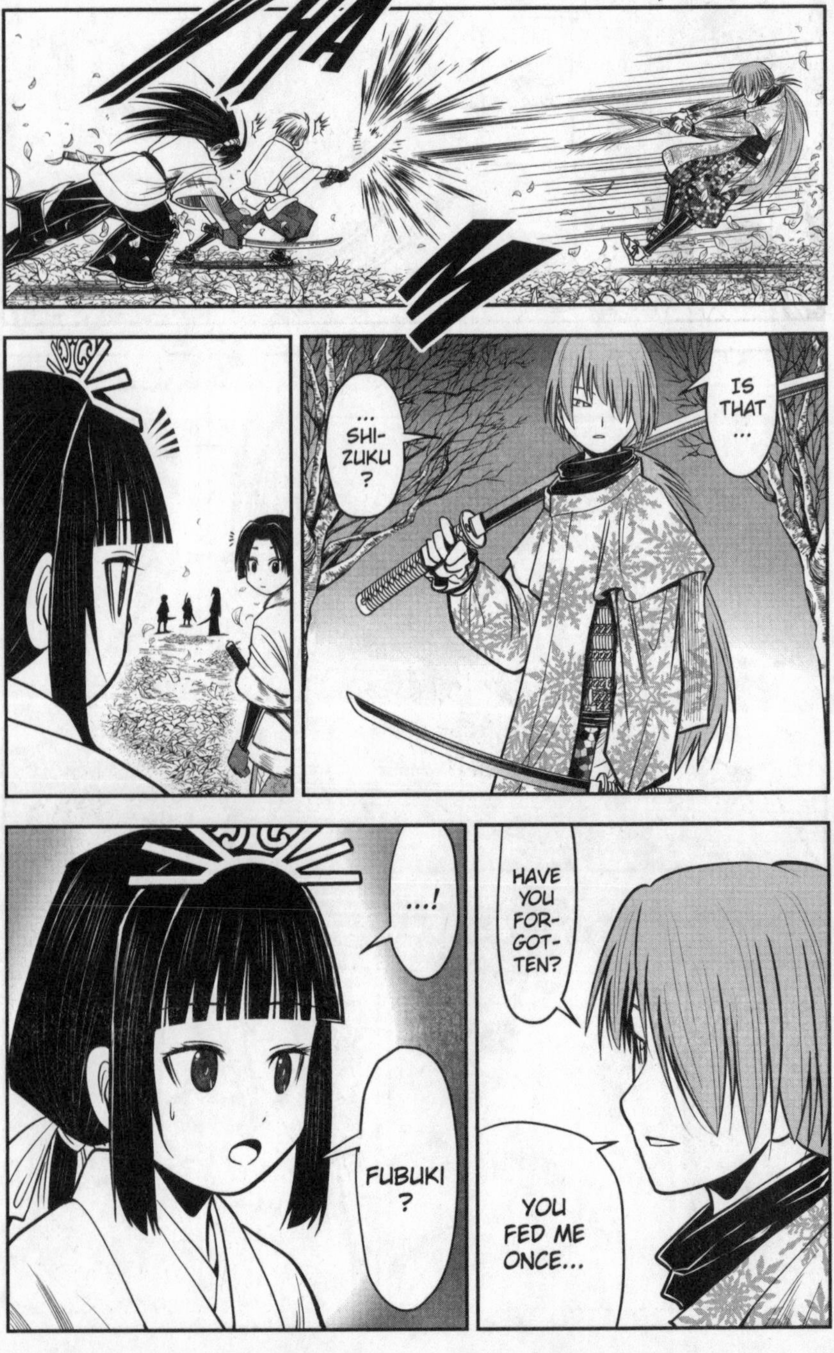
WHA
M
IS THAT ...
... SHI-ZUKU?
HAVE YOU FOR-GOT-TEN?
YOU FED ME ONCE...
...!
FUBUKI?

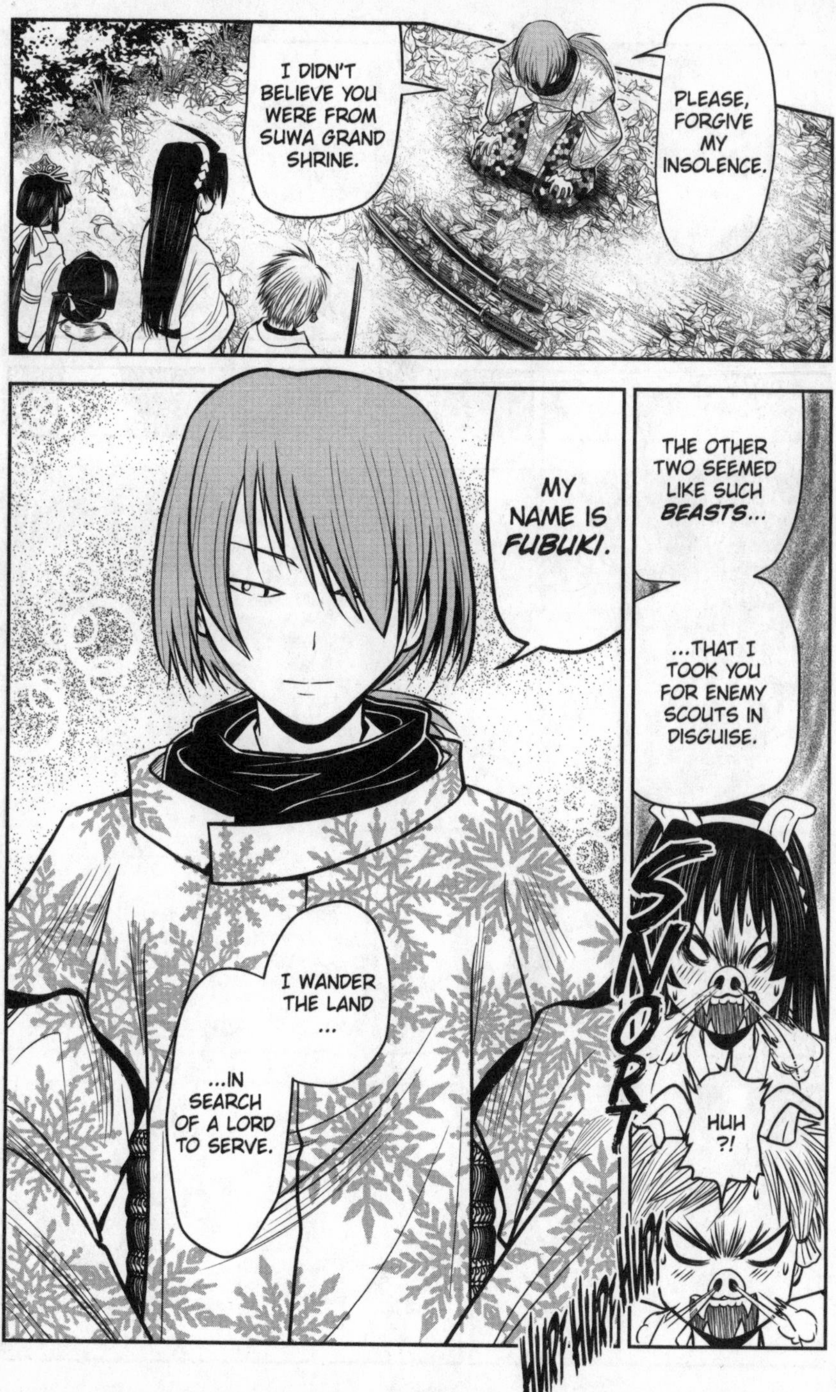
PLEASE, FORGIVE MY INSOLENCE.
I DIDN'T BELIEVE YOU WERE FROM SUWA GRAND SHRINE.
THE OTHER TWO SEEMED LIKE SUCH *BEASTS*...
...THAT I TOOK YOU FOR ENEMY SCOUTS IN DISGUISE.
SNORT
HUH ?!
HUFF HUFF HUFF
MY NAME IS *FUBUKI*.
I WANDER THE LAND ...
...IN SEARCH OF A LORD TO SERVE.

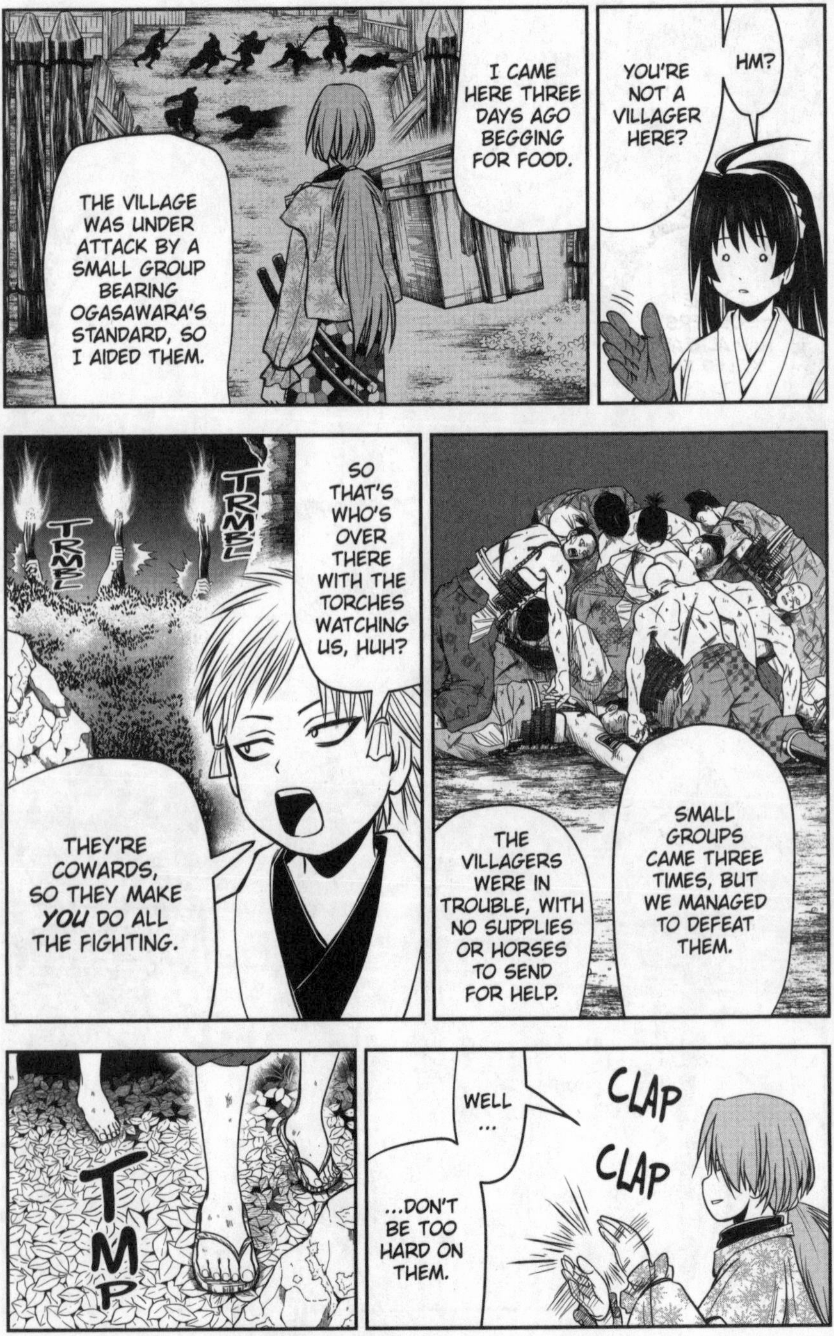
HM?
YOU'RE NOT A VILLAGER HERE?
I CAME HERE THREE DAYS AGO BEGGING FOR FOOD.
THE VILLAGE WAS UNDER ATTACK BY A SMALL GROUP BEARING OGASAWARA'S STANDARD, SO I AIDED THEM.
SMALL GROUPS CAME THREE TIMES, BUT WE MANAGED TO DEFEAT THEM.
THE VILLAGERS WERE IN TROUBLE, WITH NO SUPPLIES OR HORSES TO SEND FOR HELP.
SO THAT'S WHO'S OVER THERE WITH THE TORCHES WATCHING US, HUH?
TRMBL
TRMBL
THEY'RE COWARDS, SO THEY MAKE *YOU* DO ALL THE FIGHTING.
CLAP
CLAP
WELL...
...DON'T BE TOO HARD ON THEM.
TMP

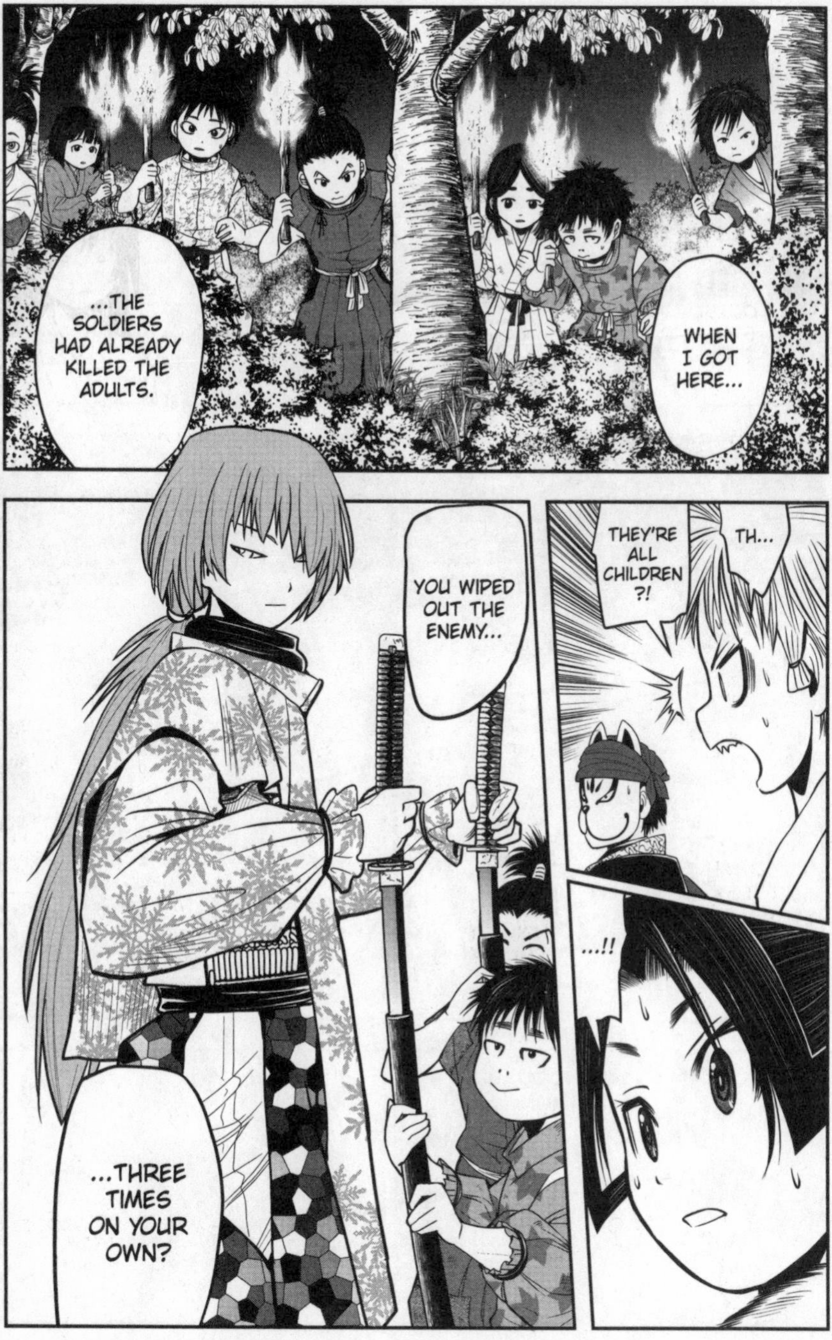
WHEN I GOT HERE...
...THE SOLDIERS HAD ALREADY KILLED THE ADULTS.
TH...
THEY'RE ALL CHILDREN ?!
...!!
YOU WIPED OUT THE ENEMY...
...THREE TIMES ON YOUR OWN?

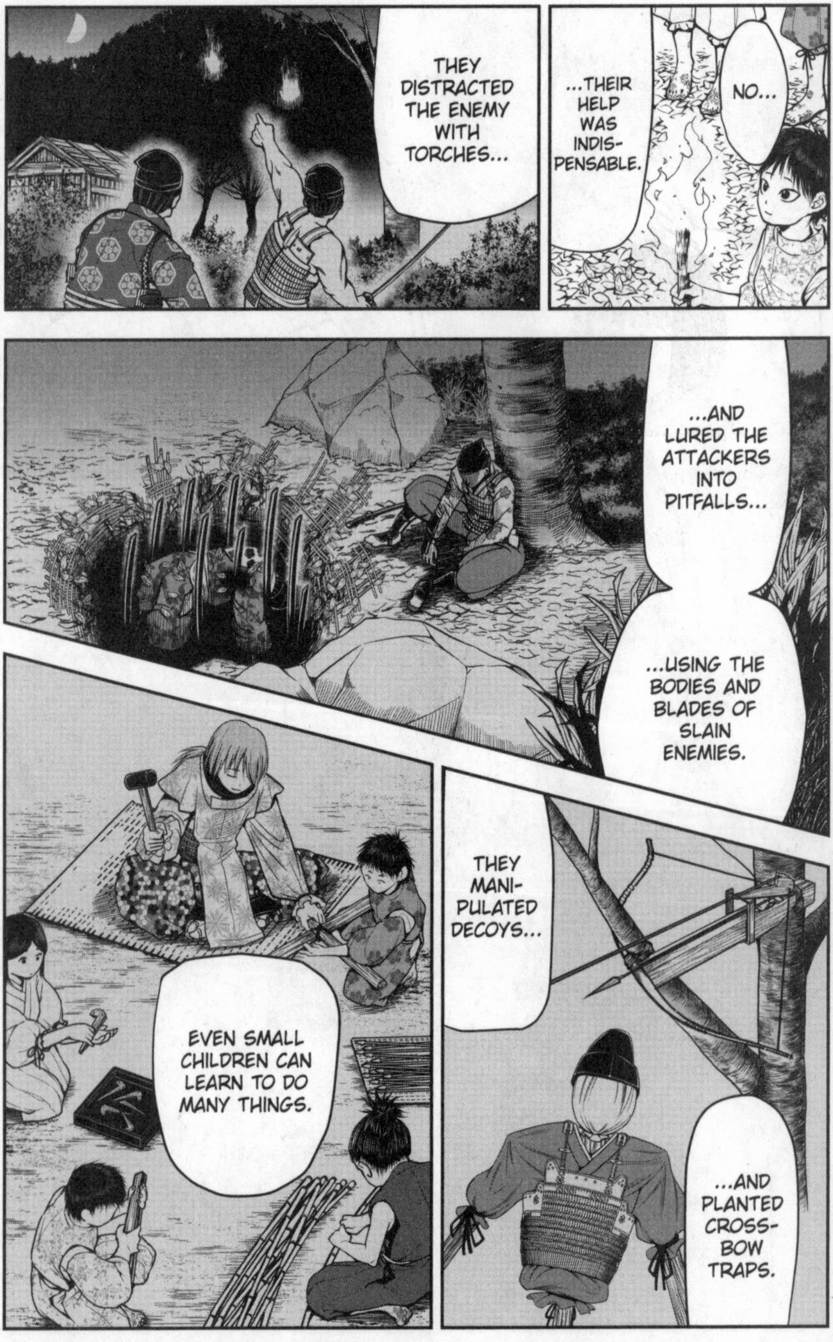
NO...
...THEIR HELP WAS INDIS-PENSABLE.
THEY DISTRACTED THE ENEMY WITH TORCHES...
...AND LURED THE ATTACKERS INTO PITFALLS...
...USING THE BODIES AND BLADES OF SLAIN ENEMIES.
THEY MANI-PULATED DECOYS...
...AND PLANTED CROSS-BOW TRAPS.
EVEN SMALL CHILDREN CAN LEARN TO DO MANY THINGS.

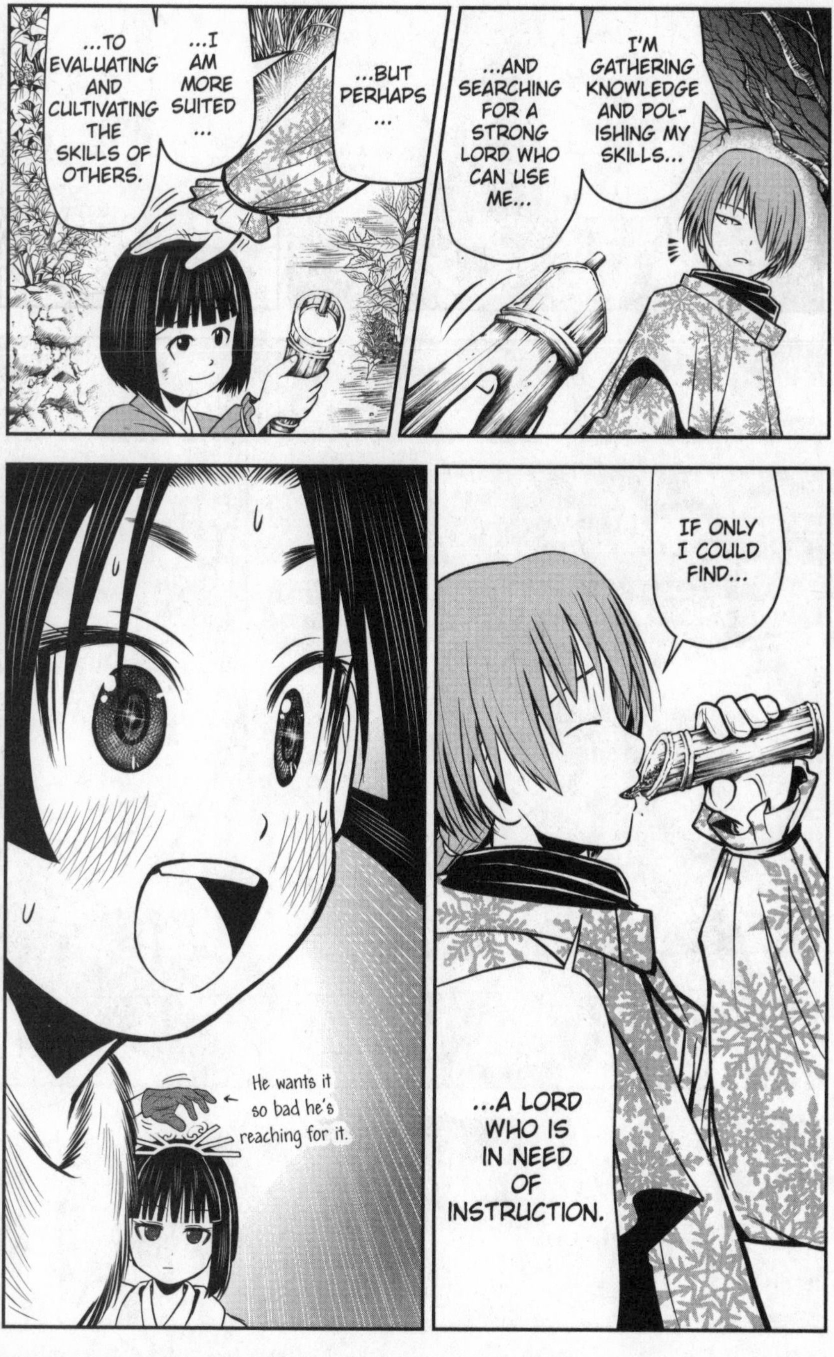
I'M GATHERING KNOWLEDGE AND POL-ISHING MY SKILLS...
...AND SEARCHING FOR A STRONG LORD WHO CAN USE ME...
...BUT PERHAPS...
...I AM MORE SUITED...
...TO EVALUATING AND CULTIVATING THE SKILLS OF OTHERS.
IF ONLY I COULD FIND...
...A LORD WHO IS IN NEED OF INSTRUCTION.
He wants it so bad he's reaching for it.

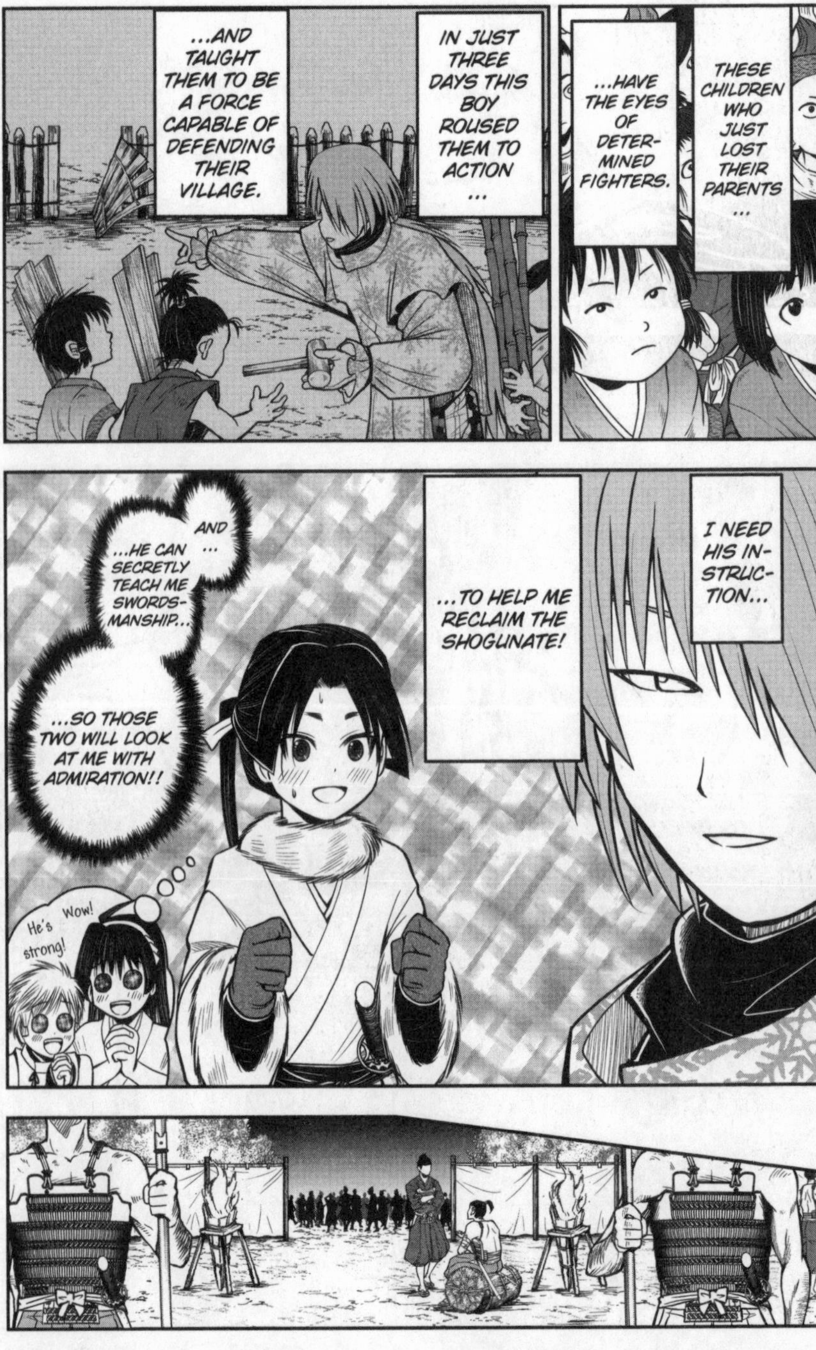
THESE CHILDREN WHO JUST LOST THEIR PARENTS...
...HAVE THE EYES OF DETERMINED FIGHTERS.
IN JUST THREE DAYS THIS BOY ROUSED THEM TO ACTION...
...AND TAUGHT THEM TO BE A FORCE CAPABLE OF DEFENDING THEIR VILLAGE.
I NEED HIS INSTRUCTION...
...TO HELP ME RECLAIM THE SHOGUNATE!
AND ... ...HE CAN SECRETLY TEACH ME SWORDSMANSHIP...
...SO THOSE TWO WILL LOOK AT ME WITH ADMIRATION!!
Wow!
He's strong!

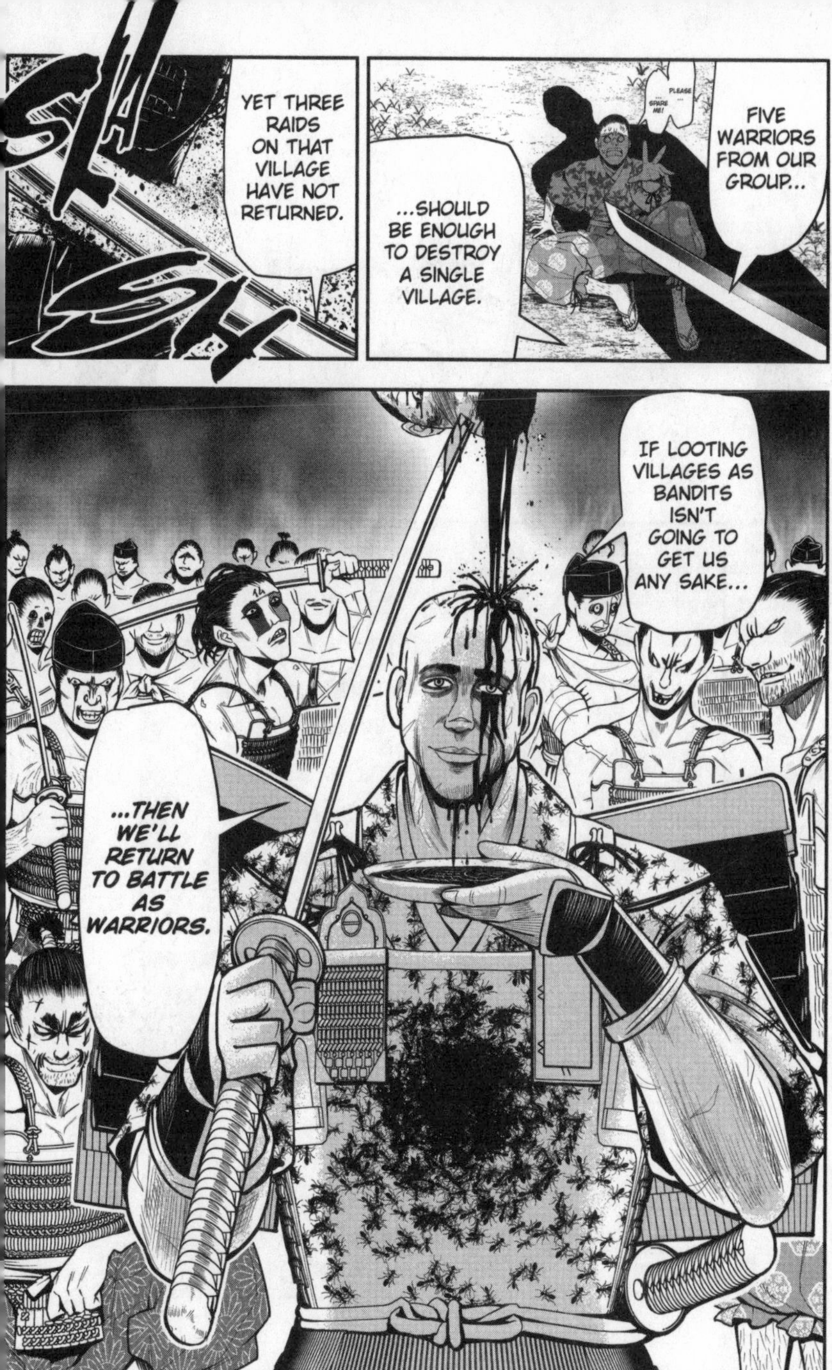
FIVE WARRIORS FROM OUR GROUP...
PLEASE... ...SPARE ME!
...SHOULD BE ENOUGH TO DESTROY A SINGLE VILLAGE.
YET THREE RAIDS ON THAT VILLAGE HAVE NOT RETURNED.
IF LOOTING VILLAGES AS BANDITS ISN'T GOING TO GET US ANY SAKE...
...THEN WE'LL RETURN TO BATTLE AS WARRIORS.

Young Lord User's Manual

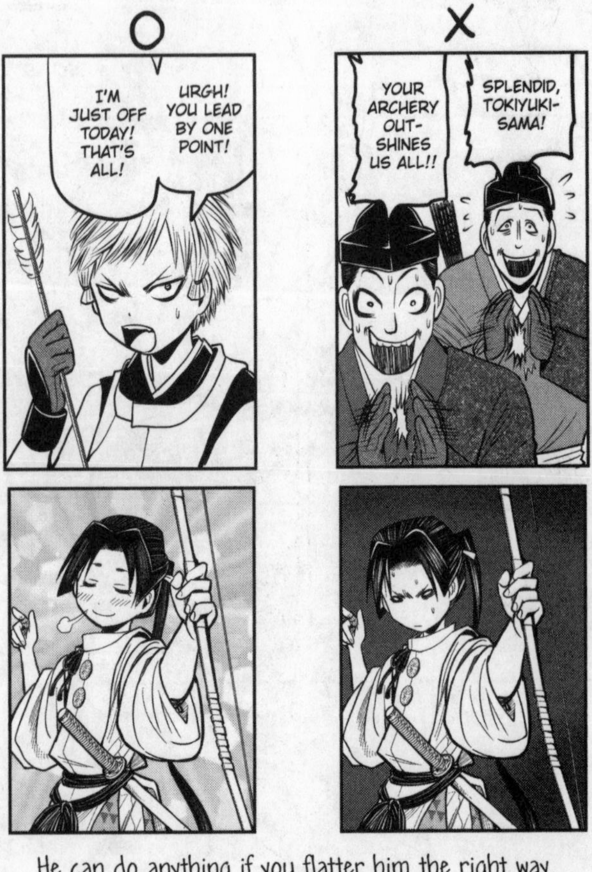
SPLENDID, TOKIYUKI-SAMA!
YOUR ARCHERY OUT-SHINES US ALL!!
URGH! YOU LEAD BY ONE POINT!
I'M JUST OFF TODAY! THAT'S ALL!

He can do anything if you flatter him the right way.

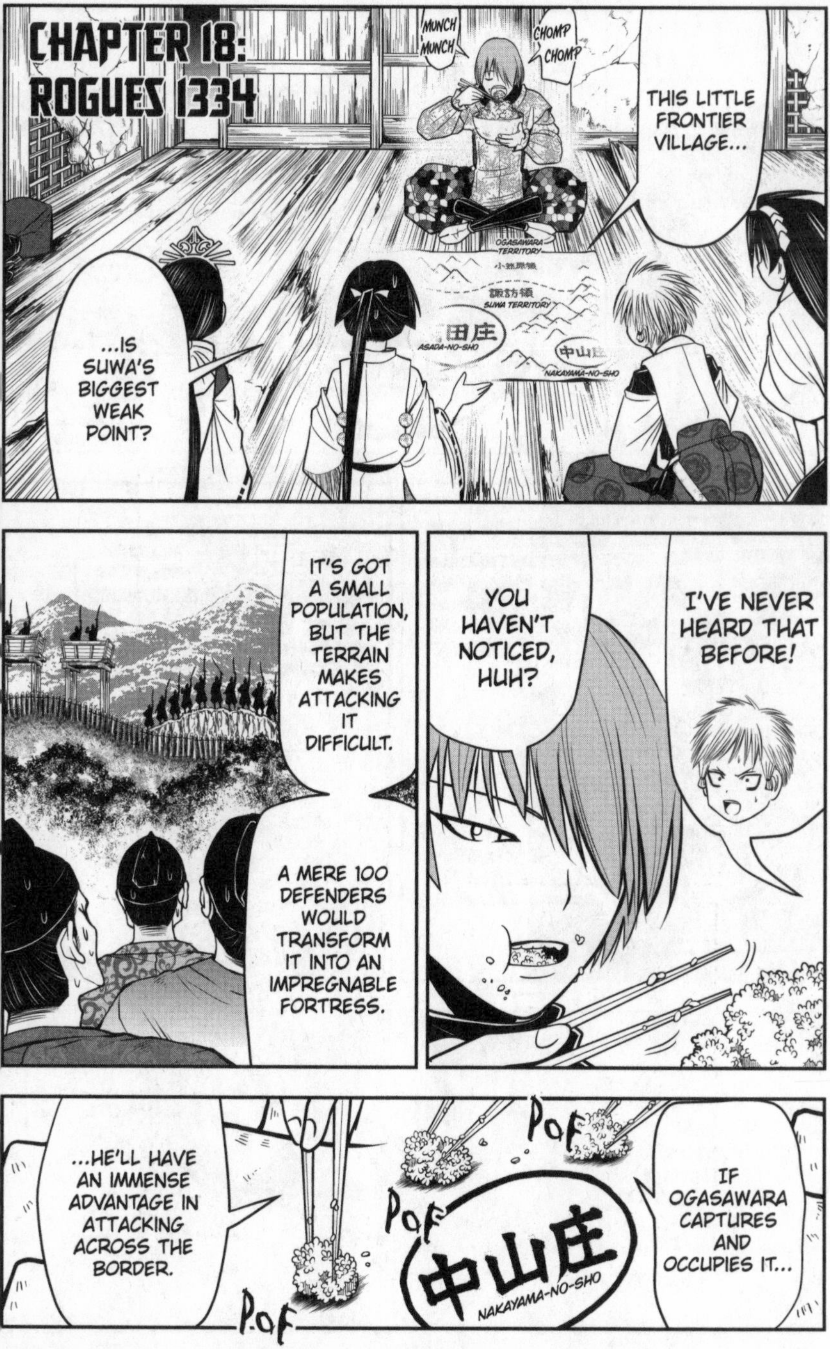
CHAPTER 18: ROGUES 1334
CHOMP CHOMP
MUNCH MUNCH
THIS LITTLE FRONTIER VILLAGE...
OGASAWARA TERRITORY
小笠原領
諏訪領
SUWA TERRITORY
中山庄
NAKAYAMA-NO-SHO
田庄
ASADA-NO-SHO
...IS SUWA'S BIGGEST WEAK POINT?
I'VE NEVER HEARD THAT BEFORE!
YOU HAVEN'T NOTICED, HUH?
IT'S GOT A SMALL POPULATION, BUT THE TERRAIN MAKES ATTACKING IT DIFFICULT.
A MERE 100 DEFENDERS WOULD TRANSFORM IT INTO AN IMPREGNABLE FORTRESS.
IF OGASAWARA CAPTURES AND OCCUPIES IT...
POF
中山庄
NAKAYAMA-NO-SHO
POF
POF
...HE'LL HAVE AN IMMENSE ADVANTAGE IN ATTACKING ACROSS THE BORDER.

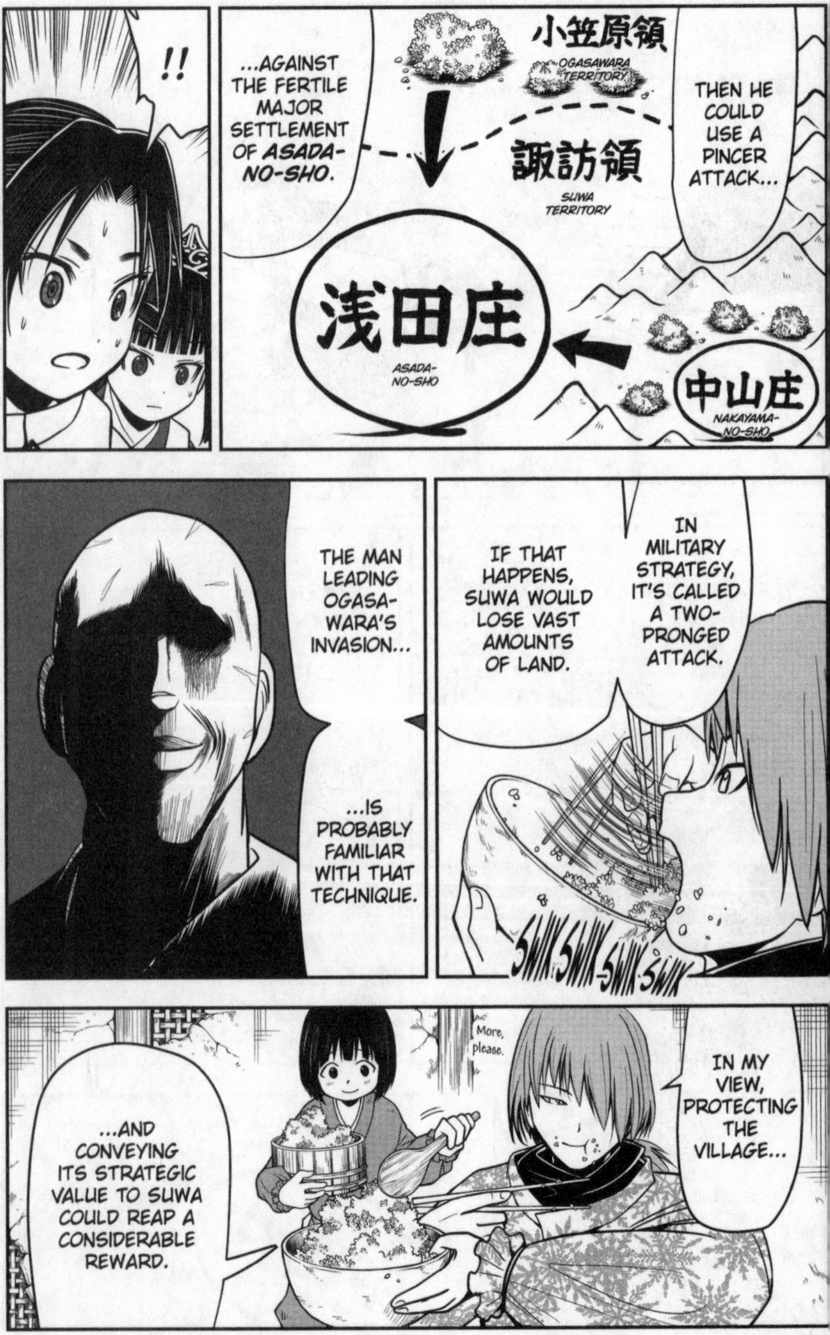
THEN HE COULD USE A PINCER ATTACK...
小笠原領
OGASAWARA TERRITORY
諏訪領
SUWA TERRITORY
中山庄
NAKAYAMA-NO-SHO
...AGAINST THE FERTILE MAJOR SETTLEMENT OF ASADA-NO-SHO.
浅田庄
ASADA-NO-SHO
!!
IN MILITARY STRATEGY, IT'S CALLED A TWO-PRONGED ATTACK.
IF THAT HAPPENS, SUWA WOULD LOSE VAST AMOUNTS OF LAND.
SWIK SWIK SWIK SWIK
THE MAN LEADING OGASAWARA'S INVASION...
...IS PROBABLY FAMILIAR WITH THAT TECHNIQUE.
IN MY VIEW, PROTECTING THE VILLAGE...
More, please.
...AND CONVEYING ITS STRATEGIC VALUE TO SUWA COULD REAP A CONSIDERABLE REWARD.

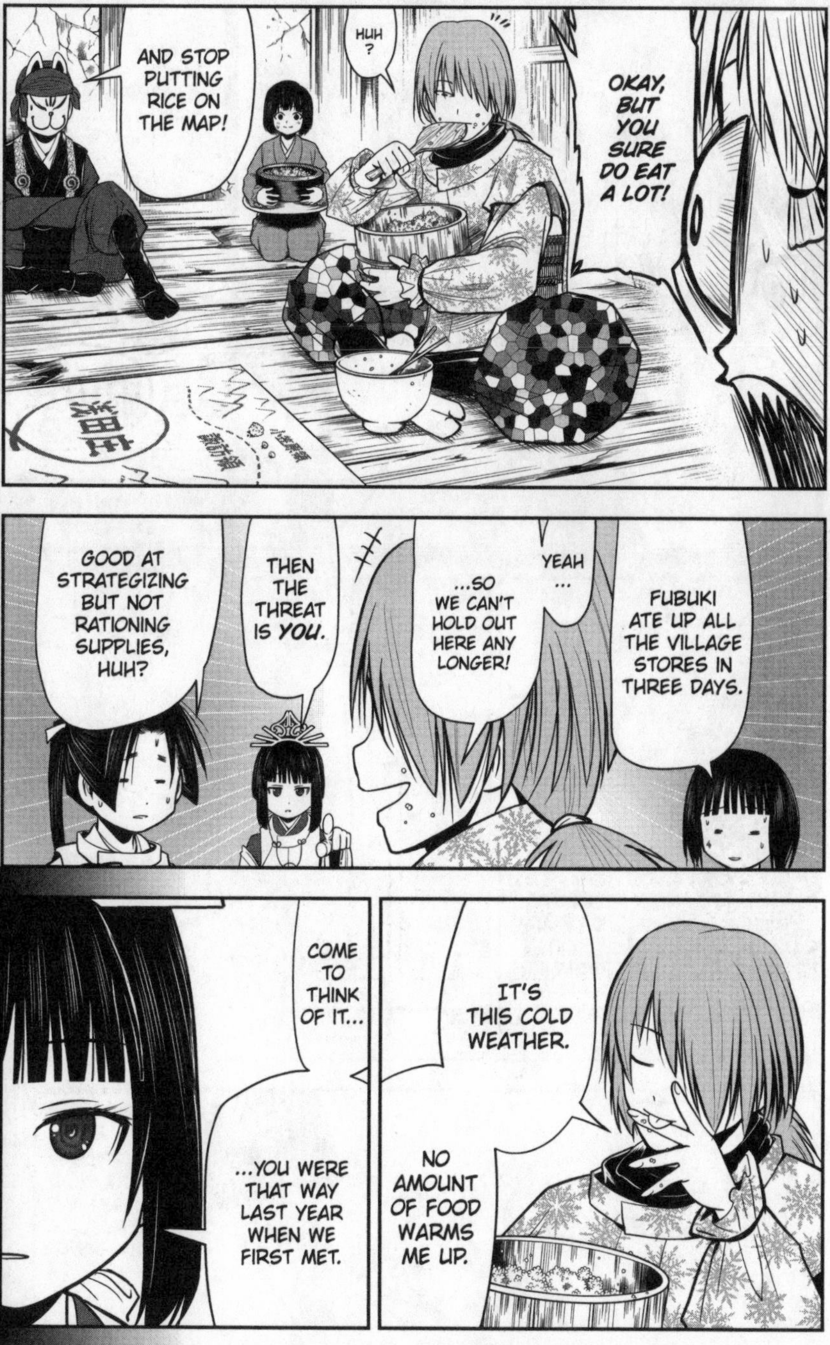
OKAY, BUT YOU SURE DO EAT A LOT!
HUH?
AND STOP PUTTING RICE ON THE MAP!
FUBUKI ATE UP ALL THE VILLAGE STORES IN THREE DAYS.
YEAH...
...SO WE CAN'T HOLD OUT HERE ANY LONGER!
THEN THE THREAT IS *YOU*.
GOOD AT STRATEGIZING BUT NOT RATIONING SUPPLIES, HUH?
IT'S THIS COLD WEATHER.
NO AMOUNT OF FOOD WARMS ME UP.
COME TO THINK OF IT...
...YOU WERE THAT WAY LAST YEAR WHEN WE FIRST MET.

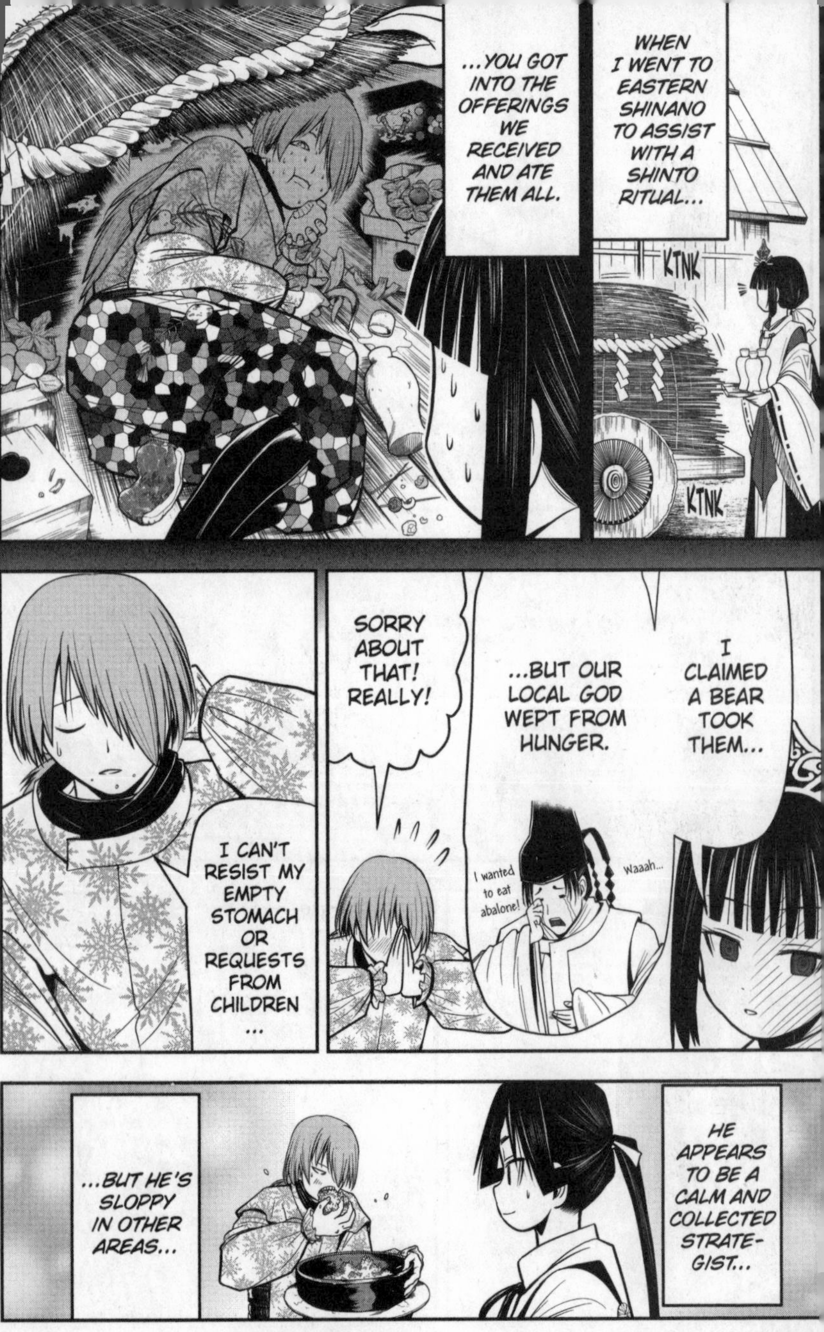
WHEN I WENT TO EASTERN SHINANO TO ASSIST WITH A SHINTO RITUAL...
KTNK
KTNK
...YOU GOT INTO THE OFFERINGS WE RECEIVED AND ATE THEM ALL.
I CLAIMED A BEAR TOOK THEM...
...BUT OUR LOCAL GOD WEPT FROM HUNGER.
Waaah...
I wanted to eat abalone!
SORRY ABOUT THAT! REALLY!
I CAN'T RESIST MY EMPTY STOMACH OR REQUESTS FROM CHILDREN...
HE APPEARS TO BE A CALM AND COLLECTED STRATEGIST...
...BUT HE'S SLOPPY IN OTHER AREAS...

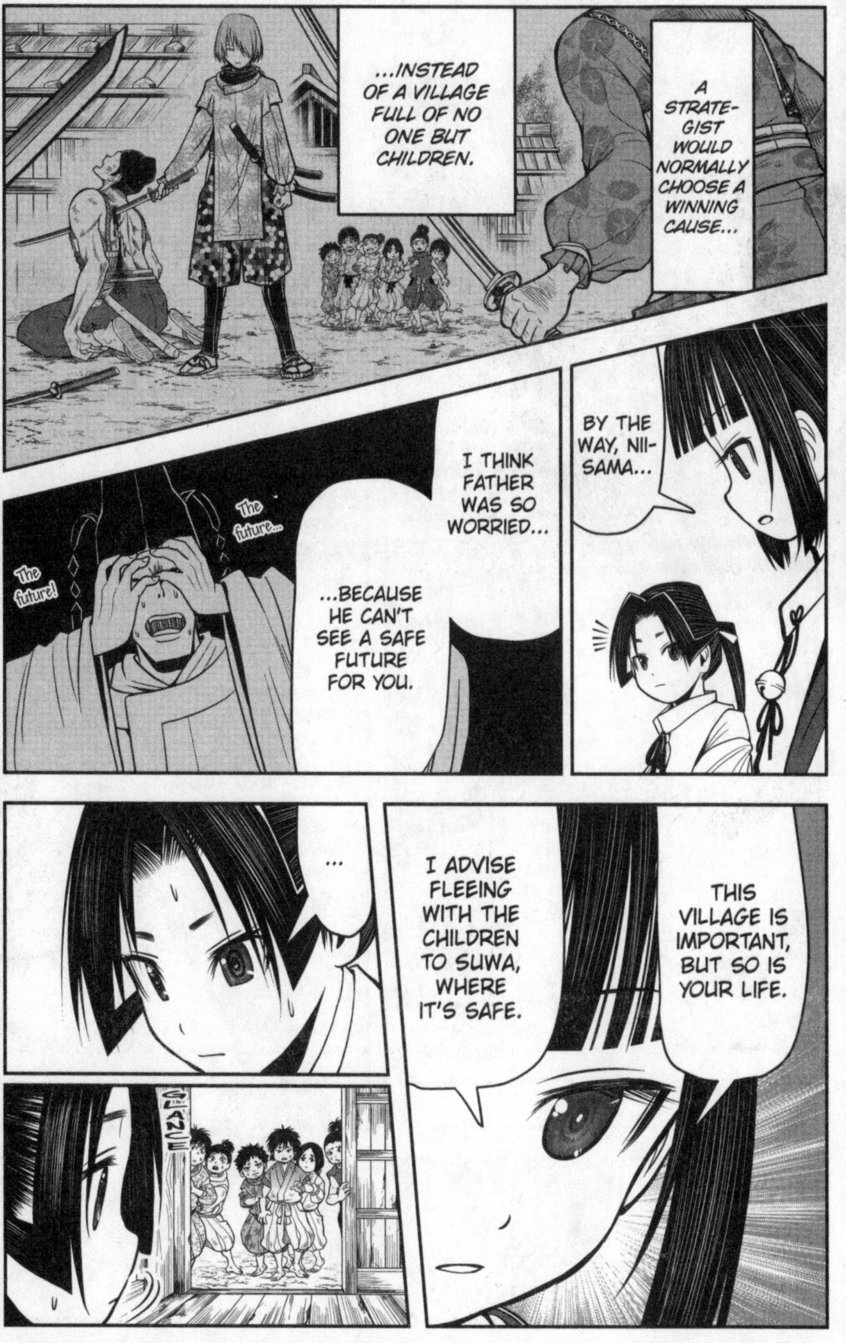
A STRATEGIST WOULD NORMALLY CHOOSE A WINNING CAUSE...
...INSTEAD OF A VILLAGE FULL OF NO ONE BUT CHILDREN.
BY THE WAY, NII-SAMA...
I THINK FATHER WAS SO WORRIED...
...BECAUSE HE CAN'T SEE A SAFE FUTURE FOR YOU.
The future...
The future!
THIS VILLAGE IS IMPORTANT, BUT SO IS YOUR LIFE.
I ADVISE FLEEING WITH THE CHILDREN TO SUWA, WHERE IT'S SAFE.
...
GLANCE

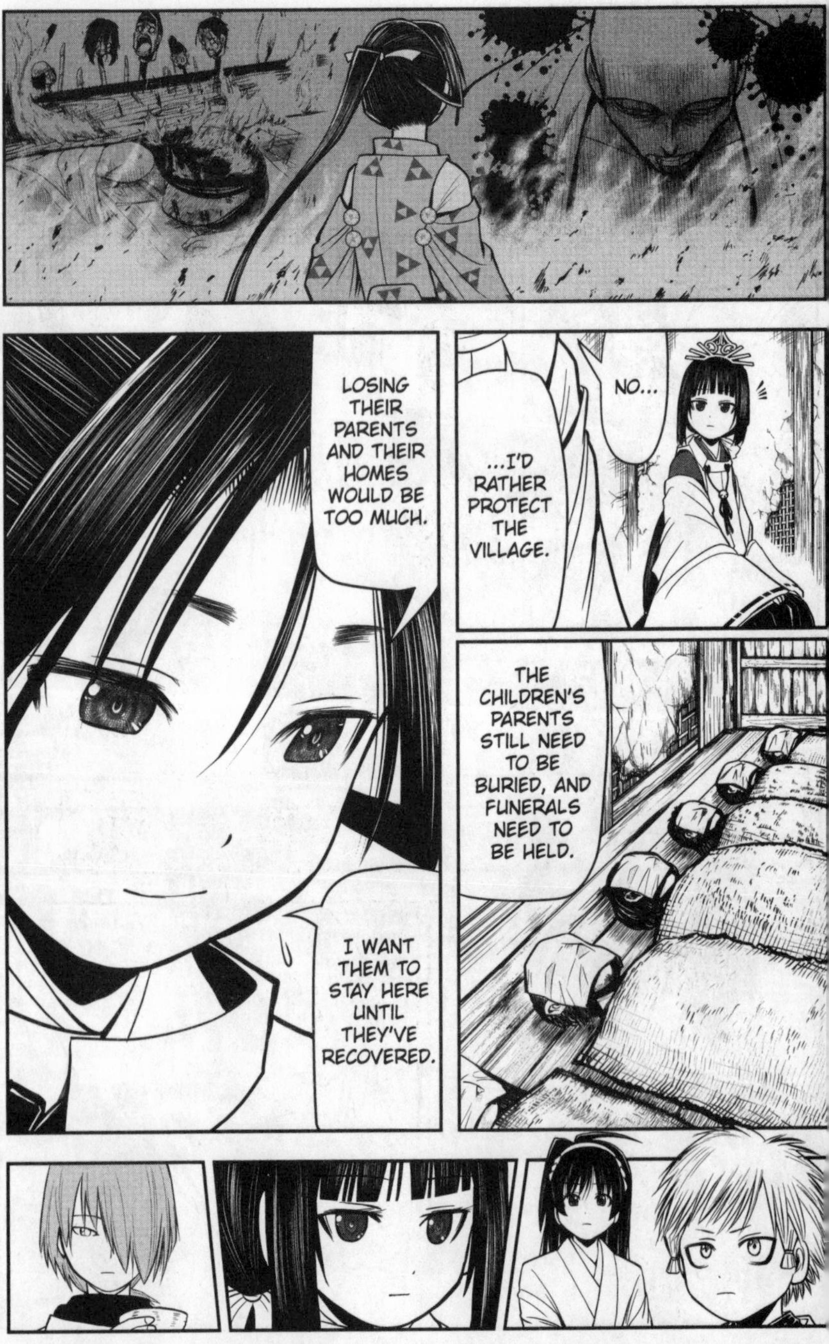
NO...
...I'D RATHER PROTECT THE VILLAGE.
THE CHILDREN'S PARENTS STILL NEED TO BE BURIED, AND FUNERALS NEED TO BE HELD.
LOSING THEIR PARENTS AND THEIR HOMES WOULD BE TOO MUCH.
I WANT THEM TO STAY HERE UNTIL THEY'VE RECOVERED.

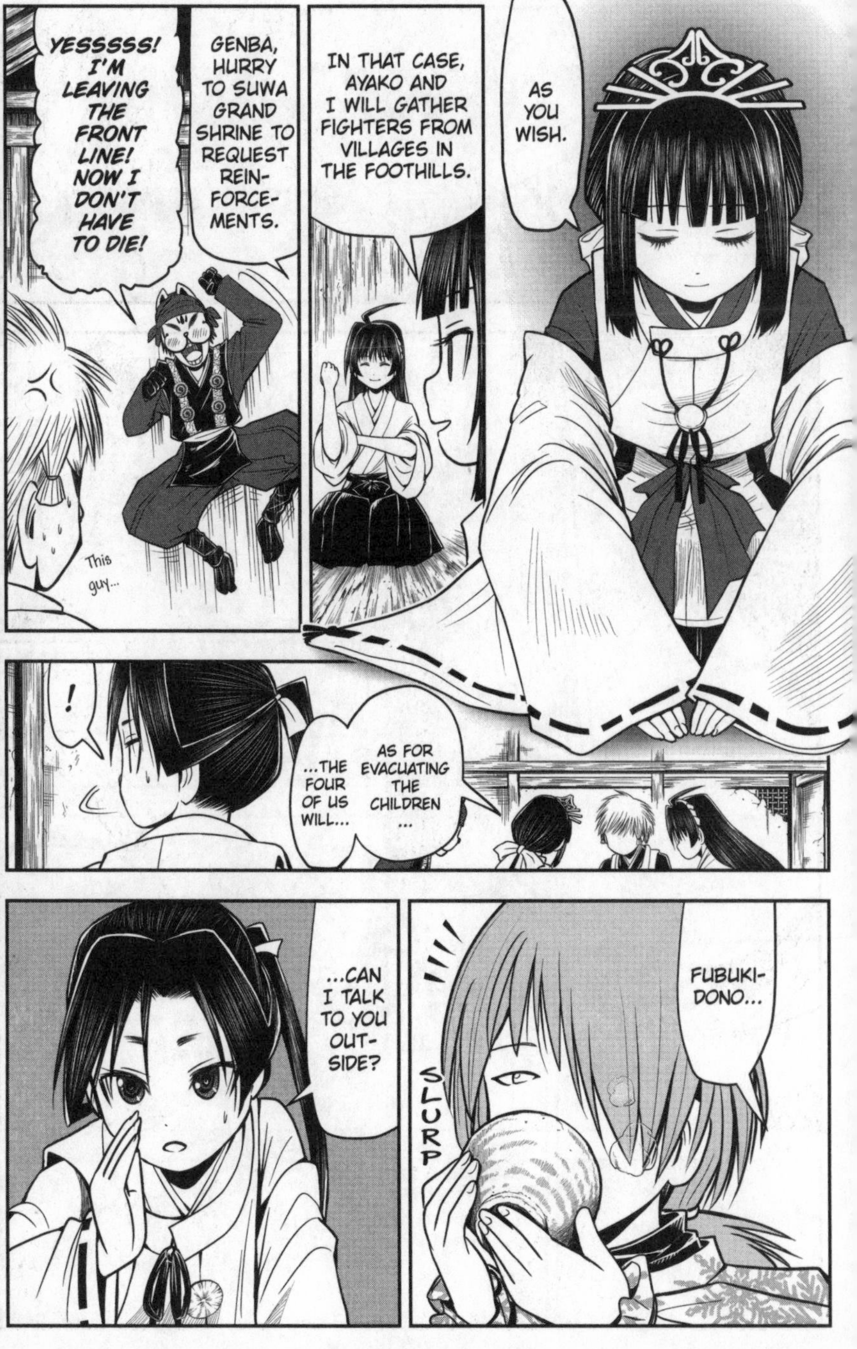
AS YOU WISH.
IN THAT CASE, AYAKO AND I WILL GATHER FIGHTERS FROM VILLAGES IN THE FOOTHILLS.
GENBA, HURRY TO SUWA GRAND SHRINE TO REQUEST REIN-FORCE-MENTS.
YESSSSS! I'M LEAVING THE FRONT LINE! NOW I DON'T HAVE TO DIE!
This guy...
AS FOR EVACUATING THE CHILDREN ...
...THE FOUR OF US WILL...
!
FUBUKI-DONO...
SLURP
...CAN I TALK TO YOU OUT-SIDE?

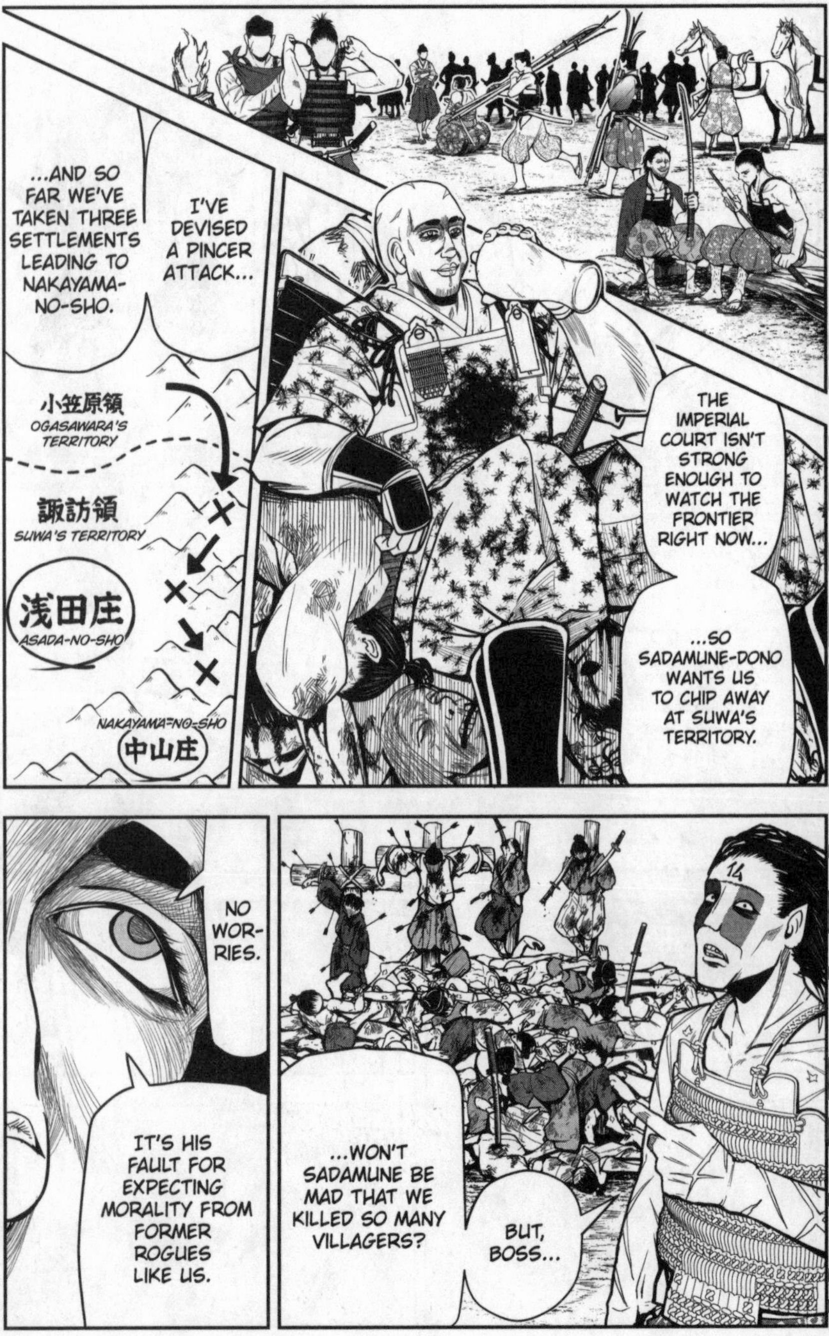
THE IMPERIAL COURT ISN'T STRONG ENOUGH TO WATCH THE FRONTIER RIGHT NOW...
...SO SADAMUNE-DONO WANTS US TO CHIP AWAY AT SUWA'S TERRITORY.
I'VE DEVISED A PINCER ATTACK...
...AND SO FAR WE'VE TAKEN THREE SETTLEMENTS LEADING TO NAKAYAMA-NO-SHO.
小笠原領
OGASAWARA'S TERRITORY
諏訪領
SUWA'S TERRITORY
浅田庄
ASADA-NO-SHO
NAKAYAMA-NO-SHO
中山庄
BUT, BOSS...
...WON'T SADAMUNE BE MAD THAT WE KILLED SO MANY VILLAGERS?
NO WORRIES.
IT'S HIS FAULT FOR EXPECTING MORALITY FROM FORMER ROGUES LIKE US.

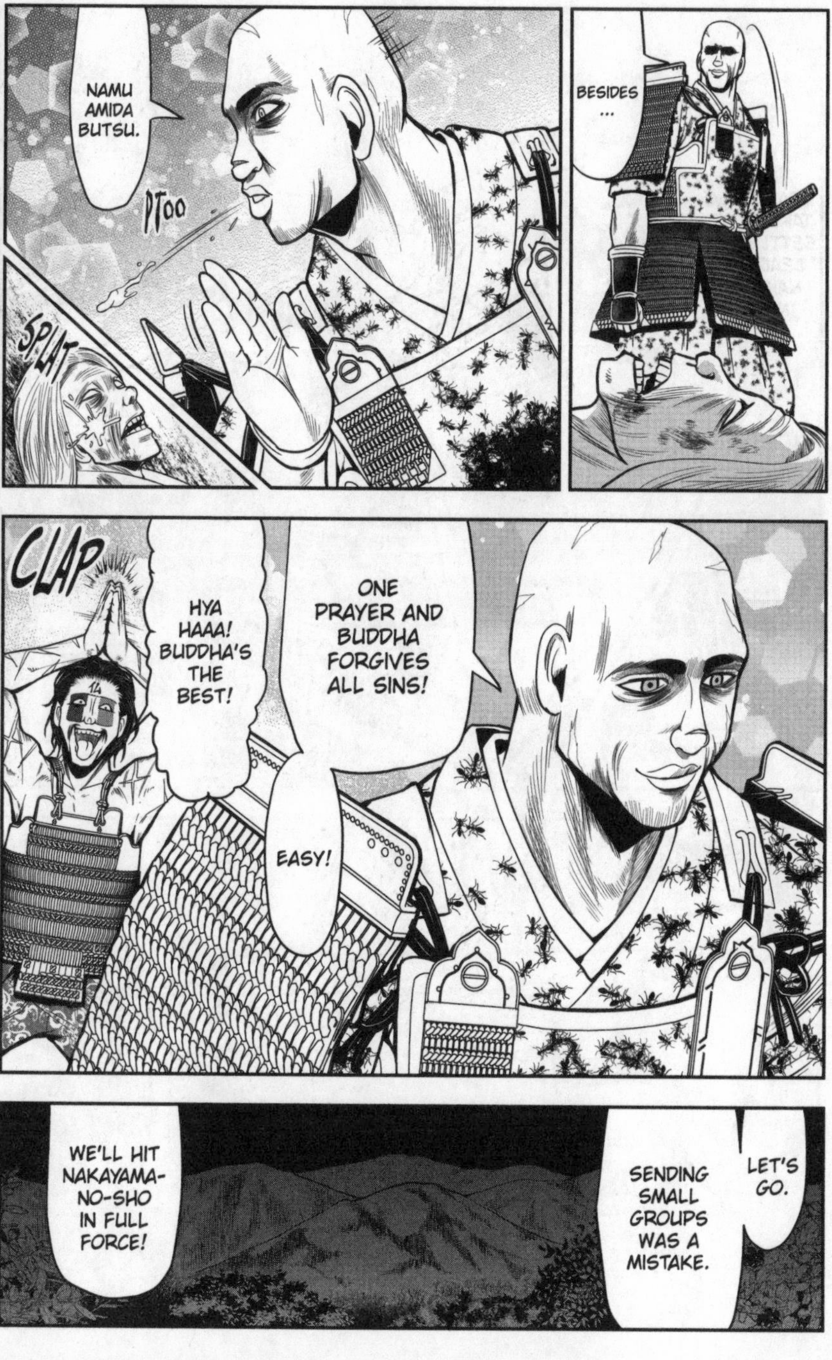
BESIDES ...
NAMU AMIDA BUTSU.
PTOO
SPLAT
ONE PRAYER AND BUDDHA FORGIVES ALL SINS!
EASY!
CLAP
HYA HAAA! BUDDHA'S THE BEST!
LET'S GO.
SENDING SMALL GROUPS WAS A MISTAKE.
WE'LL HIT NAKAYAMA-NO-SHO IN FULL FORCE!

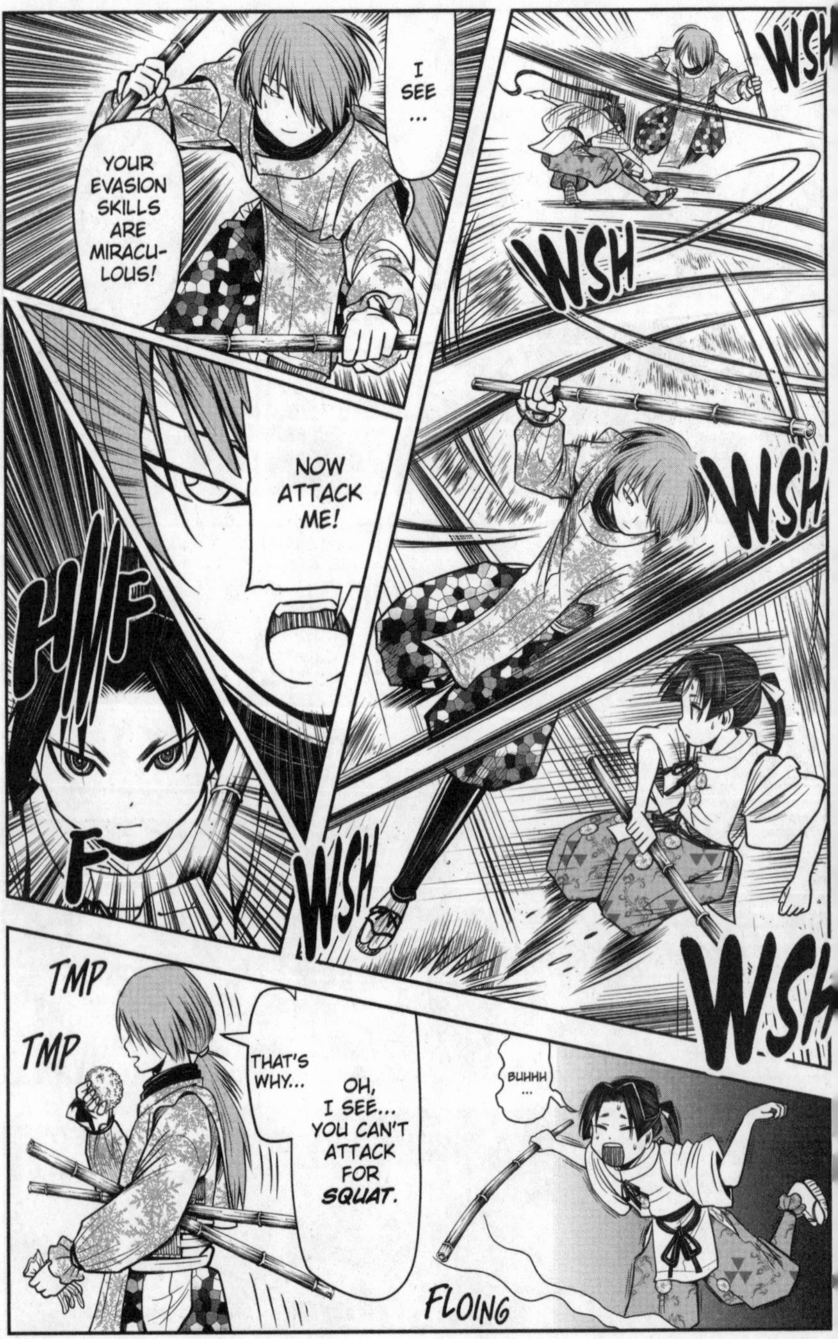
WSH
WSH
I SEE...
YOUR EVASION SKILLS ARE MIRACULOUS!
WSH
WSH
WSH
NOW ATTACK ME!
HMFF
BUHHH...
FLOING
TMP
TMP
THAT'S WHY...
OH, I SEE... YOU CAN'T ATTACK FOR SQUAT.

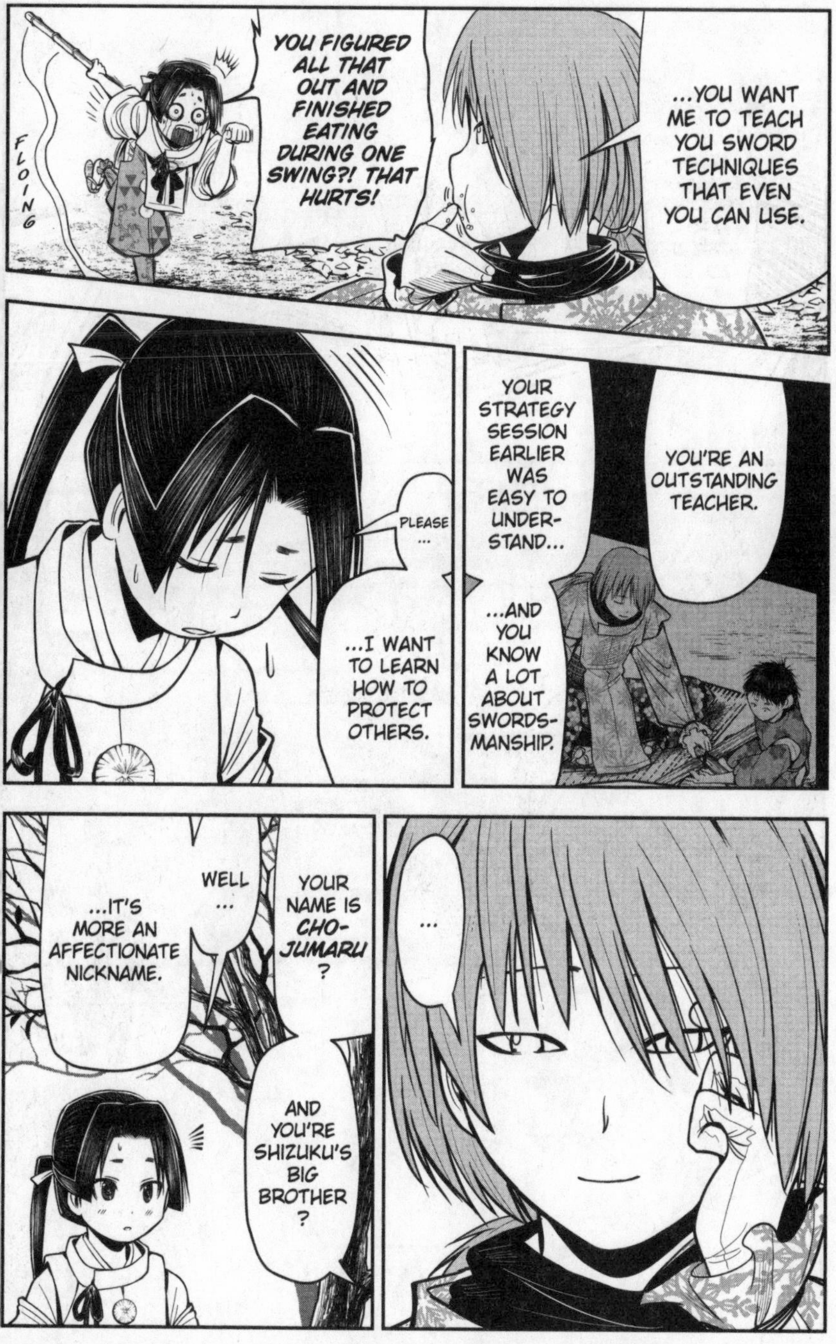
...YOU WANT ME TO TEACH YOU SWORD TECHNIQUES THAT EVEN YOU CAN USE.
YOU FIGURED ALL THAT OUT AND FINISHED EATING DURING ONE SWING?! THAT HURTS!
FLOING
YOU'RE AN OUTSTANDING TEACHER.
YOUR STRATEGY SESSION EARLIER WAS EASY TO UNDER-STAND...
...AND YOU KNOW A LOT ABOUT SWORDS-MANSHIP.
PLEASE ...
...I WANT TO LEARN HOW TO PROTECT OTHERS.
...
YOUR NAME IS CHO-JUMARU ?
AND YOU'RE SHIZUKU'S BIG BROTHER ?
WELL ...
...IT'S MORE AN AFFECTIONATE NICKNAME.

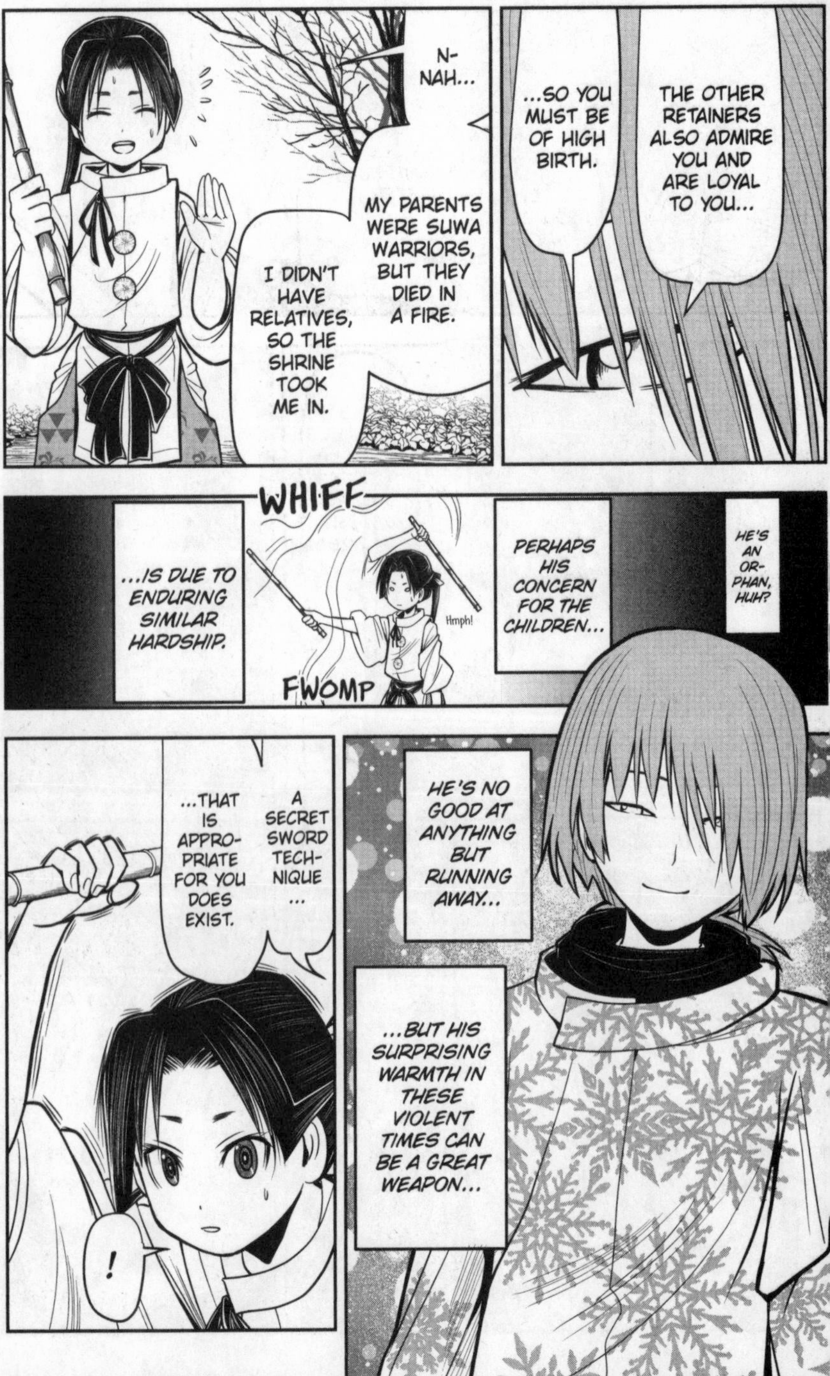
THE OTHER RETAINERS ALSO ADMIRE YOU AND ARE LOYAL TO YOU...
...SO YOU MUST BE OF HIGH BIRTH.
N-NAH...
MY PARENTS WERE SUWA WARRIORS, BUT THEY DIED IN A FIRE.
I DIDN'T HAVE RELATIVES, SO THE SHRINE TOOK ME IN.
HE'S AN ORPHAN, HUH?
PERHAPS HIS CONCERN FOR THE CHILDREN...
WHIFF
Hmph!
FWOMP
...IS DUE TO ENDURING SIMILAR HARDSHIP.
HE'S NO GOOD AT ANYTHING BUT RUNNING AWAY...
...BUT HIS SURPRISING WARMTH IN THESE VIOLENT TIMES CAN BE A GREAT WEAPON...
A SECRET SWORD TECHNIQUE...
...THAT IS APPROPRIATE FOR YOU DOES EXIST.
!

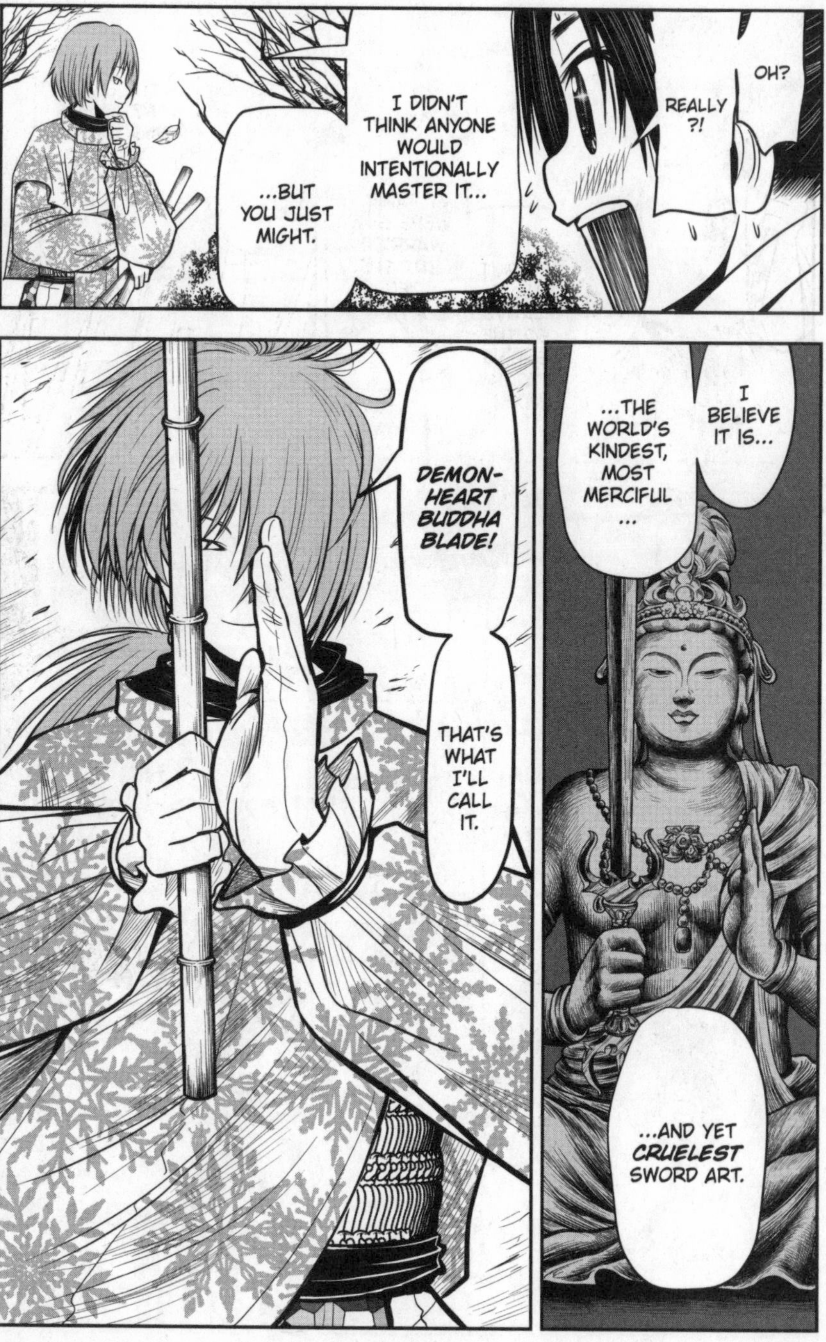

OH?
REALLY?!
I DIDN'T THINK ANYONE WOULD INTENTIONALLY MASTER IT...
...BUT YOU JUST MIGHT.
I BELIEVE IT IS...
...THE WORLD'S KINDEST, MOST MERCIFUL...
...AND YET *CRUELEST* SWORD ART.
DEMON-HEART BUDDHA BLADE!
THAT'S WHAT I'LL CALL IT.

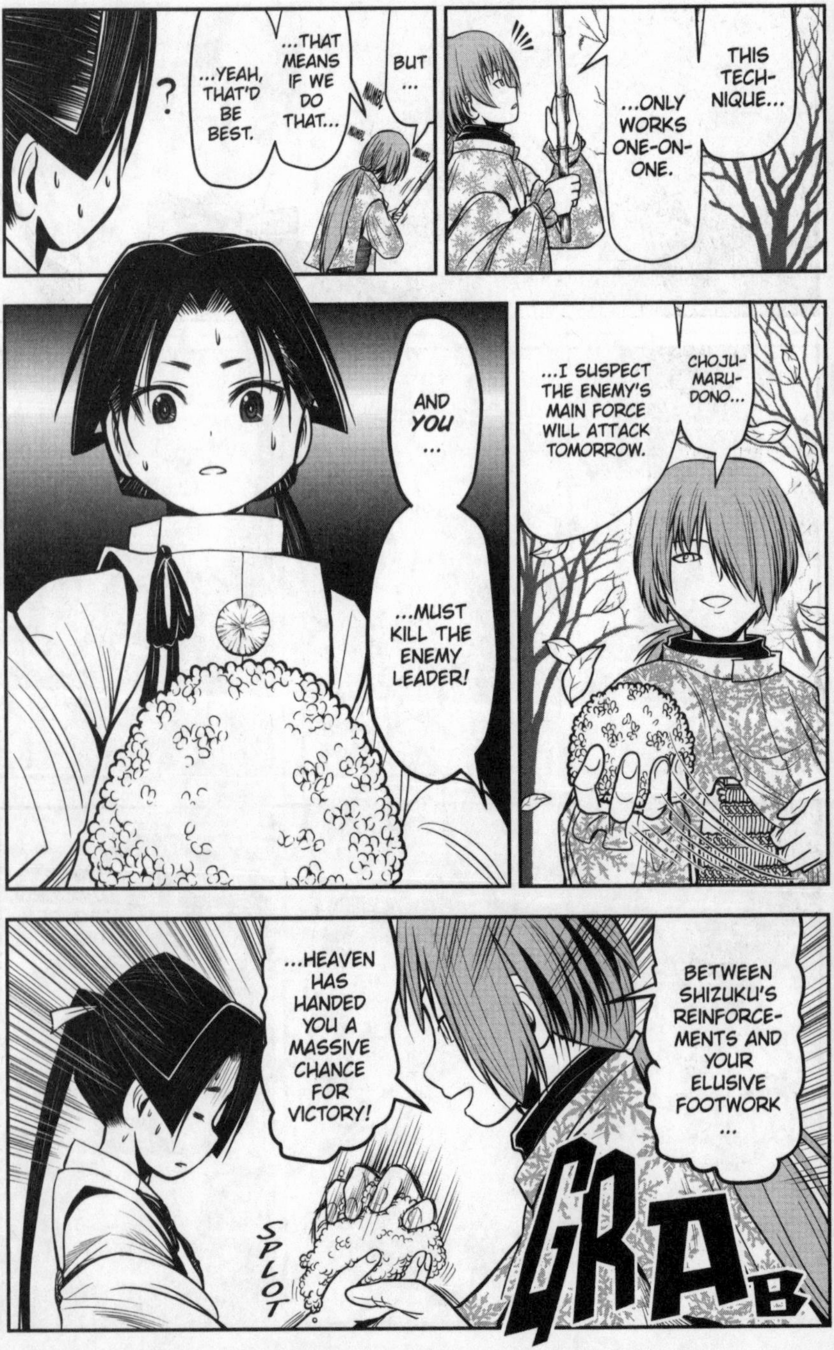
THIS TECHNIQUE...
...ONLY WORKS ONE-ON-ONE.
BUT ...
MUMBL MUMBL MUMBL
...THAT MEANS IF WE DO THAT...
...YEAH, THAT'D BE BEST.
?
CHOJUMARU-DONO...
...I SUSPECT THE ENEMY'S MAIN FORCE WILL ATTACK TOMORROW.
AND *YOU* ...
...MUST KILL THE ENEMY LEADER!
BETWEEN SHIZUKU'S REINFORCEMENTS AND YOUR ELUSIVE FOOTWORK ...
...HEAVEN HAS HANDED YOU A MASSIVE CHANCE FOR VICTORY!
GRAB
SPLOT

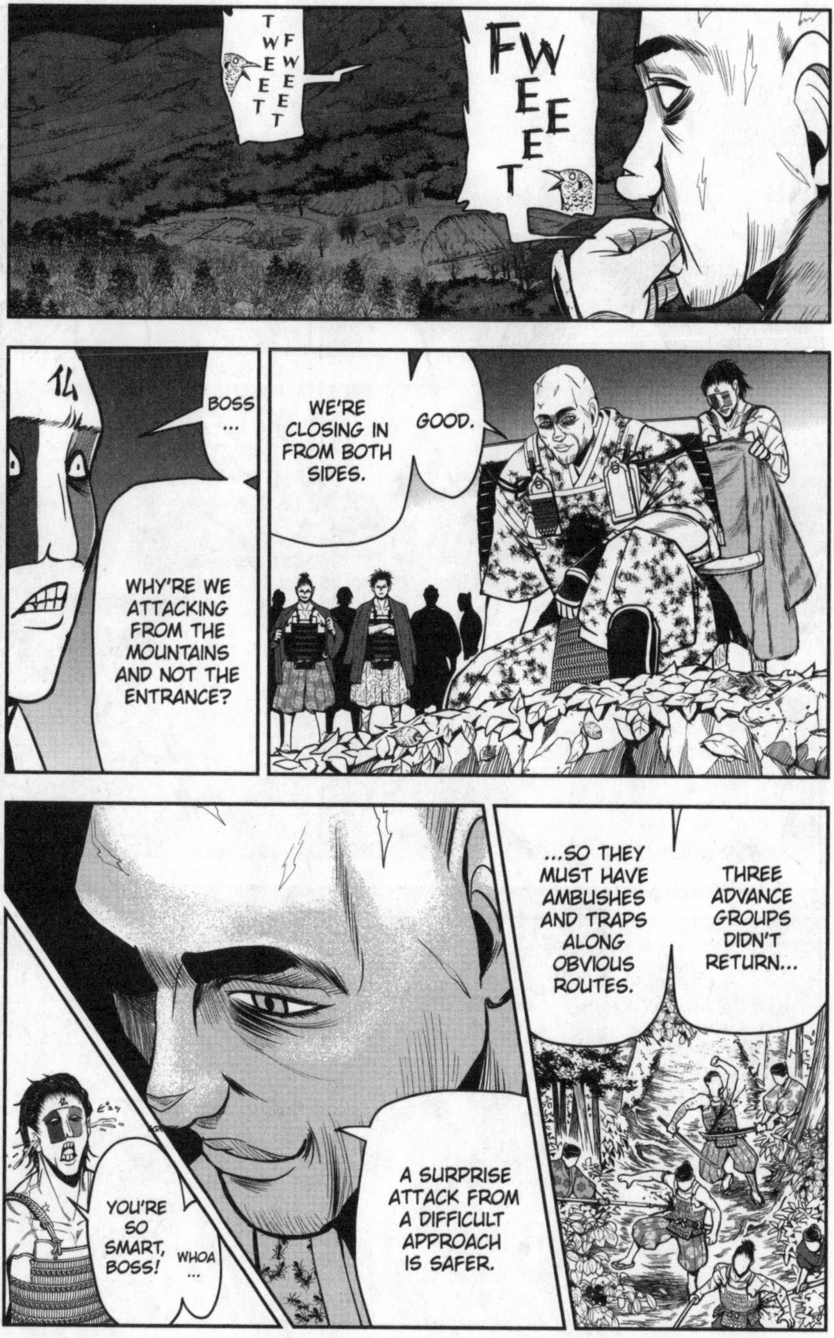
FWEET
FWEET
TWEET
GOOD.
WE'RE CLOSING IN FROM BOTH SIDES.
BOSS...
WHY'RE WE ATTACKING FROM THE MOUNTAINS AND NOT THE ENTRANCE?
THREE ADVANCE GROUPS DIDN'T RETURN...
...SO THEY MUST HAVE AMBUSHES AND TRAPS ALONG OBVIOUS ROUTES.
A SURPRISE ATTACK FROM A DIFFICULT APPROACH IS SAFER.
WHOA...
YOU'RE SO SMART, BOSS!

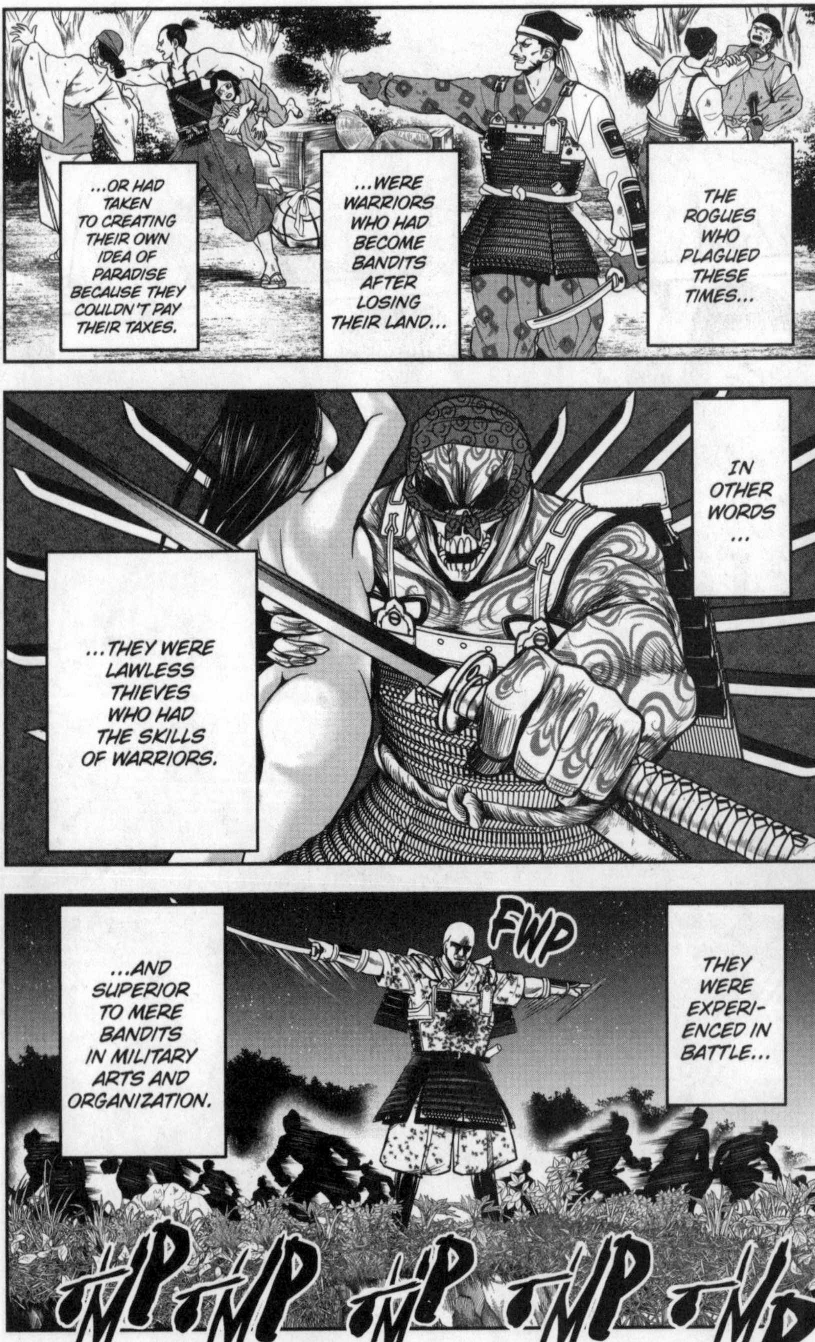
THE ROGUES WHO PLAGUED THESE TIMES...
...WERE WARRIORS WHO HAD BECOME BANDITS AFTER LOSING THEIR LAND...
...OR HAD TAKEN TO CREATING THEIR OWN IDEA OF PARADISE BECAUSE THEY COULDN'T PAY THEIR TAXES.
IN OTHER WORDS...
...THEY WERE LAWLESS THIEVES WHO HAD THE SKILLS OF WARRIORS.
THEY WERE EXPERI-ENCED IN BATTLE...
FWP
...AND SUPERIOR TO MERE BANDITS IN MILITARY ARTS AND ORGANIZATION.
TMP TMP TMP TMP TMP

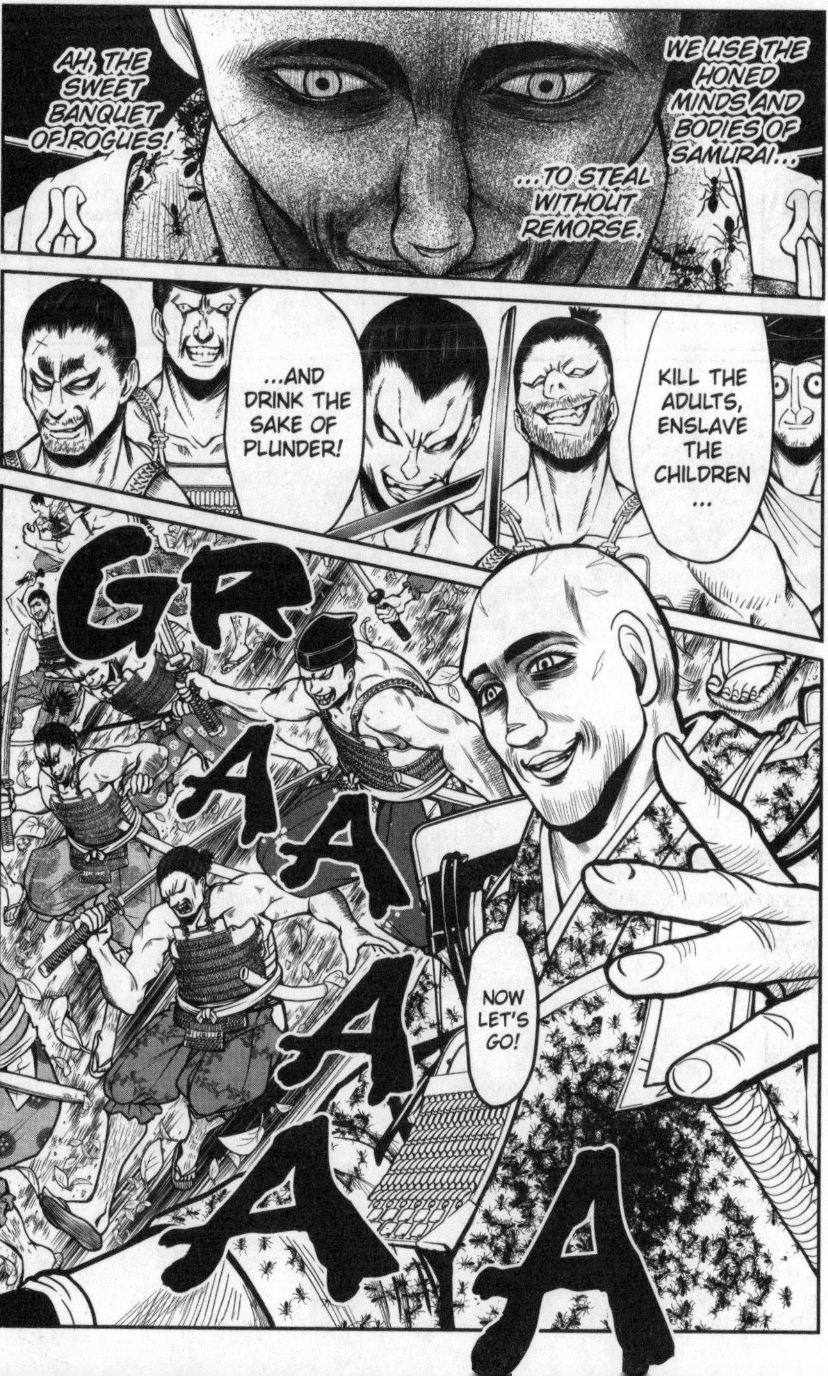
WE USE THE HONED MINDS AND BODIES OF SAMURAI...
...TO STEAL WITHOUT REMORSE.
AH, THE SWEET BANQUET OF ROGUES!
KILL THE ADULTS, ENSLAVE THE CHILDREN...
...AND DRINK THE SAKE OF PLUNDER!
NOW LET'S GO!
GRAAAAAA

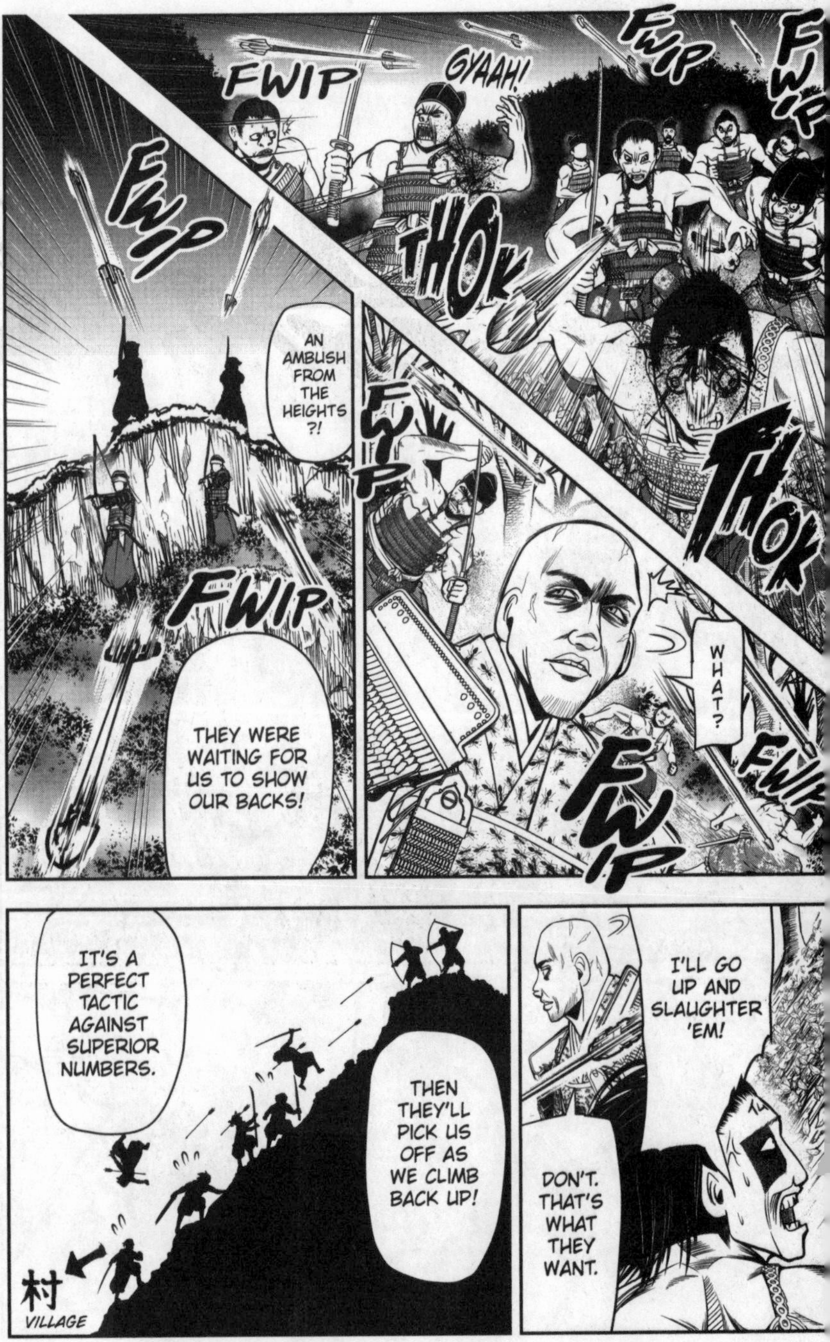
FWIP
FWIP
GYAAH!
FWIP
THOK
THOK
WHAT?
FWI
FWIP
FWIP
FWIP
AN AMBUSH FROM THE HEIGHTS?!
FWIP
FWIP
THEY WERE WAITING FOR US TO SHOW OUR BACKS!
I'LL GO UP AND SLAUGHTER 'EM!
DON'T. THAT'S WHAT THEY WANT.
IT'S A PERFECT TACTIC AGAINST SUPERIOR NUMBERS.
THEN THEY'LL PICK US OFF AS WE CLIMB BACK UP!
村
VILLAGE

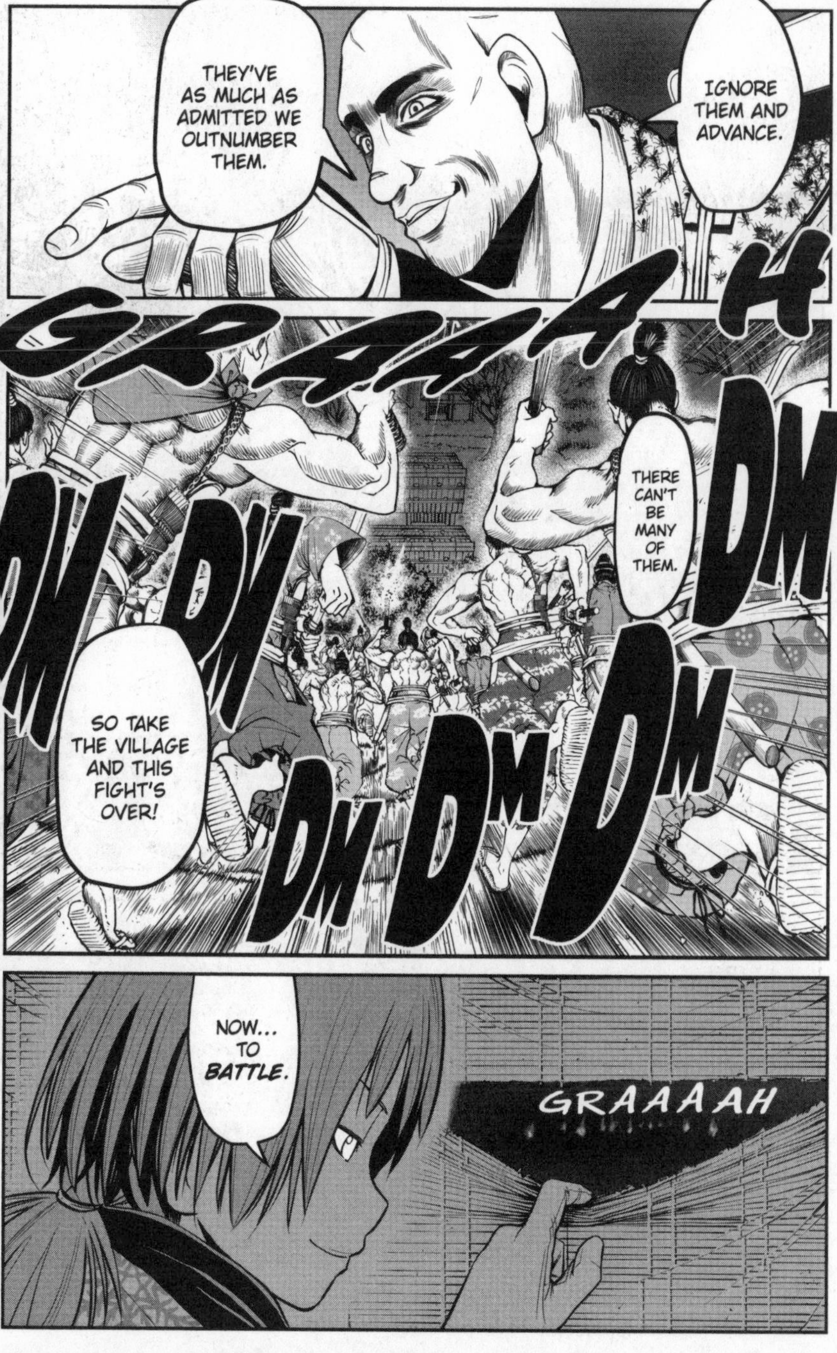
IGNORE THEM AND ADVANCE.
THEY'VE AS MUCH AS ADMITTED WE OUTNUMBER THEM.
GRAAAAH
THERE CAN'T BE MANY OF THEM.
DM DM DM DM
SO TAKE THE VILLAGE AND THIS FIGHT'S OVER!
DM DM DM DM DM
NOW... TO BATTLE.
GRAAAAH

FOX-TAIL MILLET

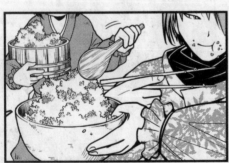

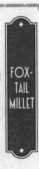

MORE DURABLE THAN RICE AND EASIER TO CULTIVATE, THIS VARIETY OF MILLET IS HIGHLY NUTRITIONAL BUT DOESN'T TASTE VERY GOOD. IT WAS AN IMPORTANT FOODSTUFF FOR THE COMMON FOLK.

I TRIED EATING 100 PERCENT MILLET. IT WAS DRY AND LACKED ALL SWEETNESS, SO IF I HAD TO CHOOSE BETWEEN MILLET AND RICE, I'D CHOOSE RICE. ON THE OTHER HAND, IT HAS A DISTINCT TASTE AND TEXTURE, AND IT'S LOW IN CALORIES. THUS, IT COULD REALLY SHINE DEPENDING ON HOW IT'S PREPARED AND SEASONED.

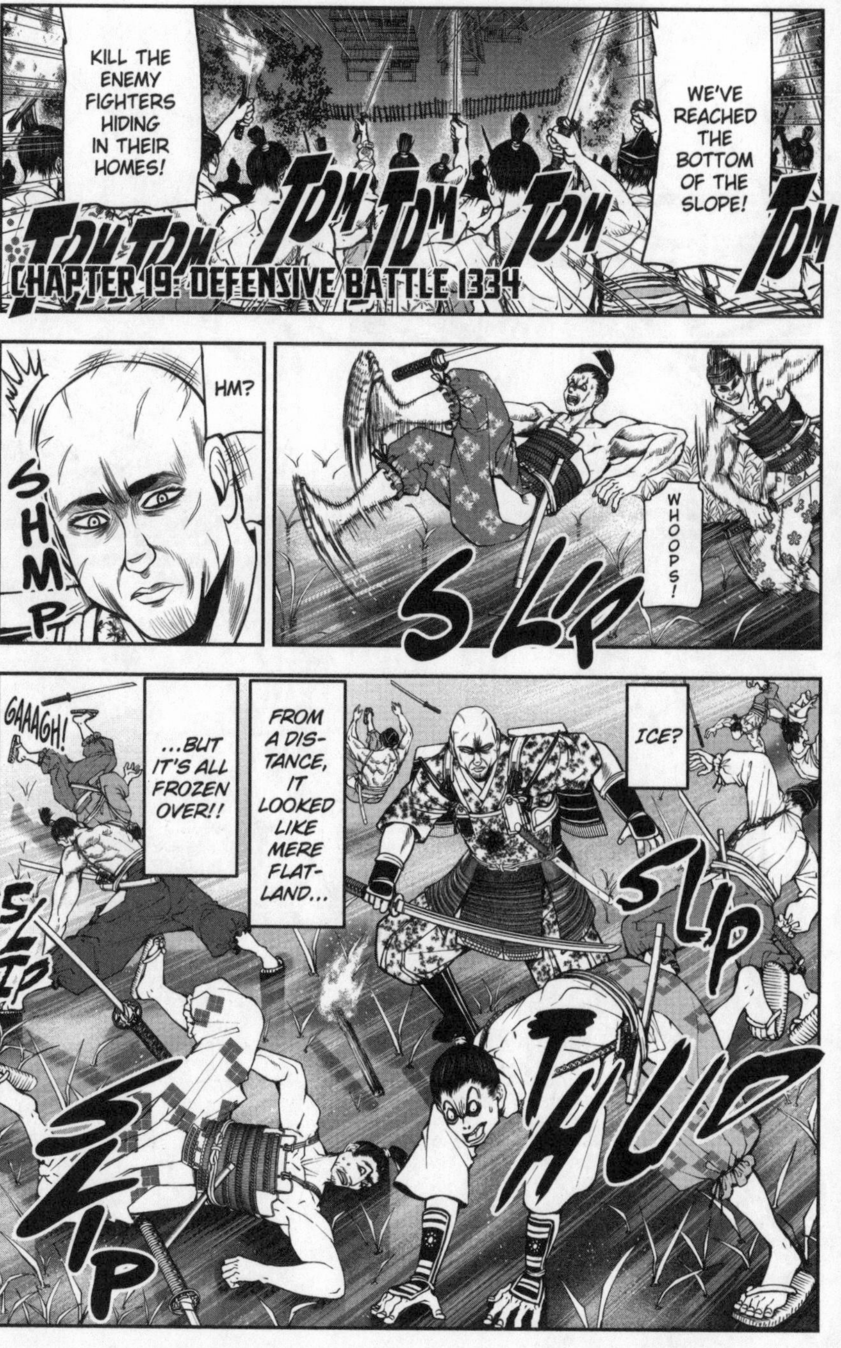
WE'VE REACHED THE BOTTOM OF THE SLOPE!
KILL THE ENEMY FIGHTERS HIDING IN THEIR HOMES!
TOM TOM TOM TOM TOM TOM TOM
CHAPTER 19: DEFENSIVE BATTLE 1334
WHOOPS!
SLIP
HM?
SHMP
ICE?
FROM A DISTANCE, IT LOOKED LIKE MERE FLATLAND...
...BUT IT'S ALL FROZEN OVER!!
SLIP
THUD
GAAAGH!
SLIP
SLIP

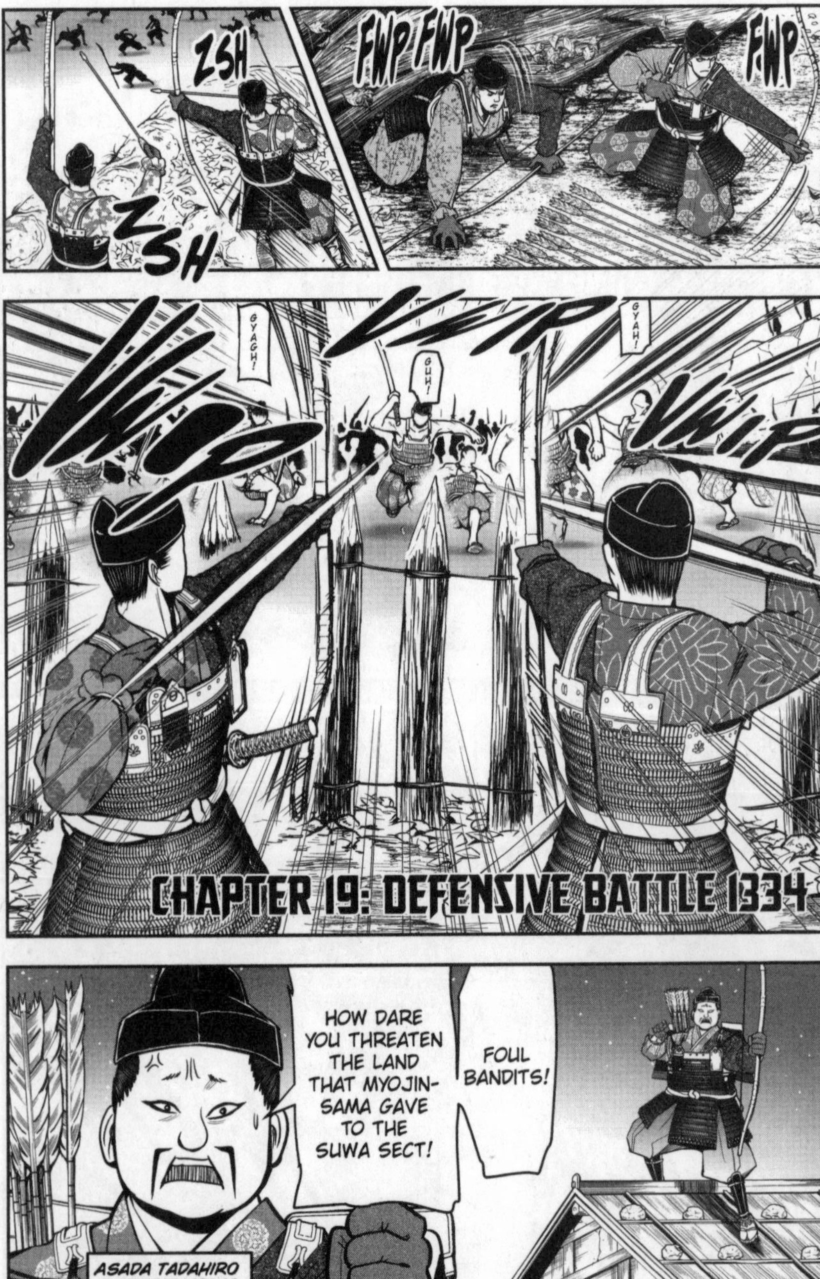
F-W-P
FWP FWP
ZSH
ZSH
GYAH!
VWIP
VWIP
GUH!
GYAGH!
VWIP
CHAPTER 19: DEFENSIVE BATTLE 1334
FOUL BANDITS!
HOW DARE YOU THREATEN THE LAND THAT MYOJIN-SAMA GAVE TO THE SUWA SECT!
ASADA TADAHIRO
SUWA SECT, LORD OF ASADA-NO-SHO

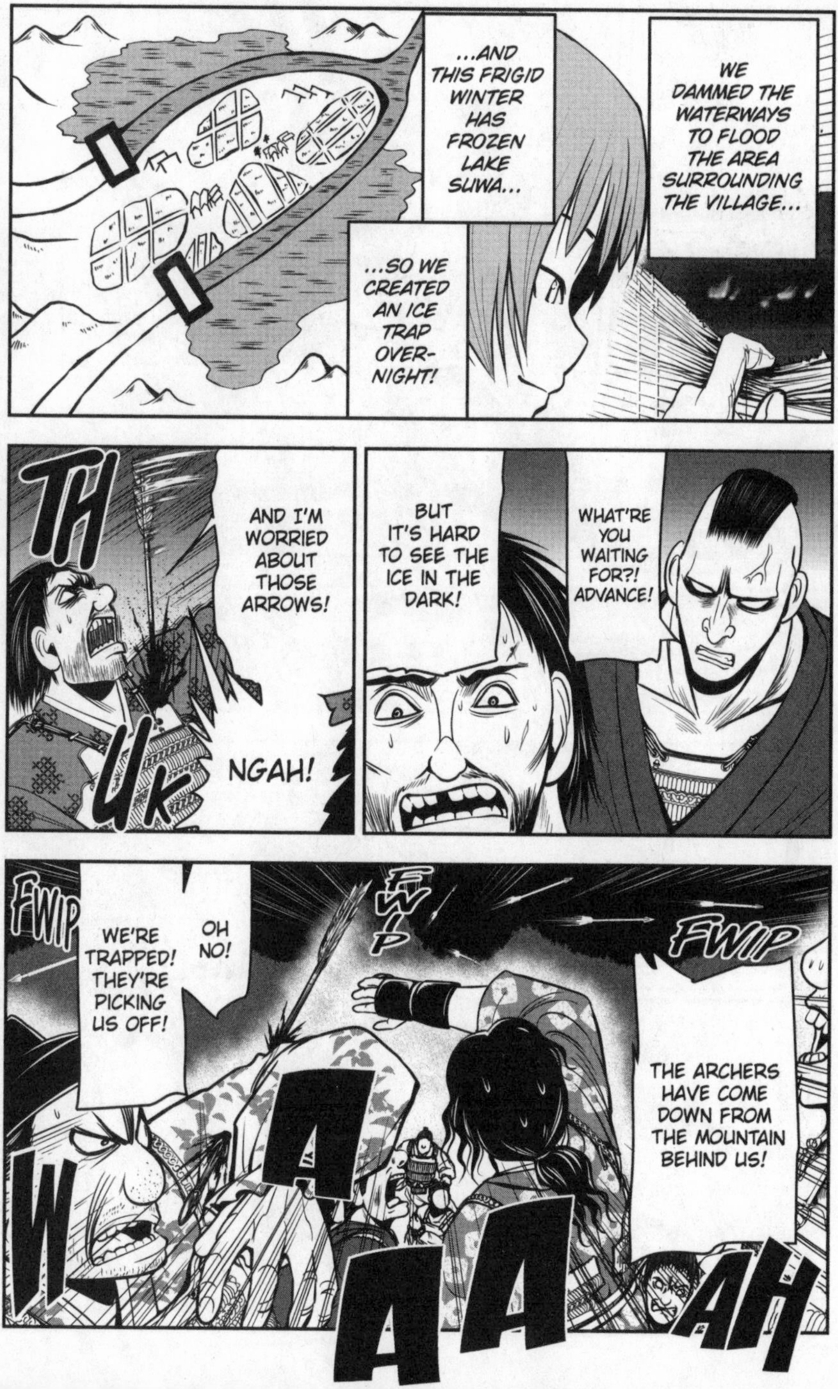
WE DAMMED THE WATERWAYS TO FLOOD THE AREA SURROUNDING THE VILLAGE...
...AND THIS FRIGID WINTER HAS FROZEN LAKE SUWA...
...SO WE CREATED AN ICE TRAP OVER-NIGHT!
WHAT'RE YOU WAITING FOR?! ADVANCE!
BUT IT'S HARD TO SEE THE ICE IN THE DARK!
AND I'M WORRIED ABOUT THOSE ARROWS!
THUK
NGAH!
FWIP
THE ARCHERS HAVE COME DOWN FROM THE MOUNTAIN BEHIND US!
FWIP
OH NO!
WE'RE TRAPPED! THEY'RE PICKING US OFF!
FWIP
WAAAAH

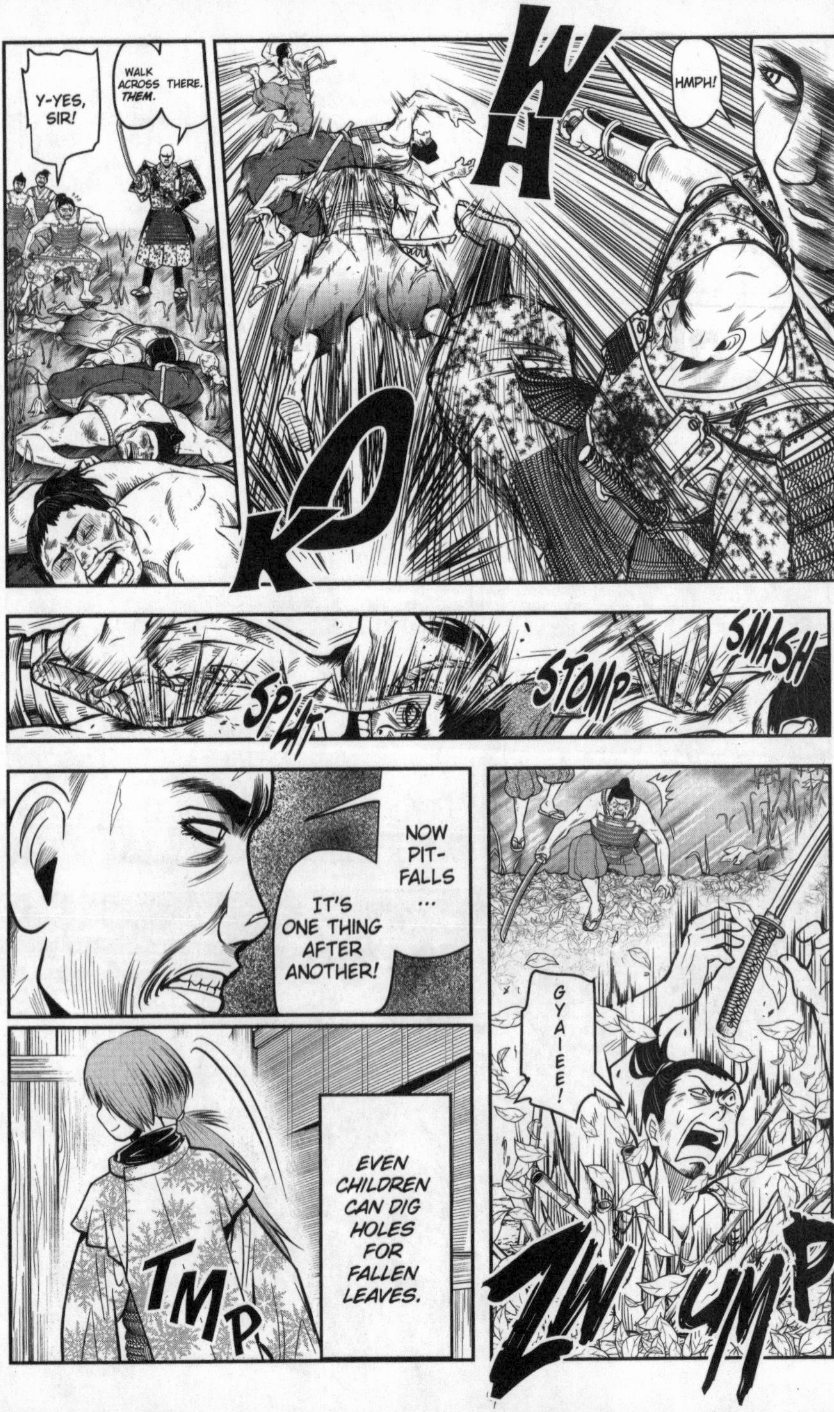
HMPH!
WHAK
WALK ACROSS THERE. THEM.
Y-YES, SIR!
SMASH
STOMP
SPLAT
GYAIEE!
ZWUMP
NOW PIT-FALLS...
IT'S ONE THING AFTER ANOTHER!
EVEN CHILDREN CAN DIG HOLES FOR FALLEN LEAVES.
TMP

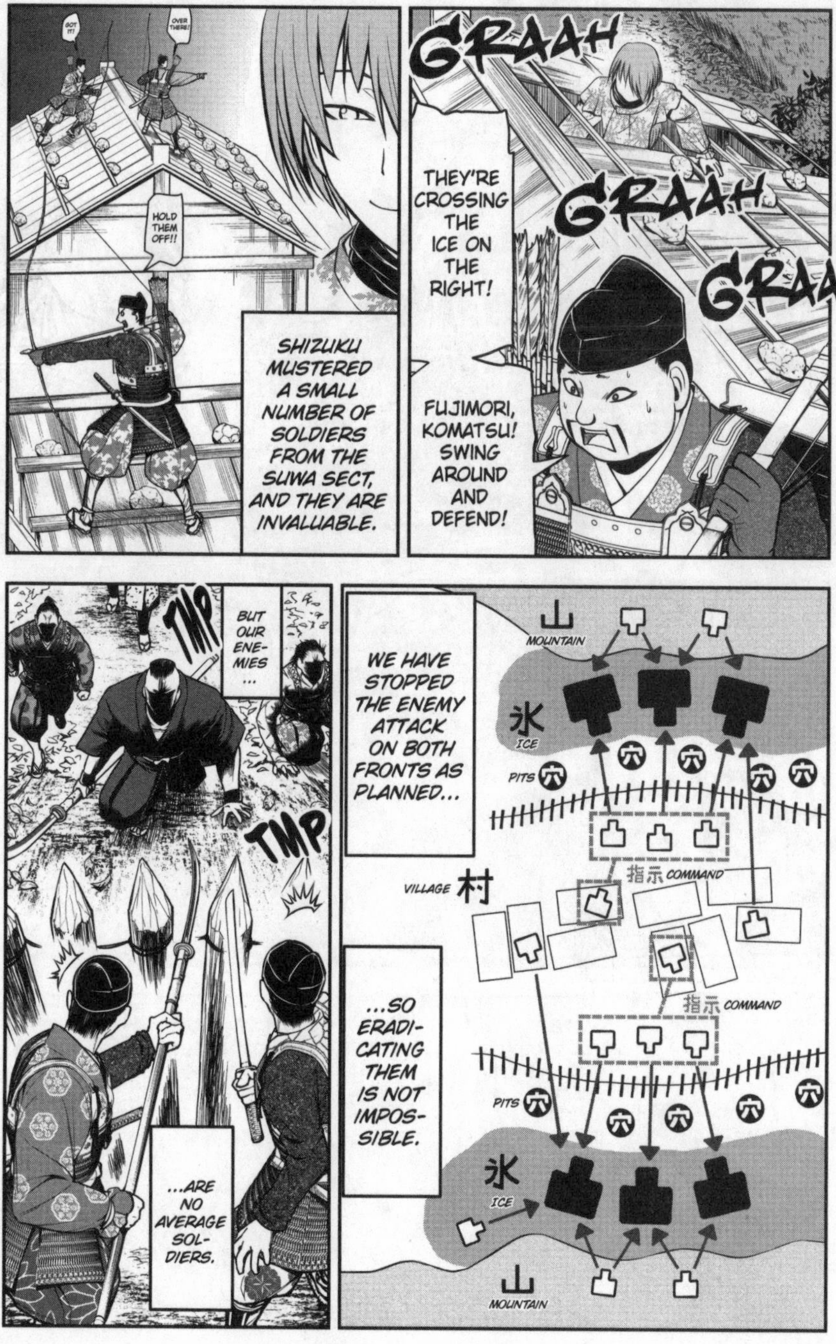
GRAAH
GRAAH
GRAA
THEY'RE CROSSING THE ICE ON THE RIGHT!
FUJIMORI, KOMATSU! SWING AROUND AND DEFEND!
OVER THERE!
GOT IT!
HOLD THEM OFF!!
SHIZUKU MUSTERED A SMALL NUMBER OF SOLDIERS FROM THE SUWA SECT, AND THEY ARE INVALUABLE.
WE HAVE STOPPED THE ENEMY ATTACK ON BOTH FRONTS AS PLANNED...
山 MOUNTAIN
氷 ICE
PITS 穴
VILLAGE 村
指示 COMMAND
指示 COMMAND
PITS 穴
氷 ICE
山 MOUNTAIN
...SO ERADICATING THEM IS NOT IMPOSSIBLE.
BUT OUR ENEMIES...
TMP
TMP
...ARE NO AVERAGE SOLDIERS.

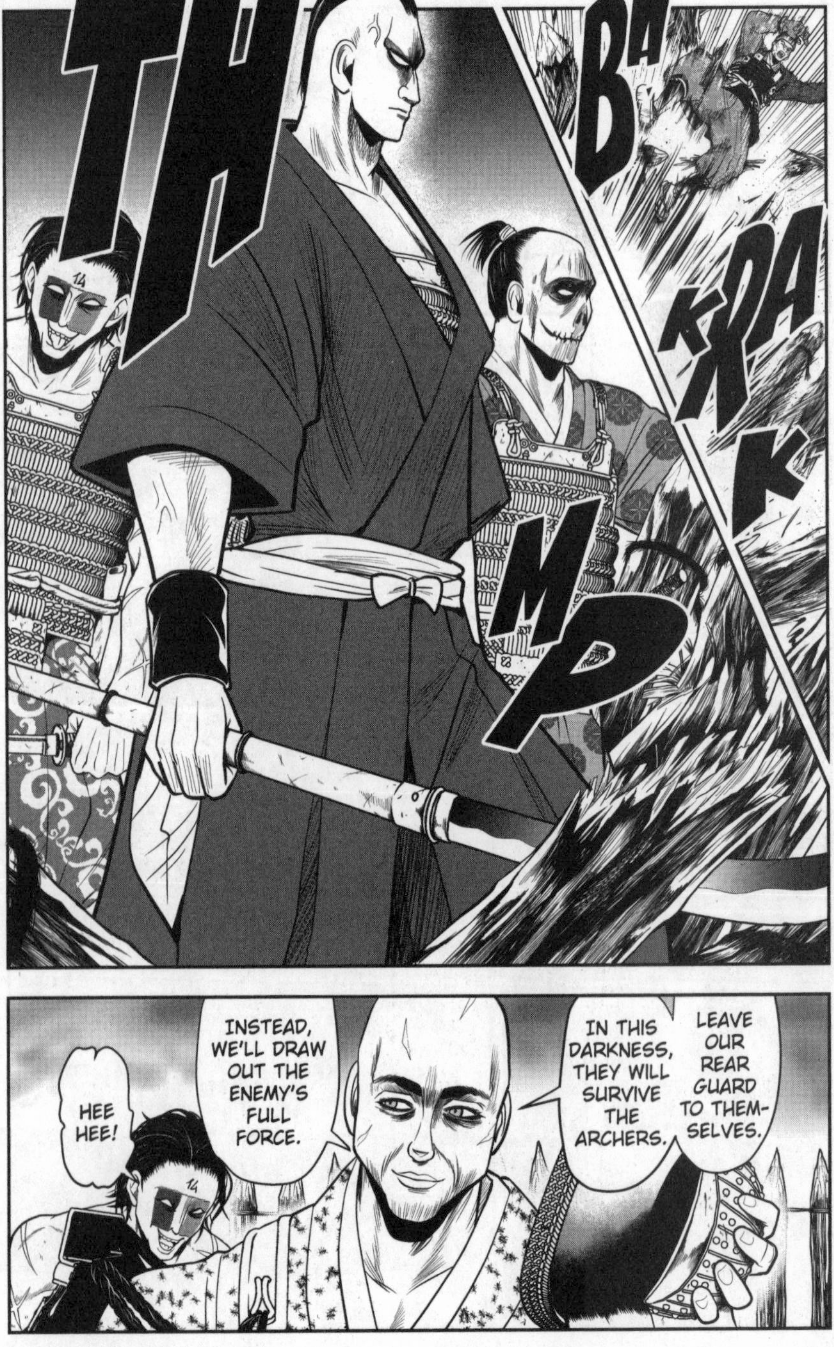
BA
KRAK
THMP
LEAVE OUR REAR GUARD TO THEMSELVES.
IN THIS DARKNESS, THEY WILL SURVIVE THE ARCHERS.
INSTEAD, WE'LL DRAW OUT THE ENEMY'S FULL FORCE.
HEE HEE!

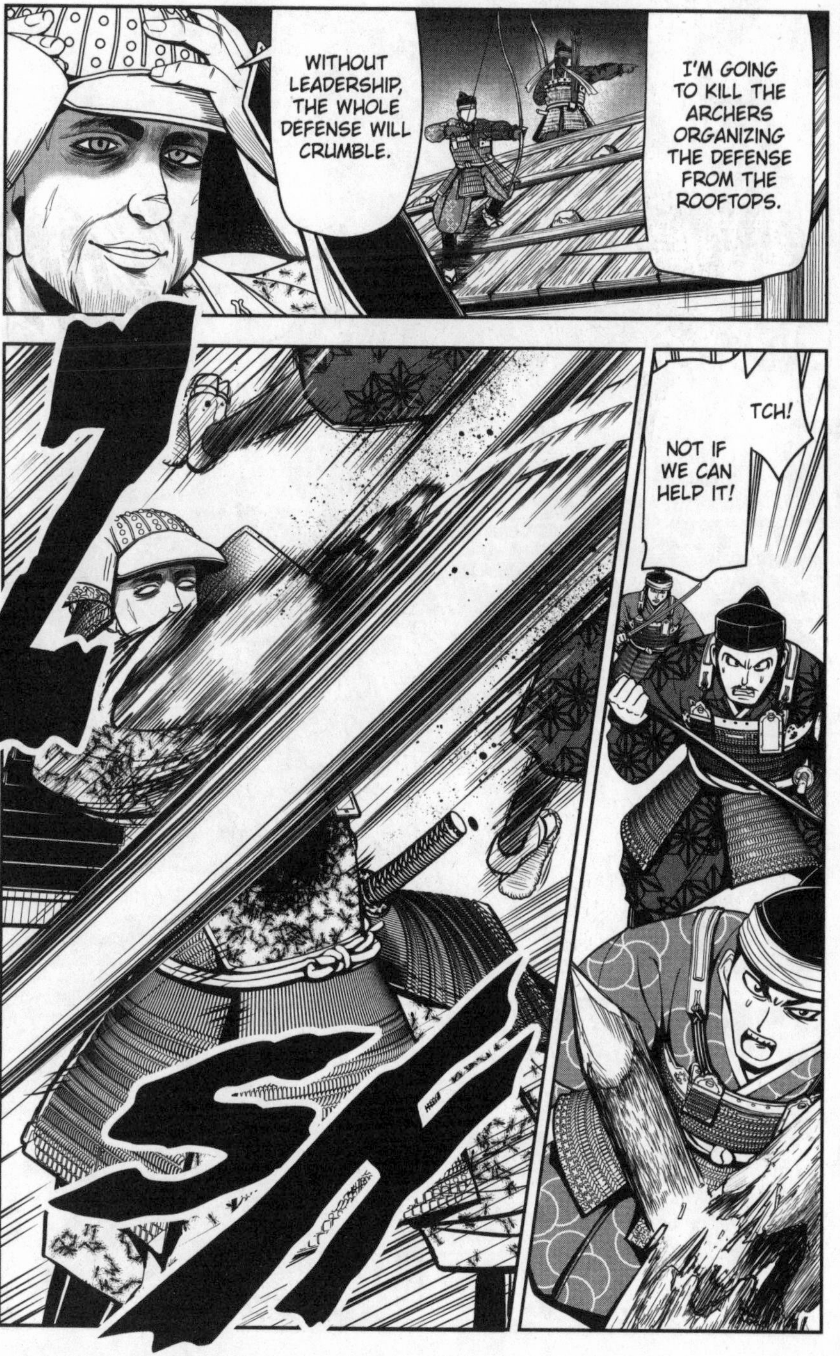
I'M GOING TO KILL THE ARCHERS ORGANIZING THE DEFENSE FROM THE ROOFTOPS.
WITHOUT LEADERSHIP, THE WHOLE DEFENSE WILL CRUMBLE.
TCH!
NOT IF WE CAN HELP IT!

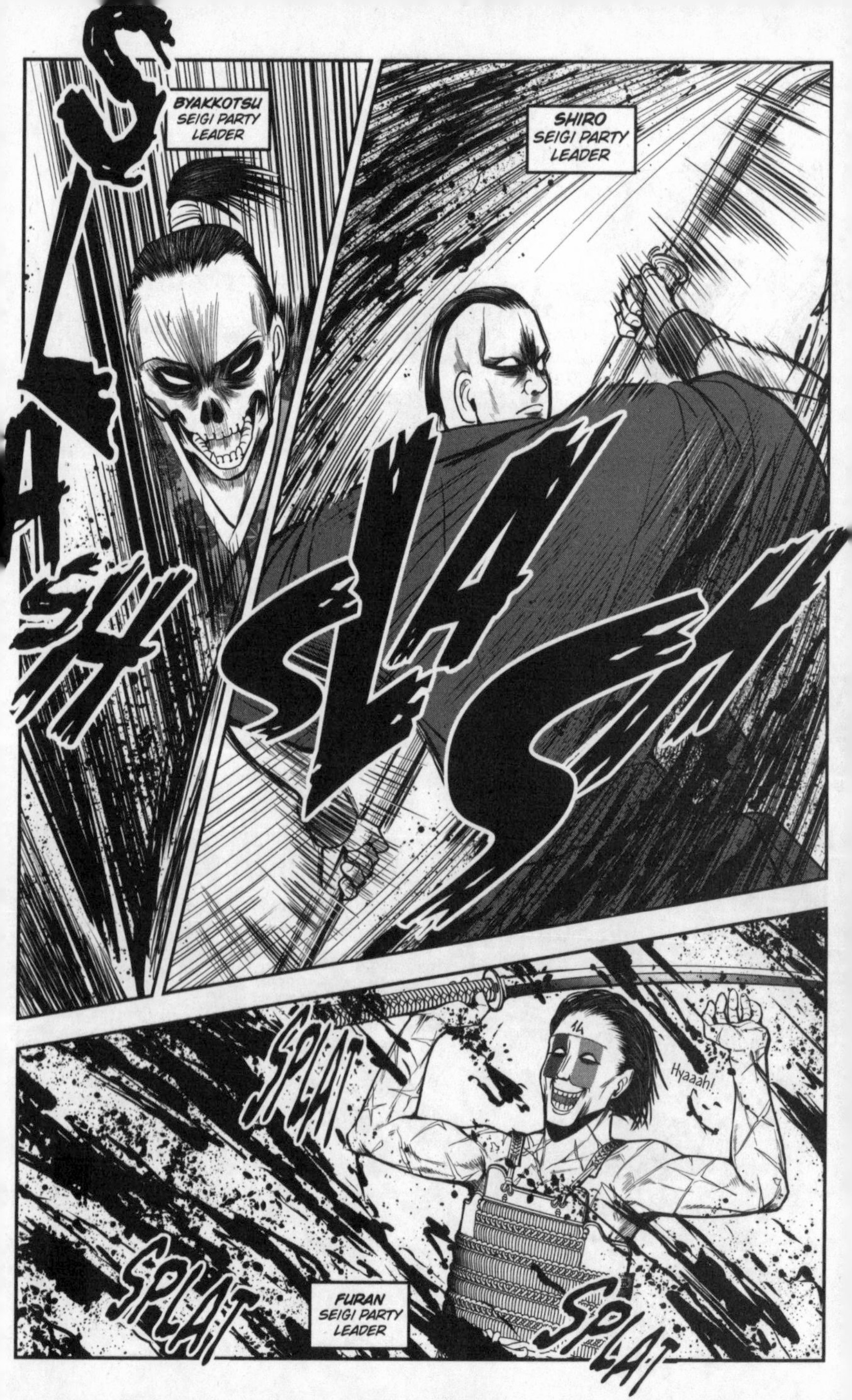
SHIRO
SEIGI PARTY
LEADER
SLASH
BYAKKOTSU
SEIGI PARTY
LEADER
SLASH
Hyaaah!
SPLAT
SPLAT
FURAN
SEIGI PARTY
LEADER
SPLAT

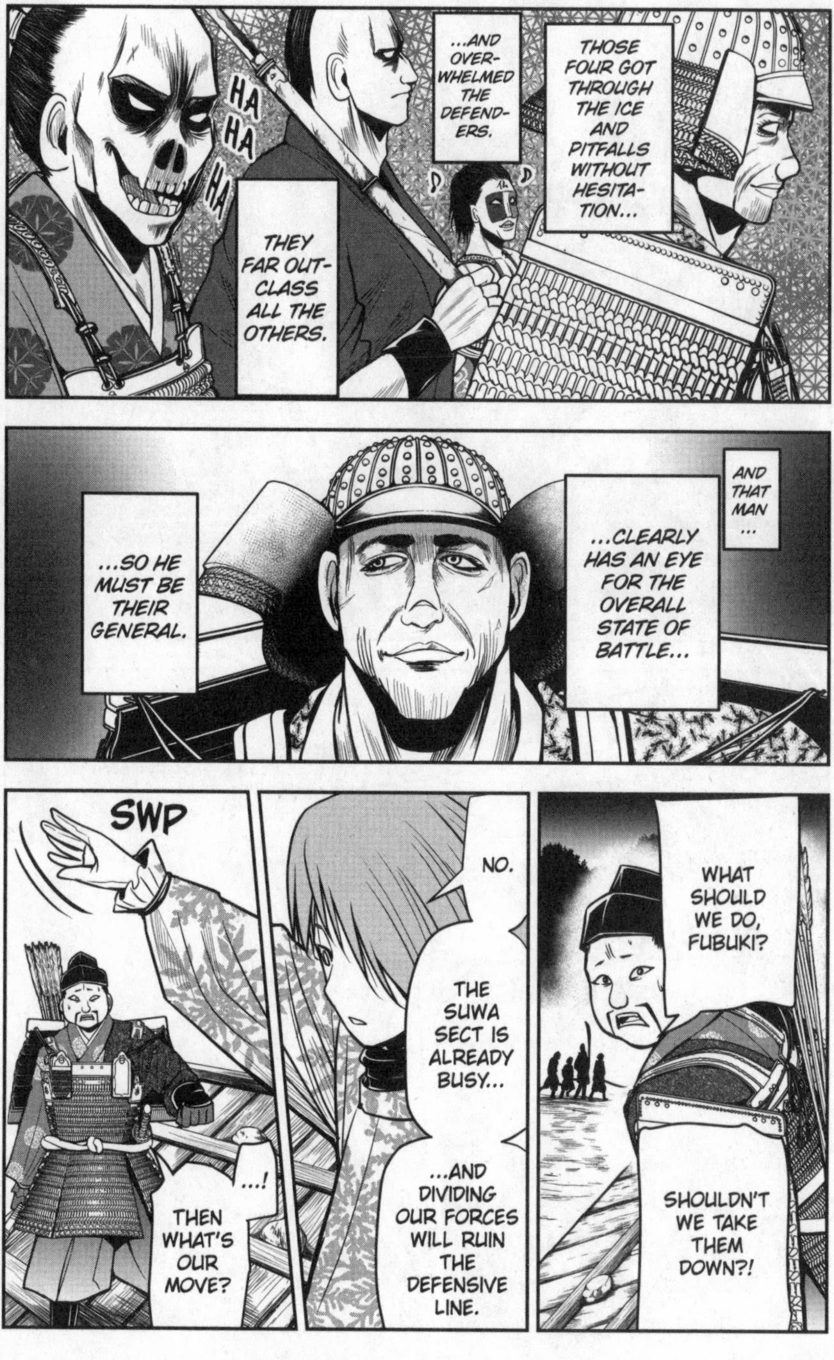
THOSE FOUR GOT THROUGH THE ICE AND PITFALLS WITHOUT HESITATION...
...AND OVERWHELMED THE DEFENDERS.
HA HA HA HA
THEY FAR OUTCLASS ALL THE OTHERS.
AND THAT MAN...
...CLEARLY HAS AN EYE FOR THE OVERALL STATE OF BATTLE...
...SO HE MUST BE THEIR GENERAL.
WHAT SHOULD WE DO, FUBUKI?
SHOULDN'T WE TAKE THEM DOWN?!
NO.
THE SUWA SECT IS ALREADY BUSY...
...AND DIVIDING OUR FORCES WILL RUIN THE DEFENSIVE LINE.
SWP
...!
THEN WHAT'S OUR MOVE?

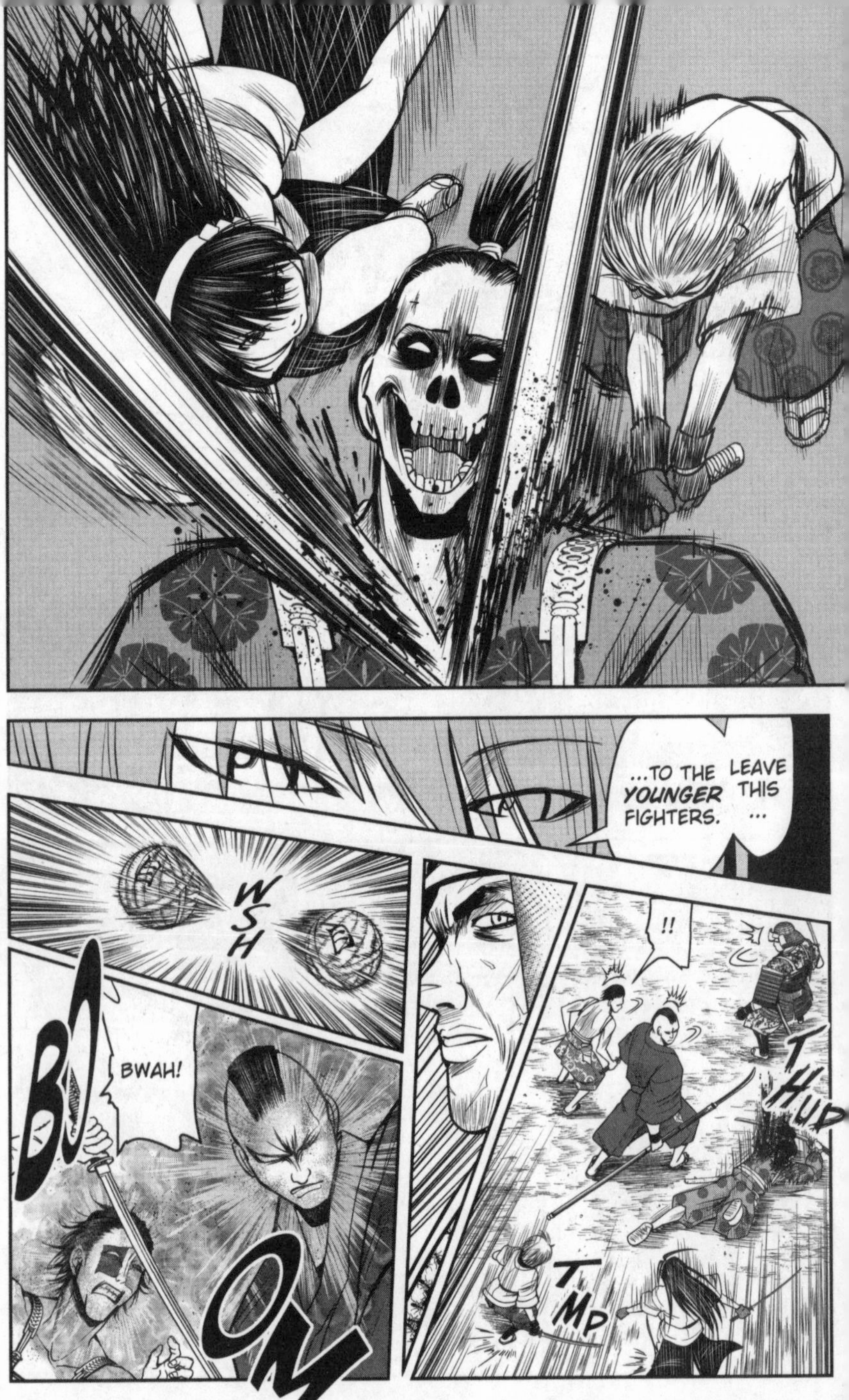
LEAVE THIS ...
...TO THE YOUNGER FIGHTERS.
!!
THUD
TMP
WSH
BOOM
BWAH!

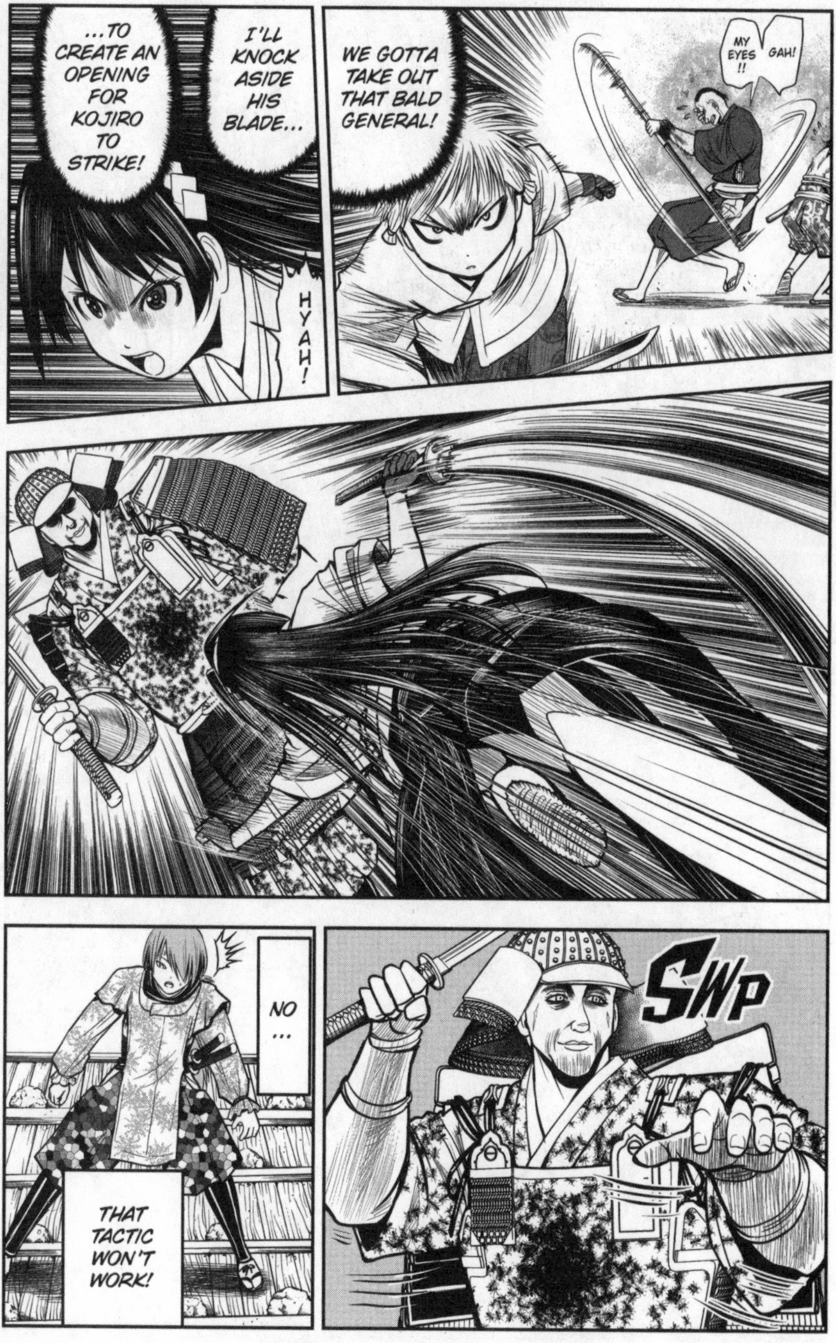
GAH!
MY EYES !!
WE GOTTA TAKE OUT THAT BALD GENERAL!
I'LL KNOCK ASIDE HIS BLADE...
...TO CREATE AN OPENING FOR KOJIRO TO STRIKE!
HYAH!
SWP
NO ...
THAT TACTIC WON'T WORK!

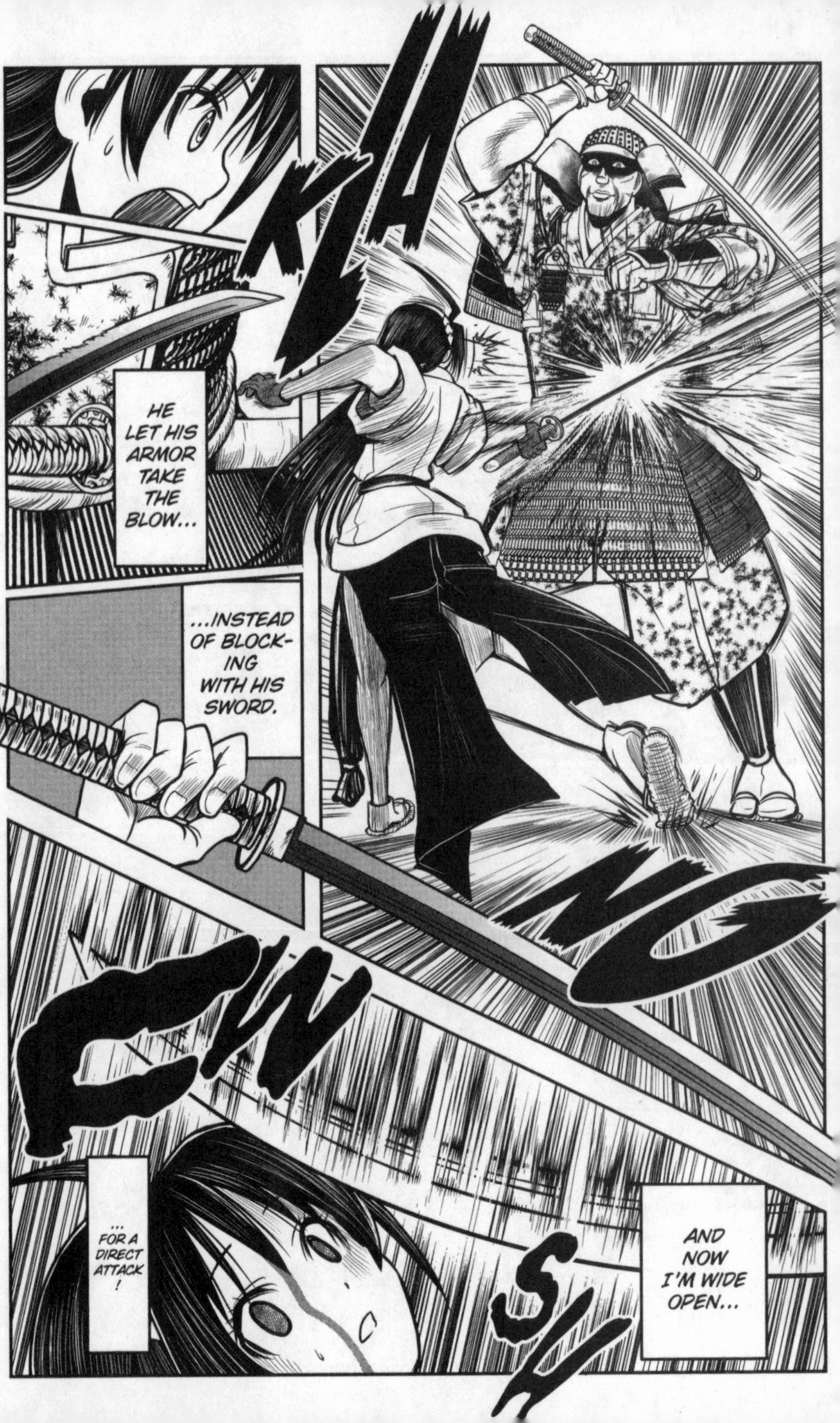
KA
HE LET HIS ARMOR TAKE THE BLOW...
...INSTEAD OF BLOCK-ING WITH HIS SWORD.
AND NOW I'M WIDE OPEN...
... FOR A DIRECT ATTACK!
SH

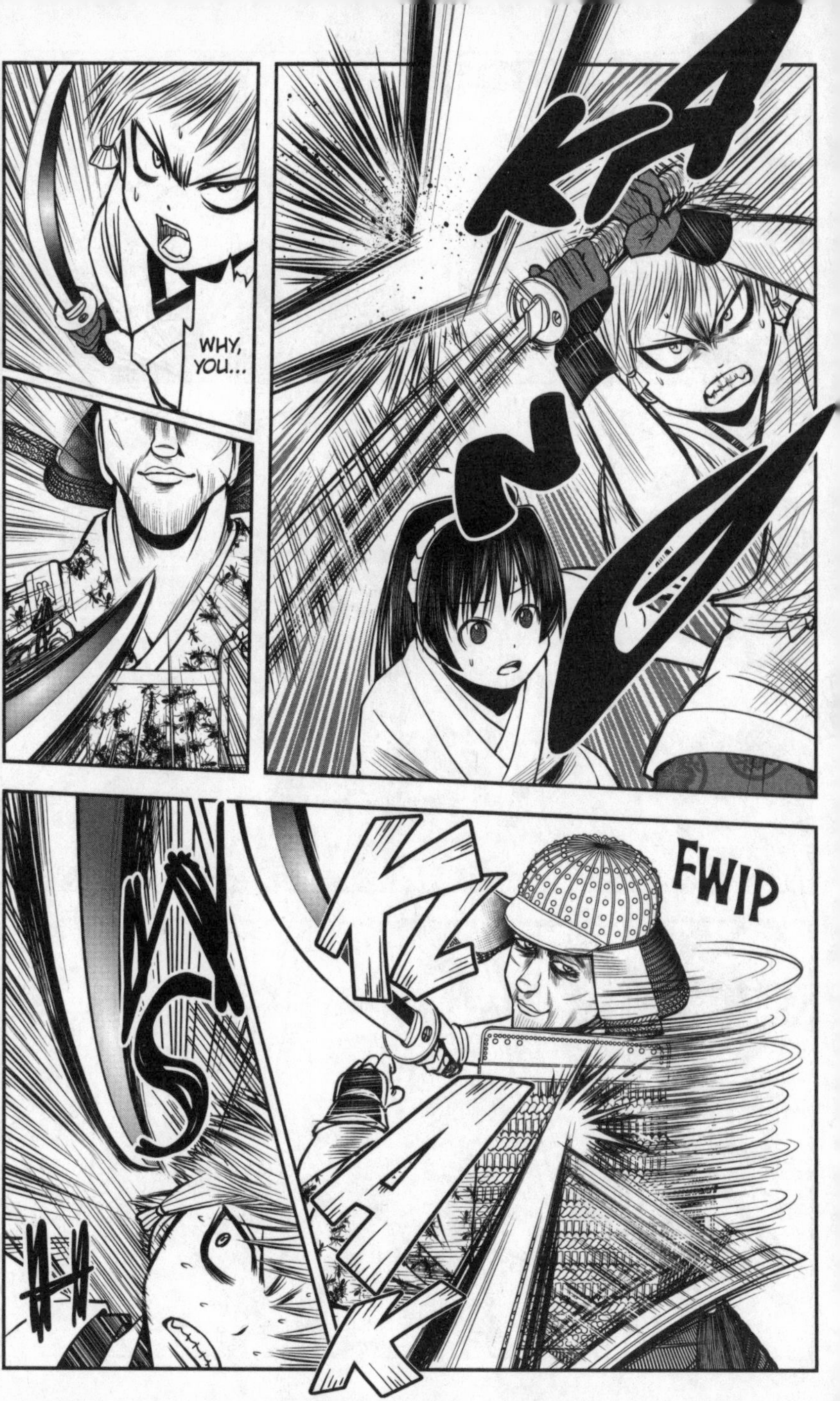
KANG
WHY, YOU...
FWIP

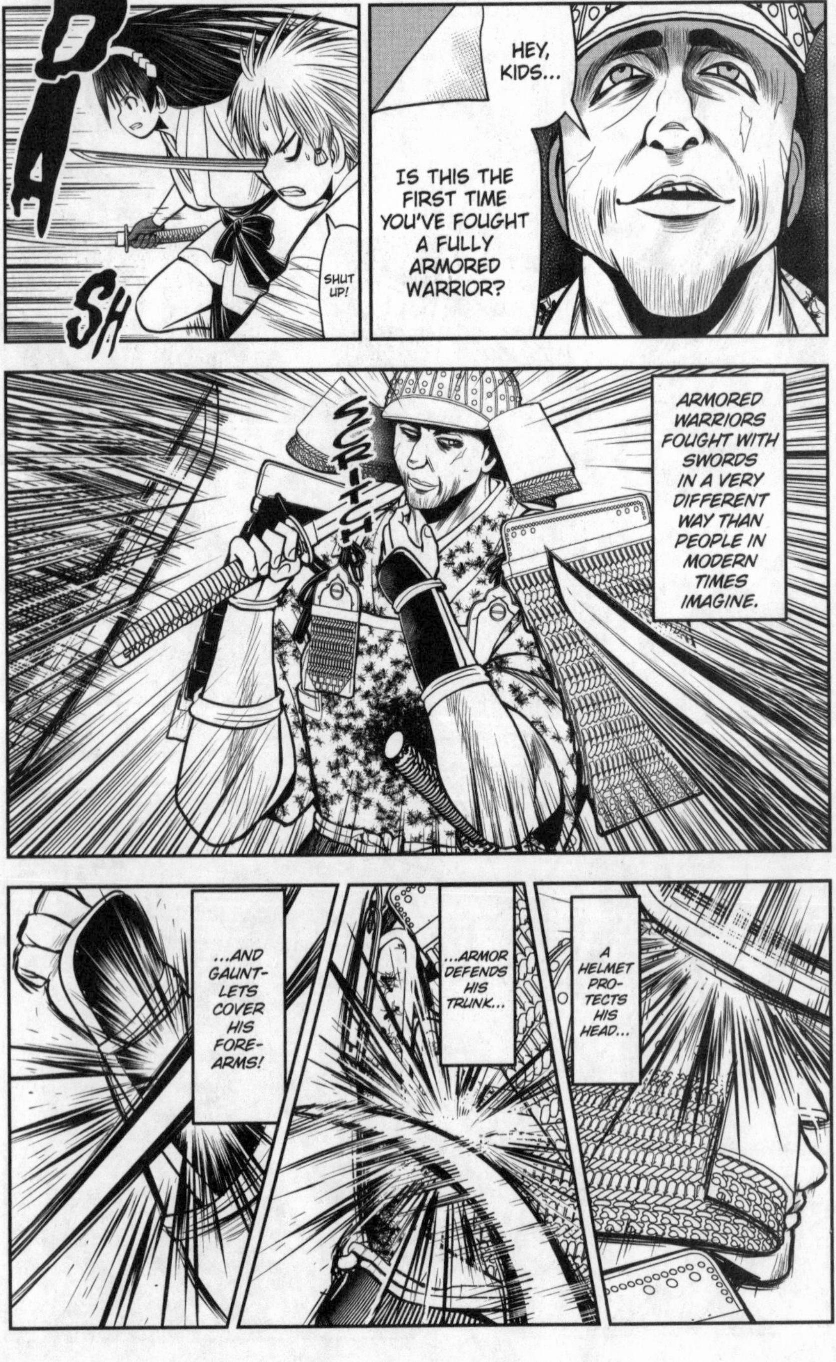
HEY, KIDS...
IS THIS THE FIRST TIME YOU'VE FOUGHT A FULLY ARMORED WARRIOR?
DA
SHUT UP!
SH
ARMORED WARRIORS FOUGHT WITH SWORDS IN A VERY DIFFERENT WAY THAN PEOPLE IN MODERN TIMES IMAGINE.
SCRITCH
A HELMET PROTECTS HIS HEAD...
...ARMOR DEFENDS HIS TRUNK...
...AND GAUNTLETS COVER HIS FOREARMS!

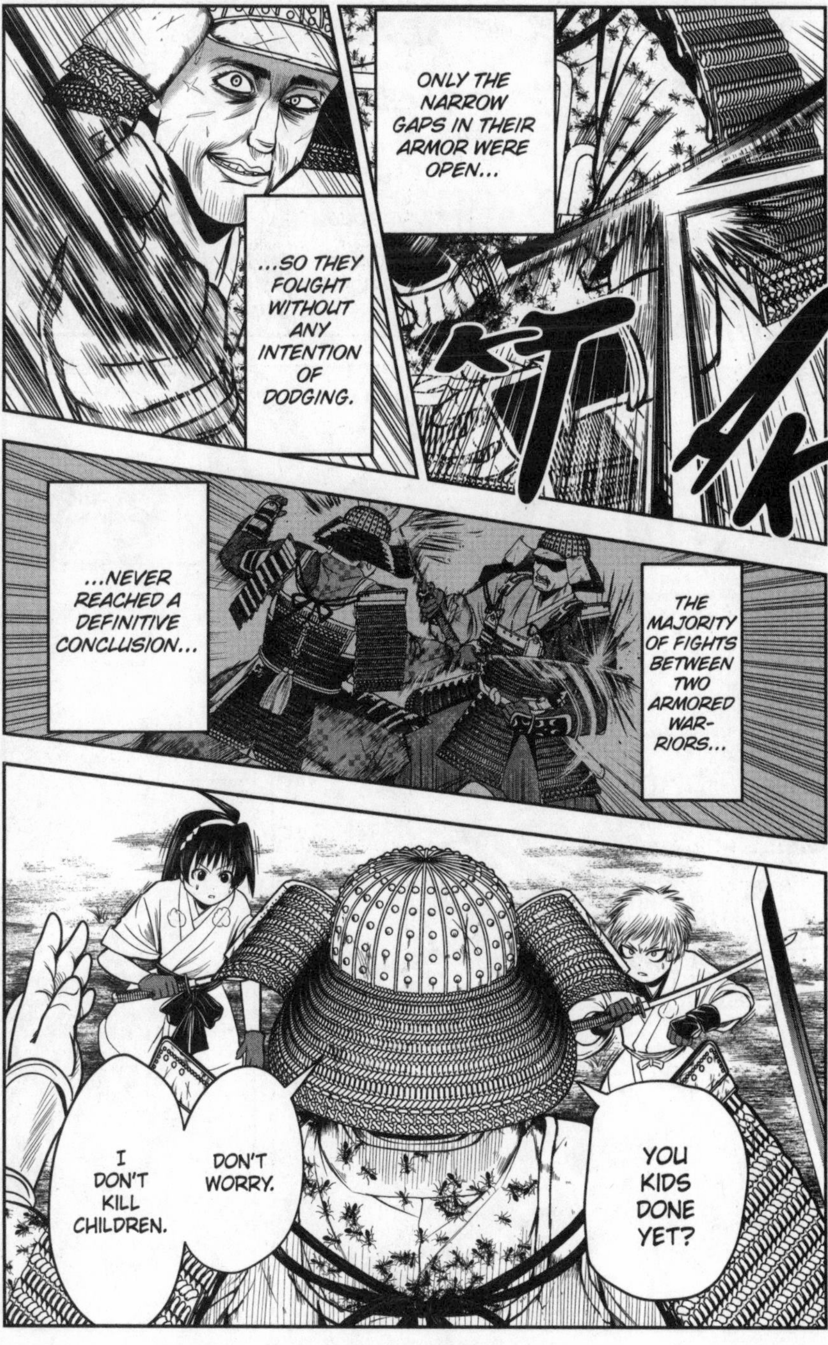
ONLY THE NARROW GAPS IN THEIR ARMOR WERE OPEN...
KTAK
...SO THEY FOUGHT WITHOUT ANY INTENTION OF DODGING.
THE MAJORITY OF FIGHTS BETWEEN TWO ARMORED WAR-RIORS...
...NEVER REACHED A DEFINITIVE CONCLUSION...
YOU KIDS DONE YET?
DON'T WORRY.
I DON'T KILL CHILDREN.

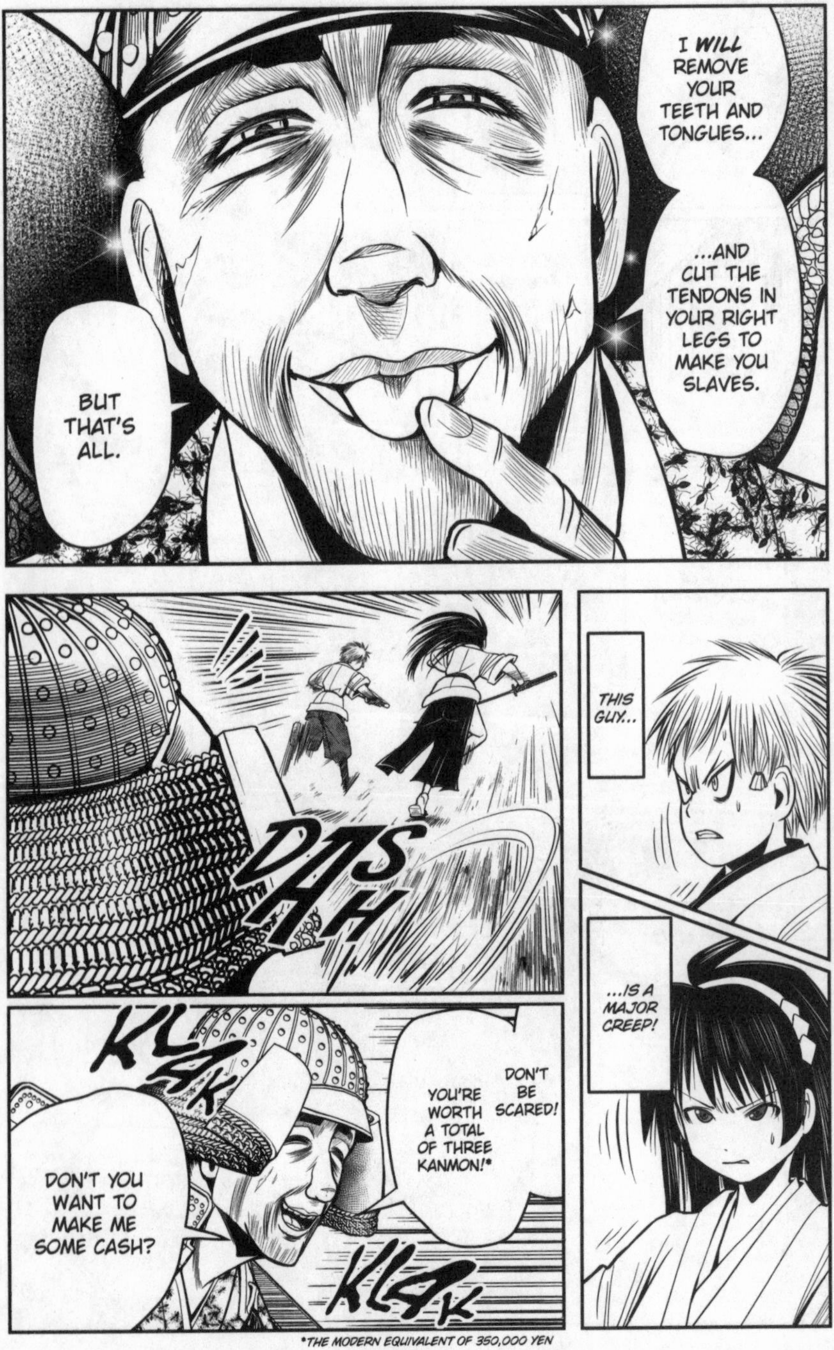

I WILL REMOVE YOUR TEETH AND TONGUES...
...AND CUT THE TENDONS IN YOUR RIGHT LEGS TO MAKE YOU SLAVES.
BUT THAT'S ALL.
THIS GUY...
...IS A MAJOR CREEP!
DASH
KLAK
DON'T BE SCARED!
YOU'RE WORTH A TOTAL OF THREE KANMON!*
DON'T YOU WANT TO MAKE ME SOME CASH?
KLAK

*THE MODERN EQUIVALENT OF 350,000 YEN

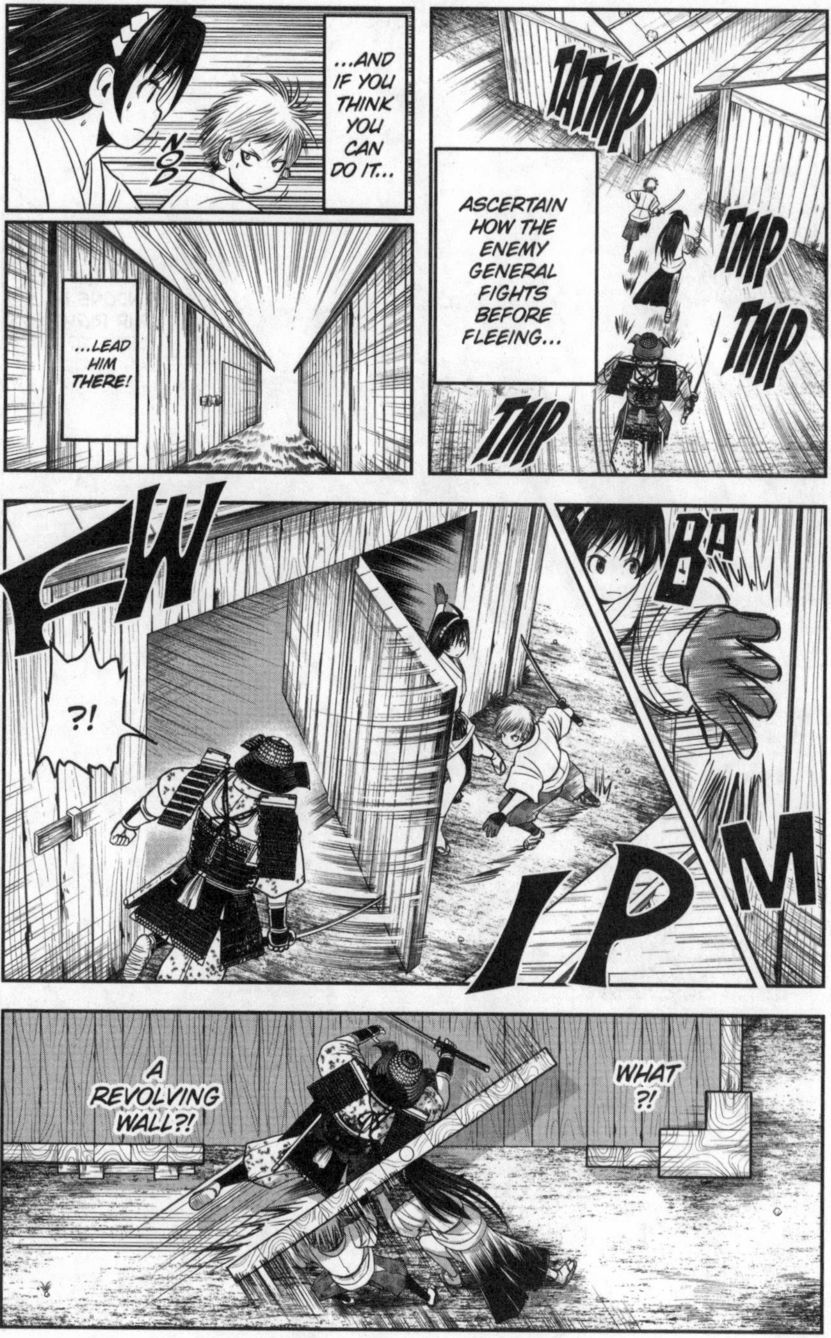
TATMP
ASCERTAIN HOW THE ENEMY GENERAL FIGHTS BEFORE FLEEING...
TMP
TMP
TMP
...AND IF YOU THINK YOU CAN DO IT...
NOD
...LEAD HIM THERE!
BAM
FWIP
?!
WHAT ?!
A REVOLVING WALL?!

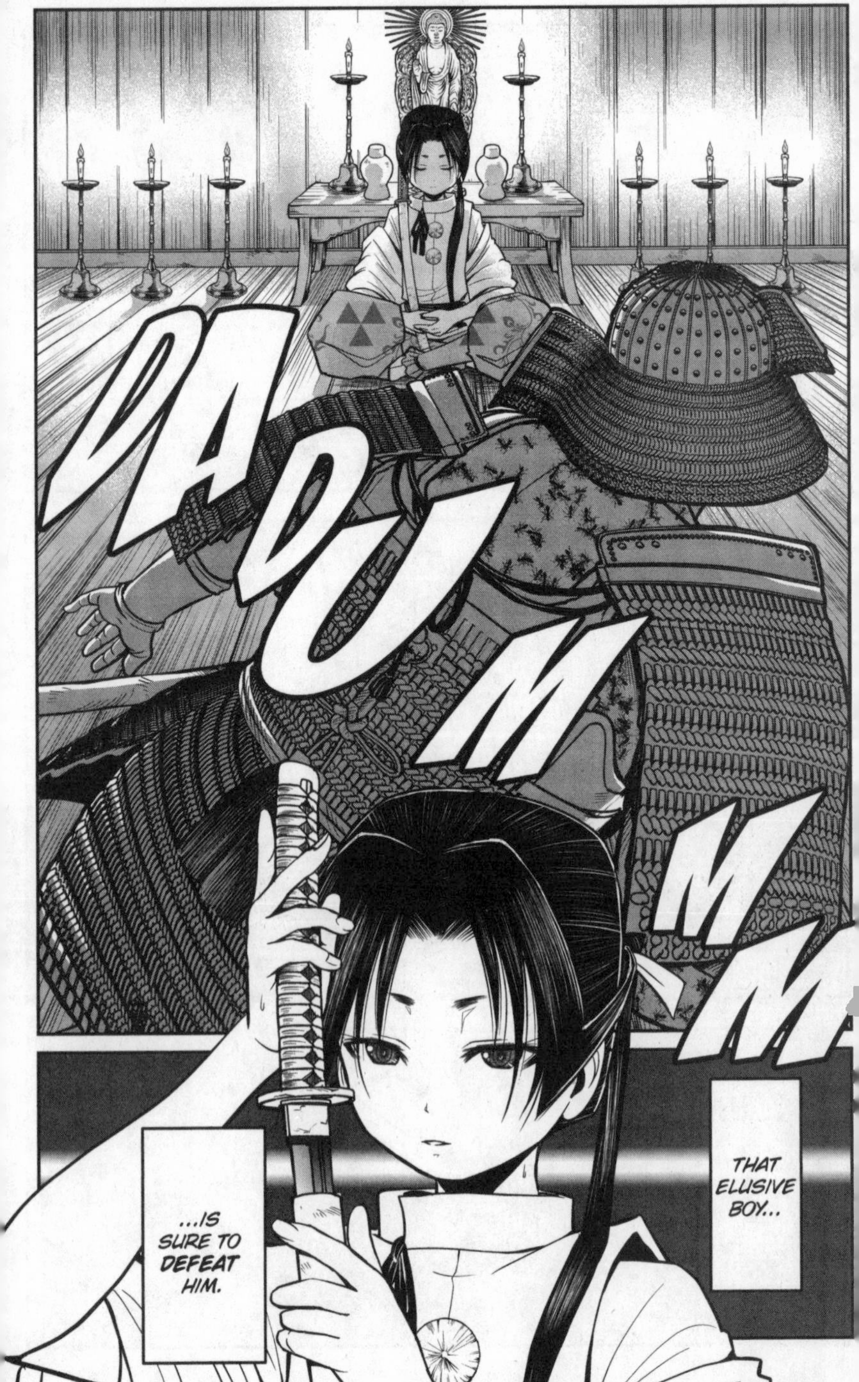
DADUMMM
THAT ELUSIVE BOY...
...IS SURE TO DEFEAT HIM.

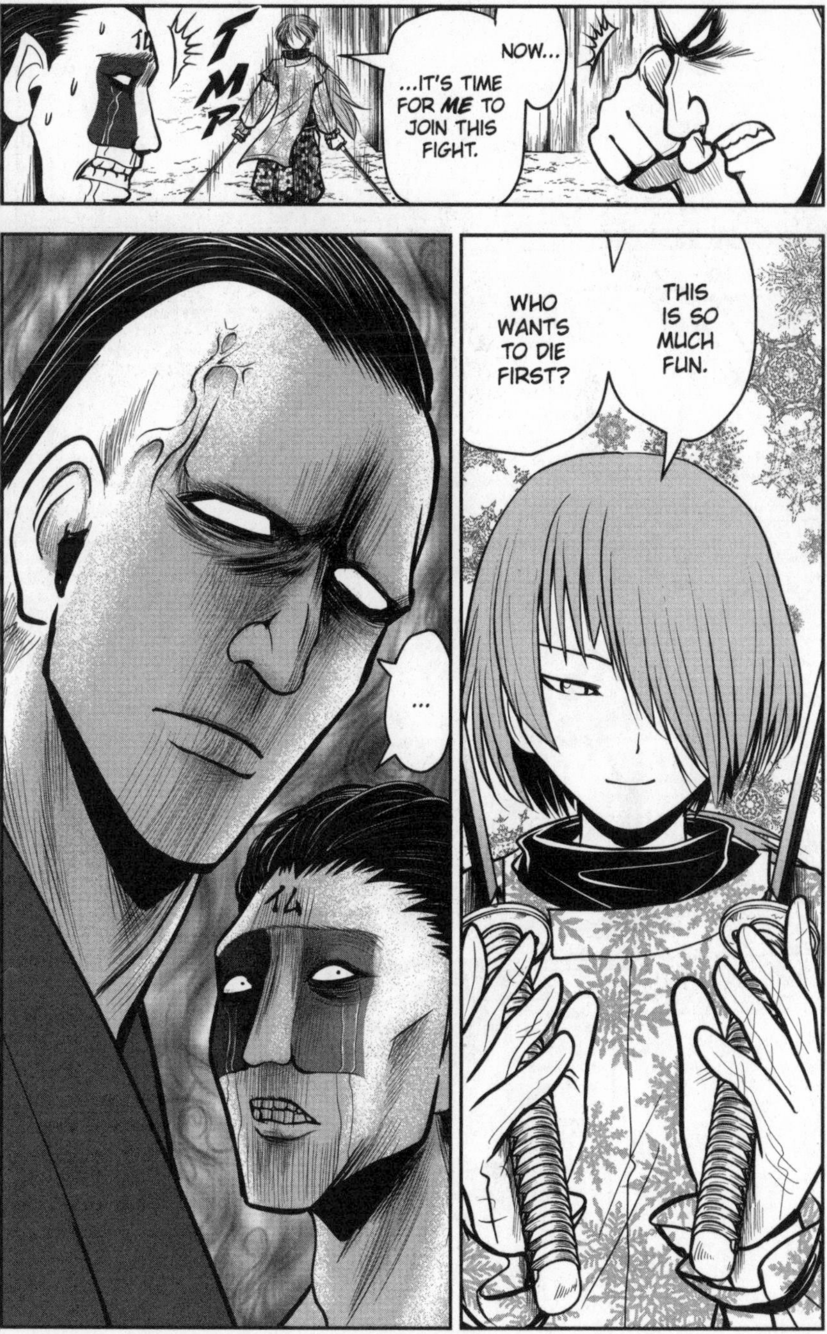
NOW... ...IT'S TIME FOR ME TO JOIN THIS FIGHT.
TMP
THIS IS SO MUCH FUN.
WHO WANTS TO DIE FIRST?
...

I WILL SCRAPE AWAY THE TARTAR...
...REMOVE BIOFILM, APPLY FLUORIDE TREATMENT, AND POLISH YOUR TEETH.
BUT THAT'S ALL.
THAT'S WHAT HE SAYS, BUT...
...I'M SURE HE'LL FIND A CAVITY TO GRIND AWAY AT!

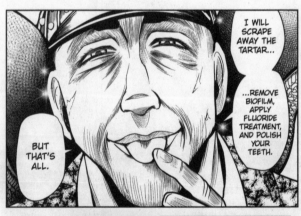

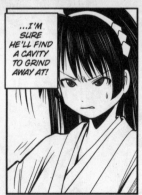

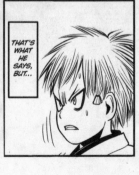

CHAPTER 20: BUDDHA 1334

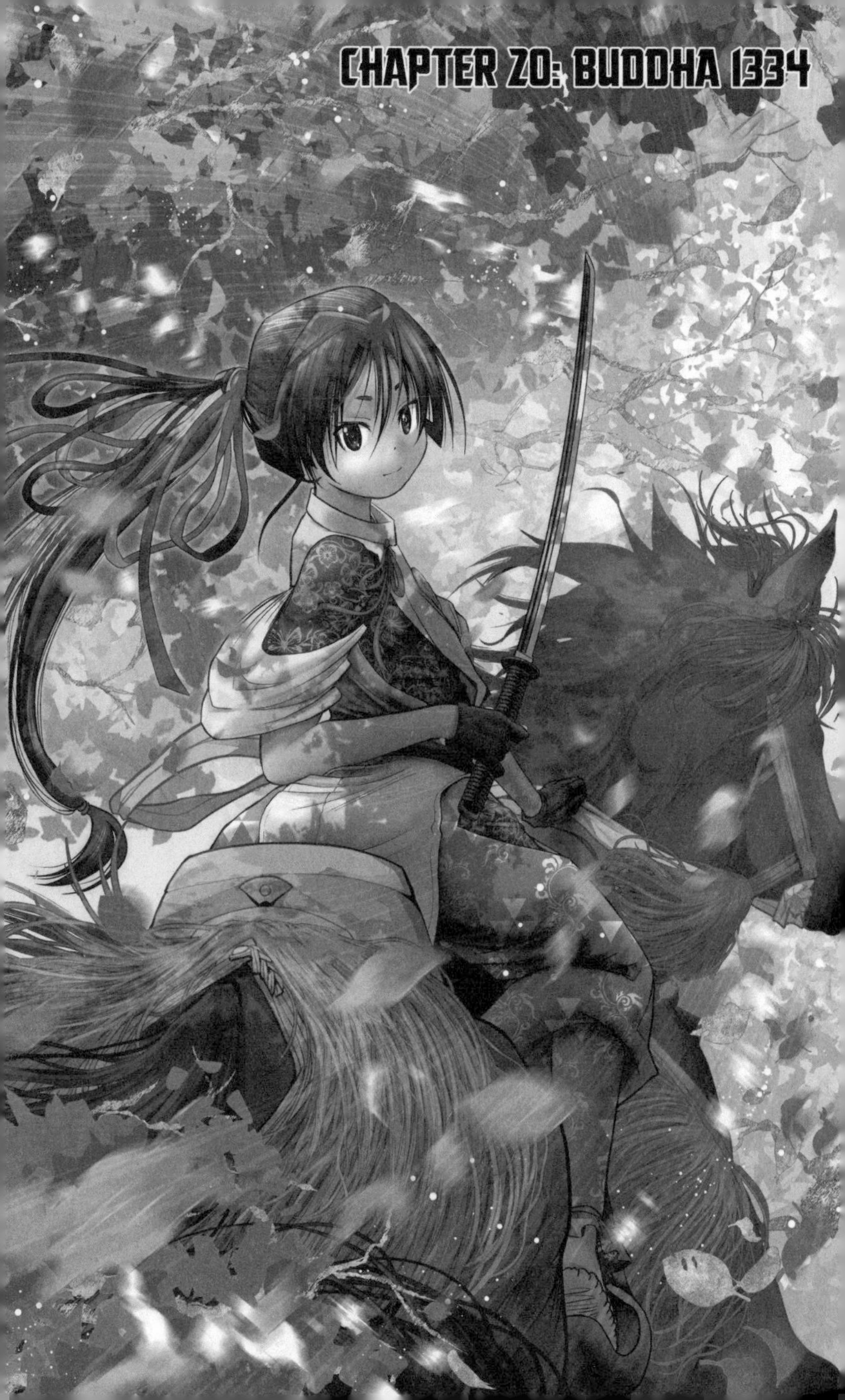

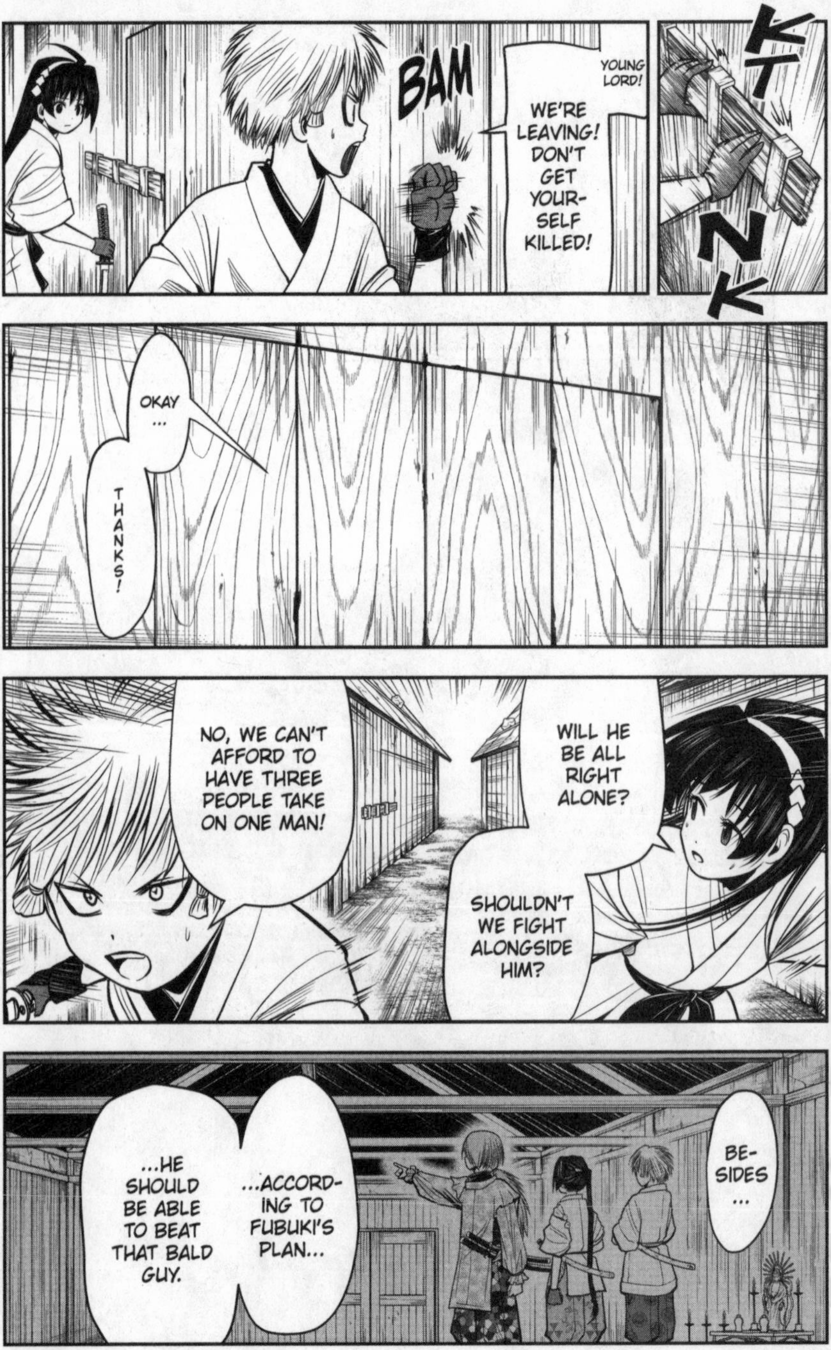
KTNK
YOUNG LORD!
WE'RE LEAVING! DON'T GET YOUR-SELF KILLED!
BAM
OKAY... THANKS!
WILL HE BE ALL RIGHT ALONE?
SHOULDN'T WE FIGHT ALONGSIDE HIM?
NO, WE CAN'T AFFORD TO HAVE THREE PEOPLE TAKE ON ONE MAN!
BE-SIDES...
...ACCORD-ING TO FUBUKI'S PLAN...
...HE SHOULD BE ABLE TO BEAT THAT BALD GUY.

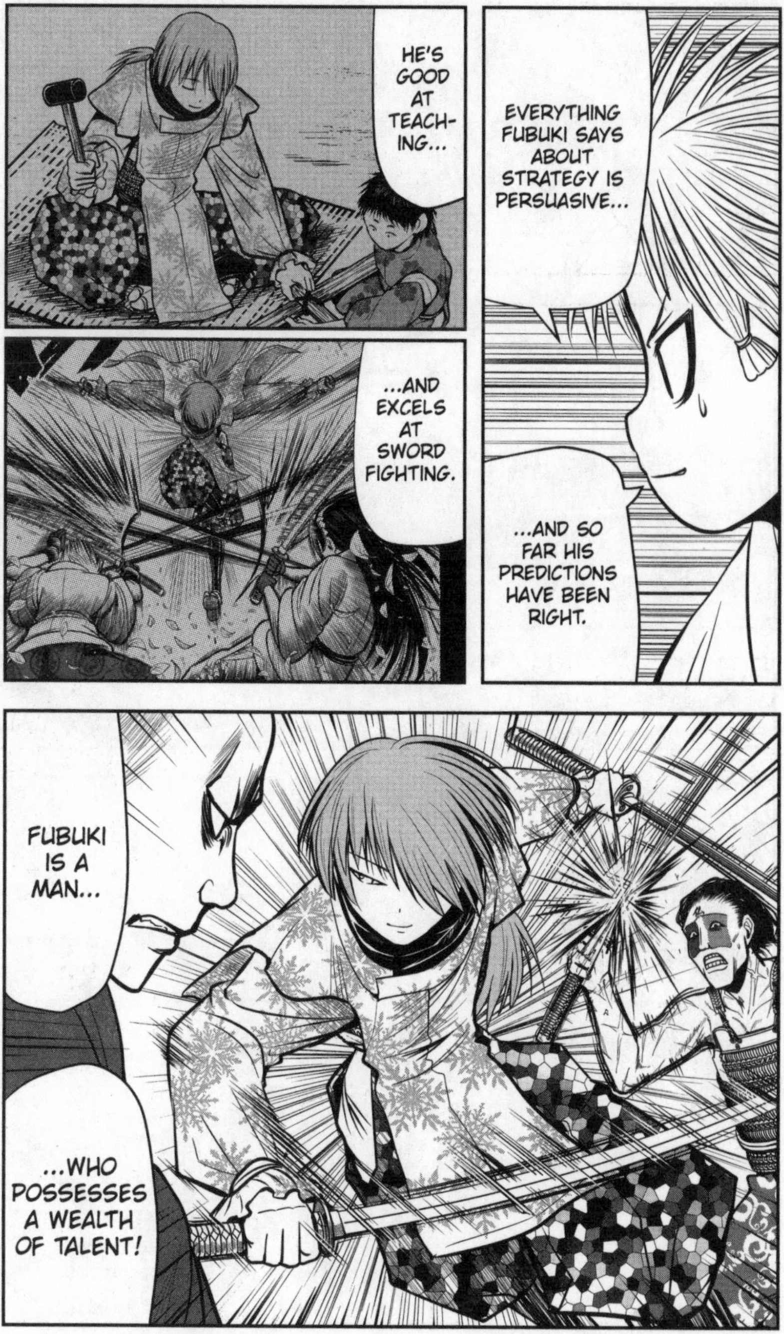
EVERYTHING FUBUKI SAYS ABOUT STRATEGY IS PERSUASIVE...
...AND SO FAR HIS PREDICTIONS HAVE BEEN RIGHT.
HE'S GOOD AT TEACHING...
...AND EXCELS AT SWORD FIGHTING.
FUBUKI IS A MAN...
...WHO POSSESSES A WEALTH OF TALENT!

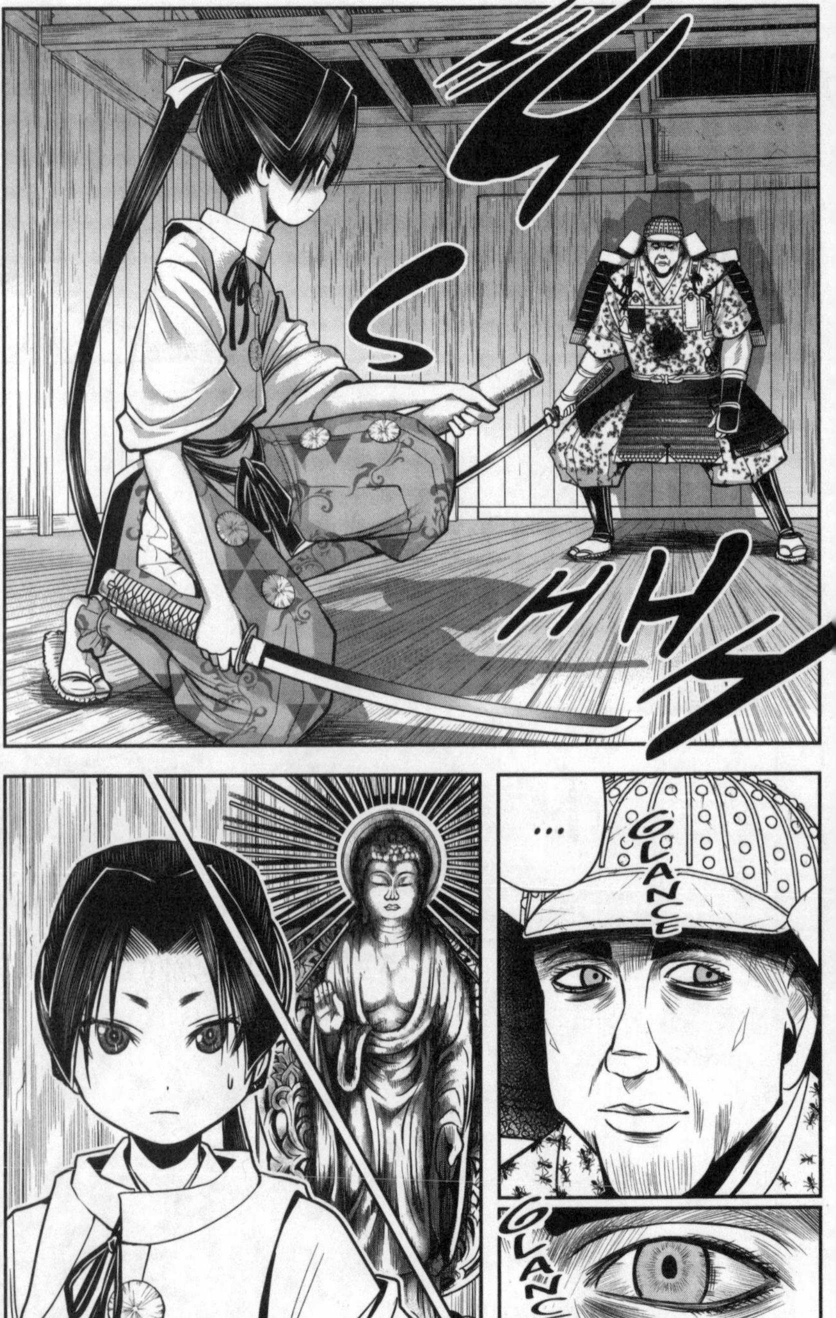
SHHHK
...
GLANCE
GLANCE

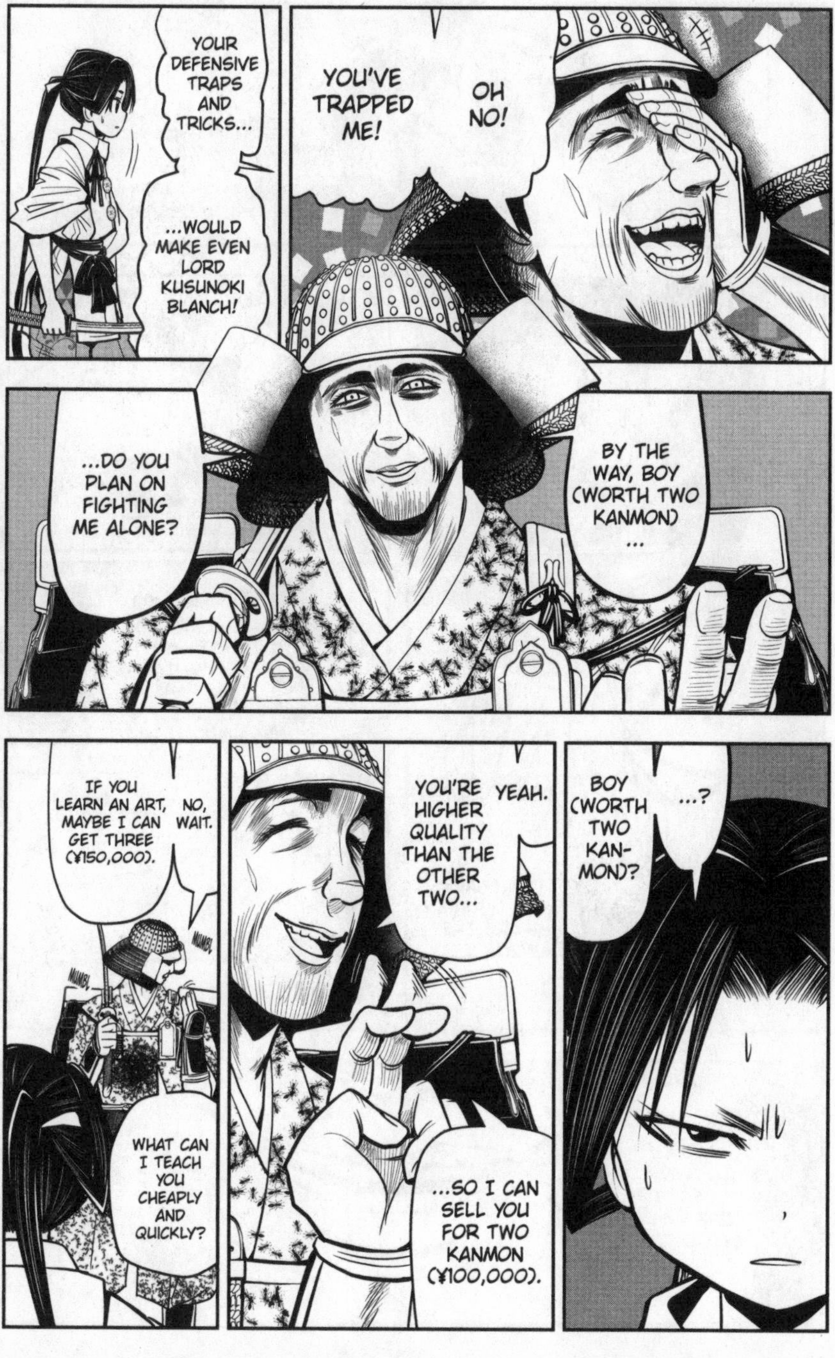
OH NO!
YOU'VE TRAPPED ME!
YOUR DEFENSIVE TRAPS AND TRICKS...
...WOULD MAKE EVEN LORD KUSUNOKI BLANCH!
BY THE WAY, BOY (WORTH TWO KANMON)...
...DO YOU PLAN ON FIGHTING ME ALONE?
...?
BOY (WORTH TWO KAN-MON)?
YEAH.
YOU'RE HIGHER QUALITY THAN THE OTHER TWO...
...SO I CAN SELL YOU FOR TWO KANMON (¥100,000).
NO, WAIT.
IF YOU LEARN AN ART, MAYBE I CAN GET THREE (¥150,000).
MUMBL
MUMBL
WHAT CAN I TEACH YOU CHEAPLY AND QUICKLY?

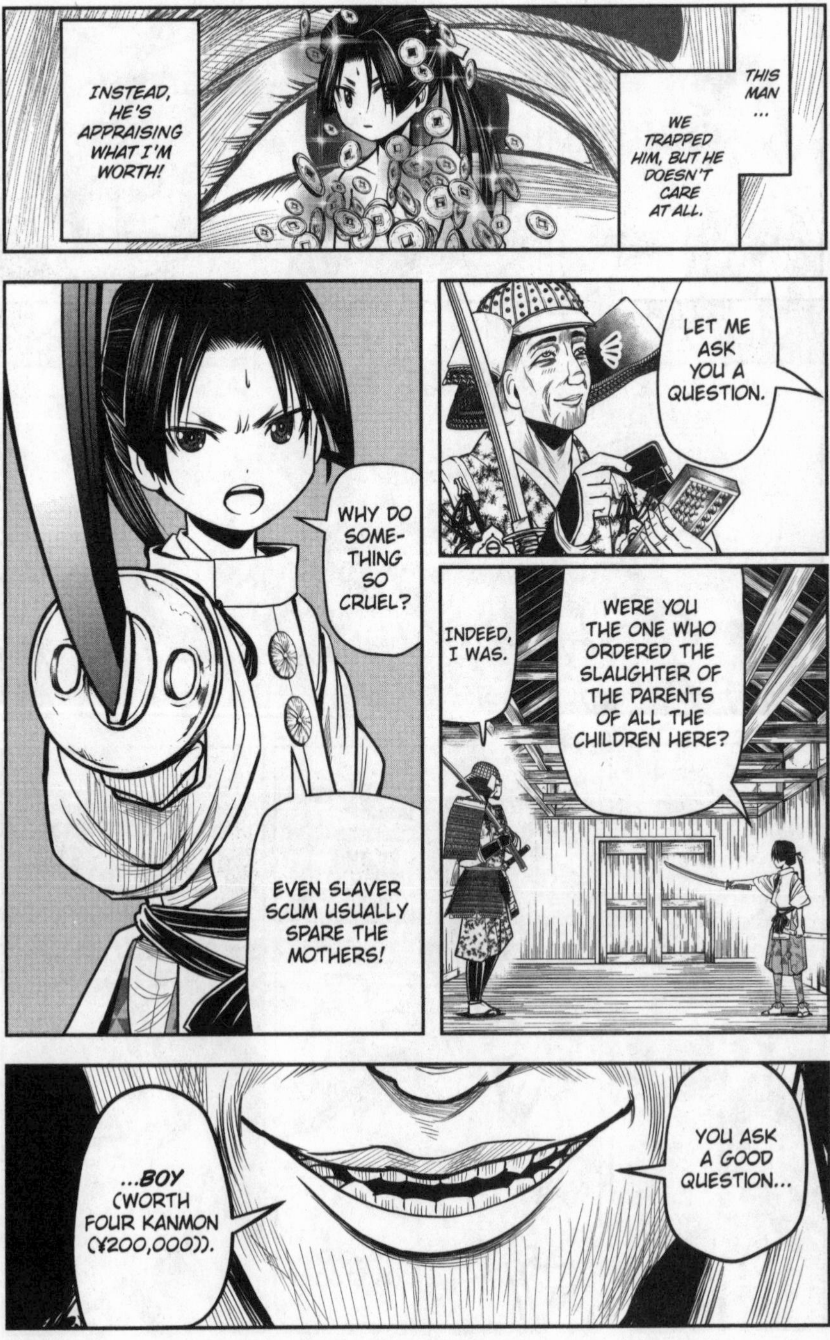
THIS MAN ...
WE TRAPPED HIM, BUT HE DOESN'T CARE AT ALL.
INSTEAD, HE'S APPRAISING WHAT I'M WORTH!
LET ME ASK YOU A QUESTION.
WERE YOU THE ONE WHO ORDERED THE SLAUGHTER OF THE PARENTS OF ALL THE CHILDREN HERE?
INDEED, I WAS.
WHY DO SOME-THING SO CRUEL?
EVEN SLAVER SCUM USUALLY SPARE THE MOTHERS!
YOU ASK A GOOD QUESTION...
...BOY (WORTH FOUR KANMON (¥200,000)).

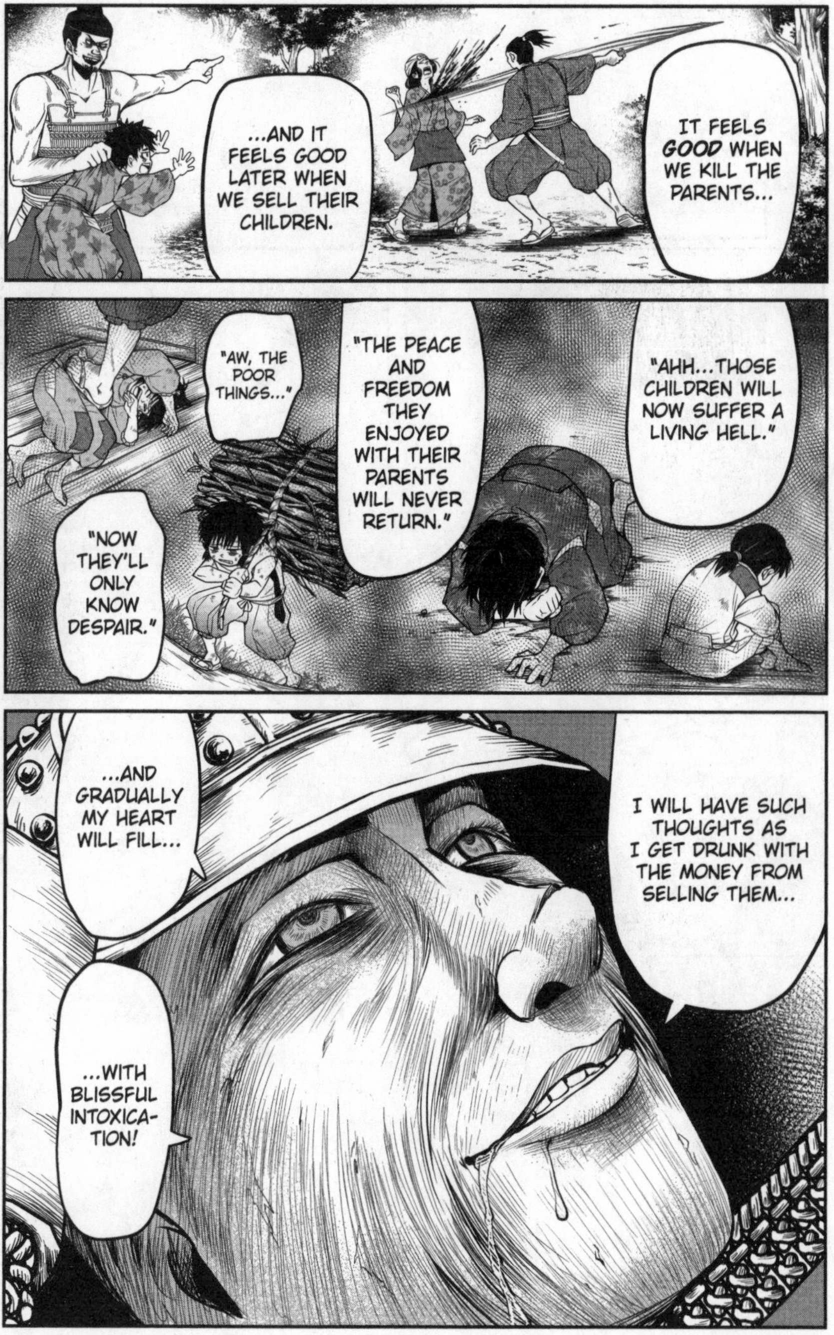
IT FEELS GOOD WHEN WE KILL THE PARENTS...
...AND IT FEELS GOOD LATER WHEN WE SELL THEIR CHILDREN.
"AHH...THOSE CHILDREN WILL NOW SUFFER A LIVING HELL."
"THE PEACE AND FREEDOM THEY ENJOYED WITH THEIR PARENTS WILL NEVER RETURN."
"AW, THE POOR THINGS..."
"NOW THEY'LL ONLY KNOW DESPAIR."
I WILL HAVE SUCH THOUGHTS AS I GET DRUNK WITH THE MONEY FROM SELLING THEM...
...AND GRADUALLY MY HEART WILL FILL...
...WITH BLISSFUL INTOXICATION!

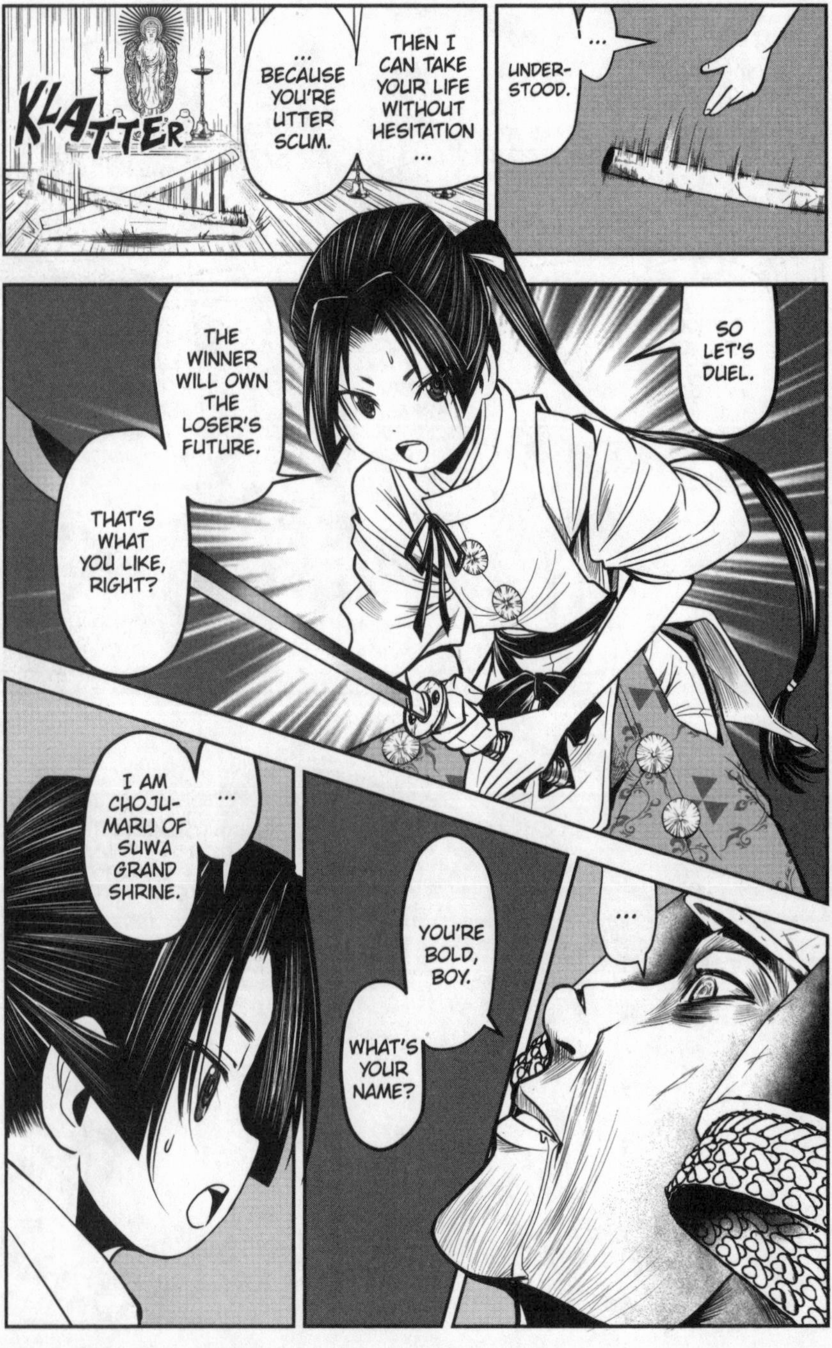
...
UNDER-STOOD.
THEN I CAN TAKE YOUR LIFE WITHOUT HESITATION ...
... BECAUSE YOU'RE UTTER SCUM.
KLATTER
SO LET'S DUEL.
THE WINNER WILL OWN THE LOSER'S FUTURE.
THAT'S WHAT YOU LIKE, RIGHT?
...
YOU'RE BOLD, BOY.
WHAT'S YOUR NAME?
...
I AM CHOJU-MARU OF SUWA GRAND SHRINE.

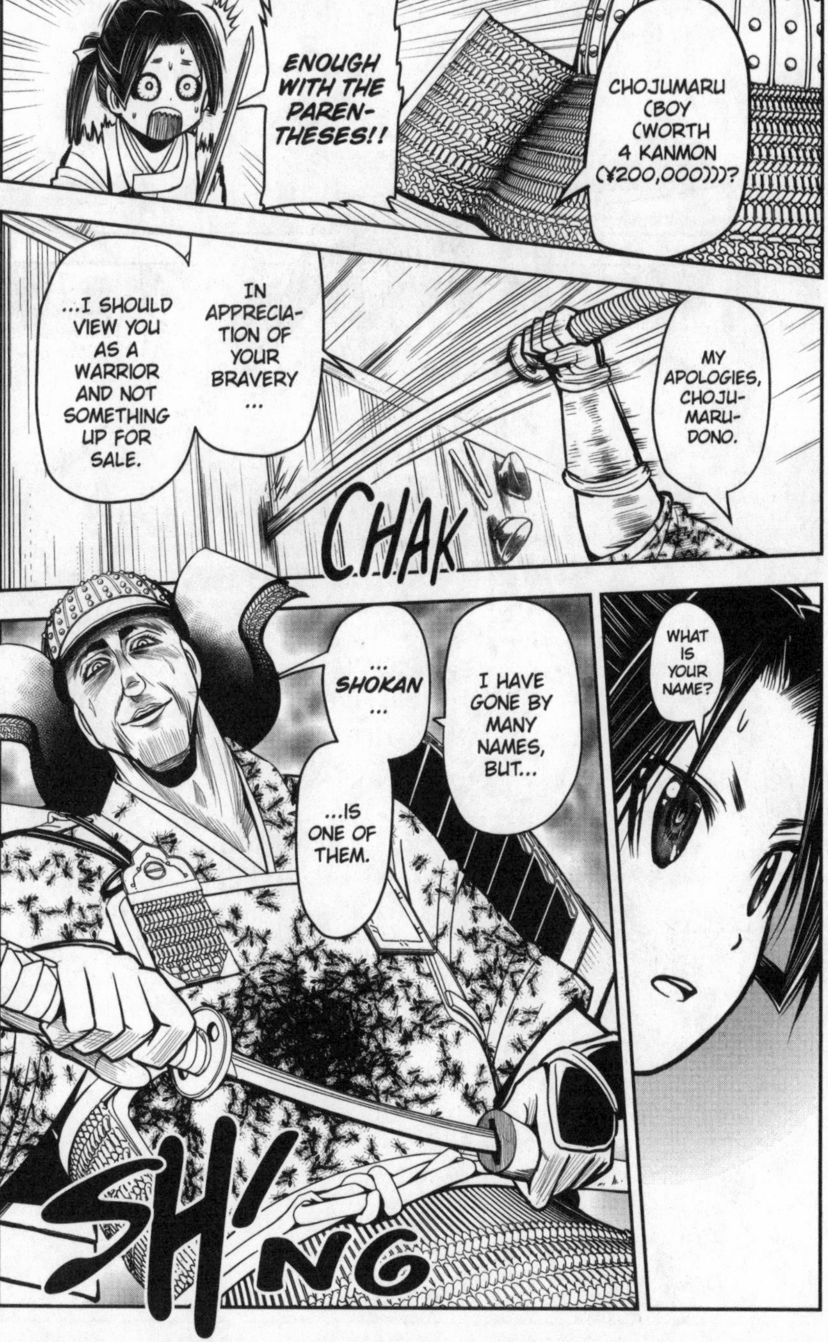
CHOJUMARU (BOY (WORTH 4 KANMON (¥200,000)))?
ENOUGH WITH THE PAREN-THESES!!
MY APOLOGIES, CHOJU-MARU-DONO.
IN APPRECIA-TION OF YOUR BRAVERY ...
...I SHOULD VIEW YOU AS A WARRIOR AND NOT SOMETHING UP FOR SALE.
CHAK
WHAT IS YOUR NAME?
I HAVE GONE BY MANY NAMES, BUT...
... SHOKAN ...
...IS ONE OF THEM.
SHING

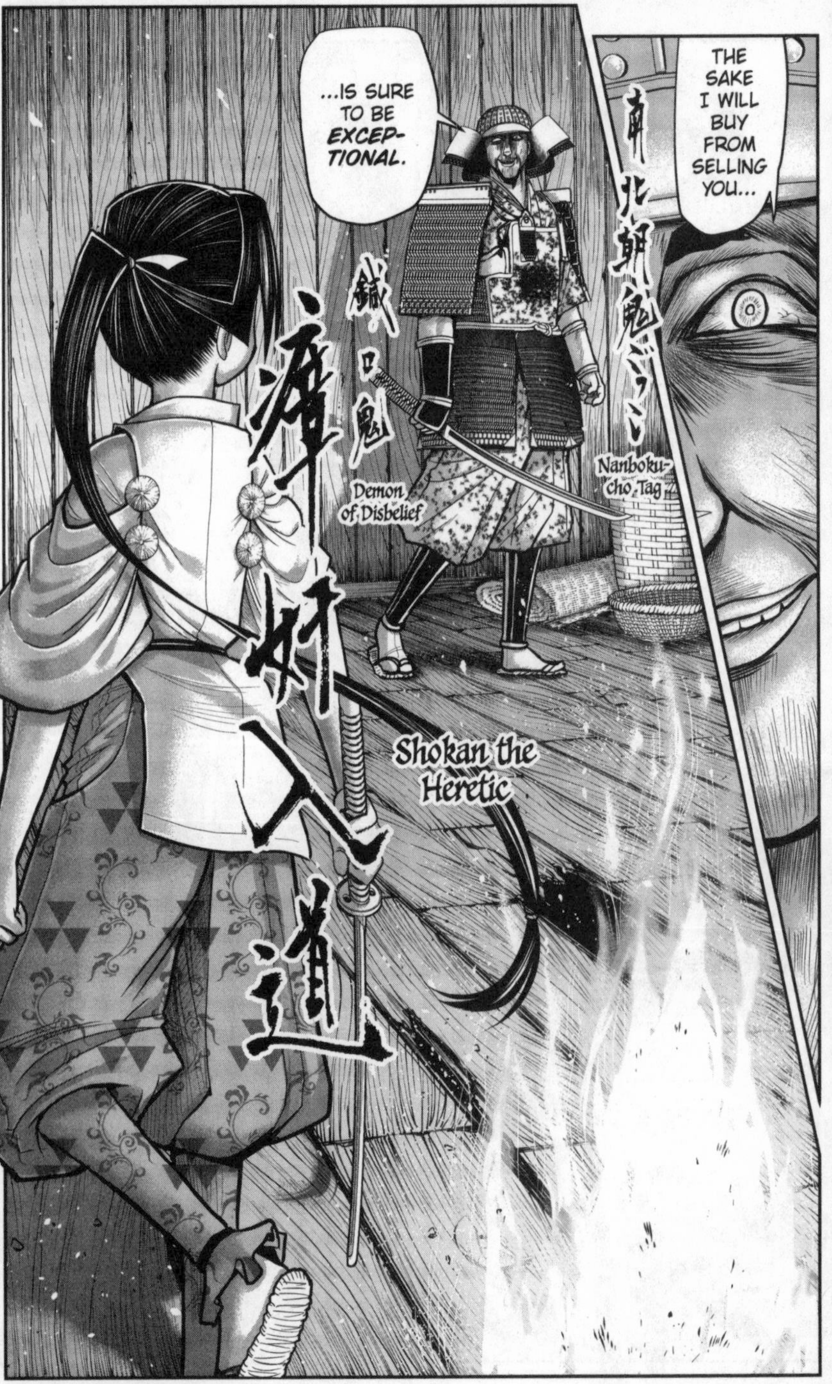
THE SAKE I WILL BUY FROM SELLING YOU...
南北朝鬼ごっこ
Nanboku-cho Tag
...IS SURE TO BE EXCEPTIONAL.
Demon of Disbelief
Shokan the Heretic

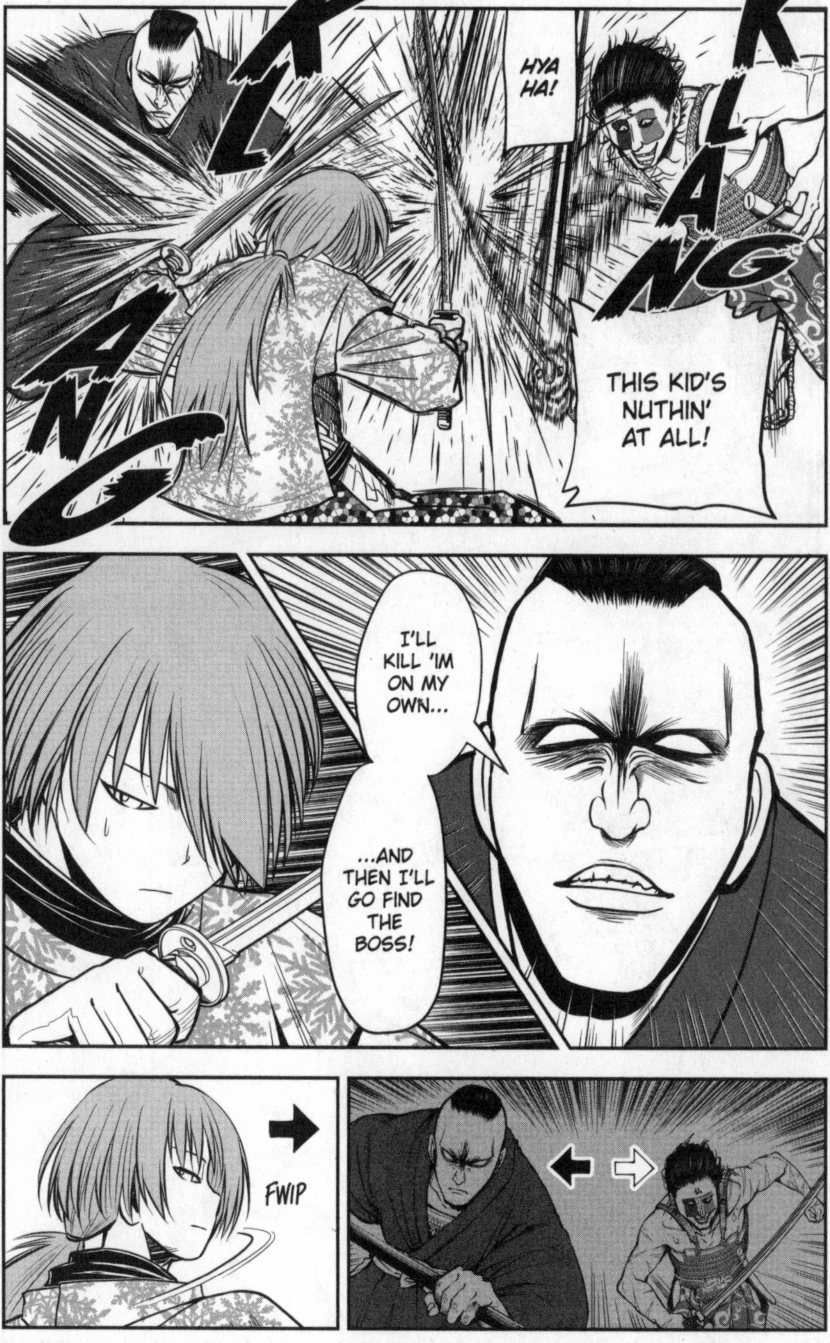
KLANG
HYA HA!
THIS KID'S NUTHIN' AT ALL!
KLANG
I'LL KILL 'IM ON MY OWN...
...AND THEN I'LL GO FIND THE BOSS!
FWIP

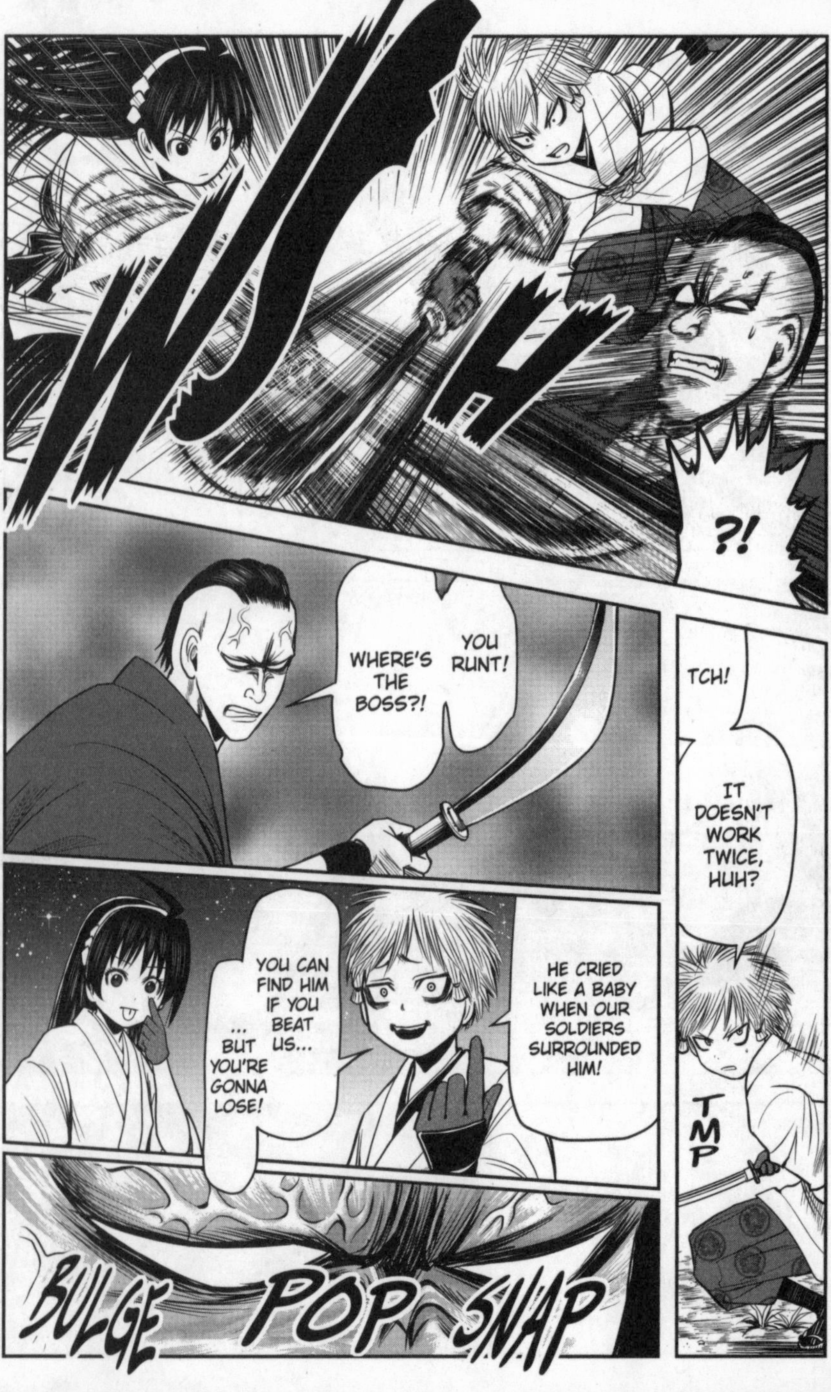
WHSH
?!
TCH!
IT DOESN'T WORK TWICE, HUH?
TMP
YOU RUNT!
WHERE'S THE BOSS?!
HE CRIED LIKE A BABY WHEN OUR SOLDIERS SURROUNDED HIM!
YOU CAN FIND HIM IF YOU BEAT US...
...BUT YOU'RE GONNA LOSE!
BULGE
POP
SNAP

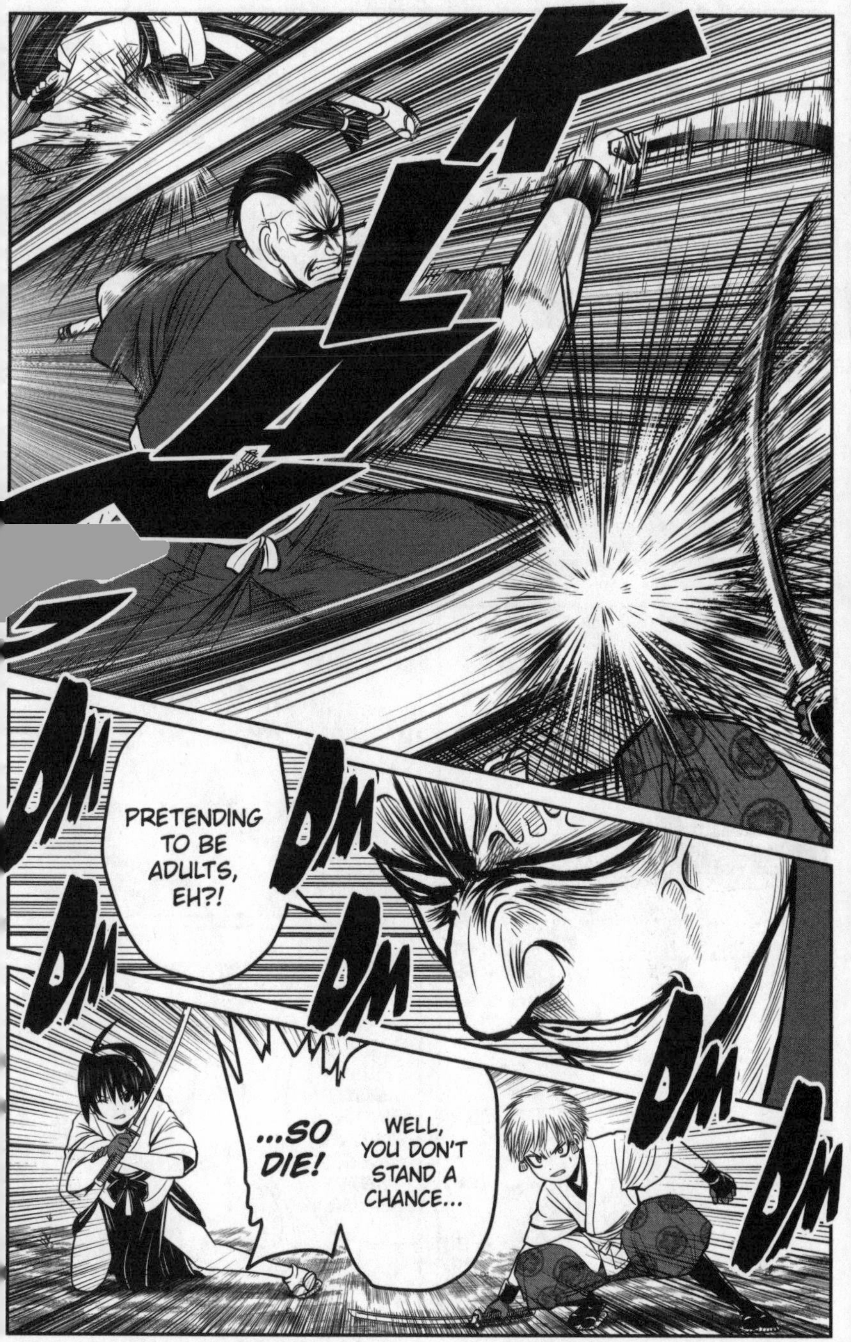

DM DM DM DM
PRETENDING TO BE ADULTS, EH?!
DM DM DM DM
WELL, YOU DON'T STAND A CHANCE...
...SO DIE!

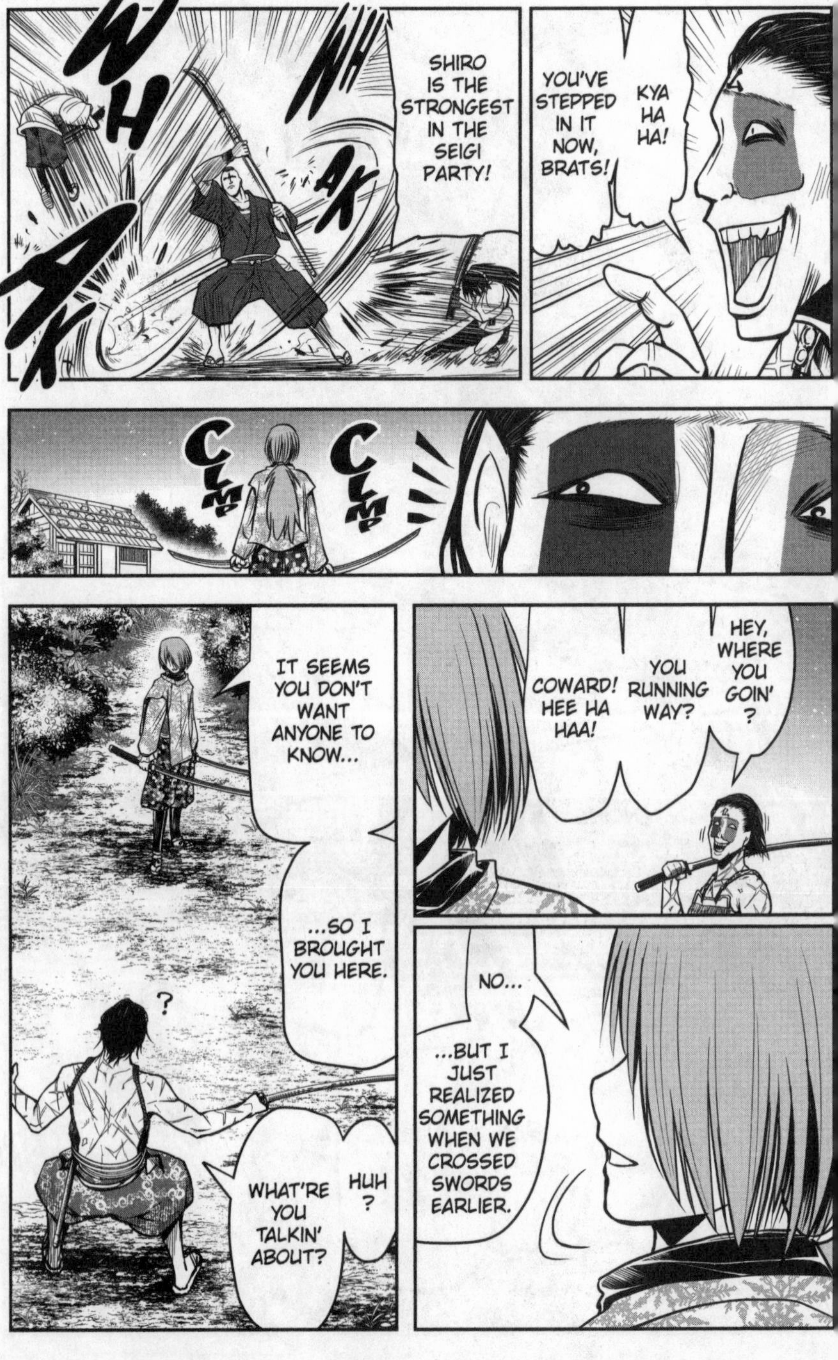
KYA HA HA!
YOU'VE STEPPED IN IT NOW, BRATS!
WHAK
SHIRO IS THE STRONGEST IN THE SEIGI PARTY!
WHAK
CLMP
CLMP
HEY, WHERE YOU GOIN'?
YOU RUNNING WAY?
COWARD! HEE HA HAA!
NO...
...BUT I JUST REALIZED SOMETHING WHEN WE CROSSED SWORDS EARLIER.
IT SEEMS YOU DON'T WANT ANYONE TO KNOW...
...SO I BROUGHT YOU HERE.
?
HUH?
WHAT'RE YOU TALKIN' ABOUT?

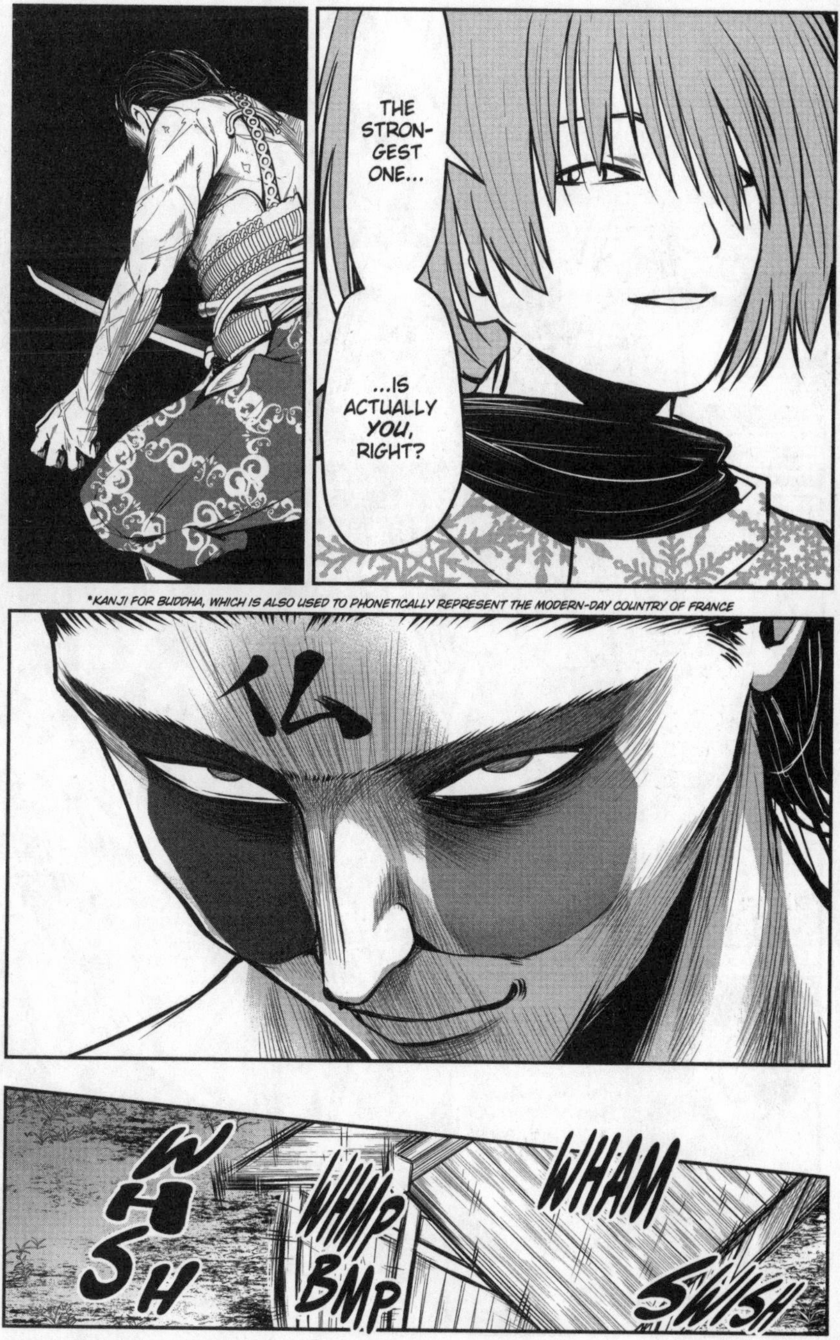
THE STRONG-GEST ONE...
...IS ACTUALLY *YOU*, RIGHT?
*KANJI FOR BUDDHA, WHICH IS ALSO USED TO PHONETICALLY REPRESENT THE MODERN-DAY COUNTRY OF FRANCE
仏
WHAM
SWISH
WHMP BMP
WHSH

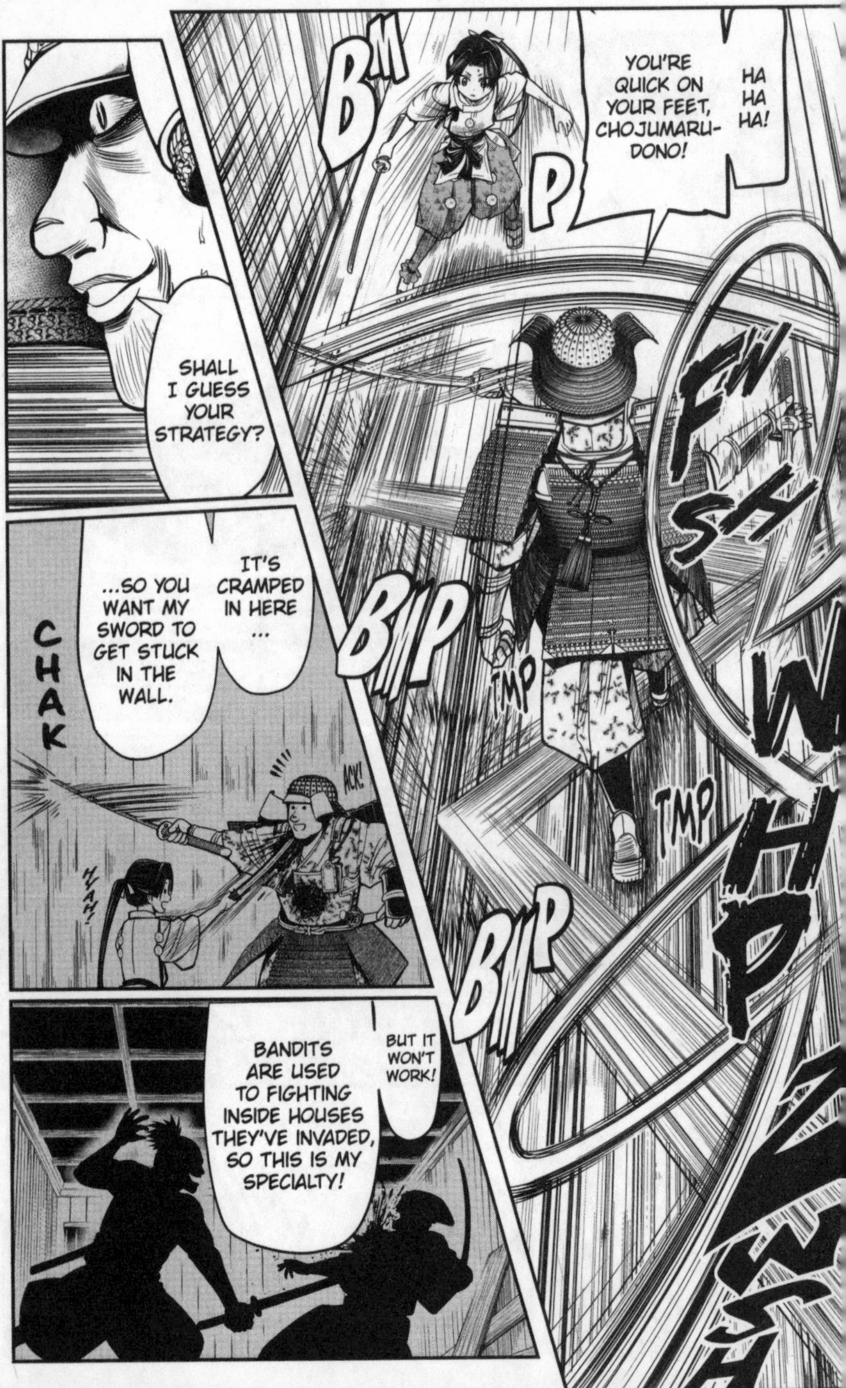
BMP
HA HA HA!
YOU'RE QUICK ON YOUR FEET, CHOJUMARU-DONO!
FWSH
BIP
TMP
TMP
BIP
WHP
SHALL I GUESS YOUR STRATEGY?
IT'S CRAMPED IN HERE ...
...SO YOU WANT MY SWORD TO GET STUCK IN THE WALL.
CHAK
ACK!
HYAH!
BUT IT WON'T WORK!
BANDITS ARE USED TO FIGHTING INSIDE HOUSES THEY'VE INVADED, SO THIS IS MY SPECIALTY!

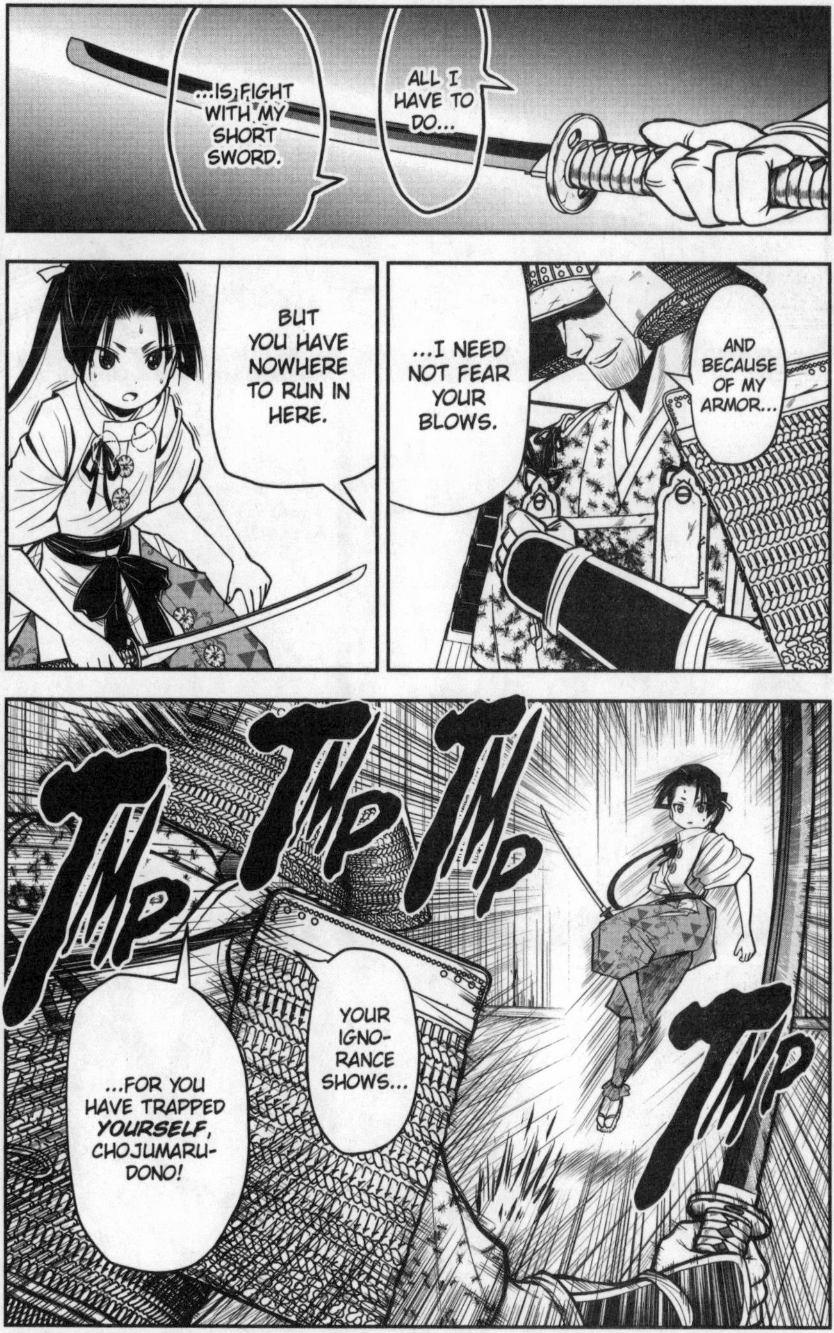
ALL I HAVE TO DO...
...IS FIGHT WITH MY SHORT SWORD.
AND BECAUSE OF MY ARMOR...
...I NEED NOT FEAR YOUR BLOWS.
BUT YOU HAVE NOWHERE TO RUN IN HERE.
TMP
TMP
TMP
TMP
YOUR IGNO-RANCE SHOWS...
...FOR YOU HAVE TRAPPED *YOURSELF*, CHOJUMARU-DONO!

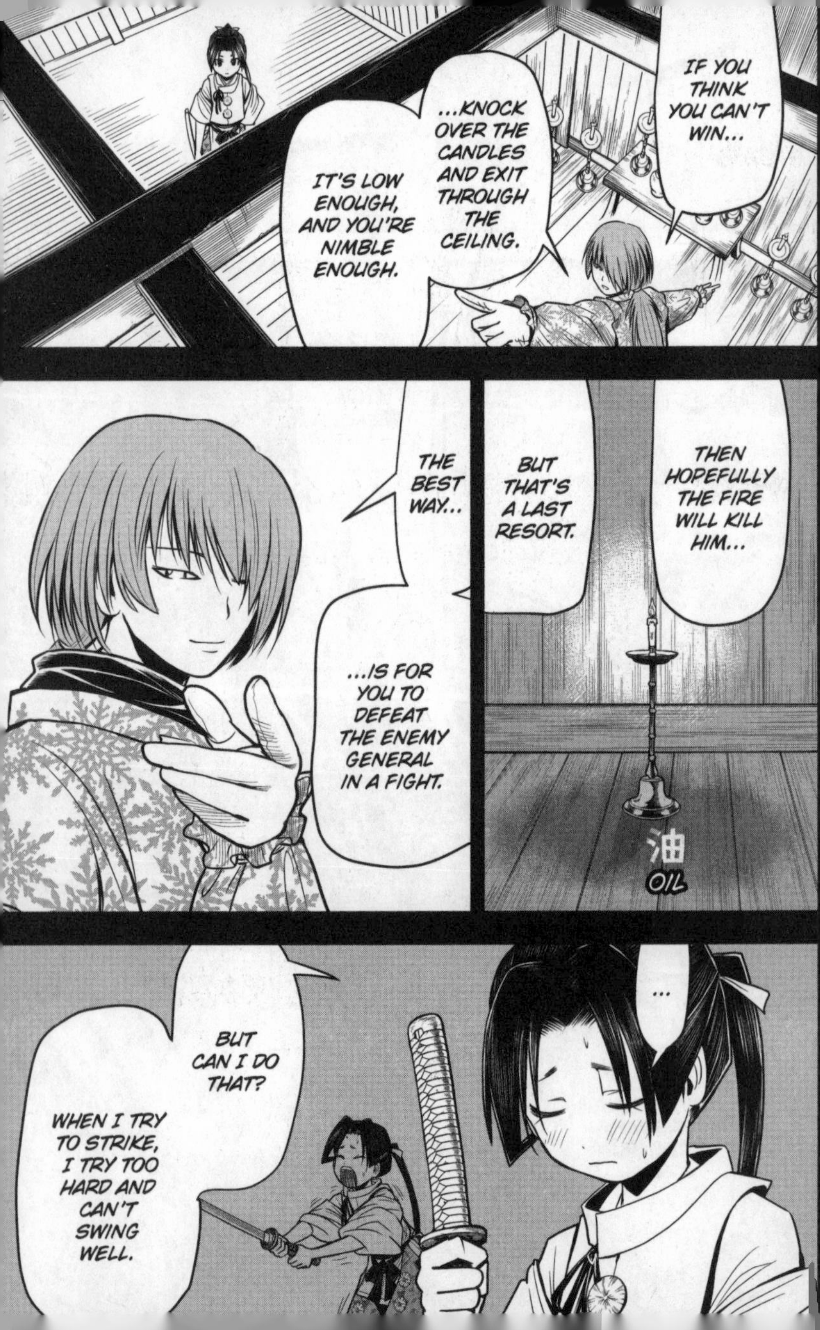
IF YOU THINK YOU CAN'T WIN...
...KNOCK OVER THE CANDLES AND EXIT THROUGH THE CEILING.
IT'S LOW ENOUGH, AND YOU'RE NIMBLE ENOUGH.
THEN HOPEFULLY THE FIRE WILL KILL HIM...
BUT THAT'S A LAST RESORT.
油
OIL
THE BEST WAY...
...IS FOR YOU TO DEFEAT THE ENEMY GENERAL IN A FIGHT.
...
BUT CAN I DO THAT?
WHEN I TRY TO STRIKE, I TRY TOO HARD AND CAN'T SWING WELL.

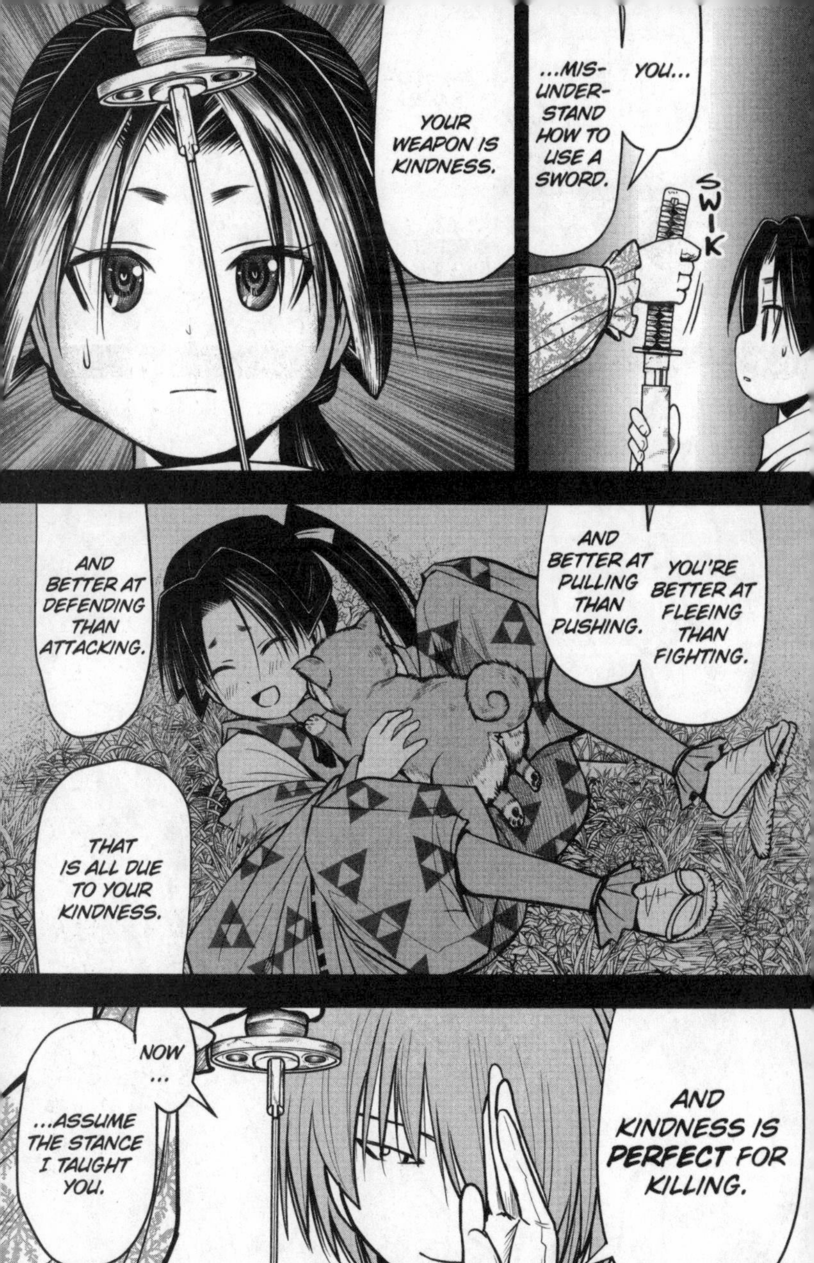
YOU...
...MISUNDERSTAND HOW TO USE A SWORD.
SWIK
YOUR WEAPON IS KINDNESS.
YOU'RE BETTER AT FLEEING THAN FIGHTING.
AND BETTER AT PULLING THAN PUSHING.
AND BETTER AT DEFENDING THAN ATTACKING.
THAT IS ALL DUE TO YOUR KINDNESS.
AND KINDNESS IS PERFECT FOR KILLING.
NOW...
...ASSUME THE STANCE I TAUGHT YOU.

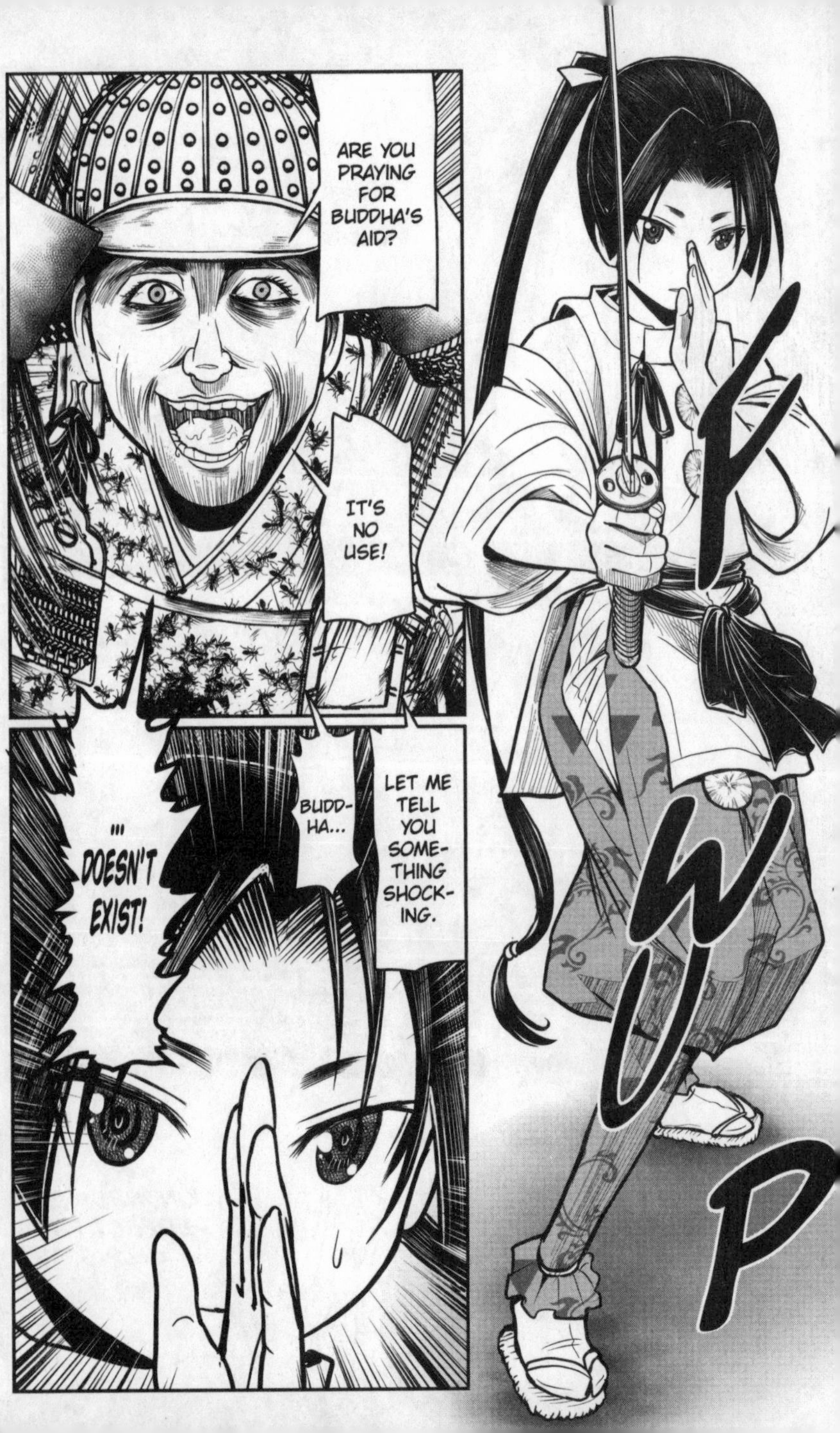
FWUP
ARE YOU PRAYING FOR BUDDHA'S AID?
IT'S NO USE!
LET ME TELL YOU SOMETHING SHOCKING.
BUDD-HA...
...DOESN'T EXIST!

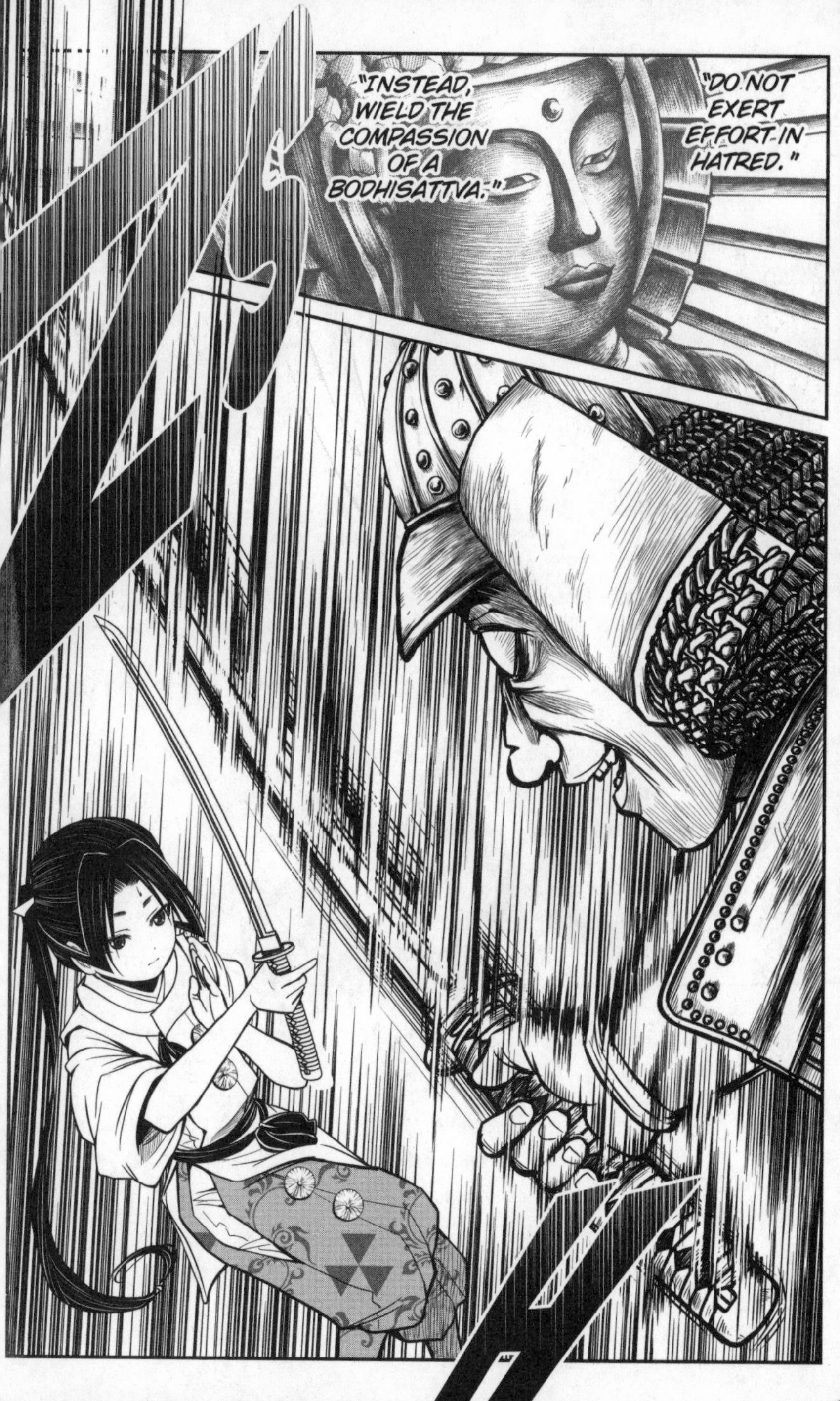
"DO NOT EXERT EFFORT IN HATRED."
"INSTEAD, WIELD THE COMPASSION OF A BODHISATTVA."

Ruined Dreams

I believed
Buddha
existed...

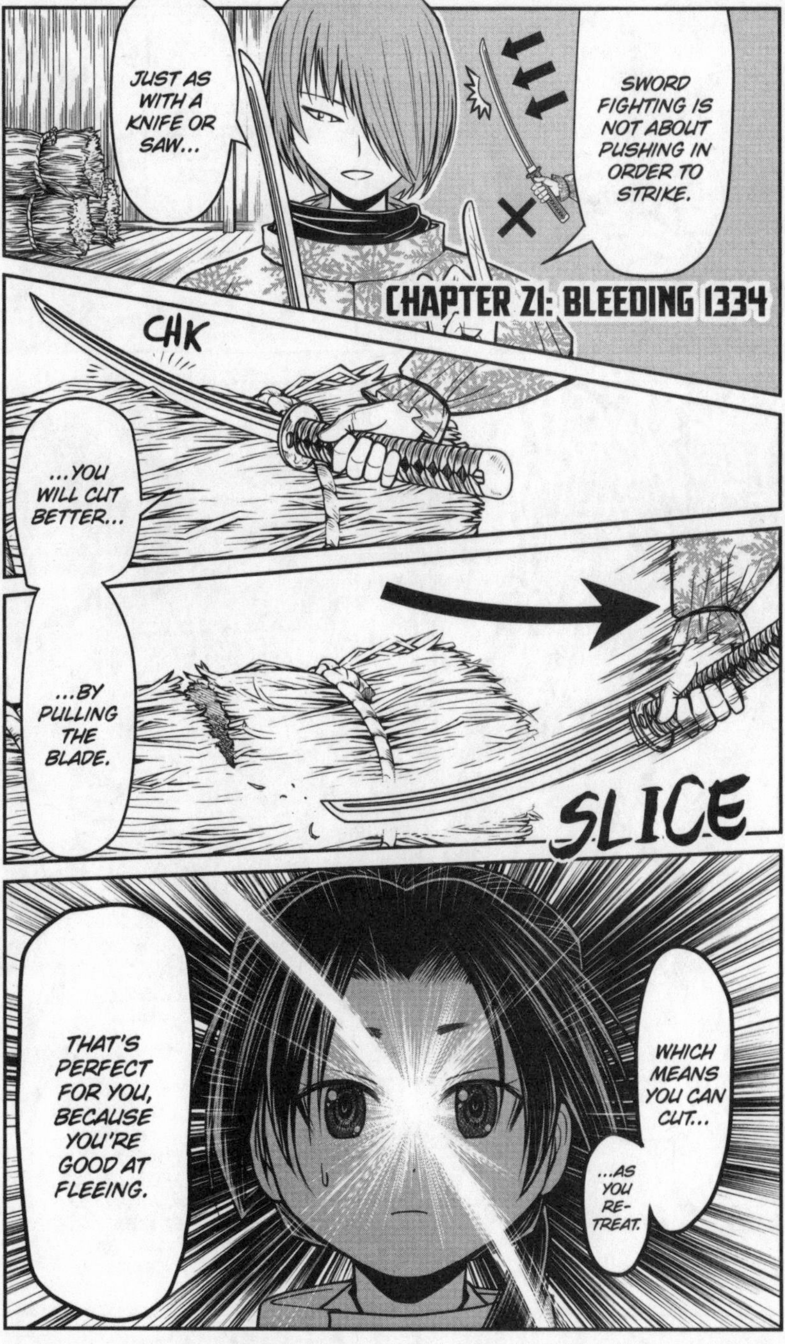
SWORD FIGHTING IS NOT ABOUT PUSHING IN ORDER TO STRIKE.
JUST AS WITH A KNIFE OR SAW...
CHAPTER 21: BLEEDING 1334
CHK
...YOU WILL CUT BETTER...
...BY PULLING THE BLADE.
SLICE
WHICH MEANS YOU CAN CUT...
...AS YOU RE-TREAT.
THAT'S PERFECT FOR YOU, BECAUSE YOU'RE GOOD AT FLEEING.

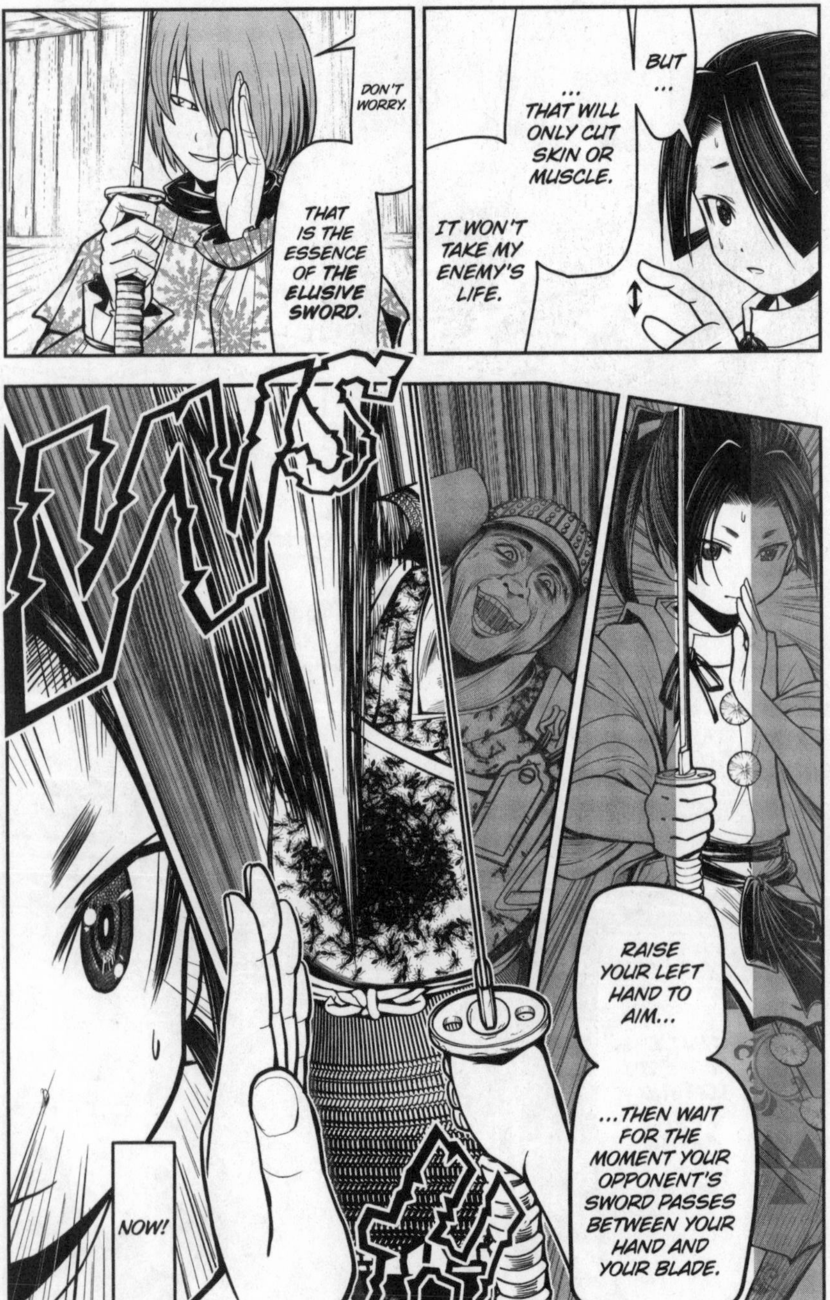
BUT ...
... THAT WILL ONLY CUT SKIN OR MUSCLE.
IT WON'T TAKE MY ENEMY'S LIFE.
DON'T WORRY.
THAT IS THE ESSENCE OF THE ELUSIVE SWORD.
RAISE YOUR LEFT HAND TO AIM...
...THEN WAIT FOR THE MOMENT YOUR OPPONENT'S SWORD PASSES BETWEEN YOUR HAND AND YOUR BLADE.
NOW!

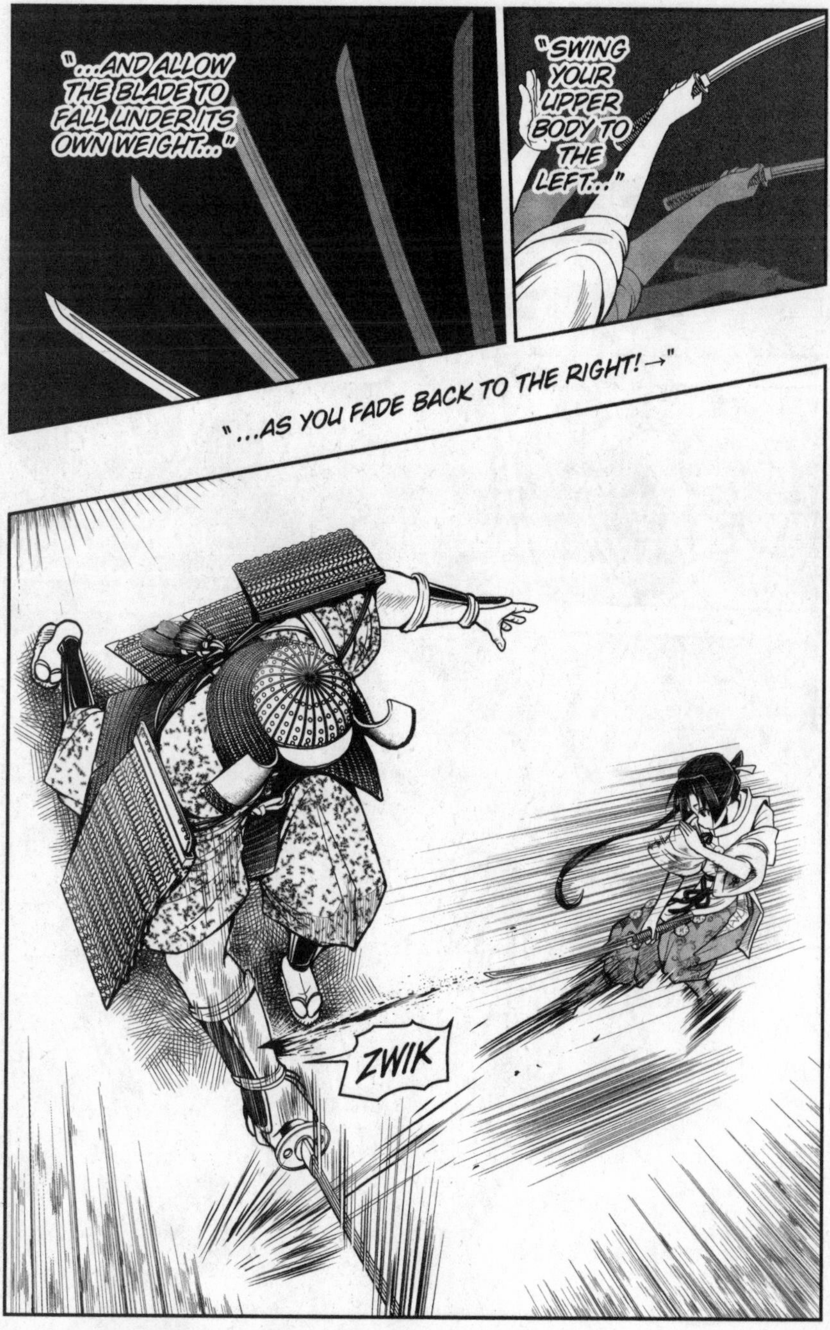
"SWING YOUR UPPER BODY TO THE LEFT..."
"...AND ALLOW THE BLADE TO FALL UNDER ITS OWN WEIGHT..."
"...AS YOU FADE BACK TO THE RIGHT!→"
ZWIK

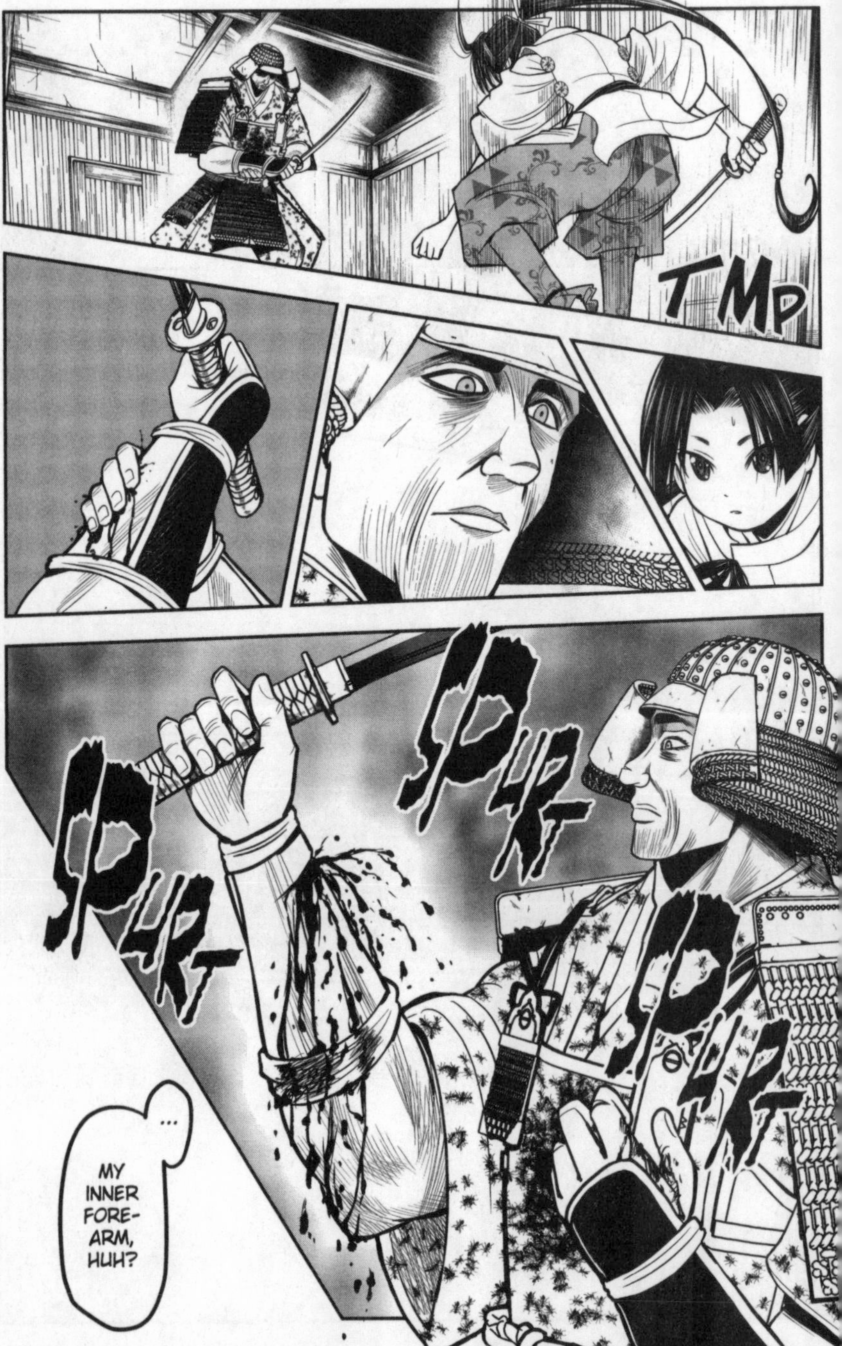
TMP
SPURT
SPURT
SPURT
...
MY INNER FORE-ARM, HUH?

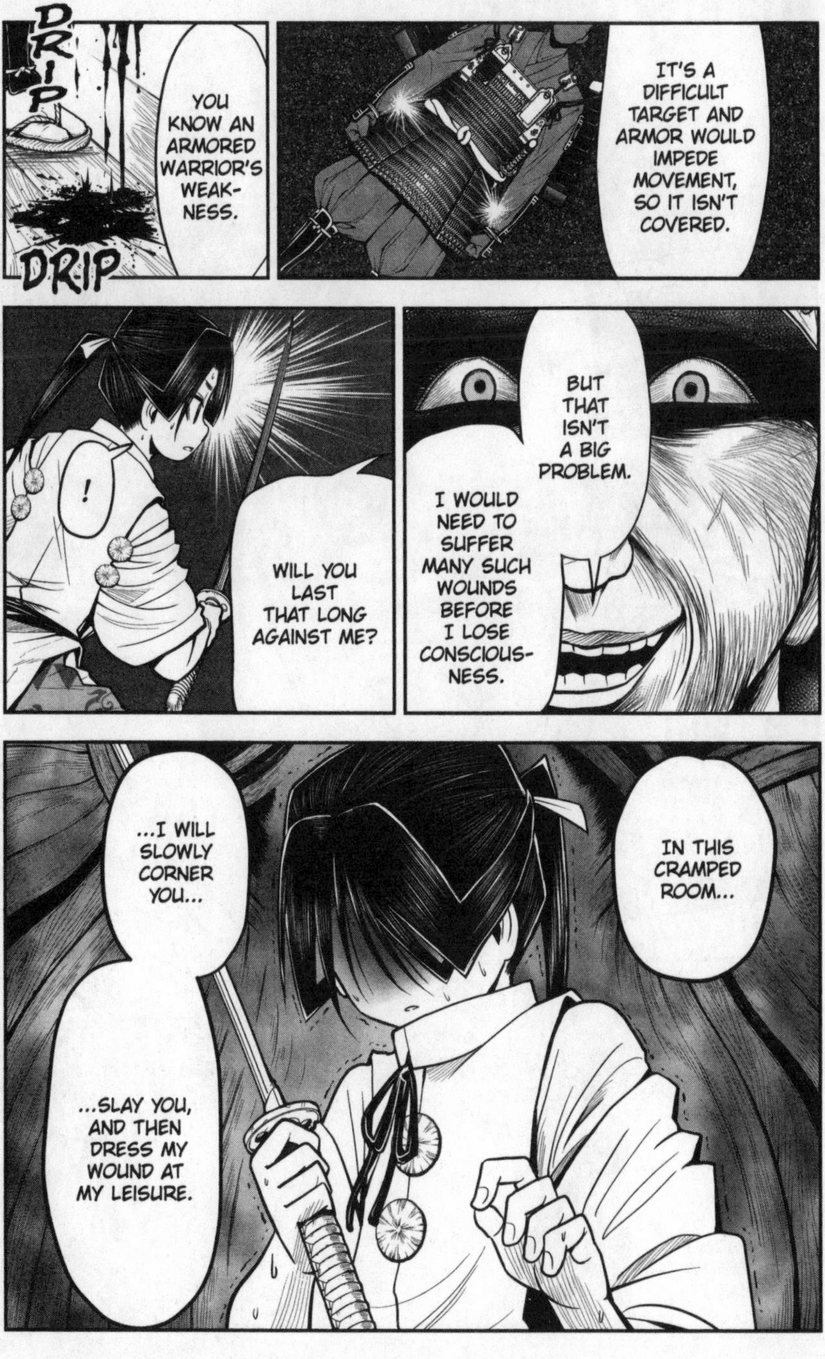
IT'S A DIFFICULT TARGET AND ARMOR WOULD IMPEDE MOVEMENT, SO IT ISN'T COVERED.
YOU KNOW AN ARMORED WARRIOR'S WEAK-NESS.
DRIP
DRIP
BUT THAT ISN'T A BIG PROBLEM.
I WOULD NEED TO SUFFER MANY SUCH WOUNDS BEFORE I LOSE CONSCIOUS-NESS.
WILL YOU LAST THAT LONG AGAINST ME?
!
IN THIS CRAMPED ROOM...
...I WILL SLOWLY CORNER YOU...
...SLAY YOU, AND THEN DRESS MY WOUND AT MY LEISURE.

CHAPTER 21: BLEEDING 1334

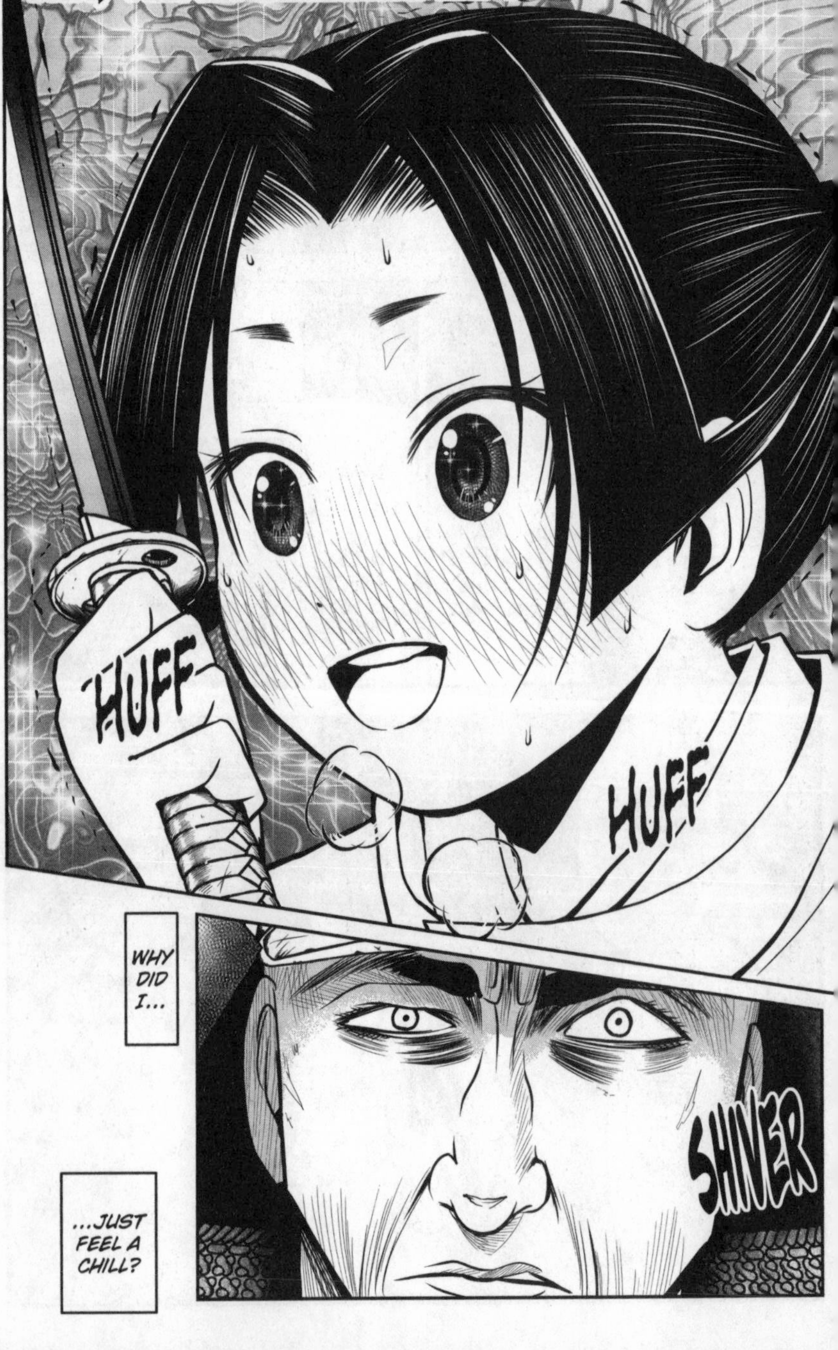
HUFF
HUFF
SHIVER
WHY DID I...
...JUST FEEL A CHILL?

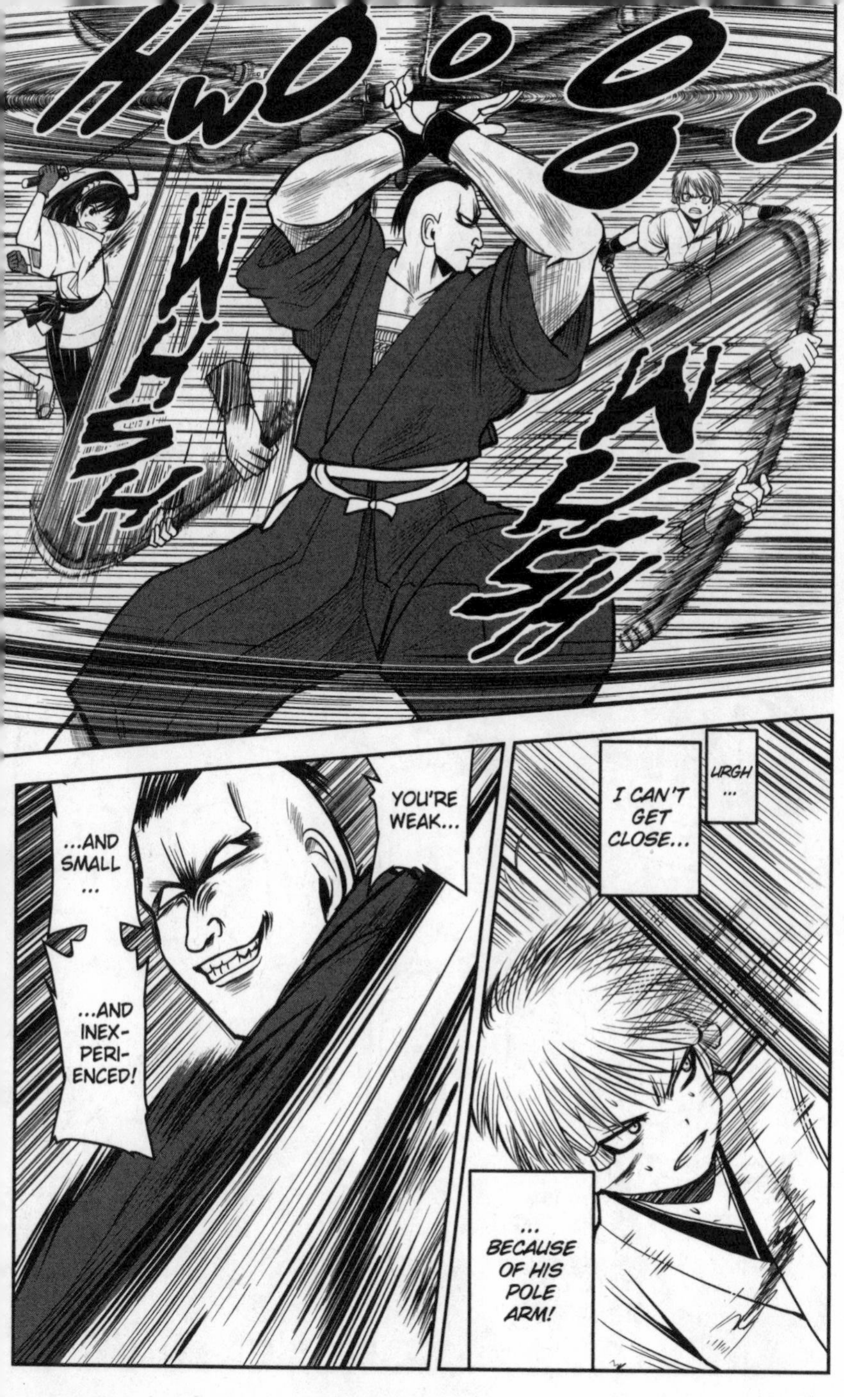
HWOOOOOO
WHSH
WHSH
URGH...
I CAN'T GET CLOSE...
...BECAUSE OF HIS POLE ARM!
YOU'RE WEAK...
...AND SMALL...
...AND INEXPERIENCED!

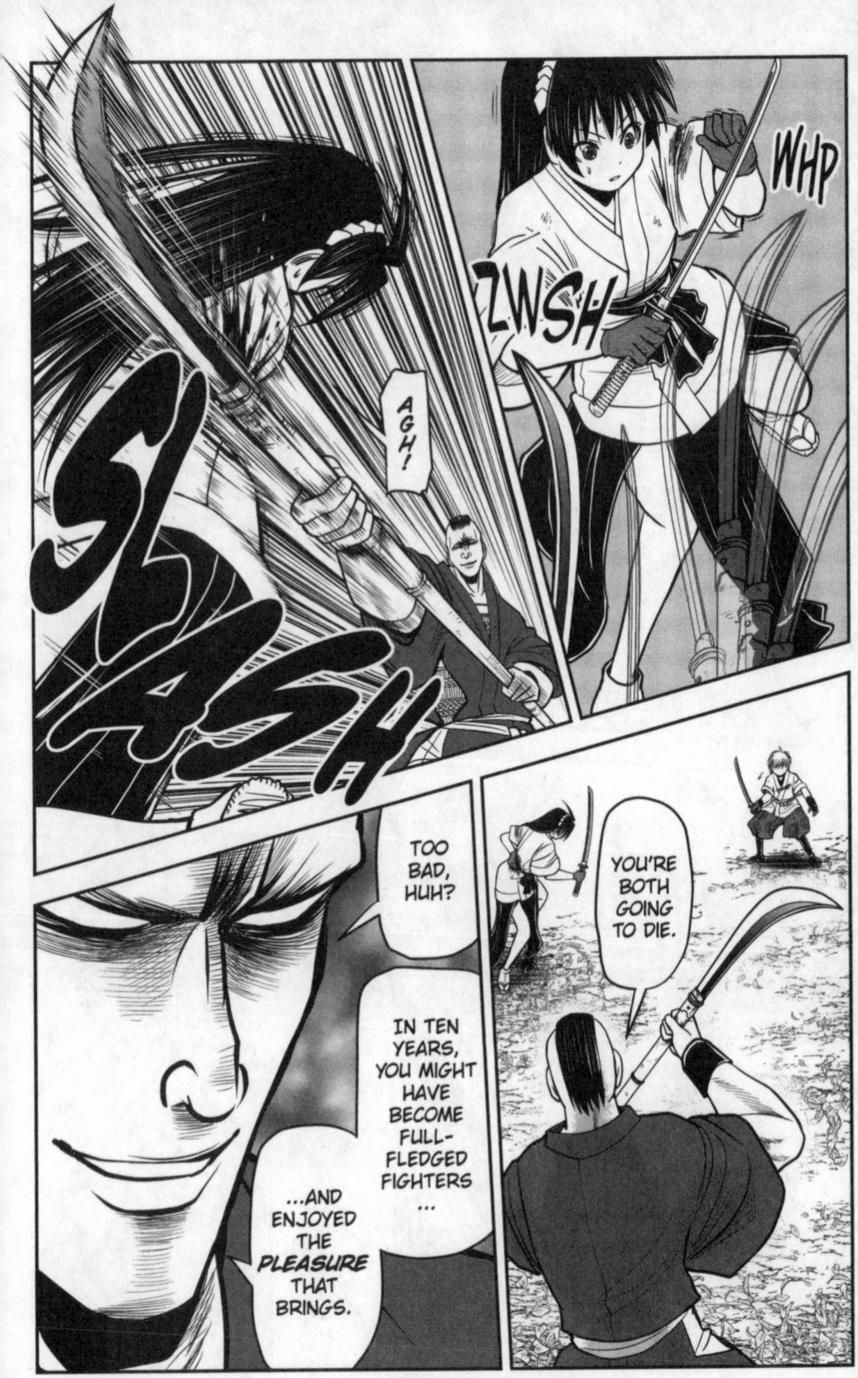
WHP
ZWSH
AGH!
SLASH
YOU'RE BOTH GOING TO DIE.
TOO BAD, HUH?
IN TEN YEARS, YOU MIGHT HAVE BECOME FULL-FLEDGED FIGHTERS...
...AND ENJOYED THE *PLEASURE* THAT BRINGS.

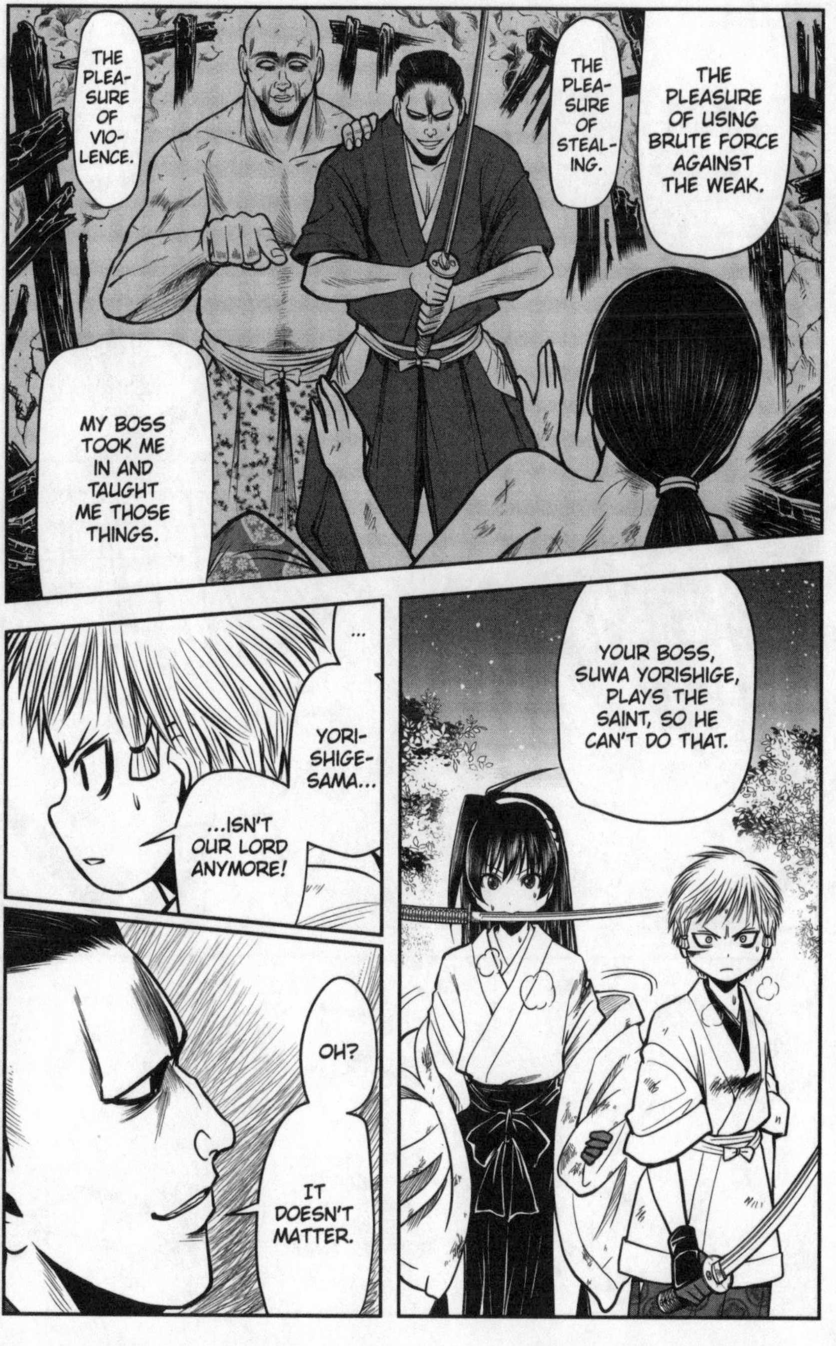
THE PLEASURE OF USING BRUTE FORCE AGAINST THE WEAK.
THE PLEA-SURE OF STEAL-ING.
THE PLEA-SURE OF VIO-LENCE.
MY BOSS TOOK ME IN AND TAUGHT ME THOSE THINGS.
YOUR BOSS, SUWA YORISHIGE, PLAYS THE SAINT, SO HE CAN'T DO THAT.
...
YORI-SHIGE-SAMA...
...ISN'T OUR LORD ANYMORE!
OH?
IT DOESN'T MATTER.

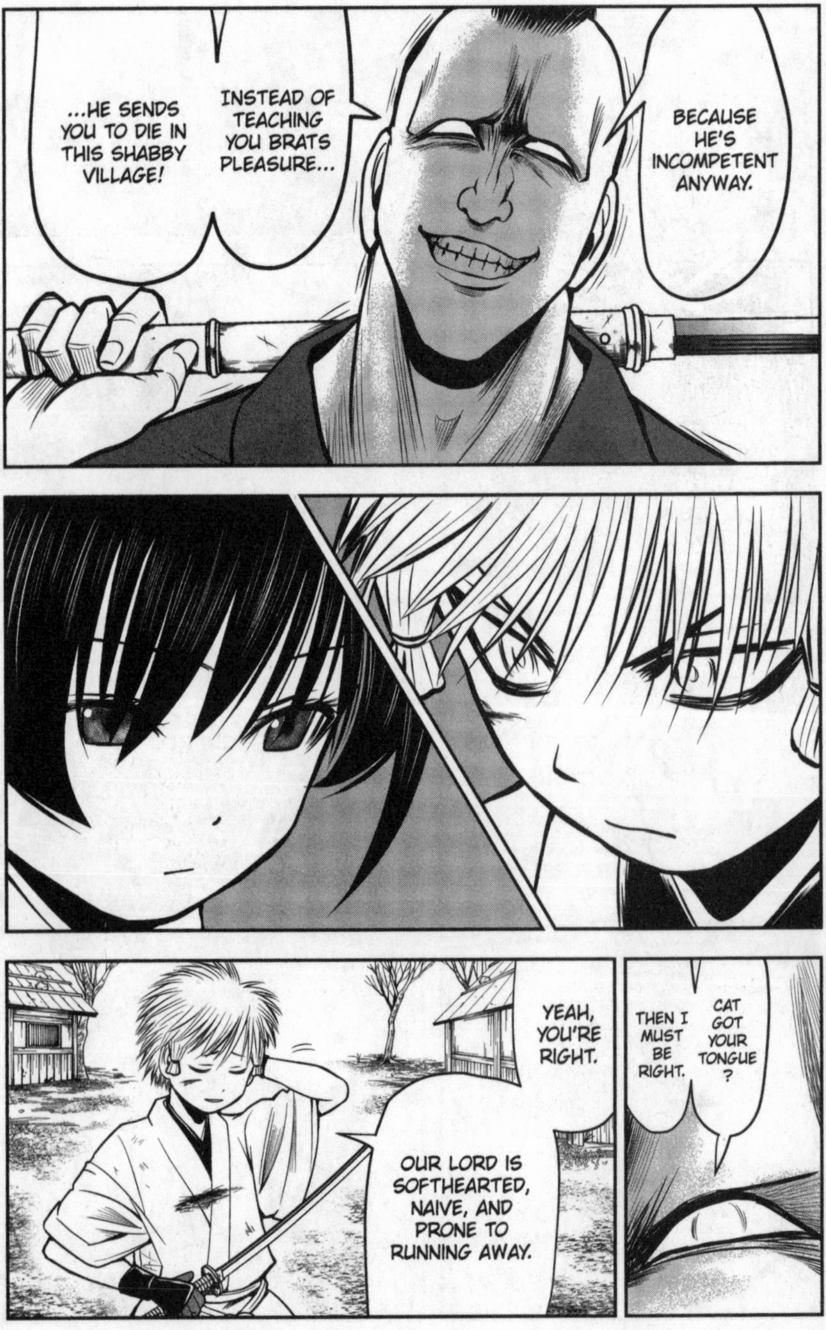
BECAUSE HE'S INCOMPETENT ANYWAY.
INSTEAD OF TEACHING YOU BRATS PLEASURE...
...HE SENDS YOU TO DIE IN THIS SHABBY VILLAGE!
CAT GOT YOUR TONGUE?
THEN I MUST BE RIGHT.
YEAH, YOU'RE RIGHT.
OUR LORD IS SOFTHEARTED, NAIVE, AND PRONE TO RUNNING AWAY.

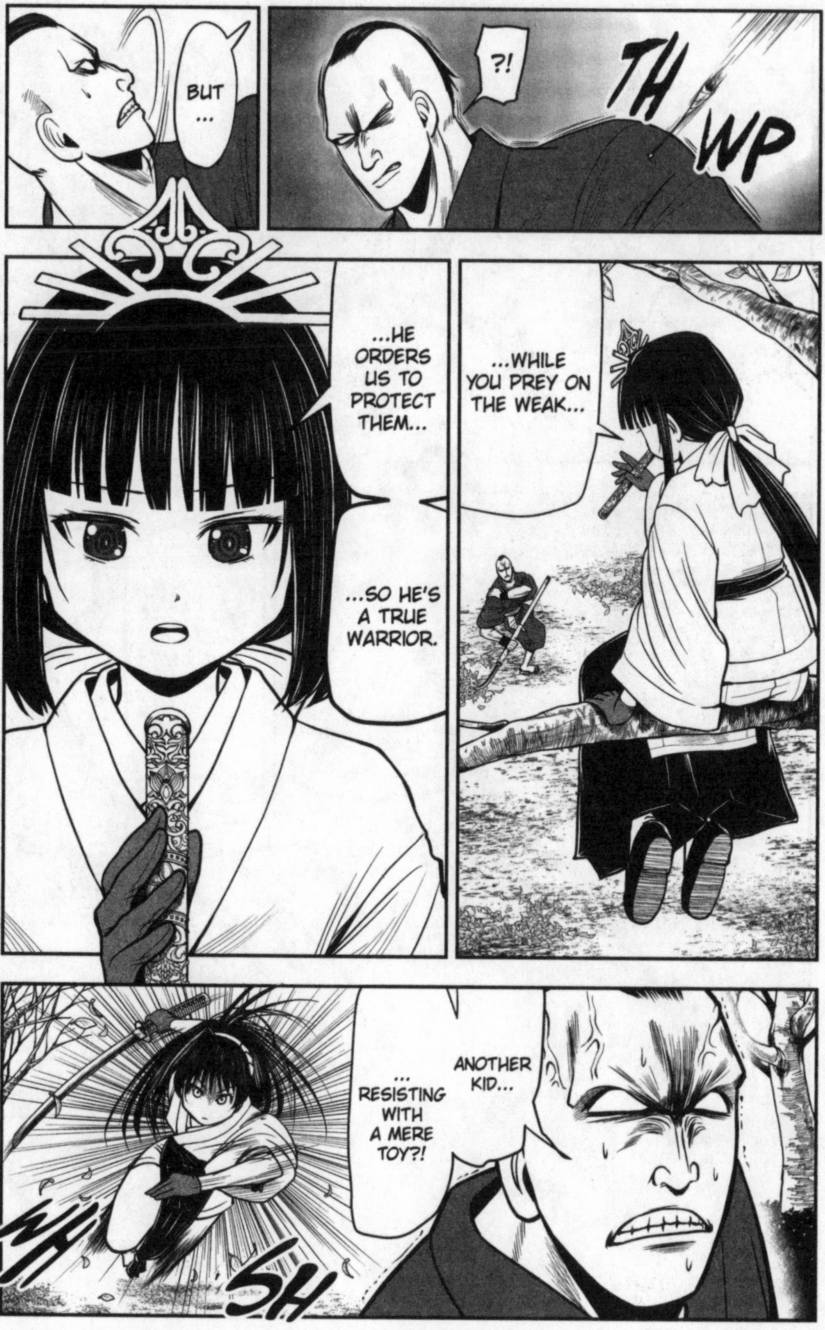
?!
THWP
BUT ...
...WHILE YOU PREY ON THE WEAK...
...HE ORDERS US TO PROTECT THEM...
...SO HE'S A TRUE WARRIOR.
ANOTHER KID...
...RESISTING WITH A MERE TOY?!
WHSH

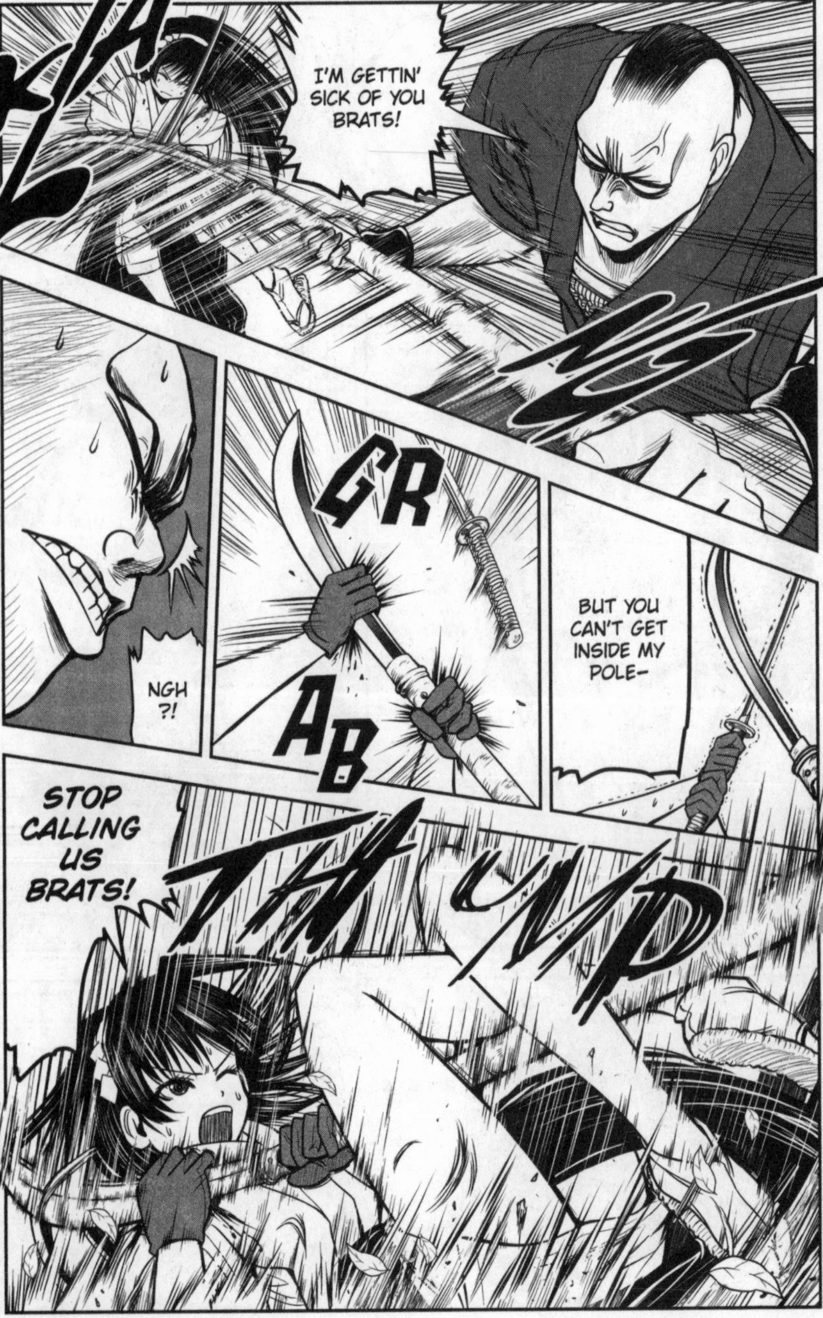
I'M GETTIN' SICK OF YOU BRATS!
BUT YOU CAN'T GET INSIDE MY POLE-
GRAB
NGH ?!
STOP CALLING US BRATS!
THUMP

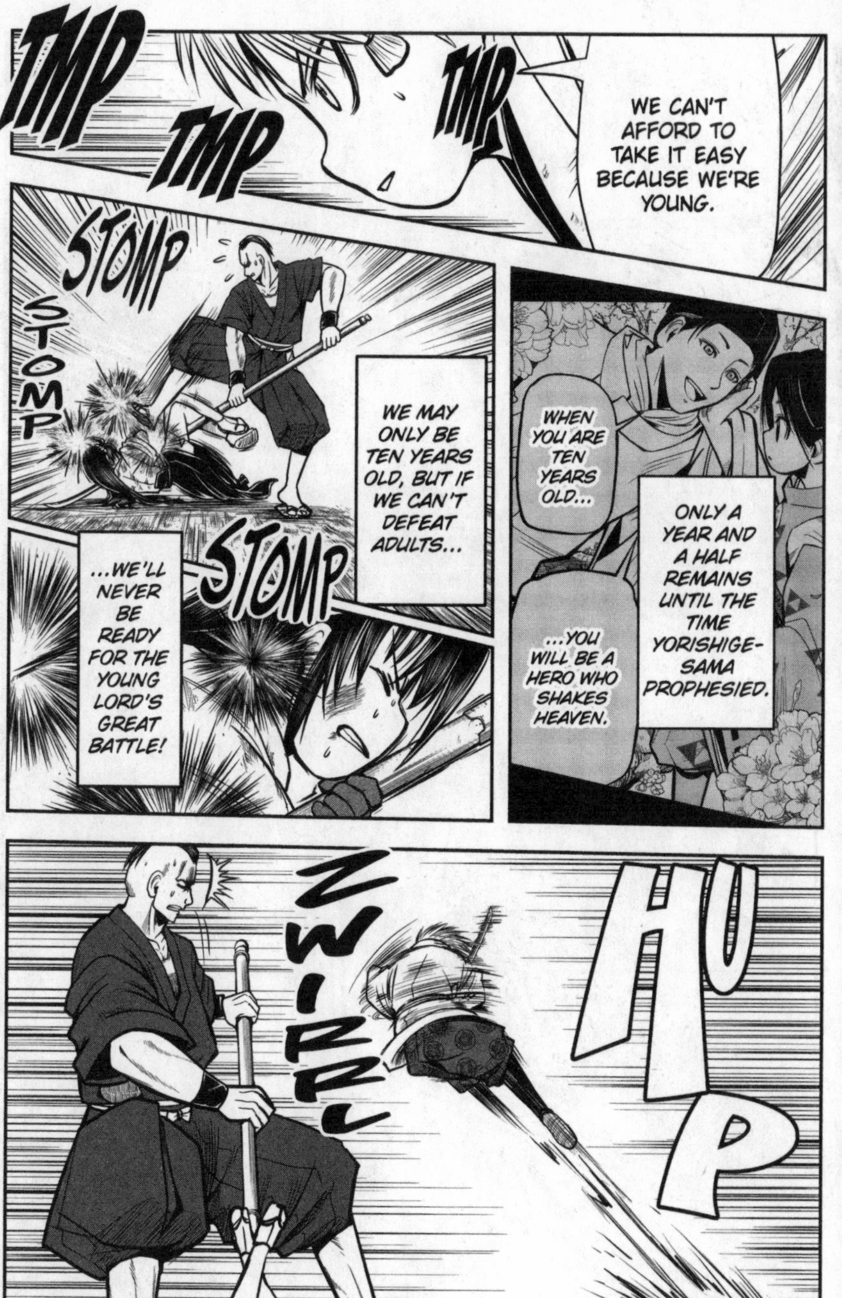

TMP
TMP
TMP
WE CAN'T AFFORD TO TAKE IT EASY BECAUSE WE'RE YOUNG.
WHEN YOU ARE TEN YEARS OLD...
...YOU WILL BE A HERO WHO SHAKES HEAVEN.
ONLY A YEAR AND A HALF REMAINS UNTIL THE TIME YORISHIGE-SAMA PROPHESIED.
STOMP
STOMP
WE MAY ONLY BE TEN YEARS OLD, BUT IF WE CAN'T DEFEAT ADULTS...
STOMP
...WE'LL NEVER BE READY FOR THE YOUNG LORD'S GREAT BATTLE!
HUP
ZWIRRL

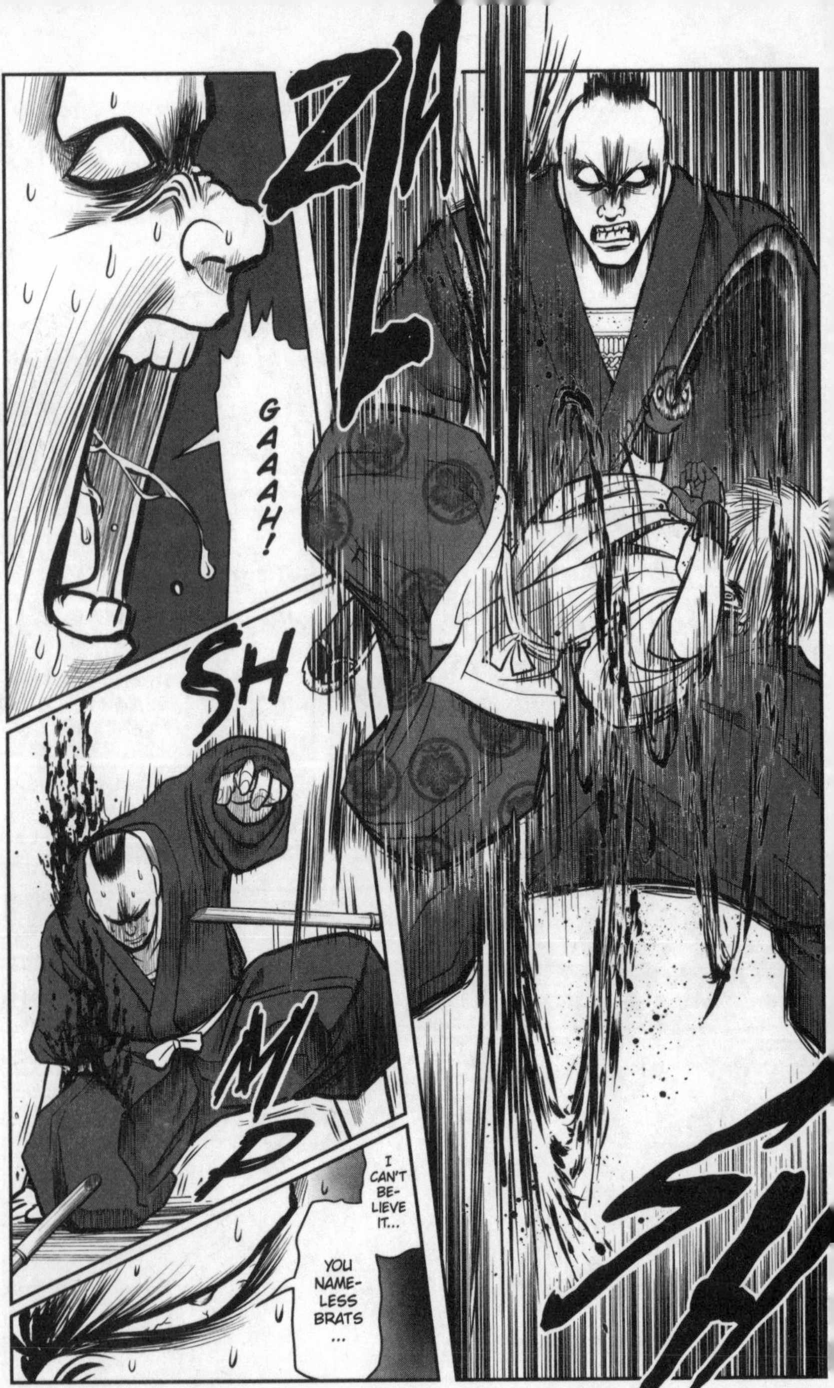
ZA
GAAAAH!
SH
MP
I CAN'T BE-LIEVE IT...
YOU NAME-LESS BRATS ...

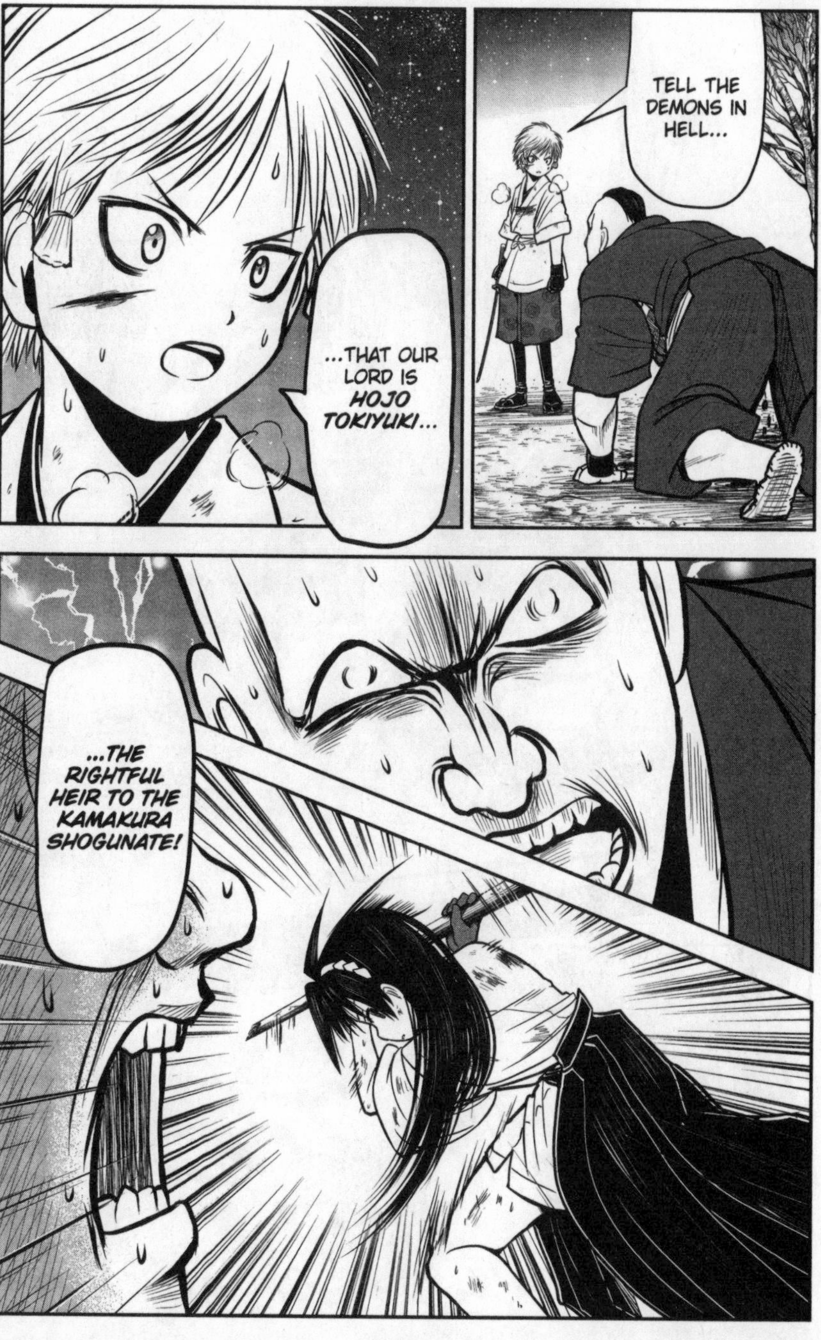
TELL THE DEMONS IN HELL...
...THAT OUR LORD IS *HOJO TOKIYUKI*...
...THE RIGHTFUL HEIR TO THE KAMAKURA SHOGUNATE!

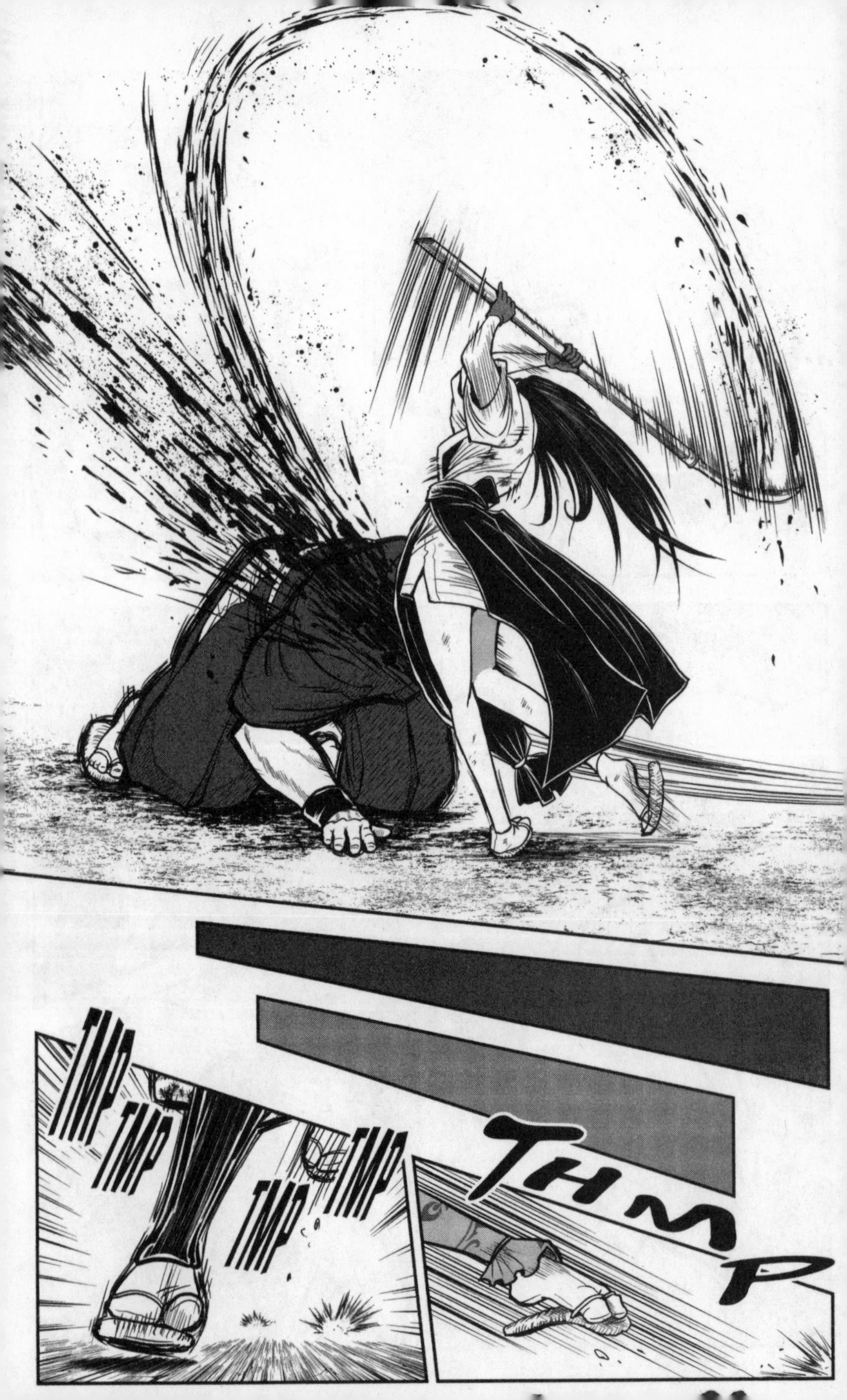
THMP
TMP
TMP
TMP
TMP

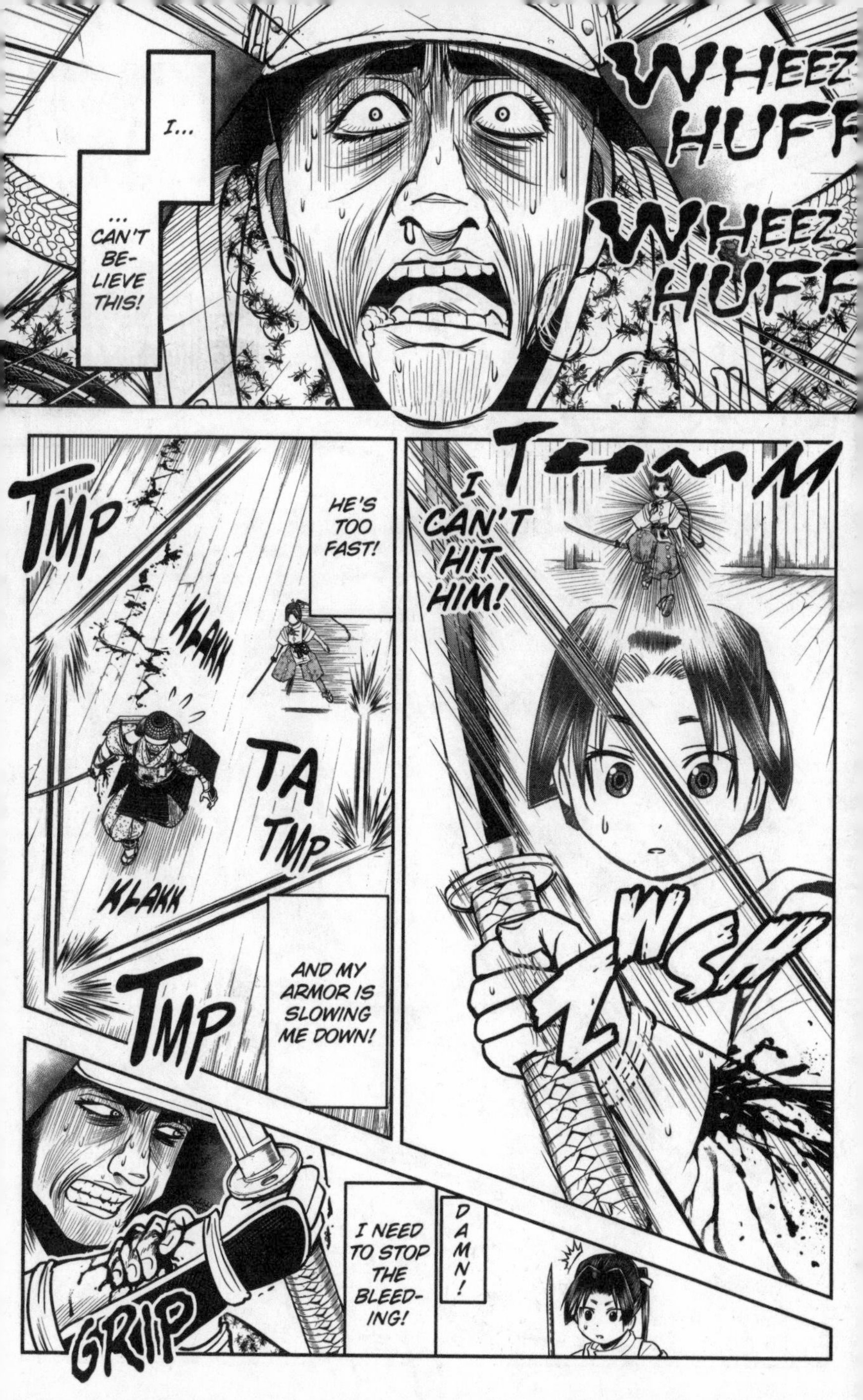
WHEEZ
HUFF
WHEEZ
HUFF
I...
...CAN'T BE-LIEVE THIS!
I CAN'T HIT HIM!
WSH
HE'S TOO FAST!
TMP
KLAKK
TA
TMP
KLAKK
TMP
AND MY ARMOR IS SLOWING ME DOWN!
DAMN!
I NEED TO STOP THE BLEED-ING!
GRIP

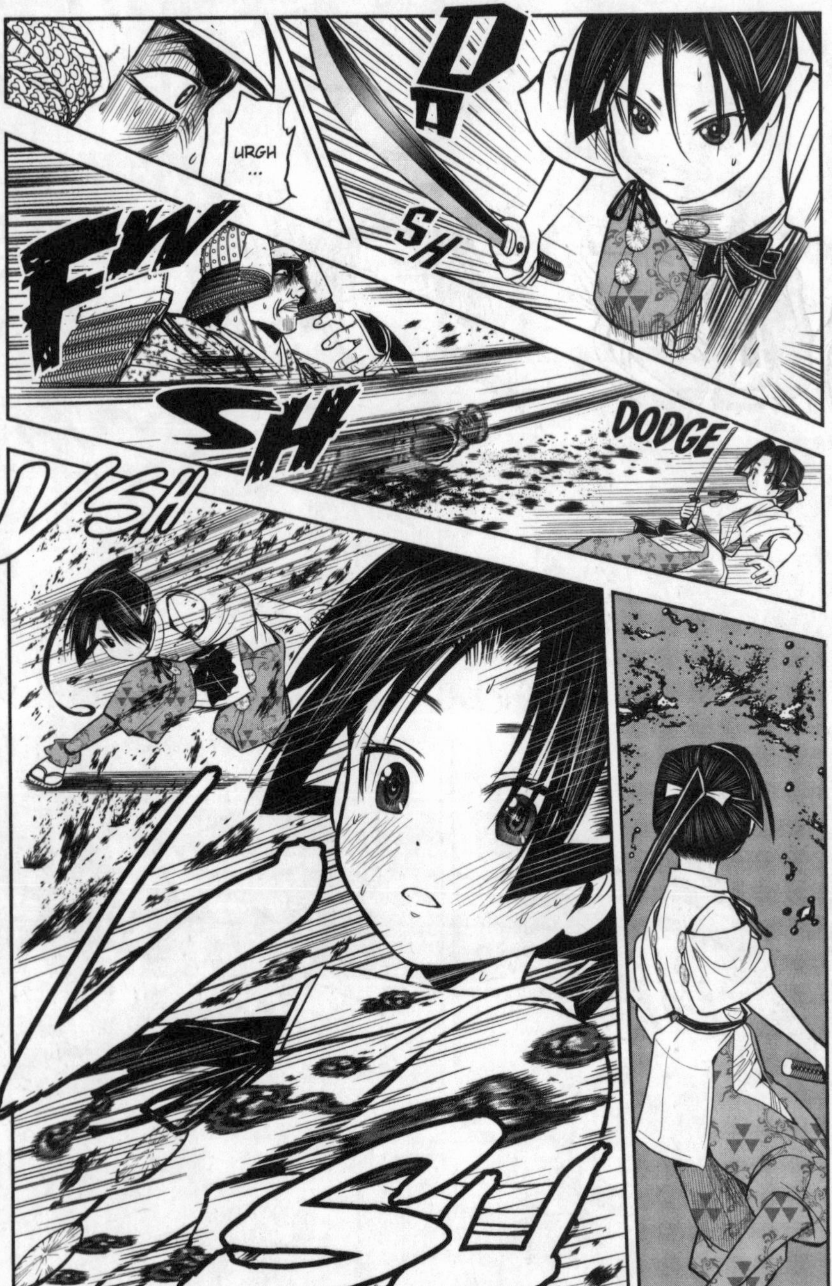
D
SH
URGH ...
FW
DODGE
SH
VSH
SH

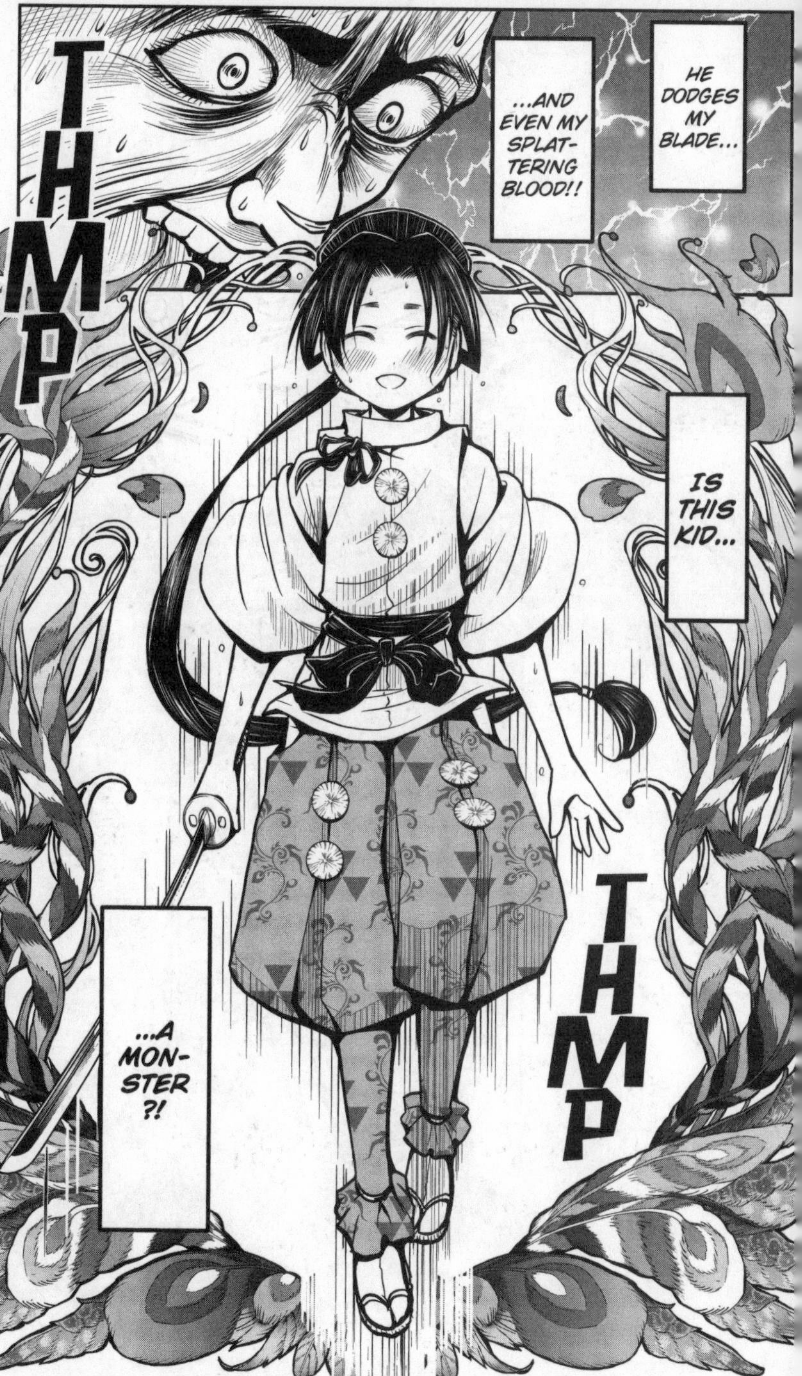
HE DODGES MY BLADE...
...AND EVEN MY SPLAT-TERING BLOOD!!
THMP
IS THIS KID...
THMP
...A MON-STER?!

Making It Brattier

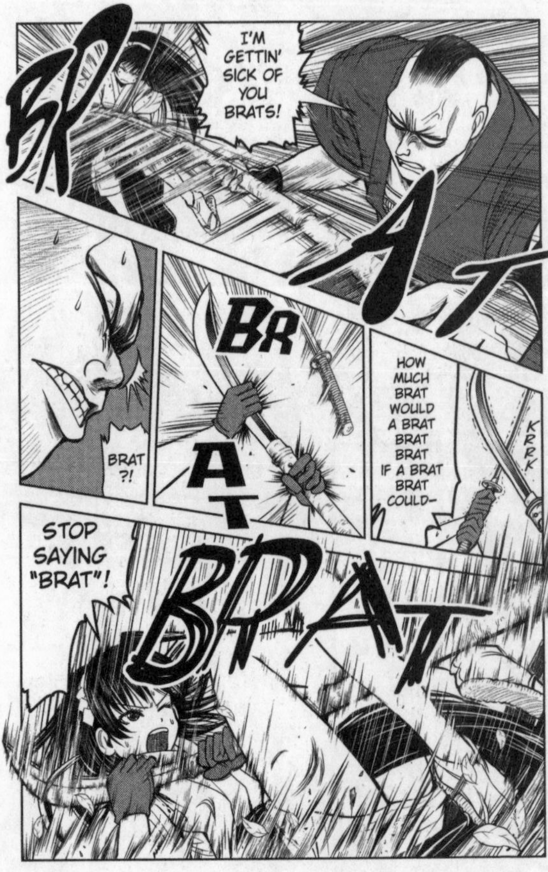
I'M GETTIN' SICK OF YOU BRATS!
BRAT
HOW MUCH BRAT WOULD A BRAT BRAT BRAT IF A BRAT BRAT COULD–
KRRK
BRAT
BRAT?!
STOP SAYING "BRAT"!
BRAT

CHAPTER 22: REVERED BUDDHA 1334

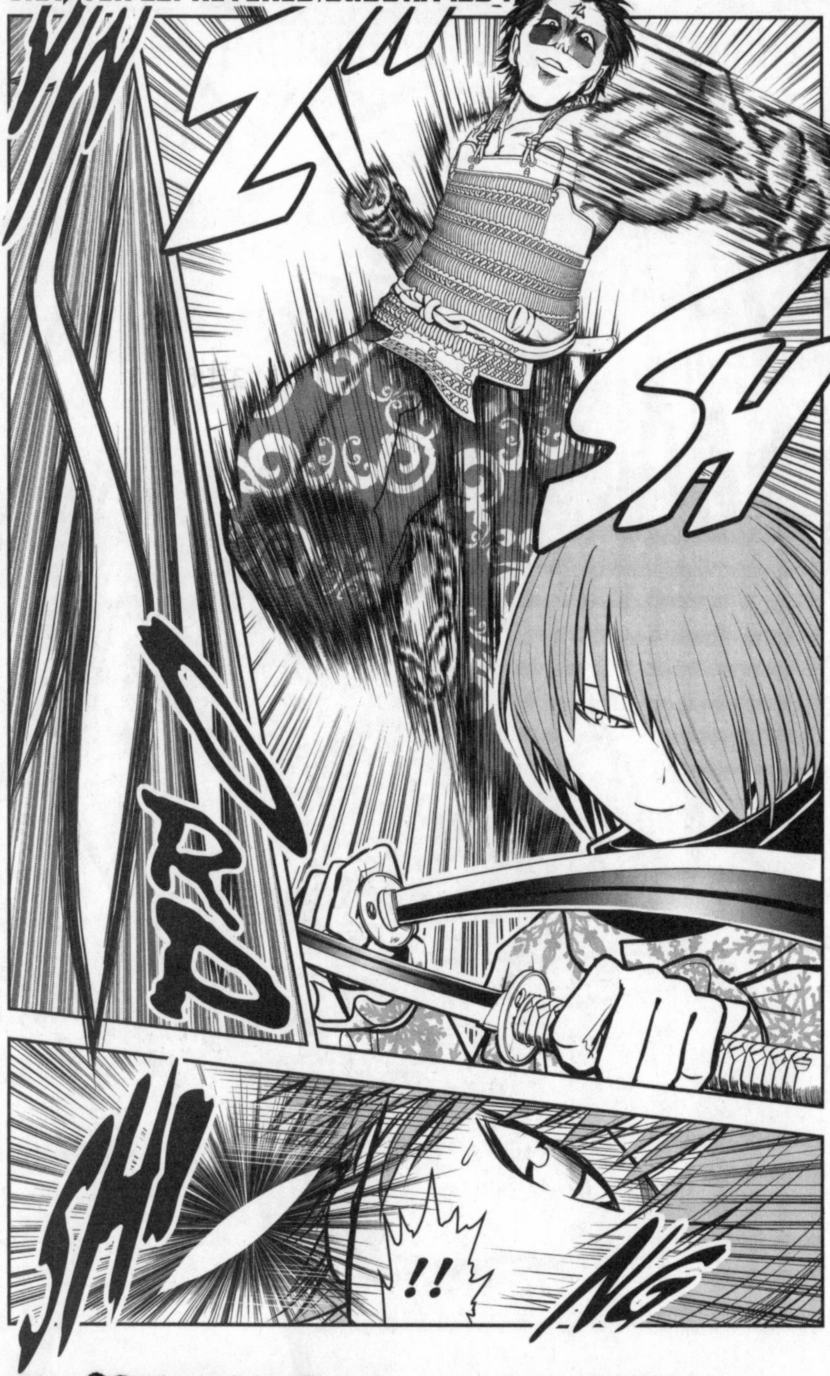
SH
!!
SHI
NG

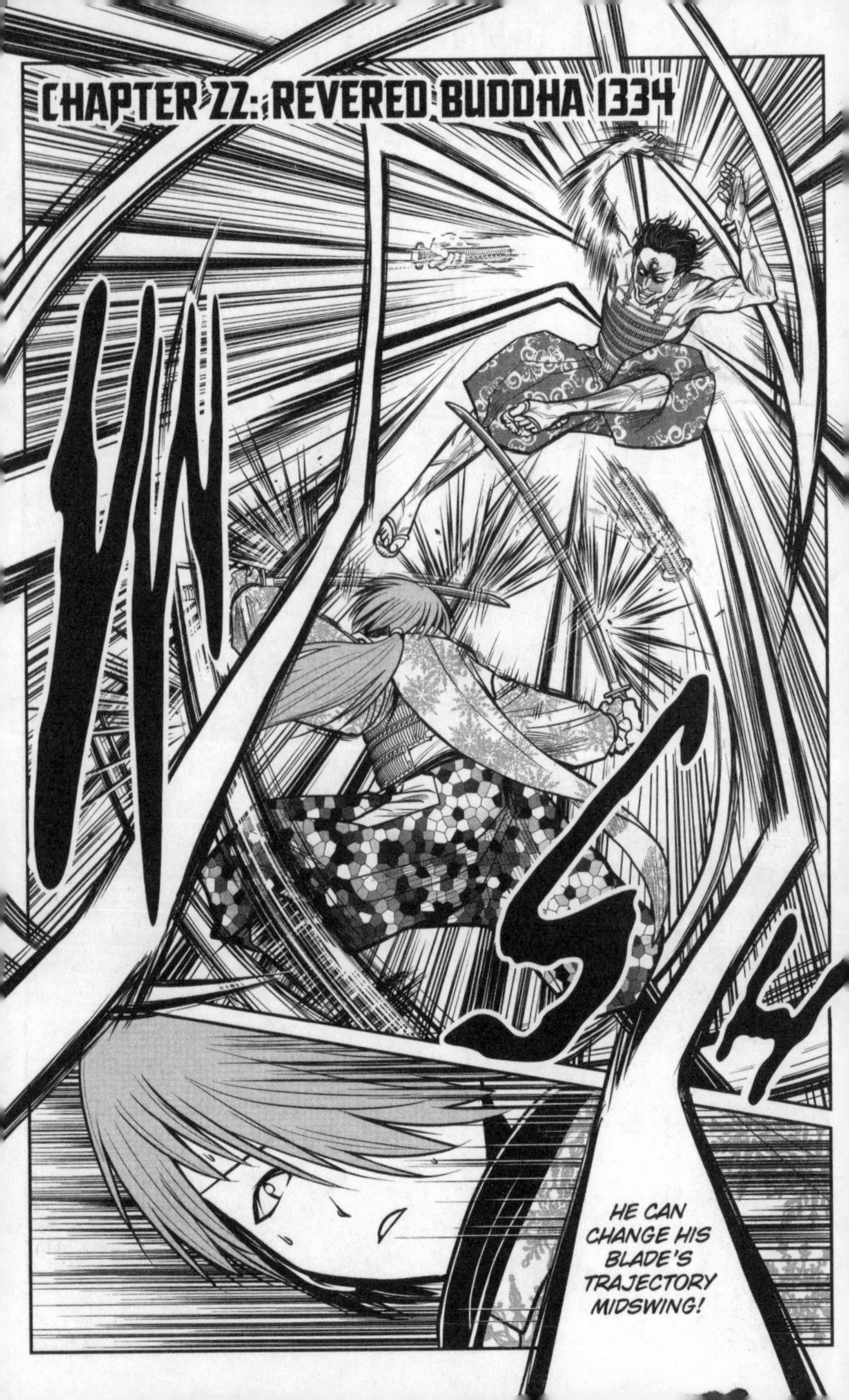
CHAPTER 22: REVERED BUDDHA 1334
WHSH
HE CAN CHANGE HIS BLADE'S TRAJECTORY MIDSWING!

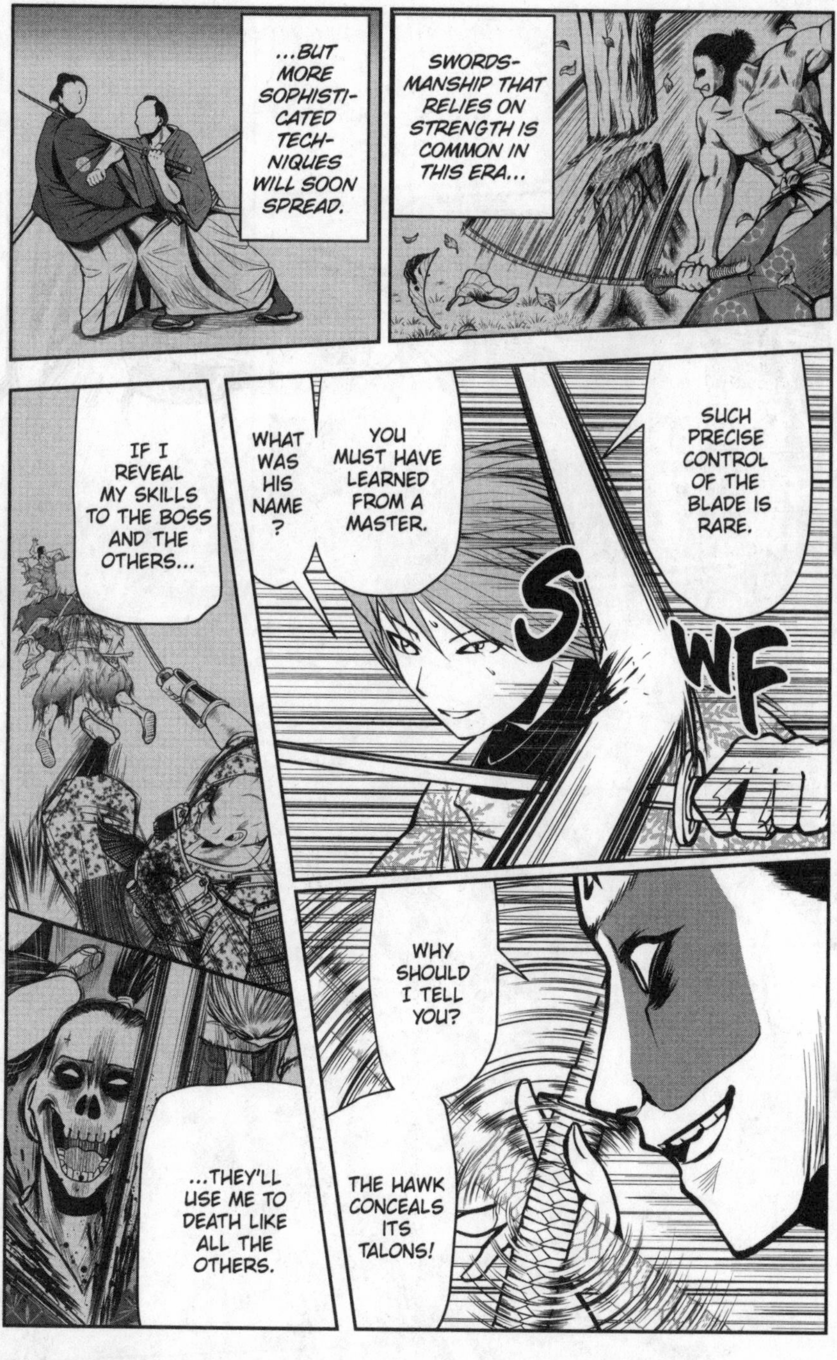
SWORDSMANSHIP THAT RELIES ON STRENGTH IS COMMON IN THIS ERA...
...BUT MORE SOPHISTICATED TECHNIQUES WILL SOON SPREAD.
SUCH PRECISE CONTROL OF THE BLADE IS RARE.
SWF
YOU MUST HAVE LEARNED FROM A MASTER.
WHAT WAS HIS NAME?
IF I REVEAL MY SKILLS TO THE BOSS AND THE OTHERS...
WHY SHOULD I TELL YOU?
THE HAWK CONCEALS ITS TALONS!
...THEY'LL USE ME TO DEATH LIKE ALL THE OTHERS.

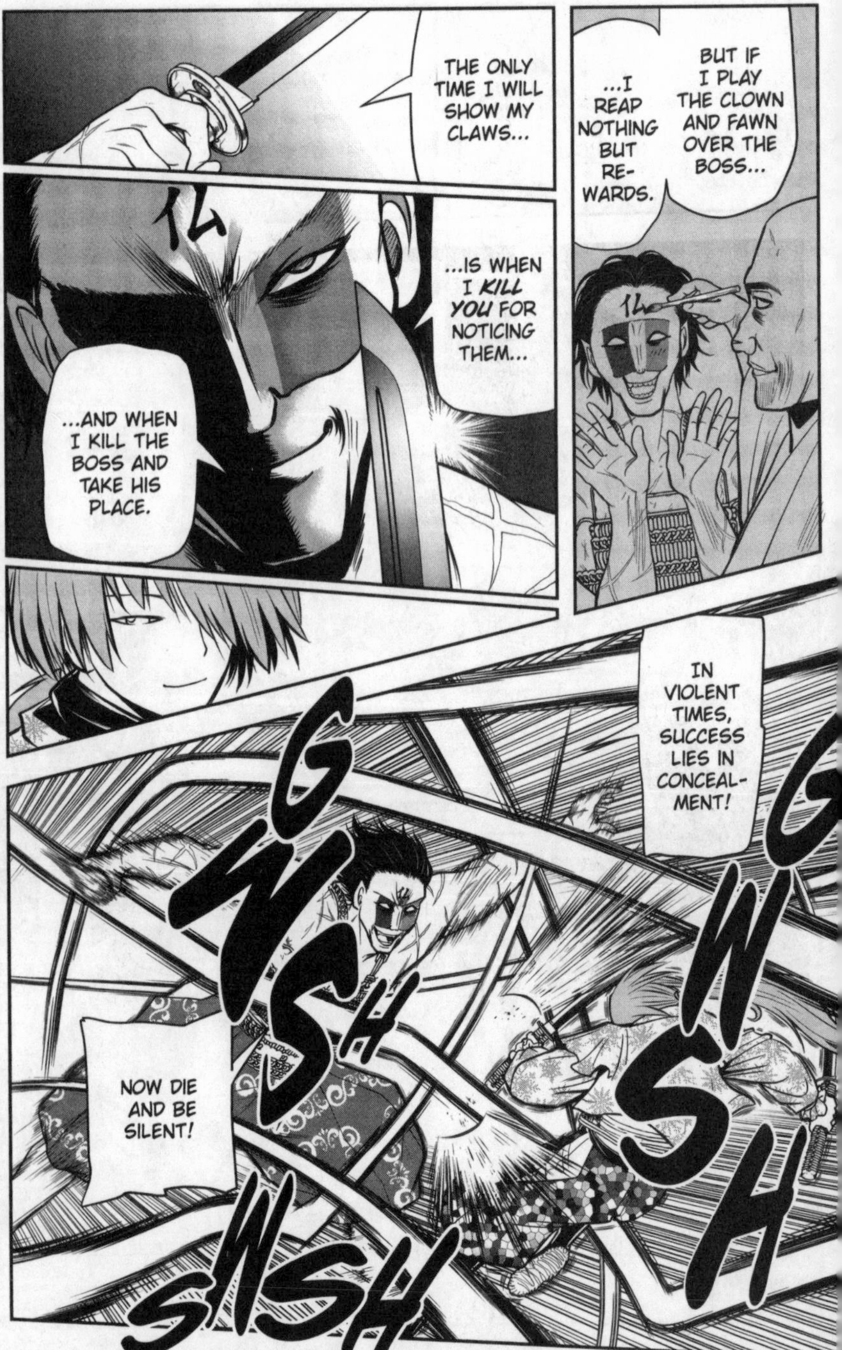
BUT IF I PLAY THE CLOWN AND FAWN OVER THE BOSS...
...I REAP NOTHING BUT RE-WARDS.
THE ONLY TIME I WILL SHOW MY CLAWS...
...IS WHEN I *KILL YOU* FOR NOTICING THEM...
...AND WHEN I KILL THE BOSS AND TAKE HIS PLACE.
IN VIOLENT TIMES, SUCCESS LIES IN CONCEAL-MENT!
GWSH
GWSH
NOW DIE AND BE SILENT!
SWSH

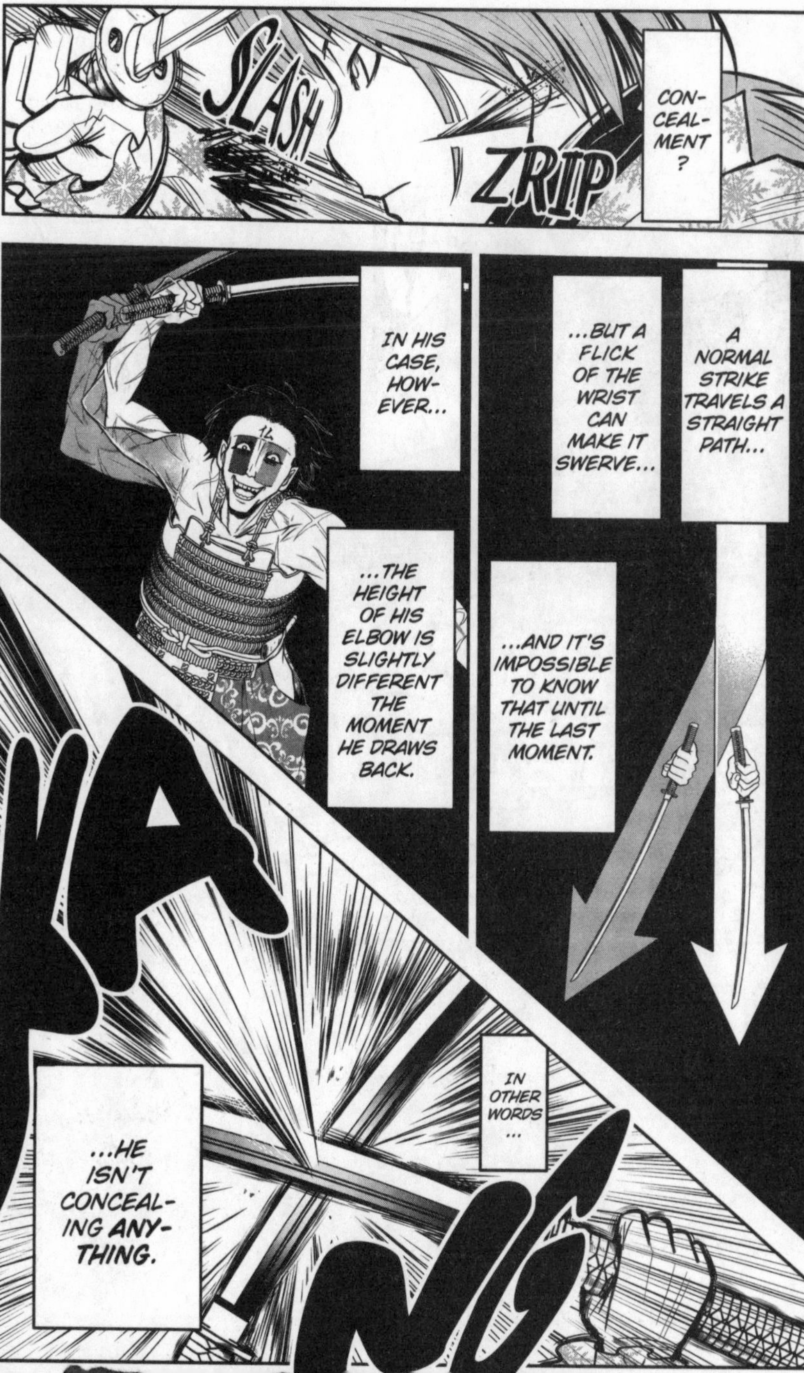
CON-CEAL-MENT?
ZRIP
SLASH
A NORMAL STRIKE TRAVELS A STRAIGHT PATH...
...BUT A FLICK OF THE WRIST CAN MAKE IT SWERVE...
...AND IT'S IMPOSSIBLE TO KNOW THAT UNTIL THE LAST MOMENT.
IN HIS CASE, HOW-EVER...
...THE HEIGHT OF HIS ELBOW IS SLIGHTLY DIFFERENT THE MOMENT HE DRAWS BACK.
IN OTHER WORDS...
...HE ISN'T CONCEAL-ING ANY-THING.

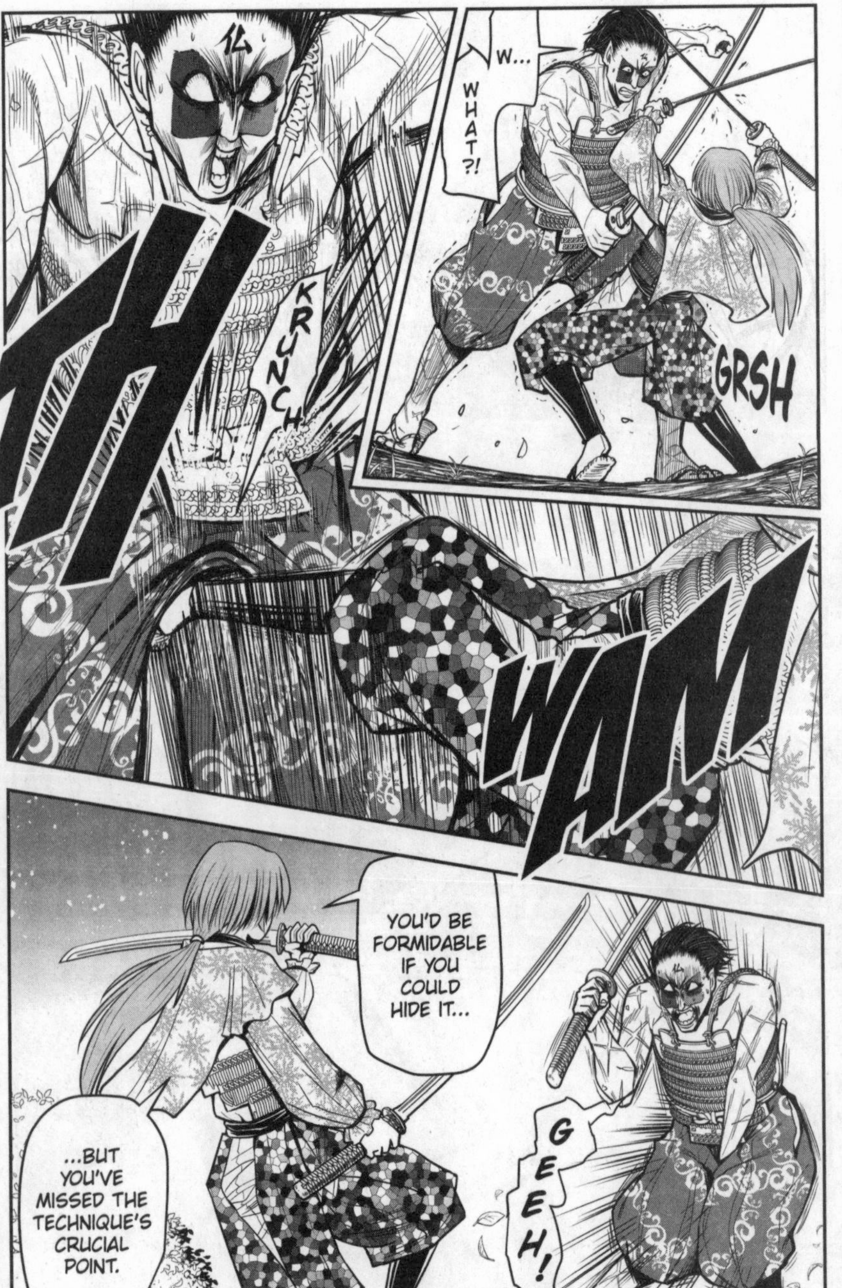
W...
WHAT?!
GRSH
仏
KRUNCH
WAM
YOU'D BE FORMIDABLE IF YOU COULD HIDE IT...
GEEH!
...BUT YOU'VE MISSED THE TECHNIQUE'S CRUCIAL POINT.

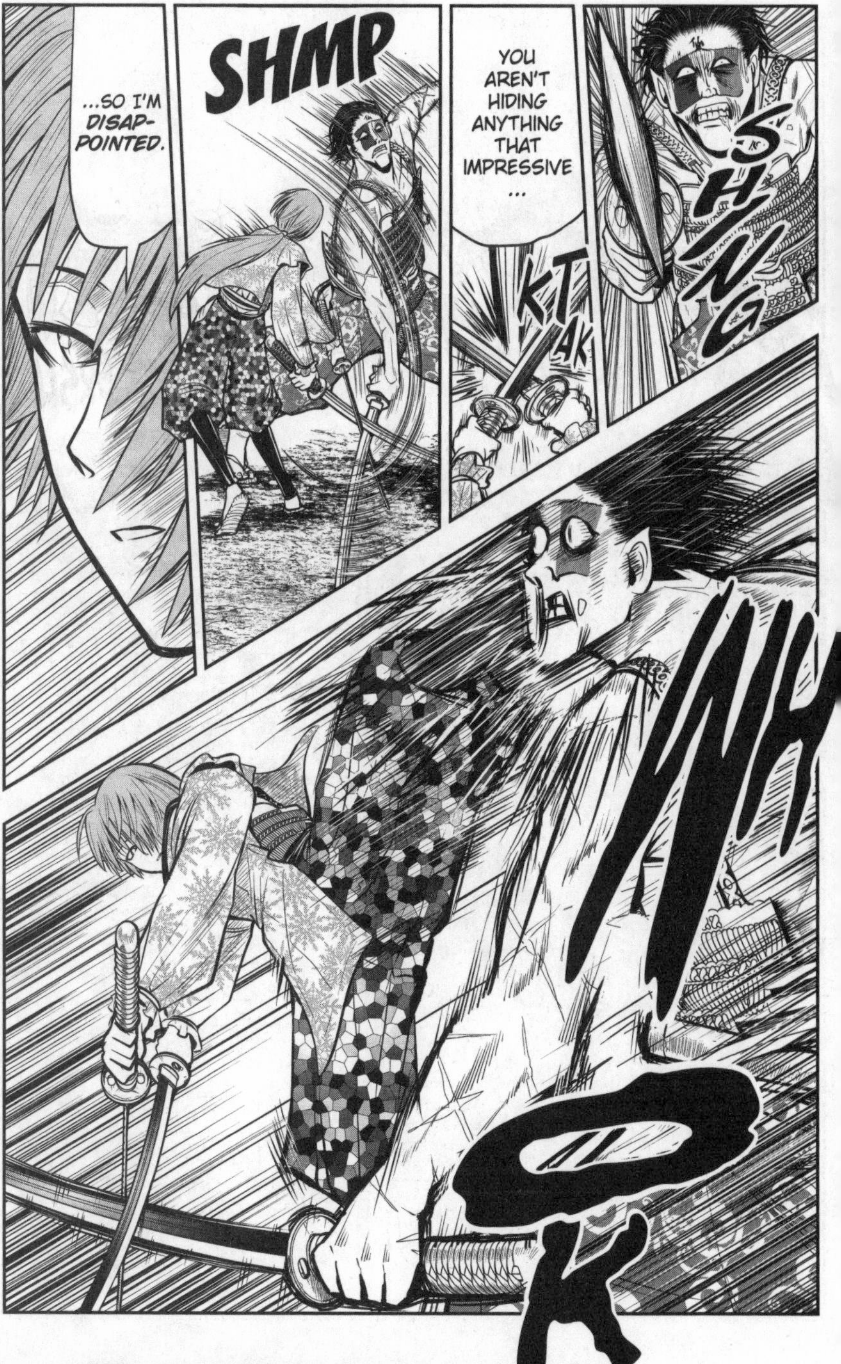
SHING
YOU AREN'T HIDING ANYTHING THAT IMPRESSIVE ...
KTAK
SHMP
...SO I'M DISAPPOINTED.

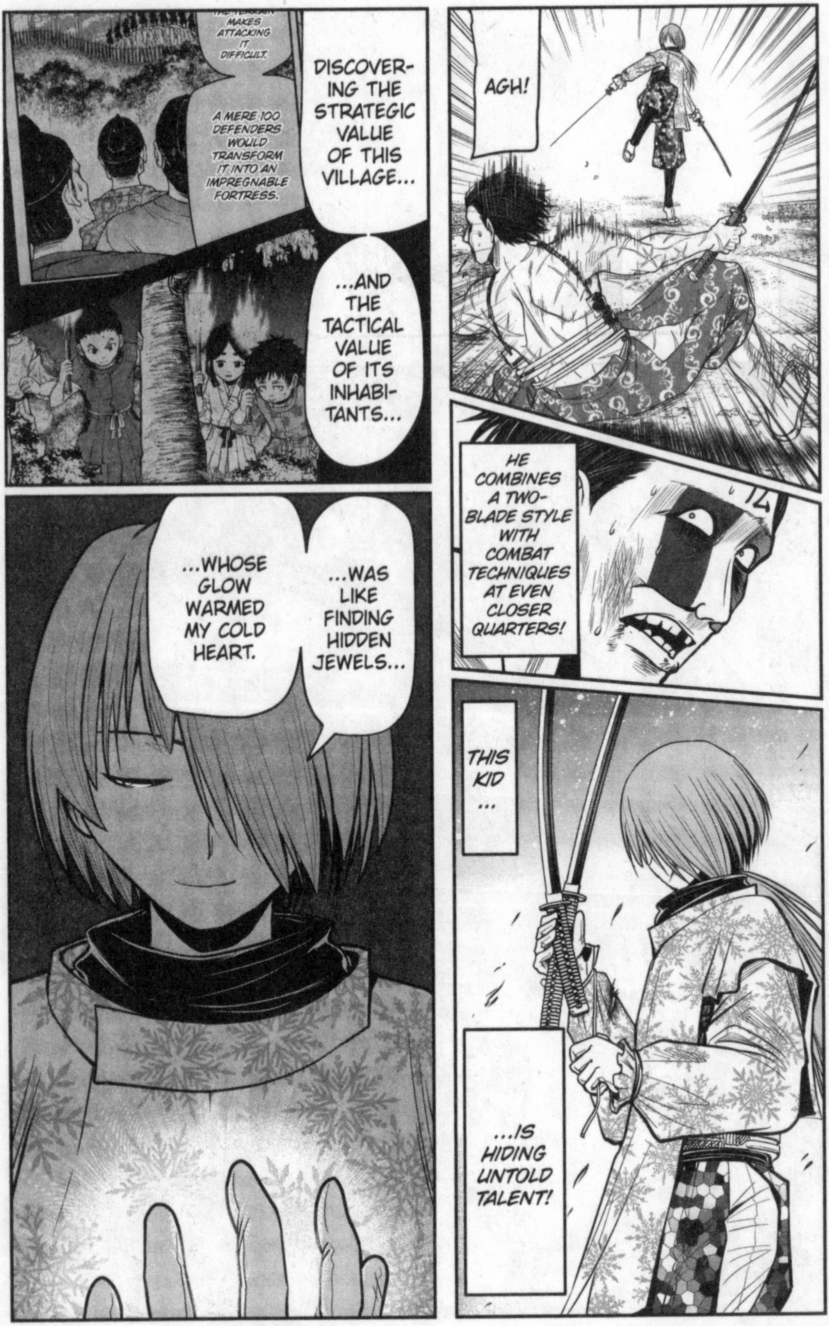
AGH!
HE COMBINES A TWO-BLADE STYLE WITH COMBAT TECHNIQUES AT EVEN CLOSER QUARTERS!
THIS KID ...
...IS HIDING UNTOLD TALENT!
MAKES ATTACKING IT DIFFICULT.
A MERE 100 DEFENDERS WOULD TRANSFORM IT INTO AN IMPREGNABLE FORTRESS.
DISCOVERING THE STRATEGIC VALUE OF THIS VILLAGE...
...AND THE TACTICAL VALUE OF ITS INHABITANTS...
...WAS LIKE FINDING HIDDEN JEWELS...
...WHOSE GLOW WARMED MY COLD HEART.

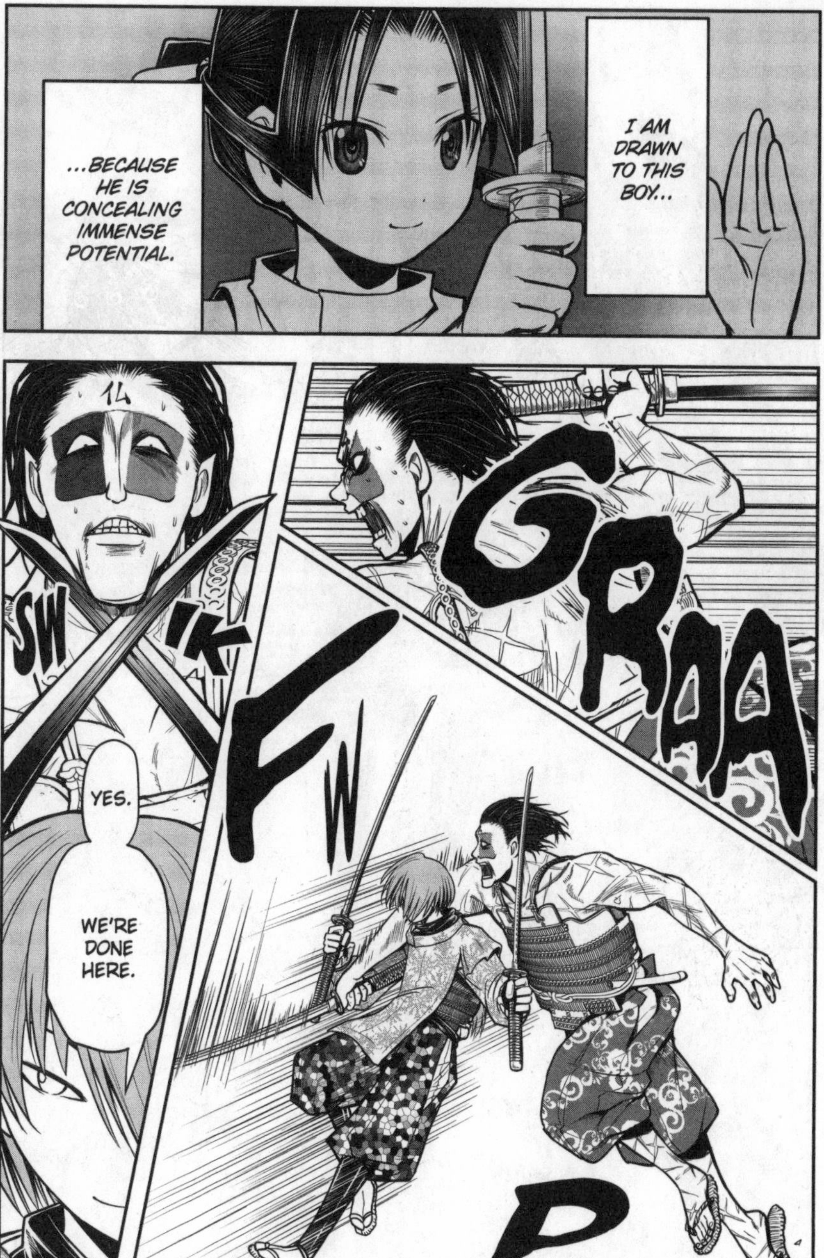
I AM DRAWN TO THIS BOY...
...BECAUSE HE IS CONCEALING IMMENSE POTENTIAL.
GRAAA
FW
P
仏
SWIK
YES.
WE'RE DONE HERE.

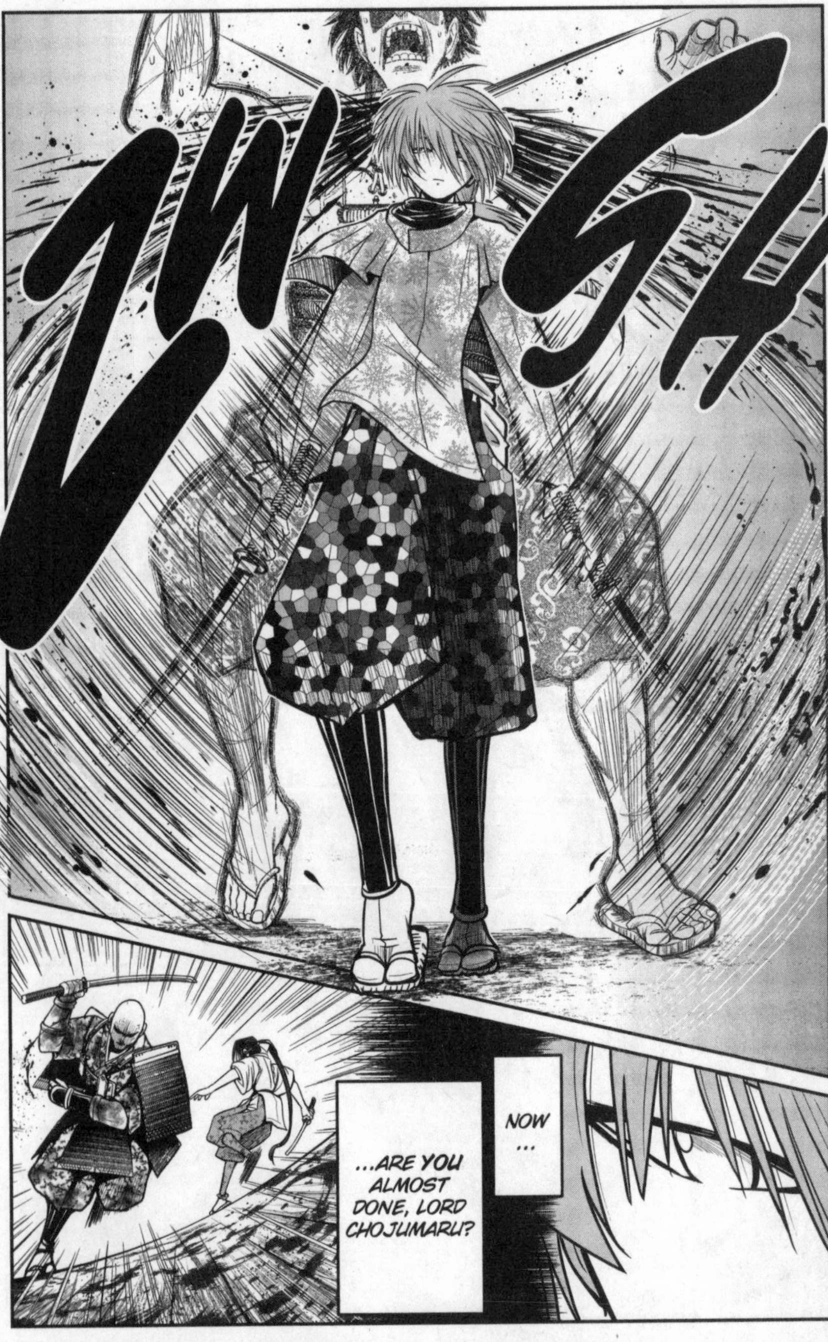
ZWSH
NOW...
...ARE YOU ALMOST DONE, LORD CHOJUMARU?

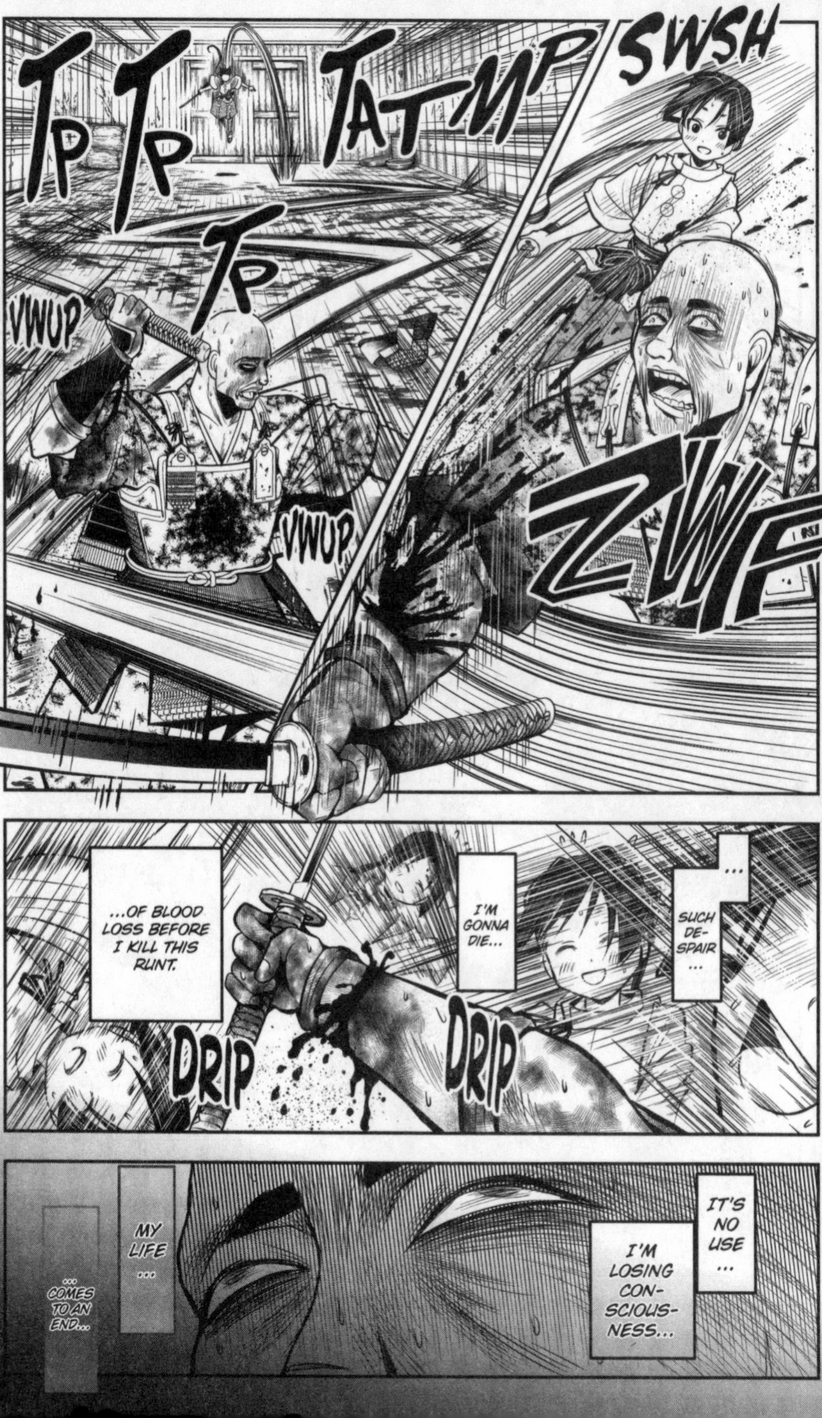
SWSH
ZWF
TP
TP
TATMP
TP
VWUP
VWUP
...
SUCH DE-SPAIR ...
I'M GONNA DIE...
...OF BLOOD LOSS BEFORE I KILL THIS RUNT.
DRIP
DRIP
IT'S NO USE ...
I'M LOSING CON-SCIOUS-NESS...
MY LIFE ...
... COMES TO AN END...

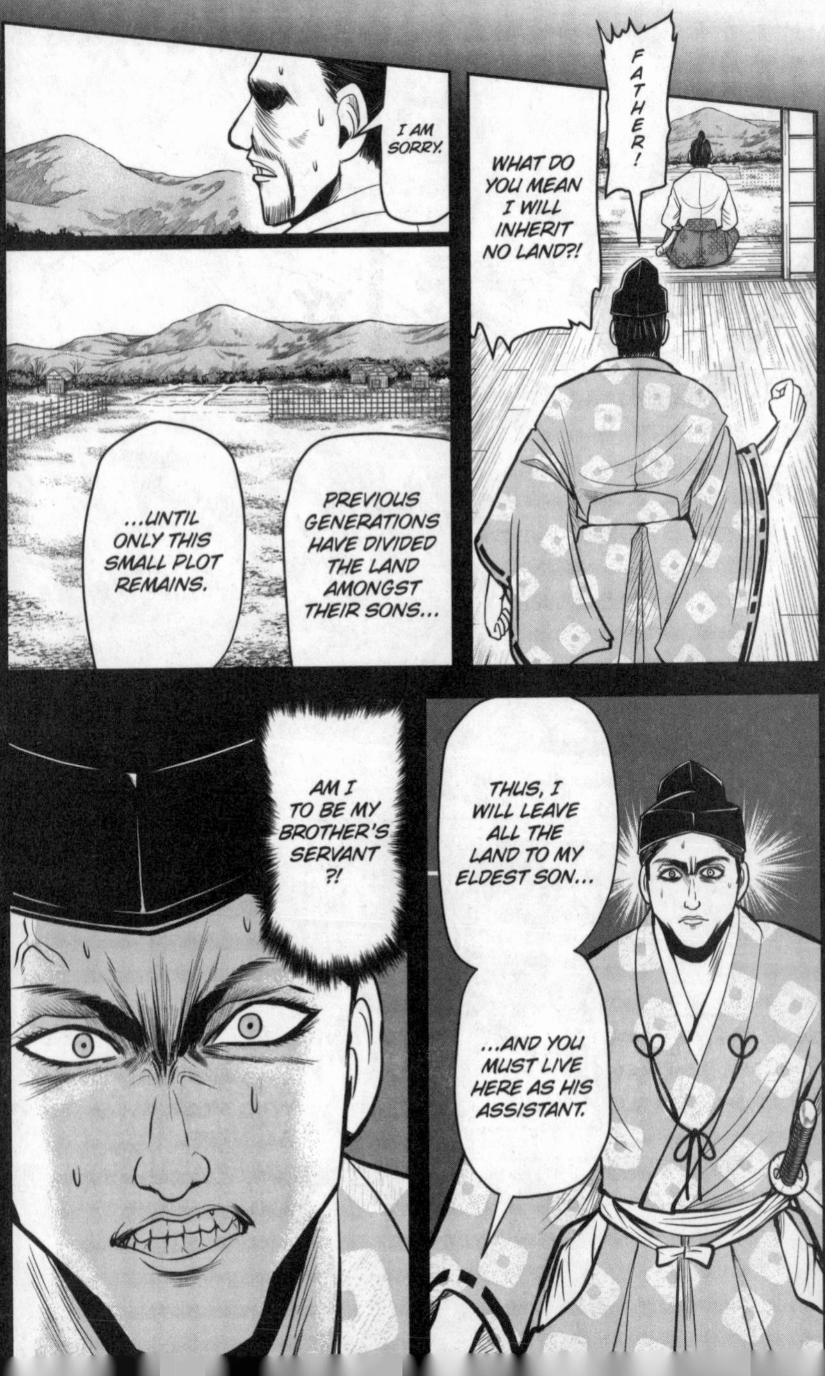
FATHER!
WHAT DO YOU MEAN I WILL INHERIT NO LAND?!
I AM SORRY.
PREVIOUS GENERATIONS HAVE DIVIDED THE LAND AMONGST THEIR SONS...
...UNTIL ONLY THIS SMALL PLOT REMAINS.
THUS, I WILL LEAVE ALL THE LAND TO MY ELDEST SON...
...AND YOU MUST LIVE HERE AS HIS ASSISTANT.
AM I TO BE MY BROTHER'S SERVANT?!

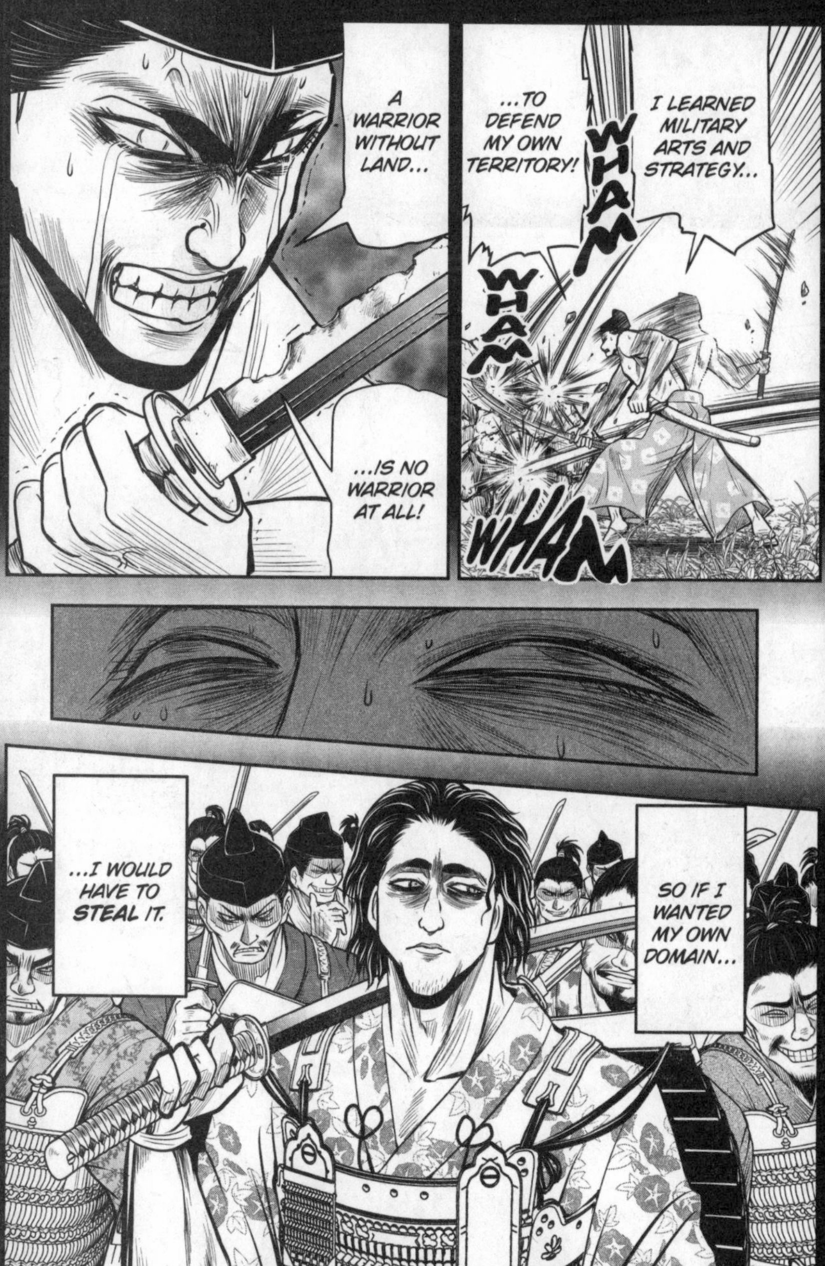
I LEARNED MILITARY ARTS AND STRATEGY...
...TO DEFEND MY OWN TERRITORY!
WHAM
WHAM
WHAM
A WARRIOR WITHOUT LAND...
...IS NO WARRIOR AT ALL!
SO IF I WANTED MY OWN DOMAIN...
...I WOULD HAVE TO STEAL IT.

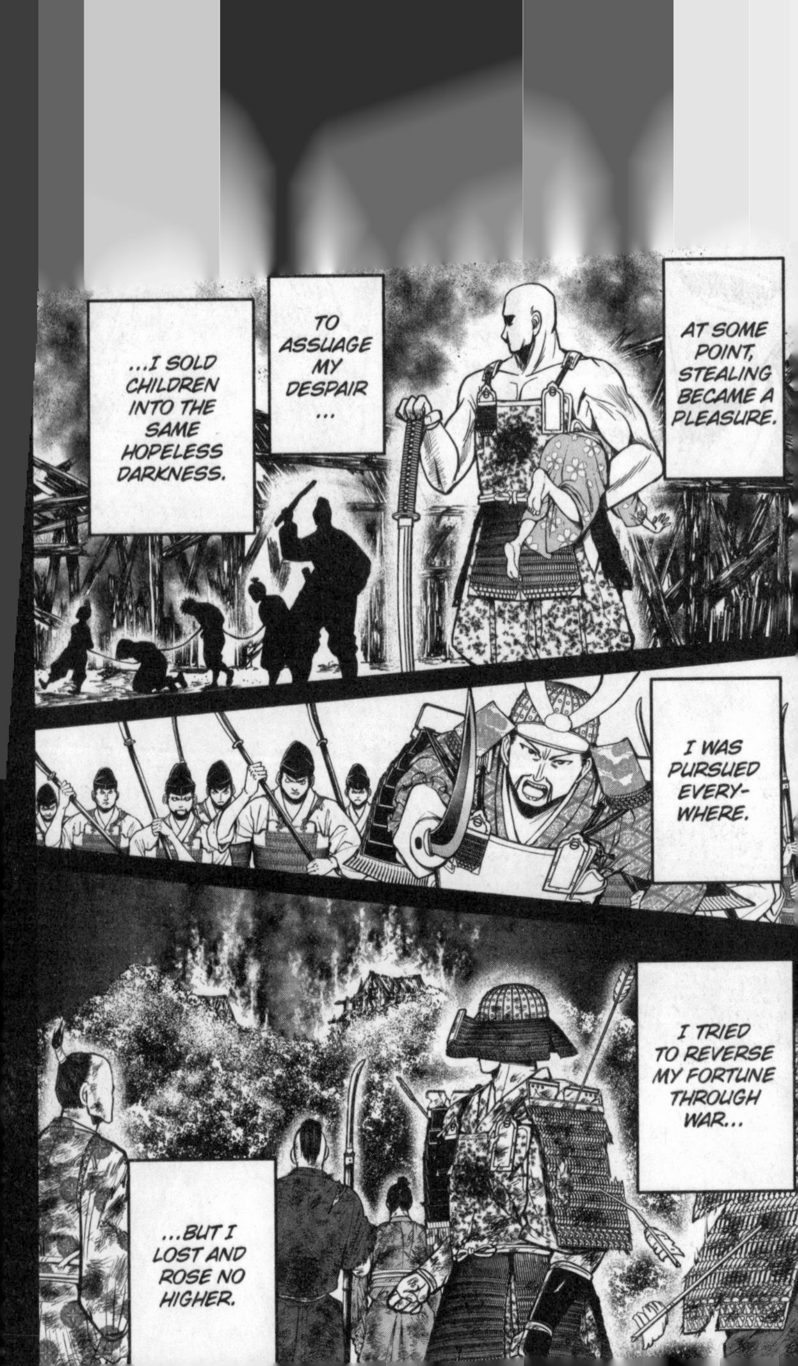
AT SOME POINT, STEALING BECAME A PLEASURE.
TO ASSUAGE MY DESPAIR...
...I SOLD CHILDREN INTO THE SAME HOPELESS DARKNESS.
I WAS PURSUED EVERY-WHERE.
I TRIED TO REVERSE MY FORTUNE THROUGH WAR...
...BUT I LOST AND ROSE NO HIGHER.

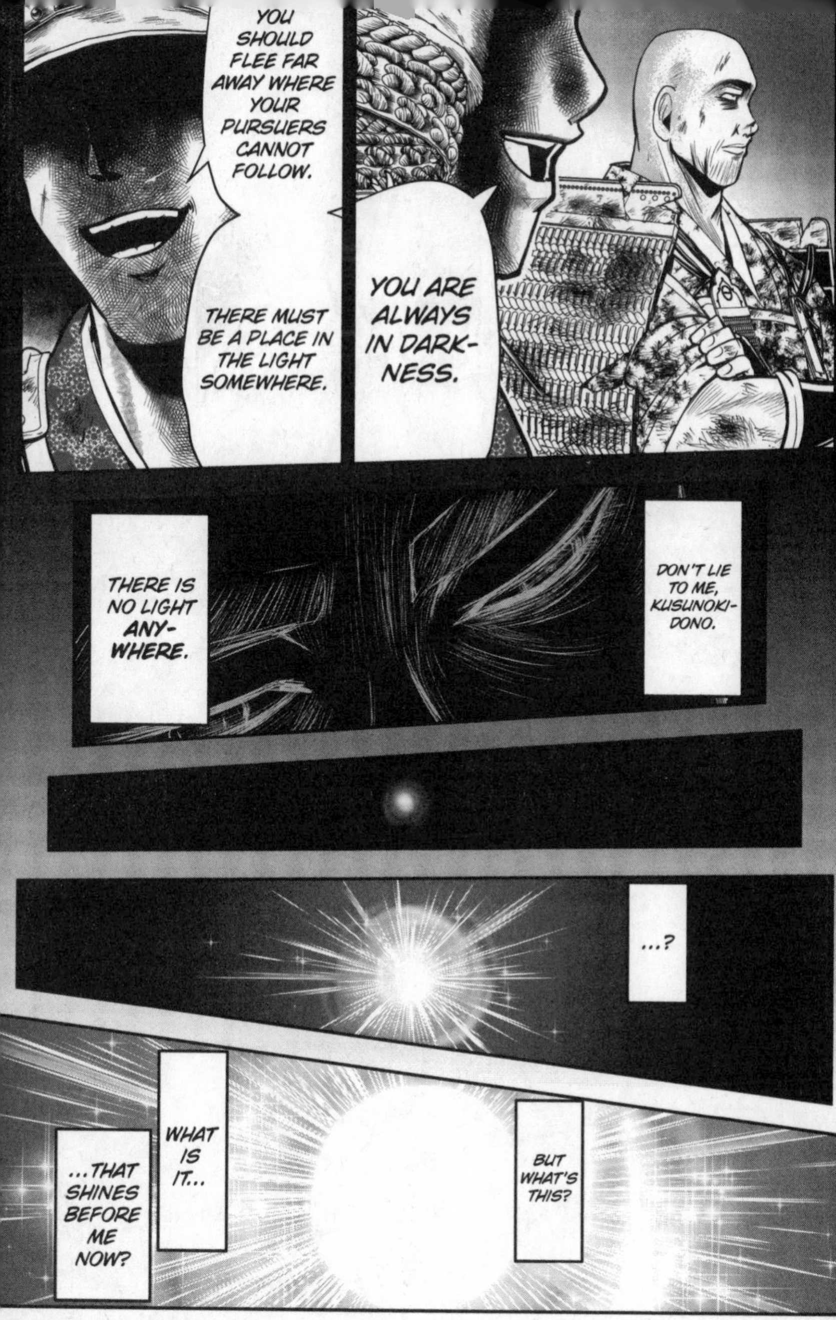
YOU ARE ALWAYS IN DARK-NESS.
YOU SHOULD FLEE FAR AWAY WHERE YOUR PURSUERS CANNOT FOLLOW.
THERE MUST BE A PLACE IN THE LIGHT SOMEWHERE.
DON'T LIE TO ME, KUSUNOKI-DONO.
THERE IS NO LIGHT ANY-WHERE.
...?
BUT WHAT'S THIS?
WHAT IS IT...
...THAT SHINES BEFORE ME NOW?

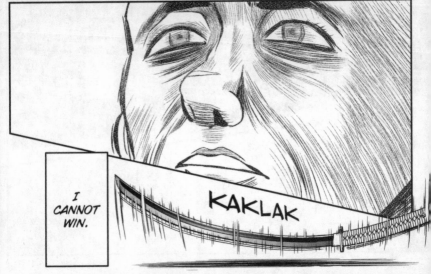

I CANNOT WIN.

KAKLAK

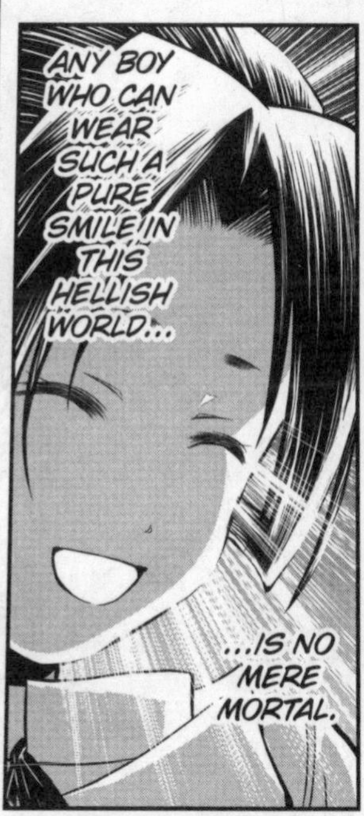
ANY BOY WHO CAN WEAR SUCH A PURE SMILE IN THIS HELLISH WORLD...
...IS NO MERE MORTAL.
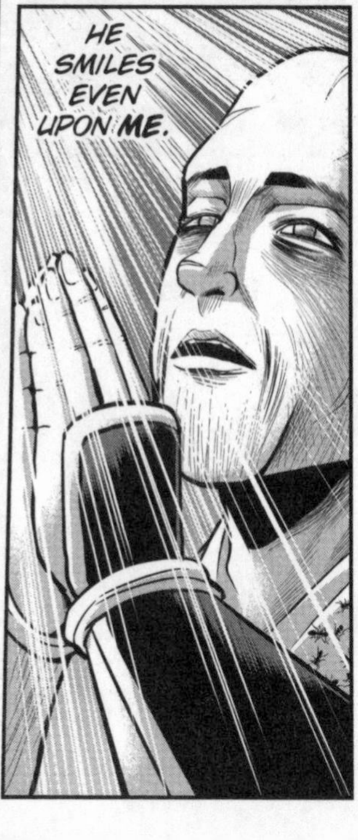
HE SMILES EVEN UPON ME.
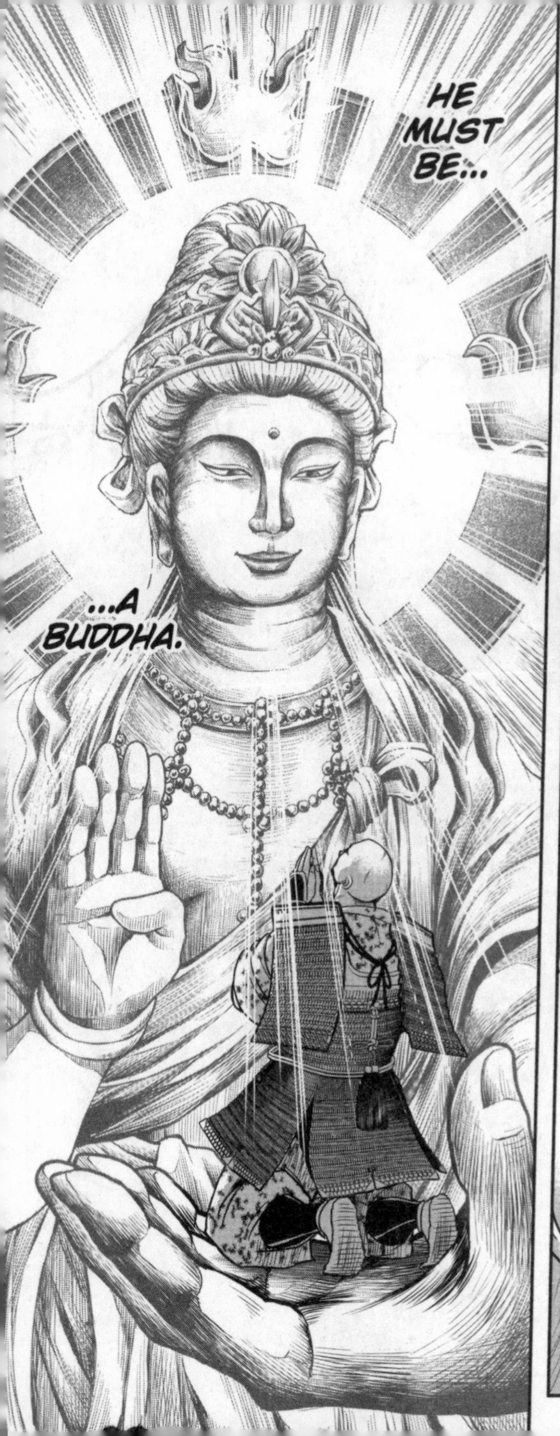
HE MUST BE...
...A BUDDHA.

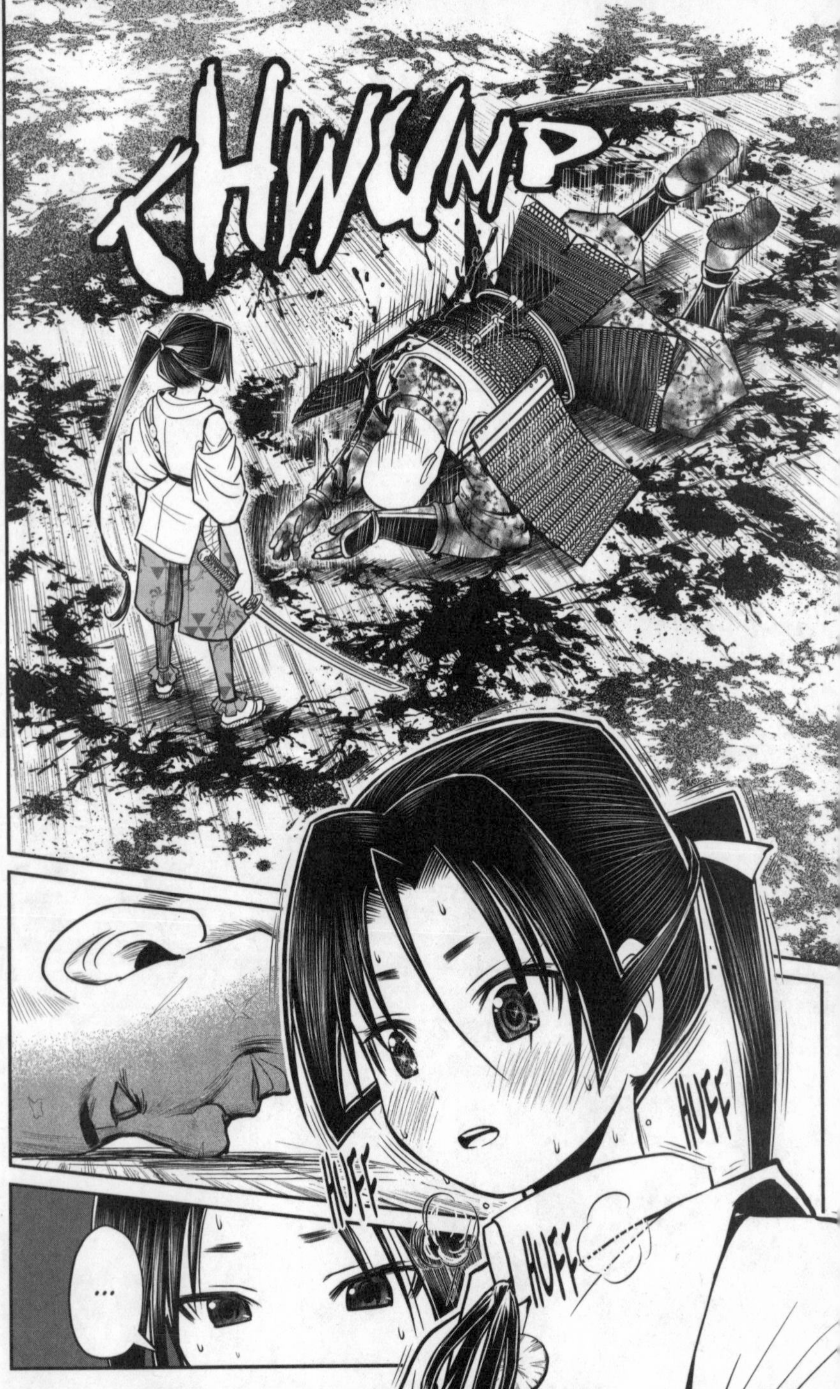
THWUMP
HUFF
HUFF
HUFF
...

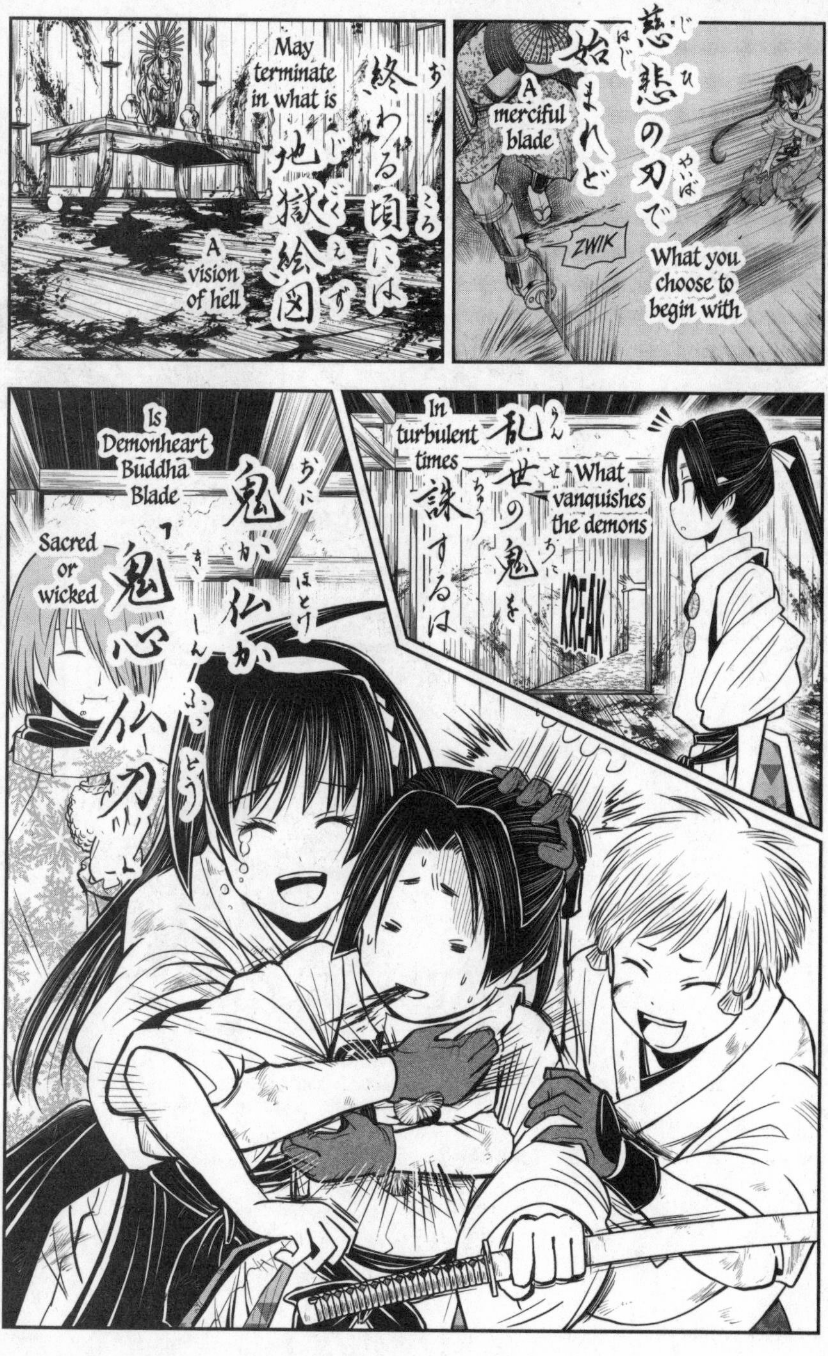
慈悲の刃で
始まれど
What you choose to begin with
A merciful blade
ZWIK
終わる頃には
地獄絵図
May terminate in what is
A vision of hell
乱世の鬼を
誅するは
In turbulent times
What vanquishes the demons
KREAK
鬼か仏か
鬼心仏刀
Sacred or wicked
Is Demonheart Buddha Blade

The Damage This Time

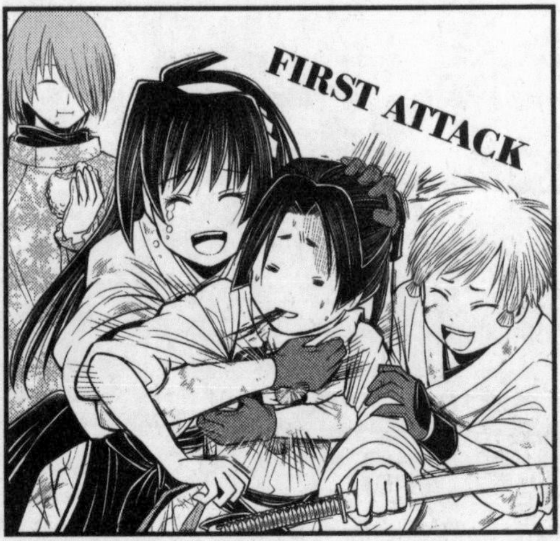
FIRST ATTACK

Fubuki	A few lacerations
Ayako	Many lacerations, abrasions, and contusions
Kojiro	Many lacerations and abrasions
Tokiyuki	Complex rib fractures

The Elusive Samurai

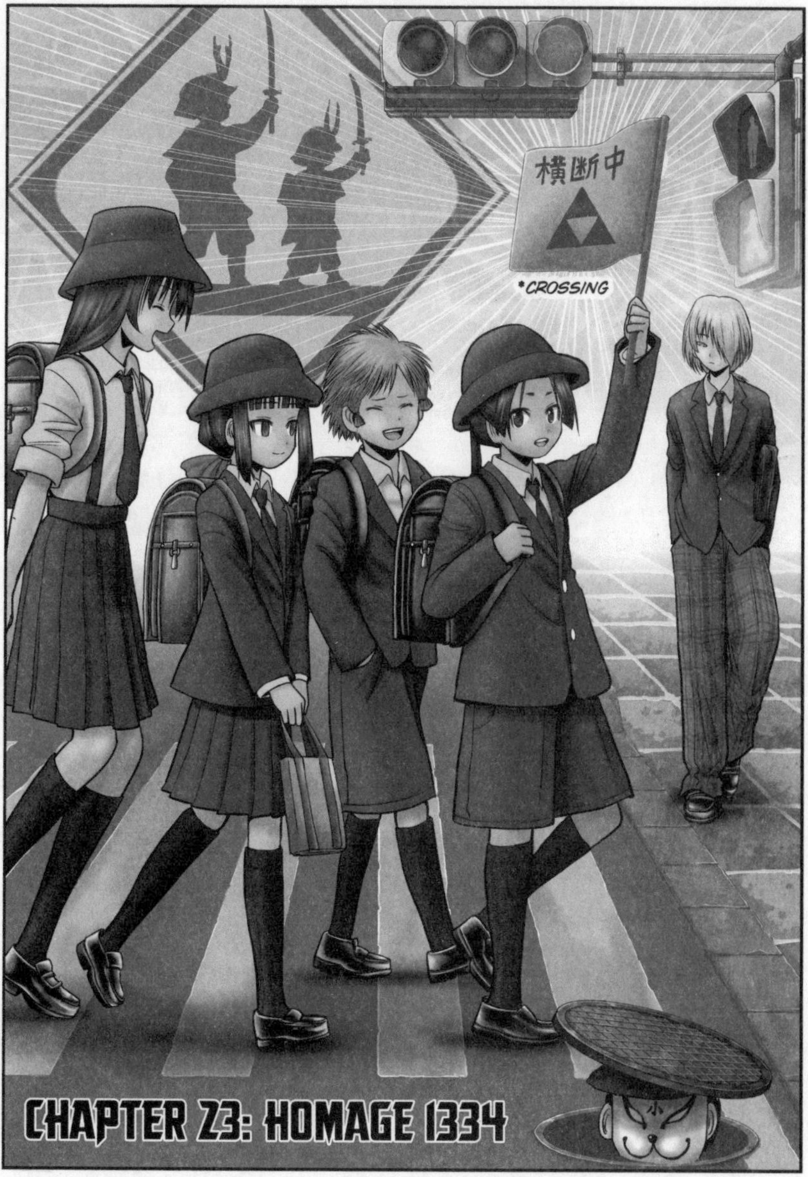
横断中
*CROSSING
CHAPTER 23: HOMAGE 1334

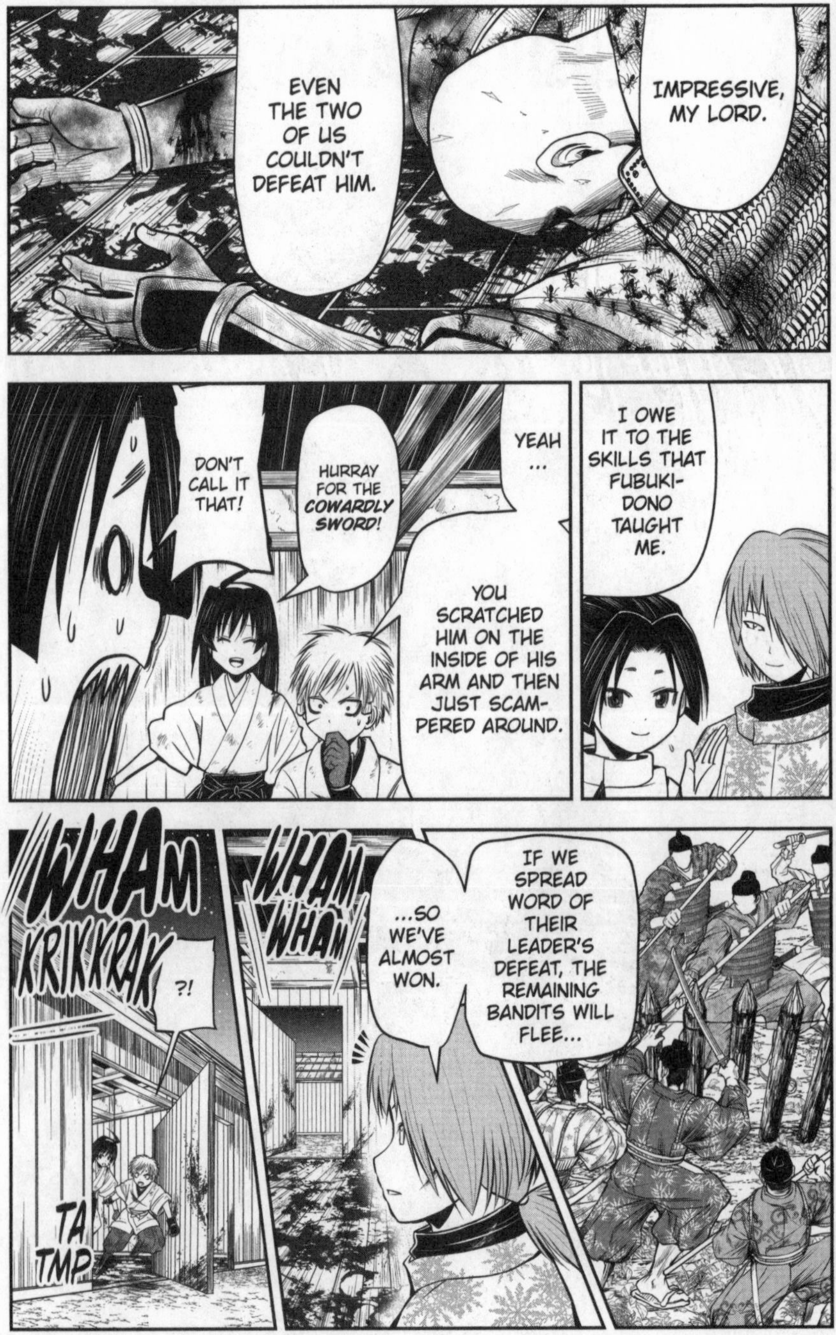
IMPRESSIVE, MY LORD.
EVEN THE TWO OF US COULDN'T DEFEAT HIM.
I OWE IT TO THE SKILLS THAT FUBUKI-DONO TAUGHT ME.
YEAH ...
YOU SCRATCHED HIM ON THE INSIDE OF HIS ARM AND THEN JUST SCAMPERED AROUND.
HURRAY FOR THE COWARDLY SWORD!
DON'T CALL IT THAT!
IF WE SPREAD WORD OF THEIR LEADER'S DEFEAT, THE REMAINING BANDITS WILL FLEE...
...SO WE'VE ALMOST WON.
WHAM WHAM
WHAM
KRIKKRAK
?!
TA TMP

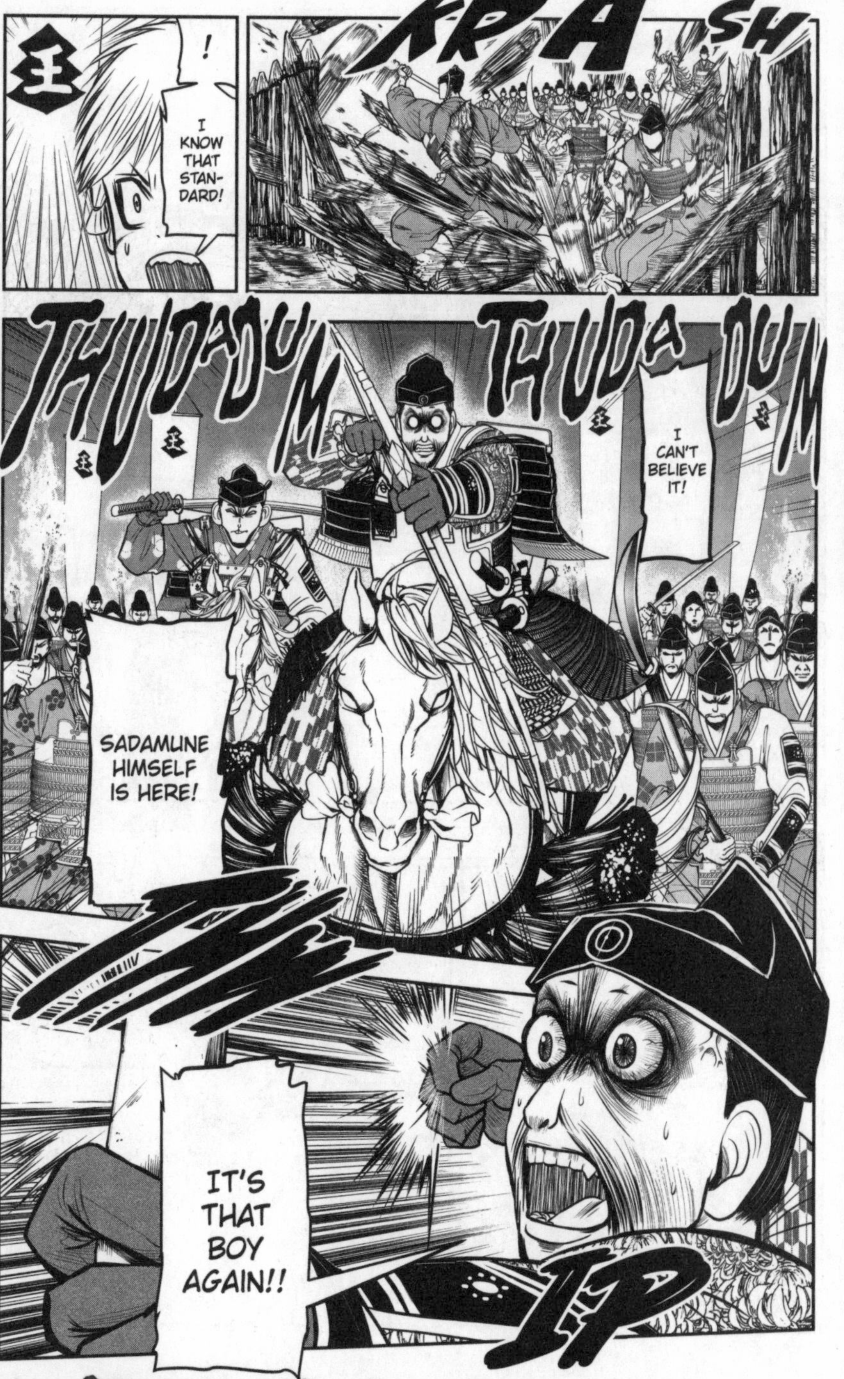
KRASH
!
I KNOW THAT STAN-DARD!
THUDADUM THUDADUM
I CAN'T BELIEVE IT!
SADAMUNE HIMSELF IS HERE!
IT'S THAT BOY AGAIN!!

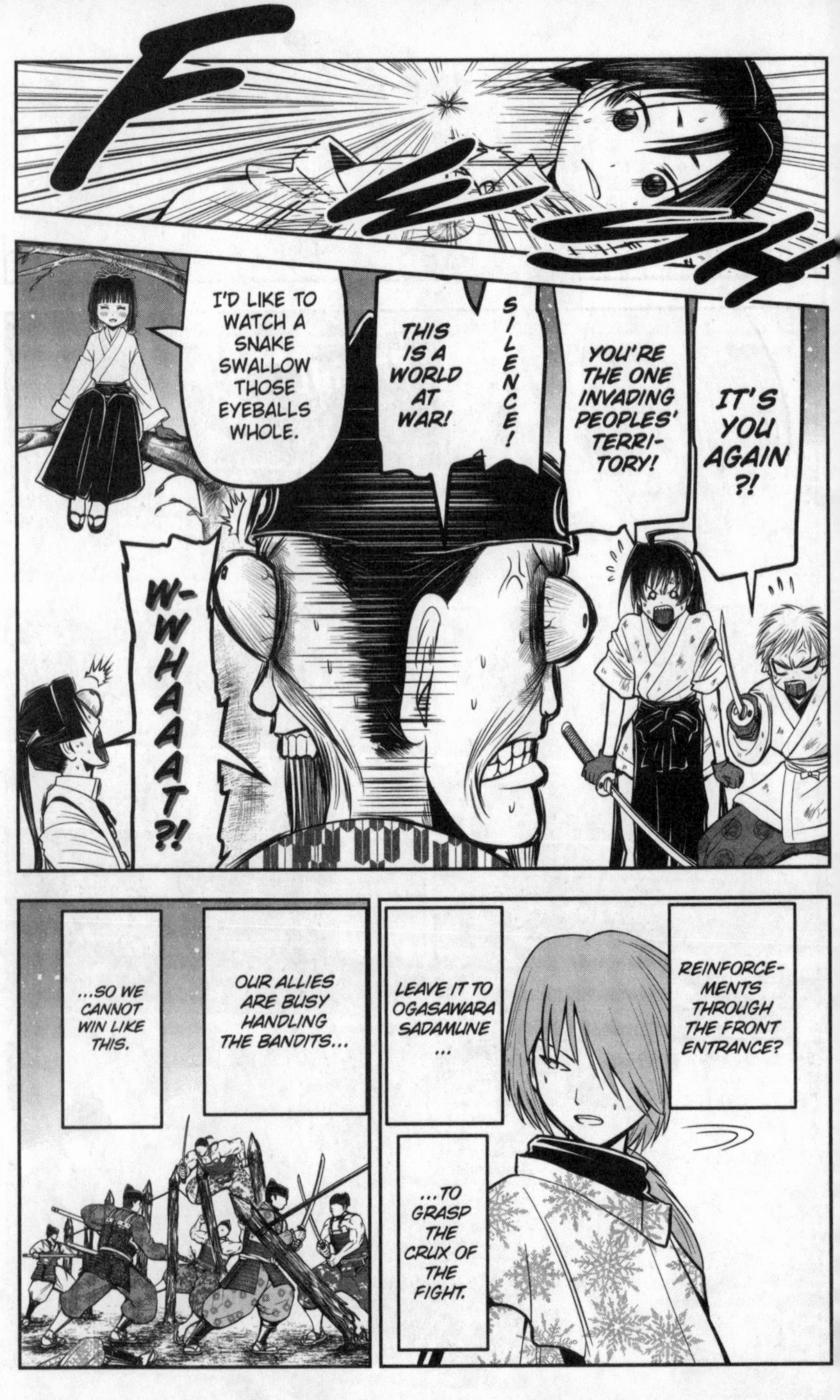
FWISSH
IT'S YOU AGAIN?!
YOU'RE THE ONE INVADING PEOPLES' TERRITORY!
SILENCE!
THIS IS A WORLD AT WAR!
I'D LIKE TO WATCH A SNAKE SWALLOW THOSE EYEBALLS WHOLE.
W-WHAAAAT?!
REINFORCEMENTS THROUGH THE FRONT ENTRANCE?
LEAVE IT TO OGASAWARA SADAMUNE...
...TO GRASP THE CRUX OF THE FIGHT.
OUR ALLIES ARE BUSY HANDLING THE BANDITS...
...SO WE CANNOT WIN LIKE THIS.

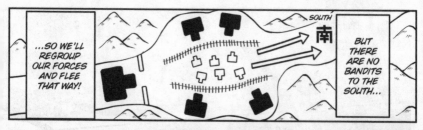

BUT THERE ARE NO BANDITS TO THE SOUTH...
SOUTH
南
...SO WE'LL REGROUP OUR FORCES AND FLEE THAT WAY!
RMMBL
WHAM
KLANG
!!
!!
TDM
TDM
TDM
WHAT?!
AN ENEMY FORCE FROM THE SOUTH TOO?!
...
NO.
POOOM
PAPOOM
!
THOSE EXPLOSIONS!

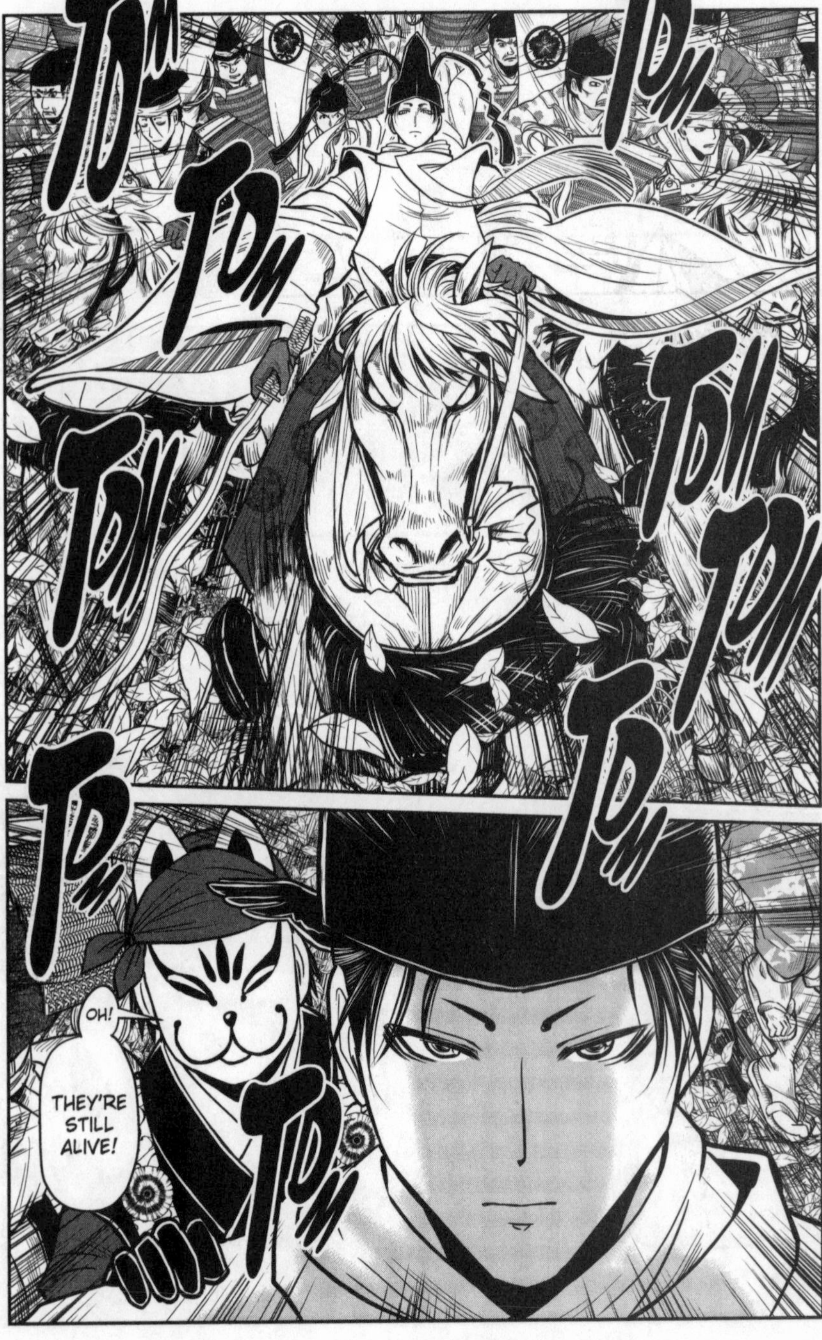

TOM
TOM TOM TOM TOM
TOM TOM
TOM TOM TOM
OH!
THEY'RE STILL ALIVE!
TOM

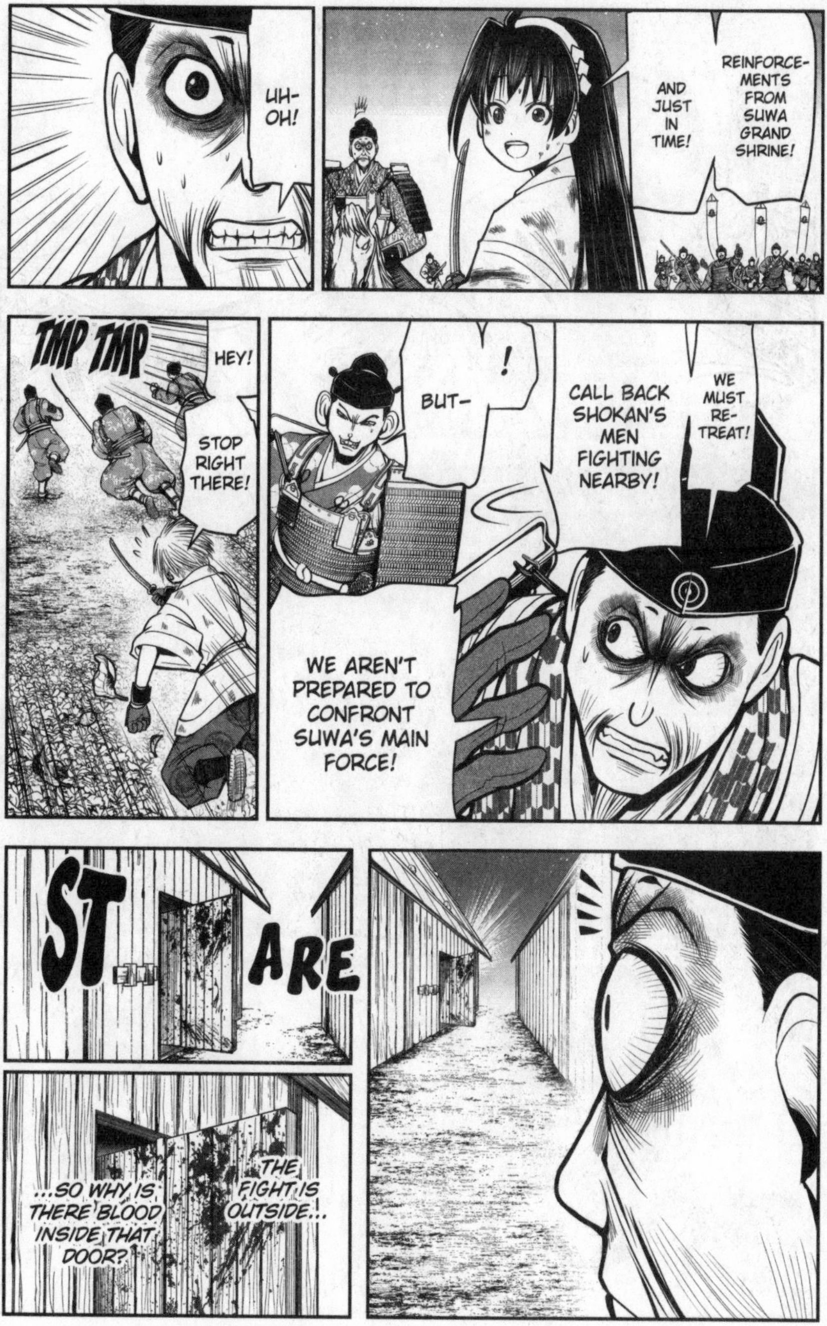
REINFORCE-
MENTS
FROM
SUWA
GRAND
SHRINE!
AND
JUST
IN
TIME!
UH-
OH!
WE
MUST
RE-
TREAT!
CALL BACK
SHOKAN'S
MEN
FIGHTING
NEARBY!
!
BUT-
WE AREN'T
PREPARED TO
CONFRONT
SUWA'S MAIN
FORCE!
TMP TMP
HEY!
STOP
RIGHT
THERE!
STARE
THE
FIGHT IS
OUTSIDE...
...SO WHY IS
THERE BLOOD
INSIDE THAT
DOOR?

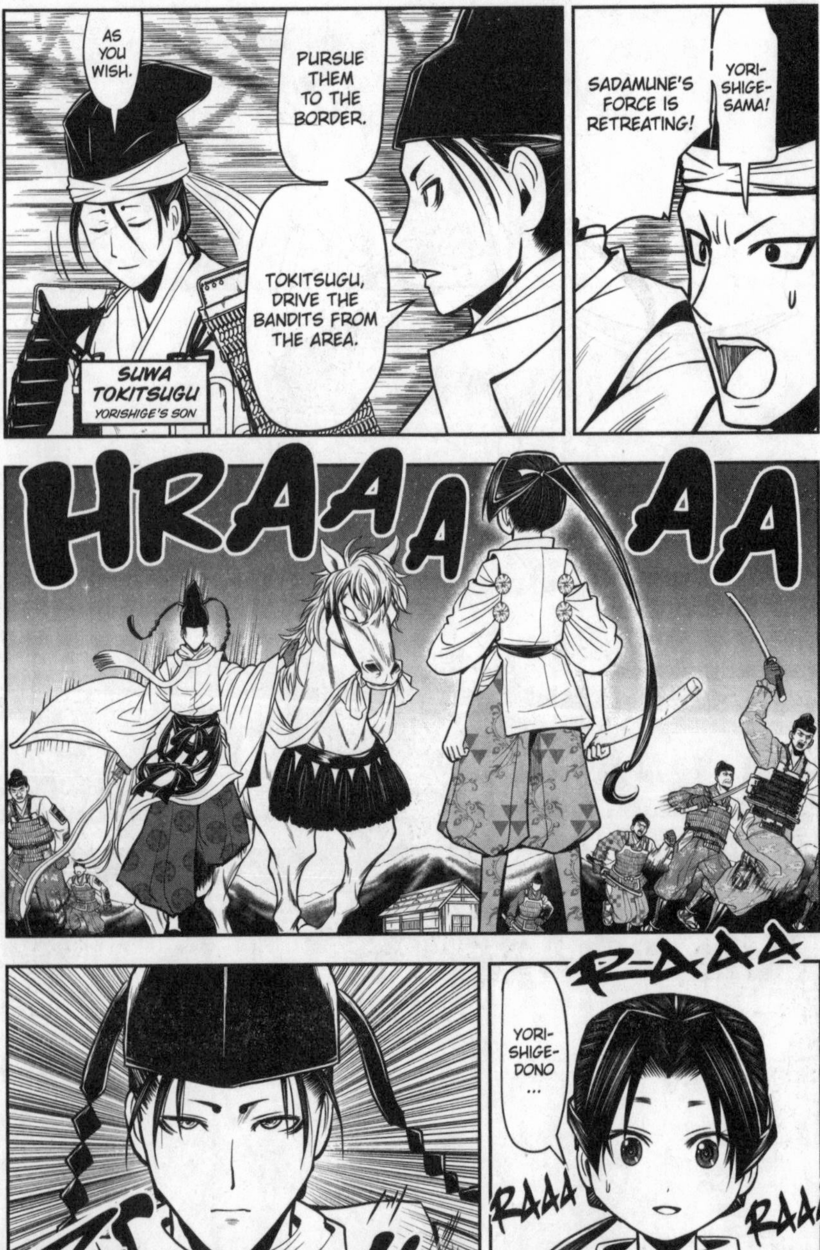
YORI-SHIGE-SAMA!
SADAMUNE'S FORCE IS RETREATING!
PURSUE THEM TO THE BORDER.
TOKITSUGU, DRIVE THE BANDITS FROM THE AREA.
AS YOU WISH.
SUWA TOKITSUGU
YORISHIGE'S SON
HRAAAAAA
RAAA
YORI-SHIGE-DONO ...
RAAA
RAAA
ZSH

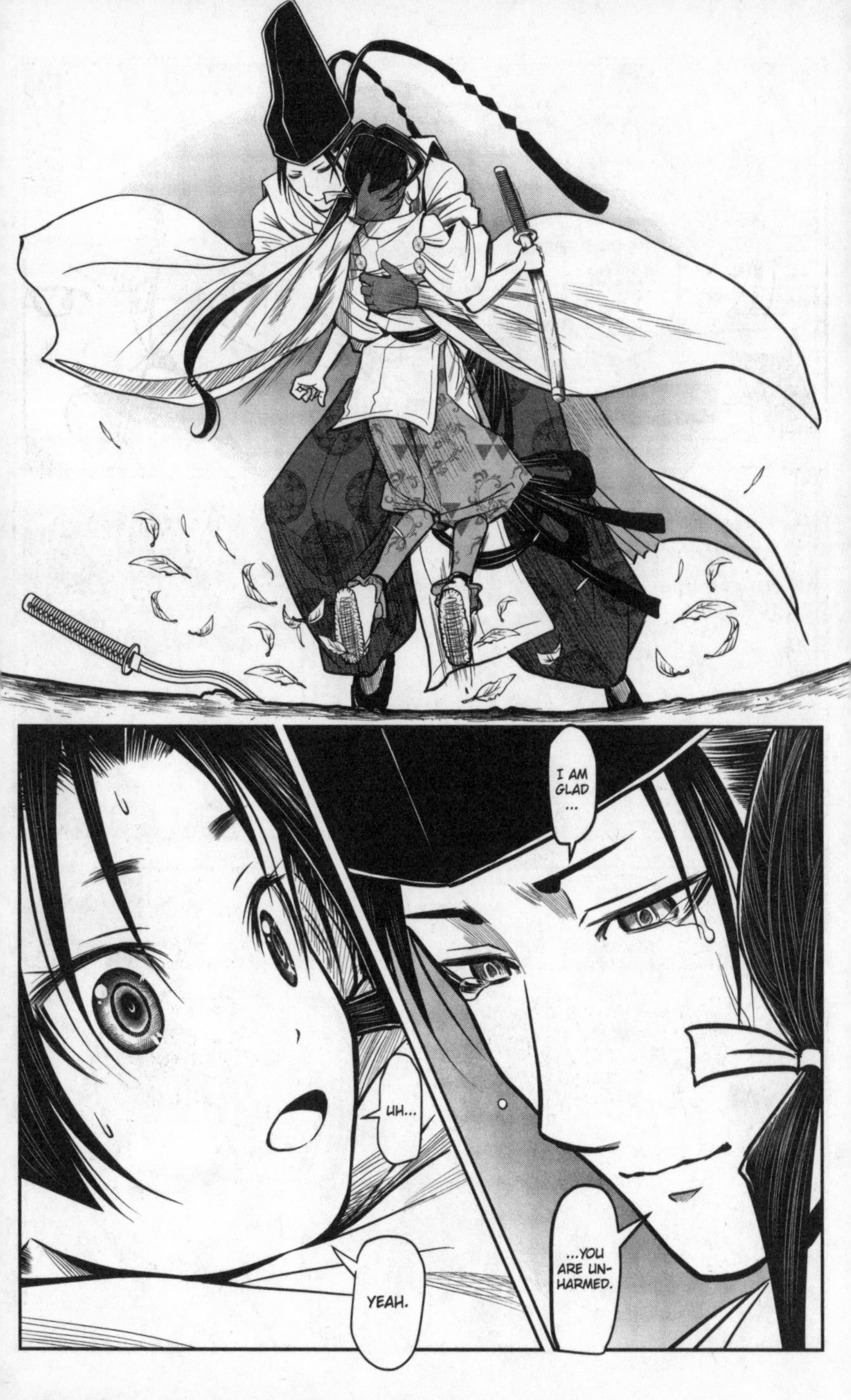
I AM GLAD ...
UH...
...YOU ARE UN-HARMED.
YEAH.

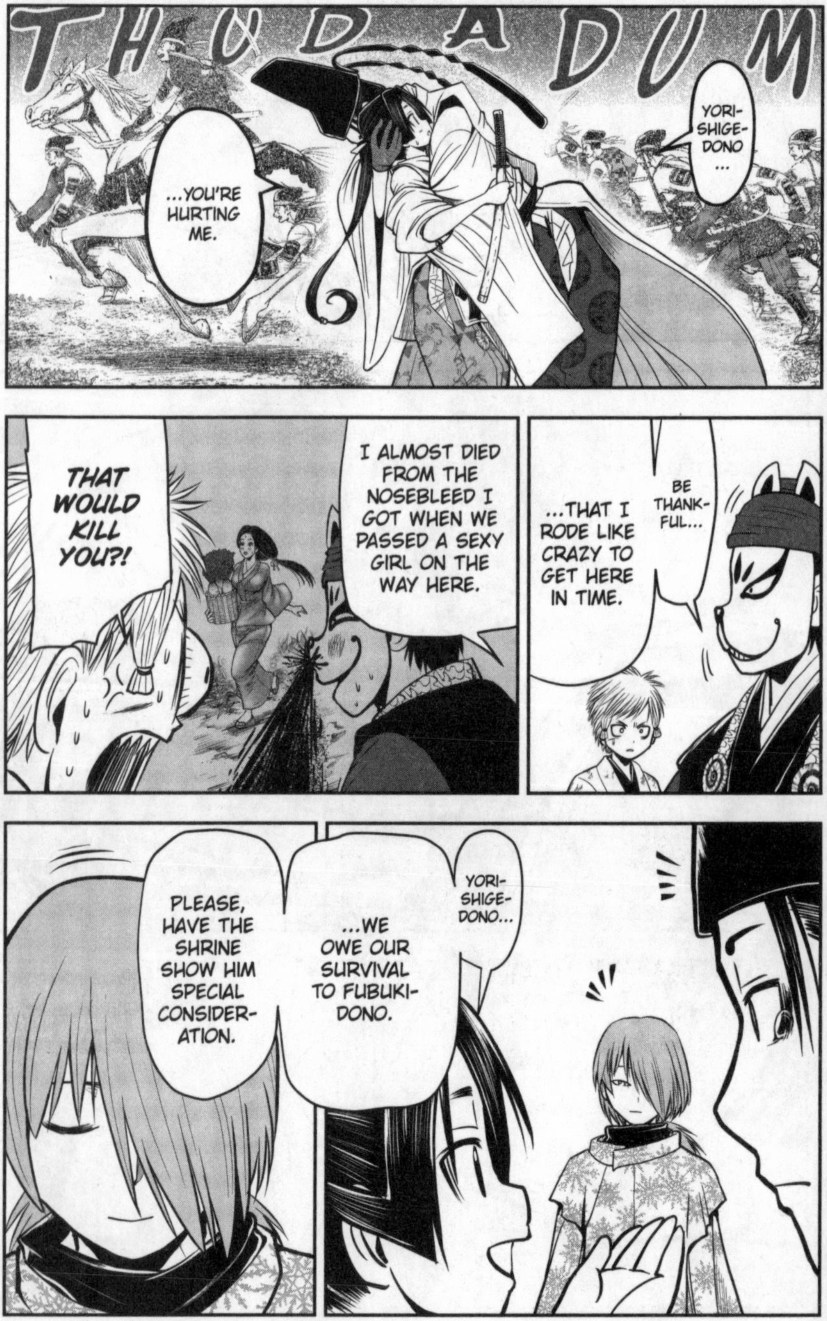
THUDADUM
YORI-SHIGE-DONO ...
...YOU'RE HURTING ME.
BE THANK-FUL...
...THAT I RODE LIKE CRAZY TO GET HERE IN TIME.
I ALMOST DIED FROM THE NOSEBLEED I GOT WHEN WE PASSED A SEXY GIRL ON THE WAY HERE.
THAT WOULD KILL YOU?!
YORI-SHIGE-DONO...
...WE OWE OUR SURVIVAL TO FUBUKI-DONO.
PLEASE, HAVE THE SHRINE SHOW HIM SPECIAL CONSIDER-ATION.

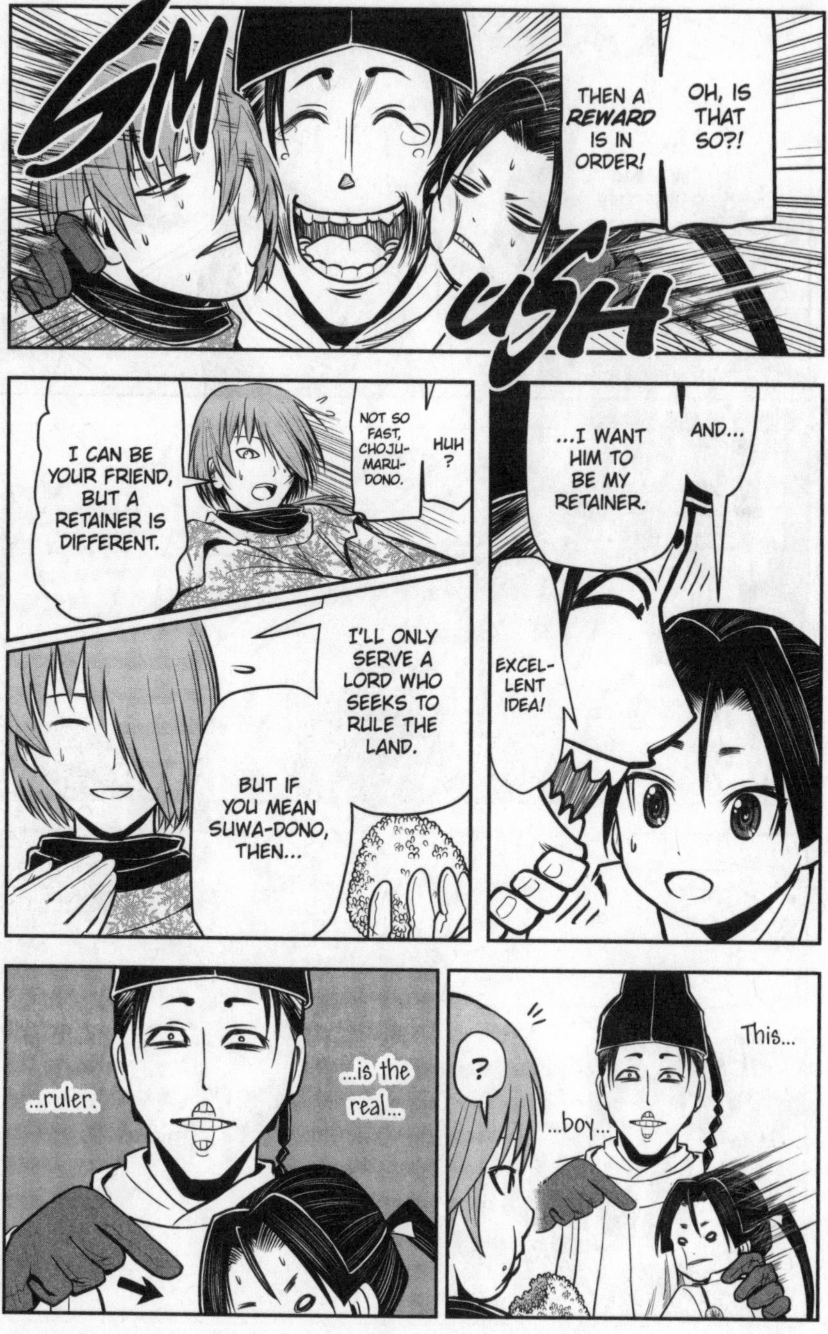
SMUSH
OH, IS THAT SO?!
THEN A REWARD IS IN ORDER!
AND...
...I WANT HIM TO BE MY RETAINER.
EXCEL-LENT IDEA!
HUH ?
NOT SO FAST, CHOJU-MARU-DONO.
I CAN BE YOUR FRIEND, BUT A RETAINER IS DIFFERENT.
I'LL ONLY SERVE A LORD WHO SEEKS TO RULE THE LAND.
BUT IF YOU MEAN SUWA-DONO, THEN...
This...
...boy...
?
...is the real...
...ruler.

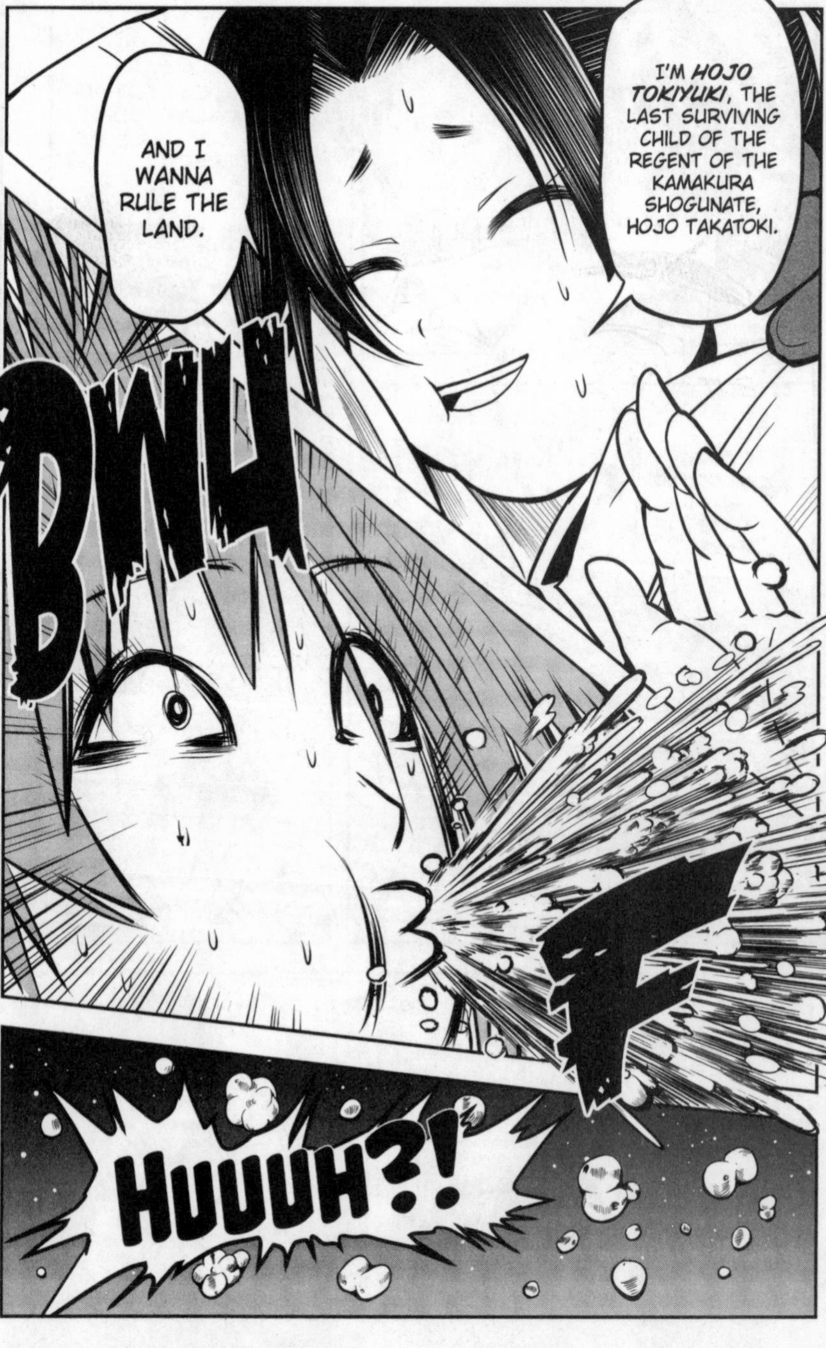
I'M *HOJO TOKIYUKI*, THE LAST SURVIVING CHILD OF THE REGENT OF THE KAMAKURA SHOGUNATE, HOJO TAKATOKI.
AND I WANNA RULE THE LAND.
HUUUH?!

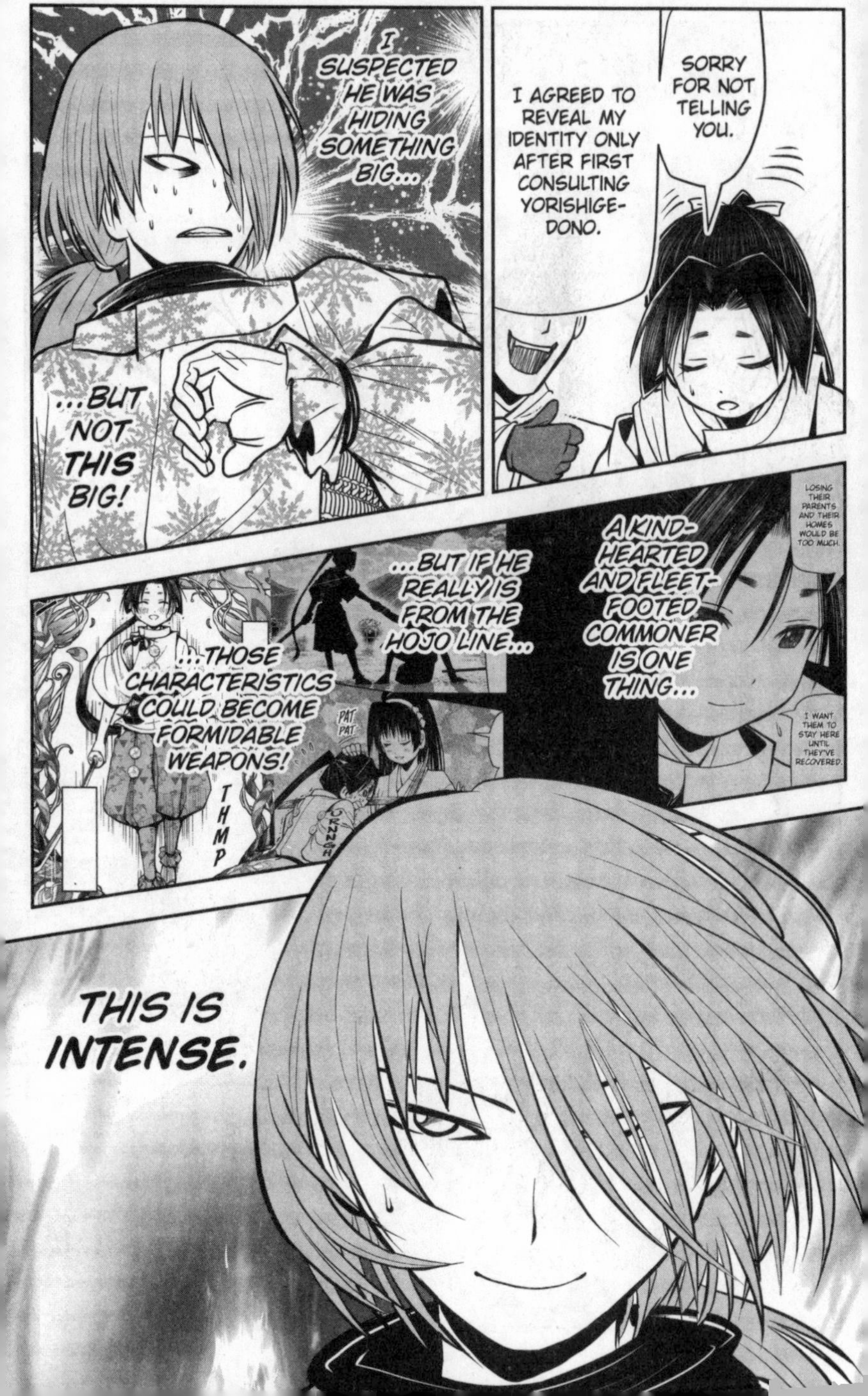
SORRY FOR NOT TELLING YOU.
I AGREED TO REVEAL MY IDENTITY ONLY AFTER FIRST CONSULTING YORISHIGE-DONO.
I SUSPECTED HE WAS HIDING SOMETHING BIG...
...BUT NOT THIS BIG!
LOSING THEIR PARENTS AND THEIR HOMES WOULD BE TOO MUCH.
A KIND-HEARTED AND FLEET-FOOTED COMMONER IS ONE THING...
I WANT THEM TO STAY HERE UNTIL THEY'VE RECOVERED.
...BUT IF HE REALLY IS FROM THE HOJO LINE...
PAT PAT
...THOSE CHARACTERISTICS COULD BECOME FORMIDABLE WEAPONS!
THMP
THIS IS INTENSE.

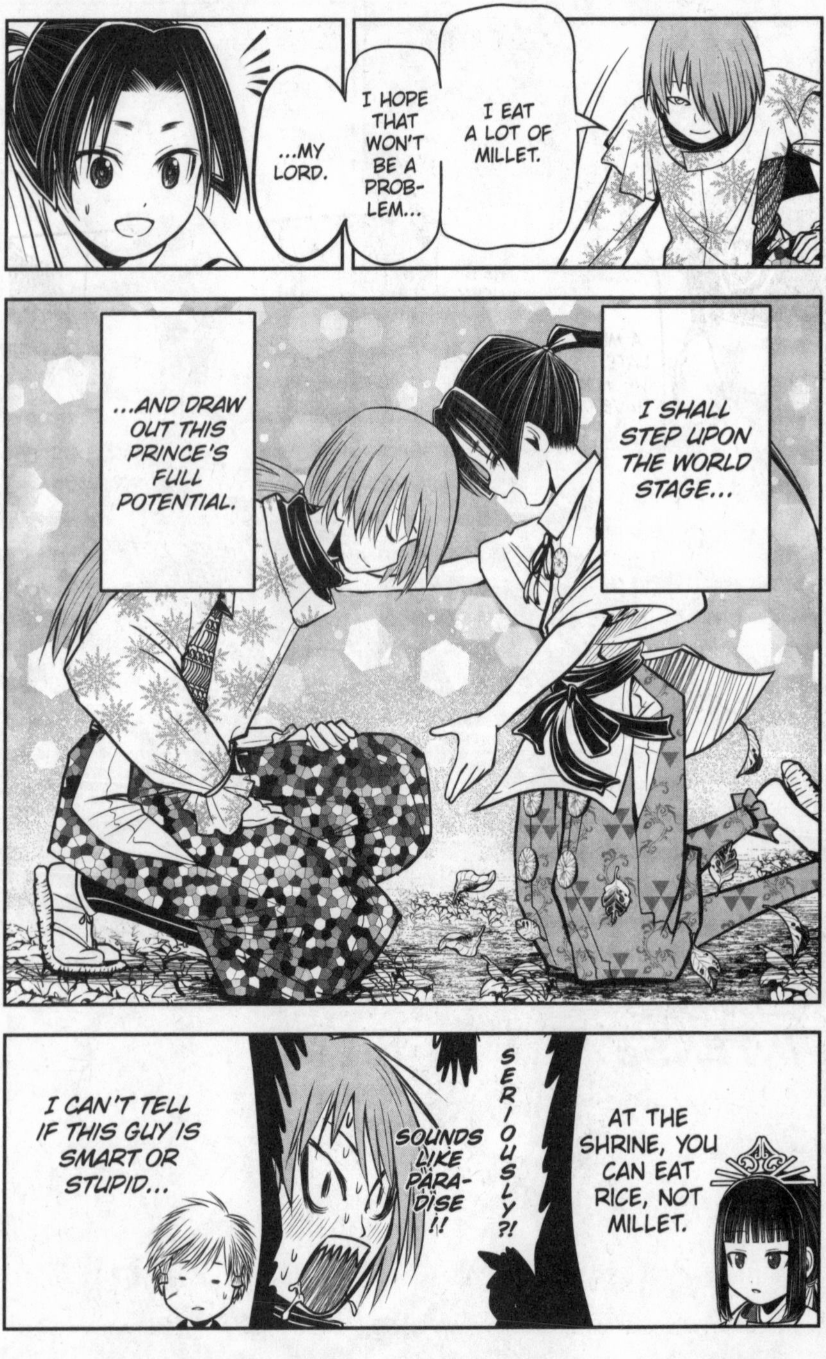
I EAT A LOT OF MILLET.
I HOPE THAT WON'T BE A PROB-LEM...
...MY LORD.
I SHALL STEP UPON THE WORLD STAGE...
...AND DRAW OUT THIS PRINCE'S FULL POTENTIAL.
AT THE SHRINE, YOU CAN EAT RICE, NOT MILLET.
SERIOUSLY?!
SOUNDS LIKE PARA-DISE!!
I CAN'T TELL IF THIS GUY IS SMART OR STUPID...

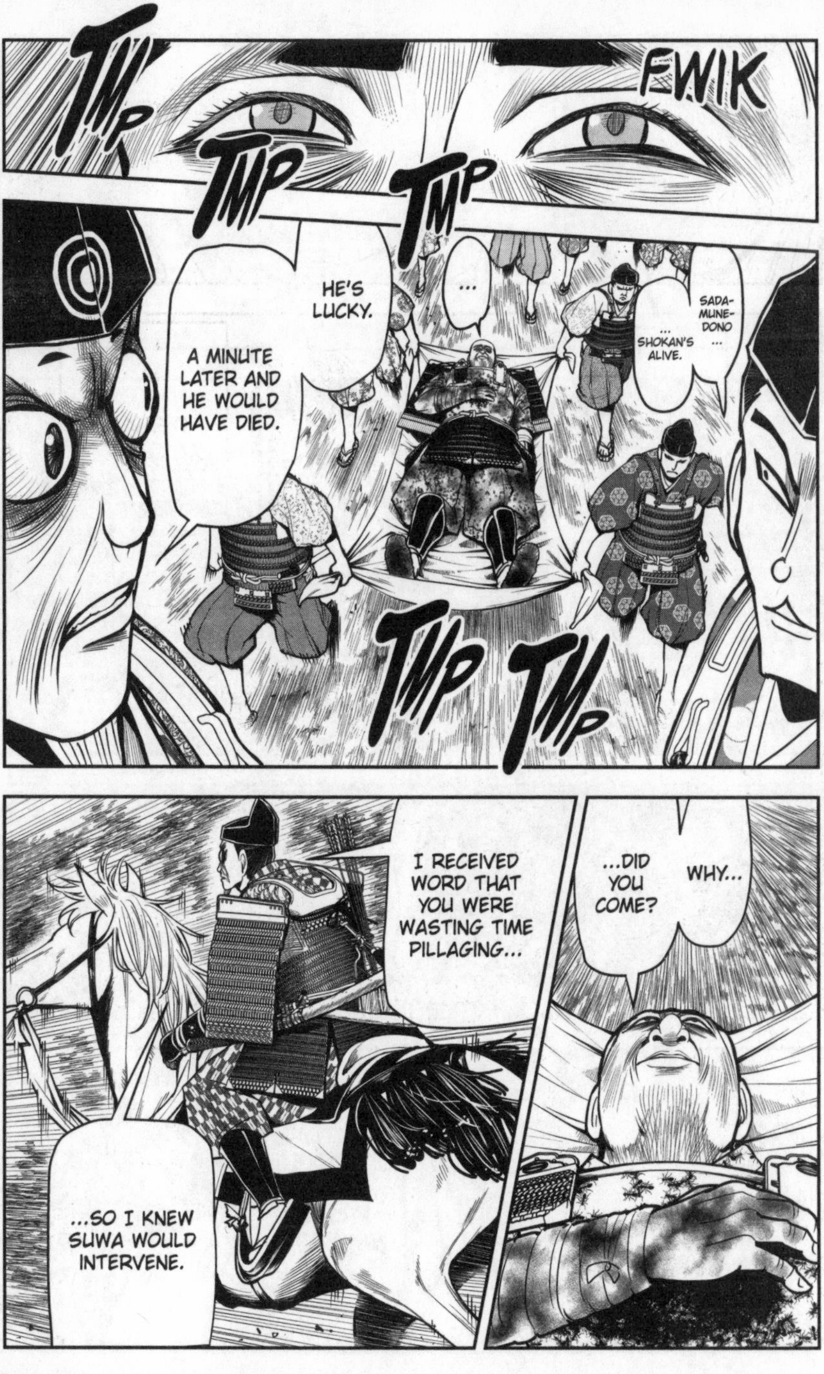
FWIK
TMP
TMP
TMP
SADA-MUNE-DONO ...
... SHOKAN'S ALIVE.
...
HE'S LUCKY.
A MINUTE LATER AND HE WOULD HAVE DIED.
TMP TMP
WHY...
...DID YOU COME?
I RECEIVED WORD THAT YOU WERE WASTING TIME PILLAGING...
...SO I KNEW SUWA WOULD INTERVENE.

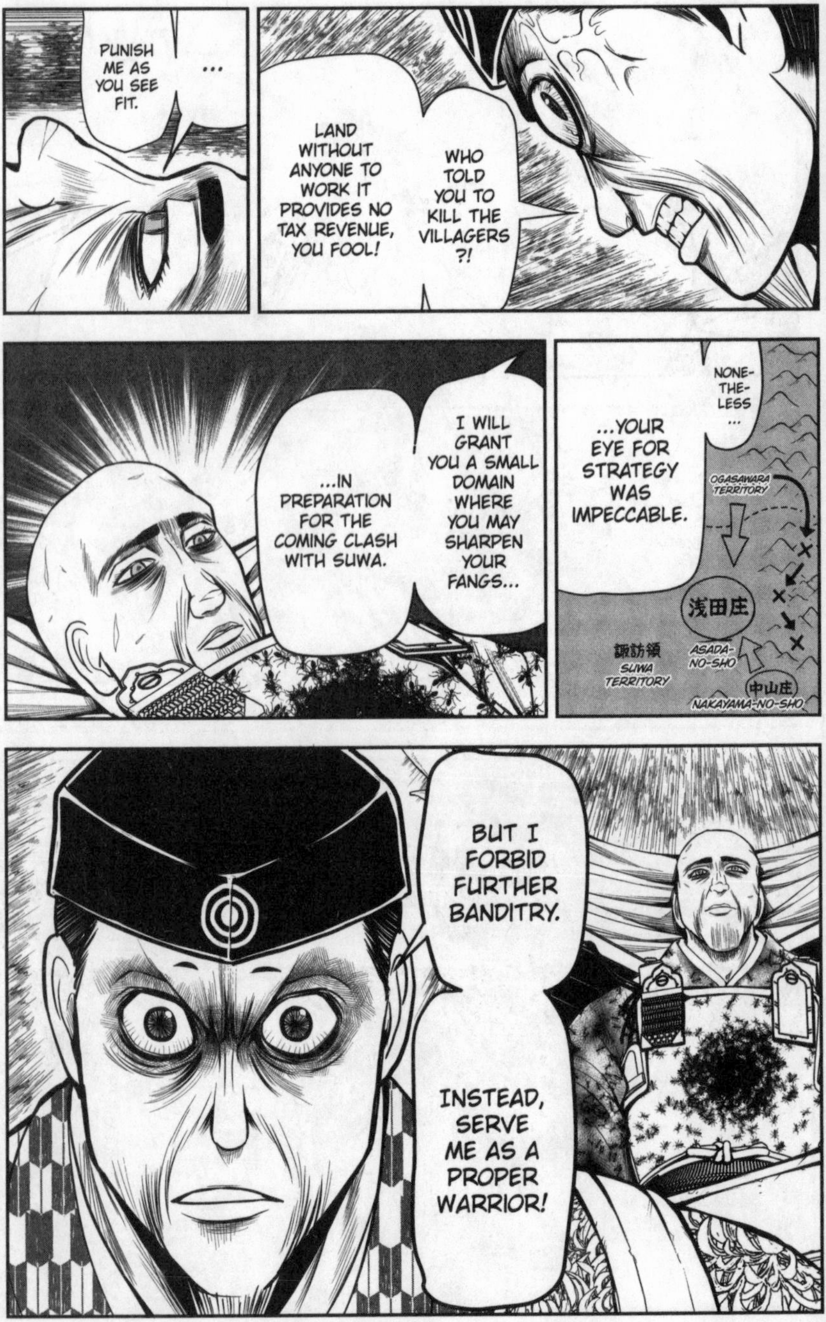
WHO TOLD YOU TO KILL THE VILLAGERS?!
LAND WITHOUT ANYONE TO WORK IT PROVIDES NO TAX REVENUE, YOU FOOL!
...
PUNISH ME AS YOU SEE FIT.
NONE-THE-LESS...
...YOUR EYE FOR STRATEGY WAS IMPECCABLE.
OGASAWARA TERRITORY
浅田庄
ASADA-NO-SHO
諏訪領
SUWA TERRITORY
中山庄
NAKAYAMA-NO-SHO
I WILL GRANT YOU A SMALL DOMAIN WHERE YOU MAY SHARPEN YOUR FANGS...
...IN PREPARATION FOR THE COMING CLASH WITH SUWA.
BUT I FORBID FURTHER BANDITRY.
INSTEAD, SERVE ME AS A PROPER WARRIOR!

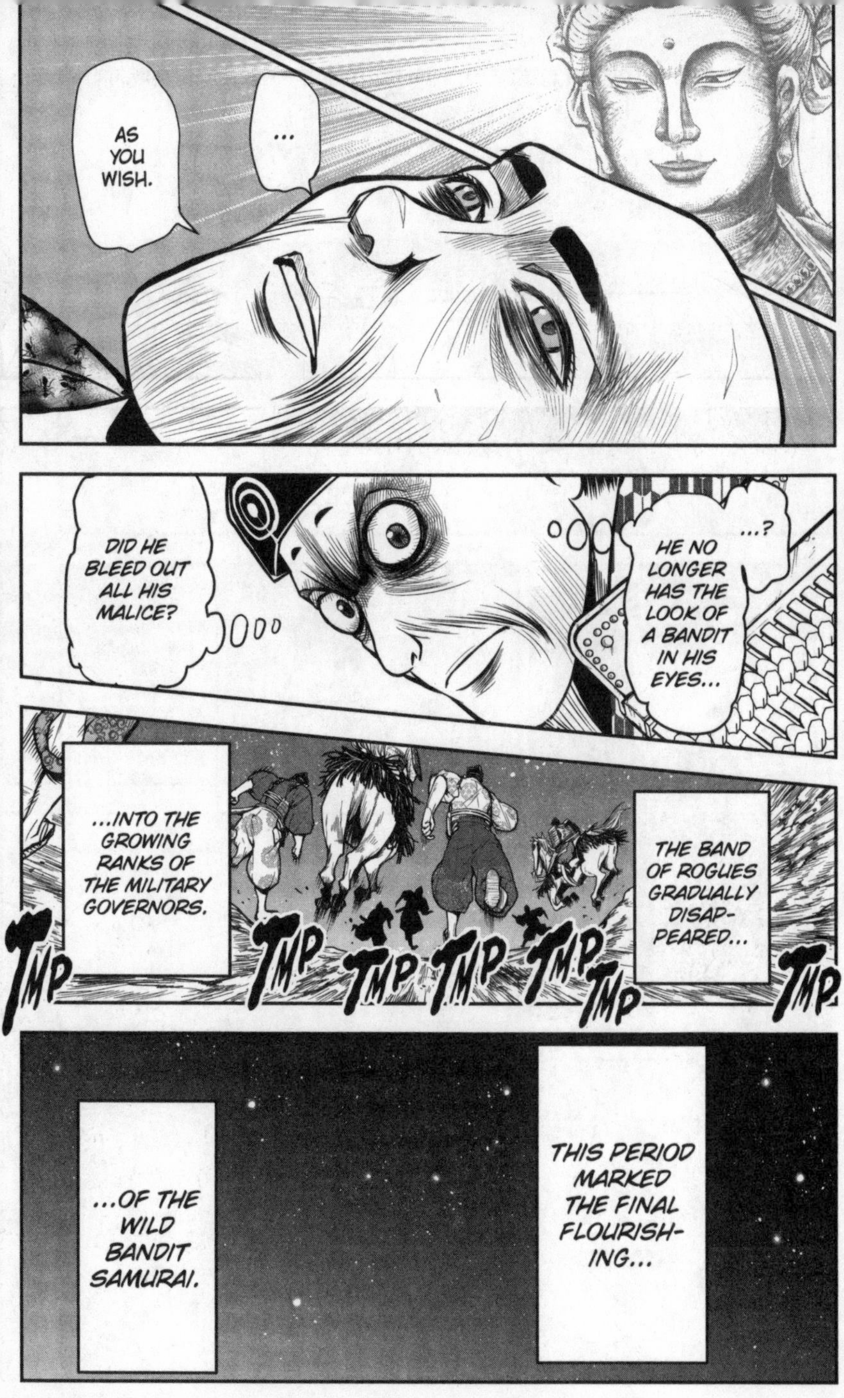
...
AS YOU WISH.
...? HE NO LONGER HAS THE LOOK OF A BANDIT IN HIS EYES...
DID HE BLEED OUT ALL HIS MALICE?
THE BAND OF ROGUES GRADUALLY DISAP-PEARED...
...INTO THE GROWING RANKS OF THE MILITARY GOVERNORS.
TMP TMP TMP TMP TMP TMP TMP
THIS PERIOD MARKED THE FINAL FLOURISH-ING...
...OF THE WILD BANDIT SAMURAI.

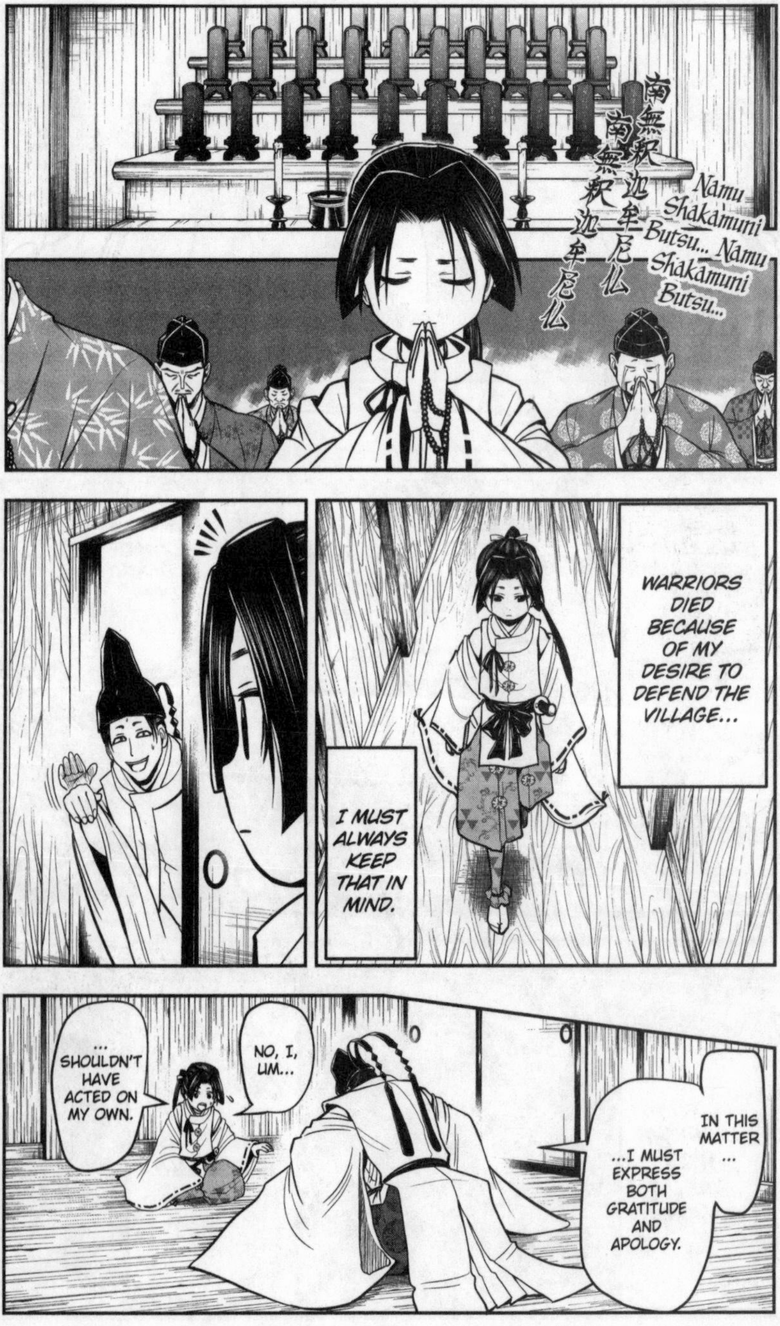
南無釈迦牟尼仏
南無釈迦牟尼仏
Namu Shakamuni Butsu... Namu Shakamuni Butsu...
WARRIORS DIED BECAUSE OF MY DESIRE TO DEFEND THE VILLAGE...
I MUST ALWAYS KEEP THAT IN MIND.
IN THIS MATTER...
...I MUST EXPRESS BOTH GRATITUDE AND APOLOGY.
NO, I, UM...
...SHOULDN'T HAVE ACTED ON MY OWN.

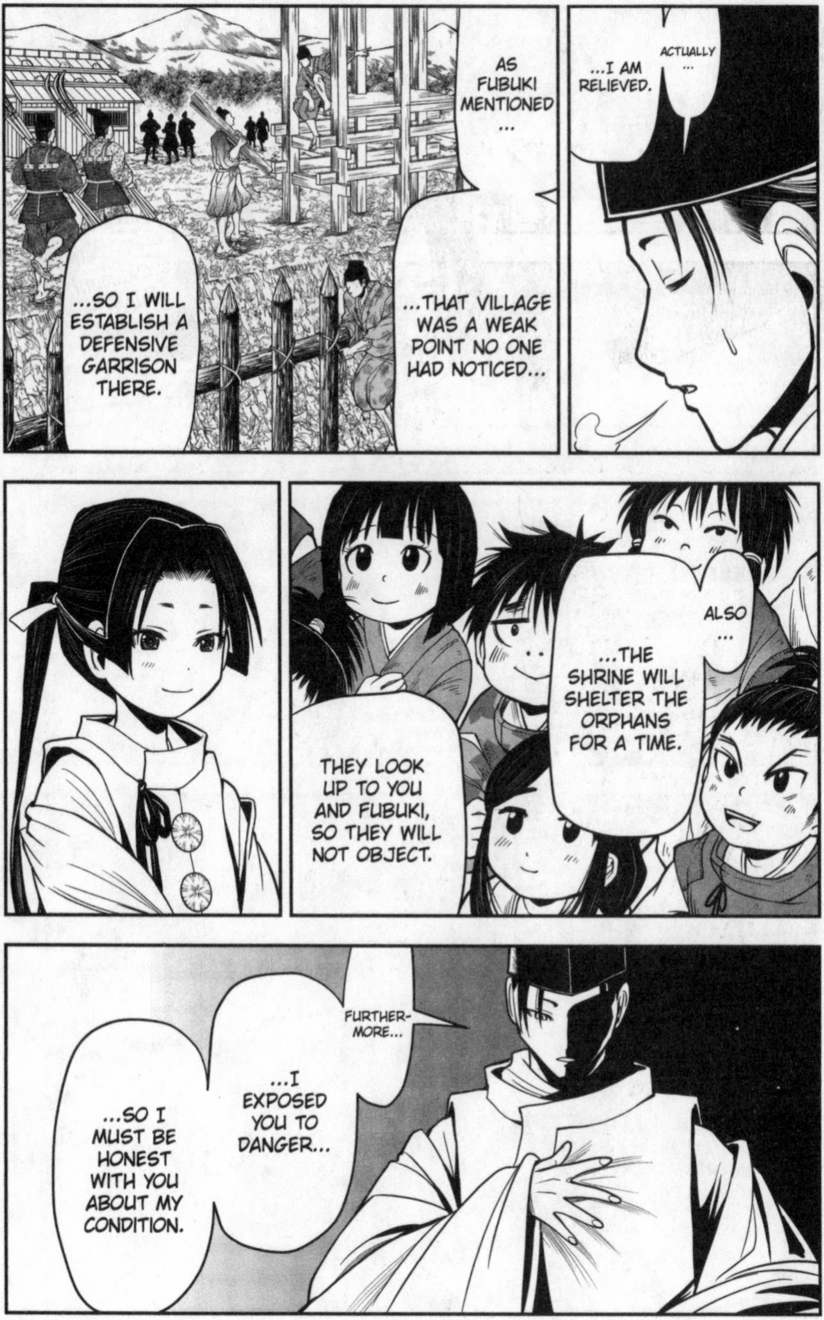
ACTUALLY...
...I AM RELIEVED.
AS FUBUKI MENTIONED...
...THAT VILLAGE WAS A WEAK POINT NO ONE HAD NOTICED...
...SO I WILL ESTABLISH A DEFENSIVE GARRISON THERE.
ALSO...
...THE SHRINE WILL SHELTER THE ORPHANS FOR A TIME.
THEY LOOK UP TO YOU AND FUBUKI, SO THEY WILL NOT OBJECT.
FURTHER-MORE...
...I EXPOSED YOU TO DANGER...
...SO I MUST BE HONEST WITH YOU ABOUT MY CONDITION.

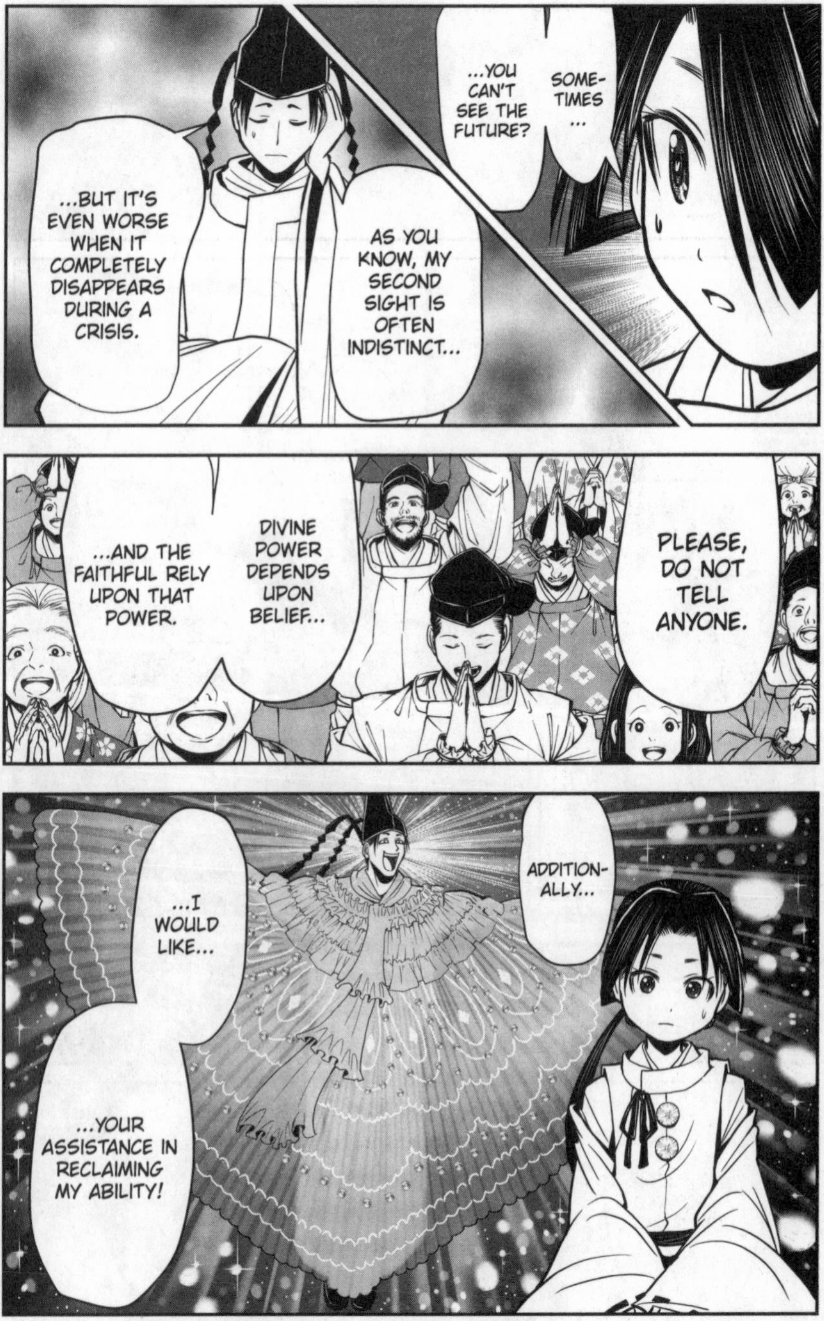
SOME-TIMES...
...YOU CAN'T SEE THE FUTURE?
AS YOU KNOW, MY SECOND SIGHT IS OFTEN INDISTINCT...
...BUT IT'S EVEN WORSE WHEN IT COMPLETELY DISAPPEARS DURING A CRISIS.
PLEASE, DO NOT TELL ANYONE.
DIVINE POWER DEPENDS UPON BELIEF...
...AND THE FAITHFUL RELY UPON THAT POWER.
ADDITION-ALLY...
...I WOULD LIKE...
...YOUR ASSISTANCE IN RECLAIMING MY ABILITY!

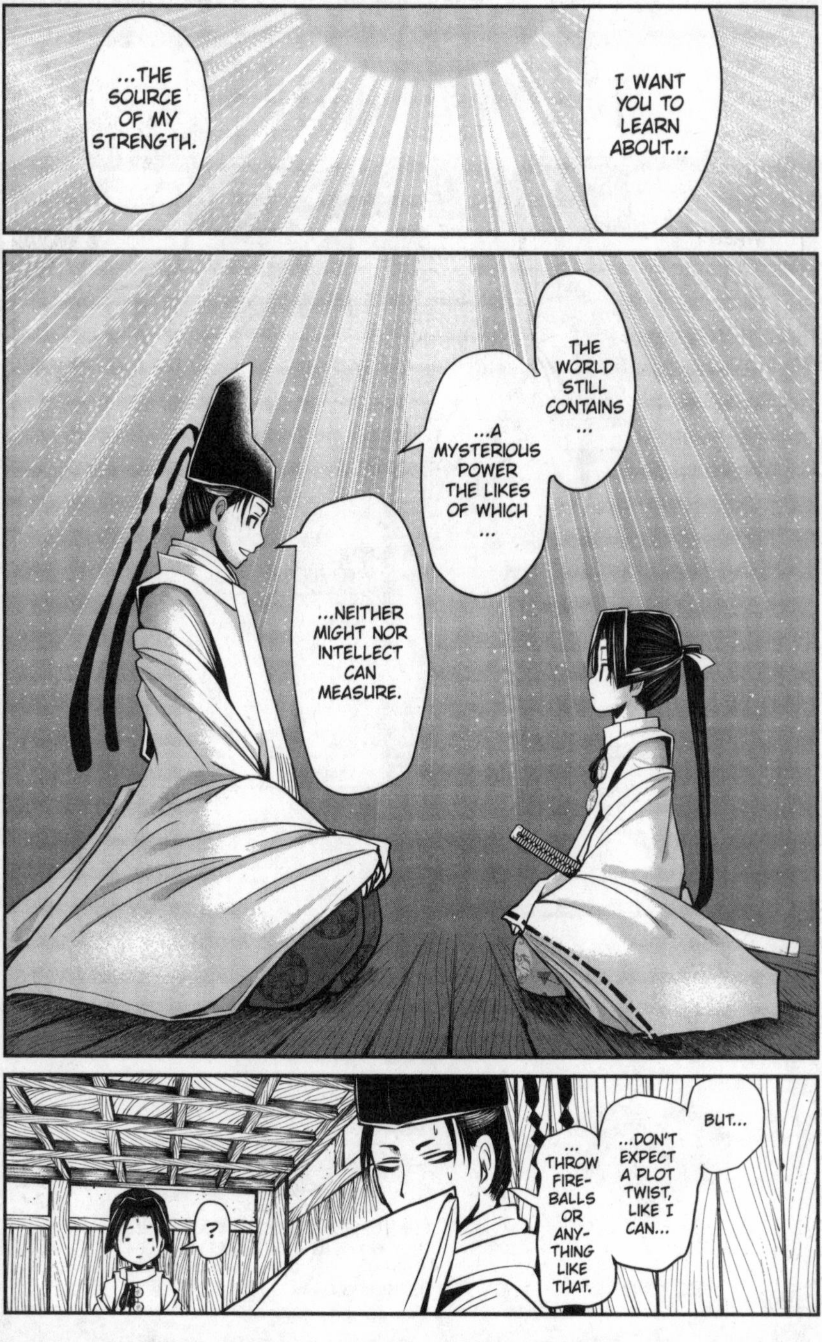
I WANT YOU TO LEARN ABOUT...
...THE SOURCE OF MY STRENGTH.
THE WORLD STILL CONTAINS...
...A MYSTERIOUS POWER THE LIKES OF WHICH...
...NEITHER MIGHT NOR INTELLECT CAN MEASURE.
BUT...
...DON'T EXPECT A PLOT TWIST, LIKE I CAN...
...THROW FIRE-BALLS OR ANY-THING LIKE THAT.
?

ICHIKAWA SUKEFUSA

★ ★ ★ **SR**

ABILITIES		NANBOKU-CHO COMPATIBILITY	
MARTIAL ARTS	79	SAVAGERY	80
INTELLIGENCE	70	LOYALTY	49
POLITICS	63	CHAOS	72
LEADERSHIP	71	INGENUITY	44
CHARM	59	RUNNING AND HIDING	49

CREST

CIRCLE WITH EARS

SKILL HELLISH EARS: 10 PERCENT INCREASE TO LEADERSHIP

SKILL SWORD FIGHTING: 20 PERCENT INCREASE TO SWORD

APTITUDE KNOWLEDGE & MEMORY: 10 PERCENT INCREASE

OTHER THINGS HIS EARS CAN DO

HE NEVER MISSES A RUMOR, SO HE HAS A COMPLETE GRASP OF THE MILITARY STRENGTH, PERSONAL AFFAIRS, AND ROMANTIC GOINGS-ON IN HIS TERRITORY AND IN OGASAWARA'S HOUSEHOLD.

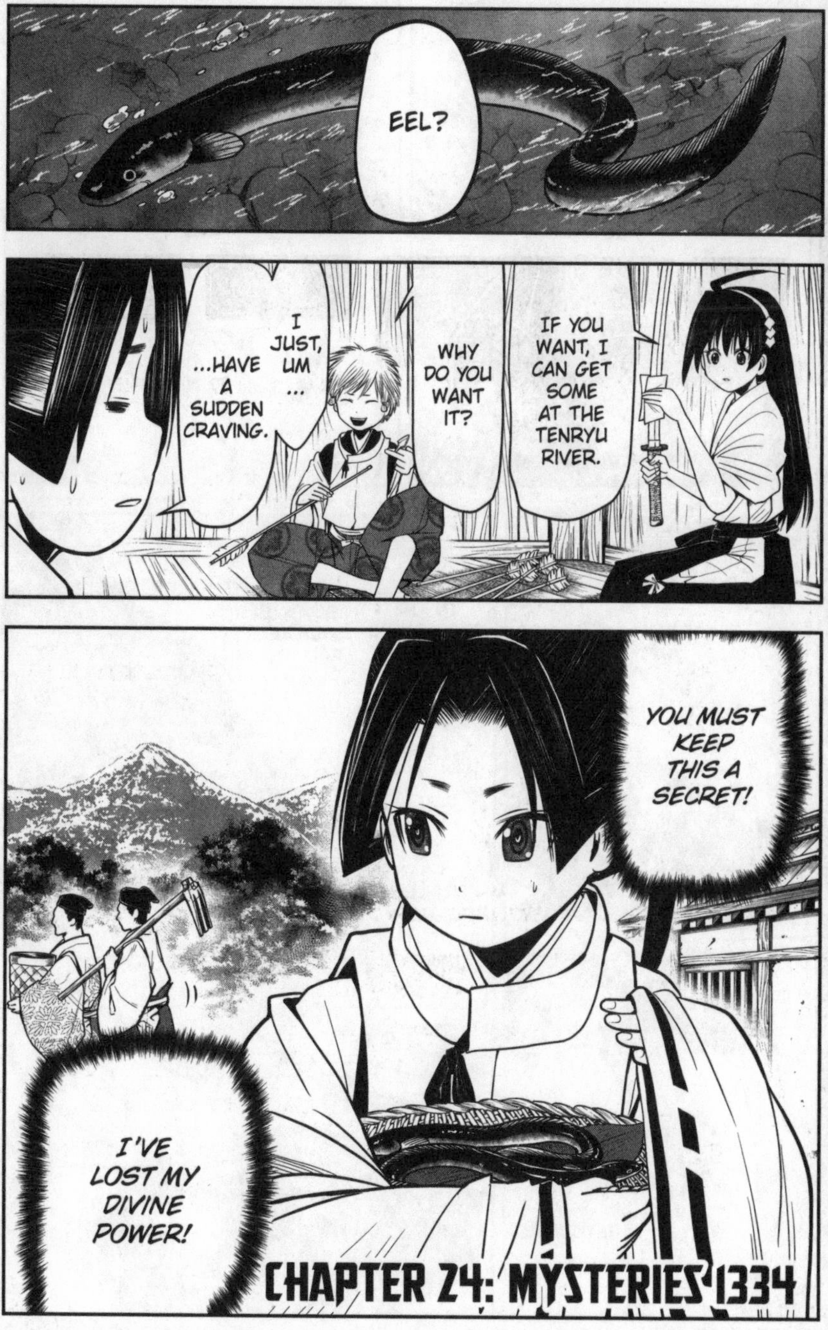
EEL?
IF YOU WANT, I CAN GET SOME AT THE TENRYU RIVER.
WHY DO YOU WANT IT?
I JUST, UM ...
...HAVE A SUDDEN CRAVING.
YOU MUST KEEP THIS A SECRET!
I'VE LOST MY DIVINE POWER!
CHAPTER 24: MYSTERIES 1334

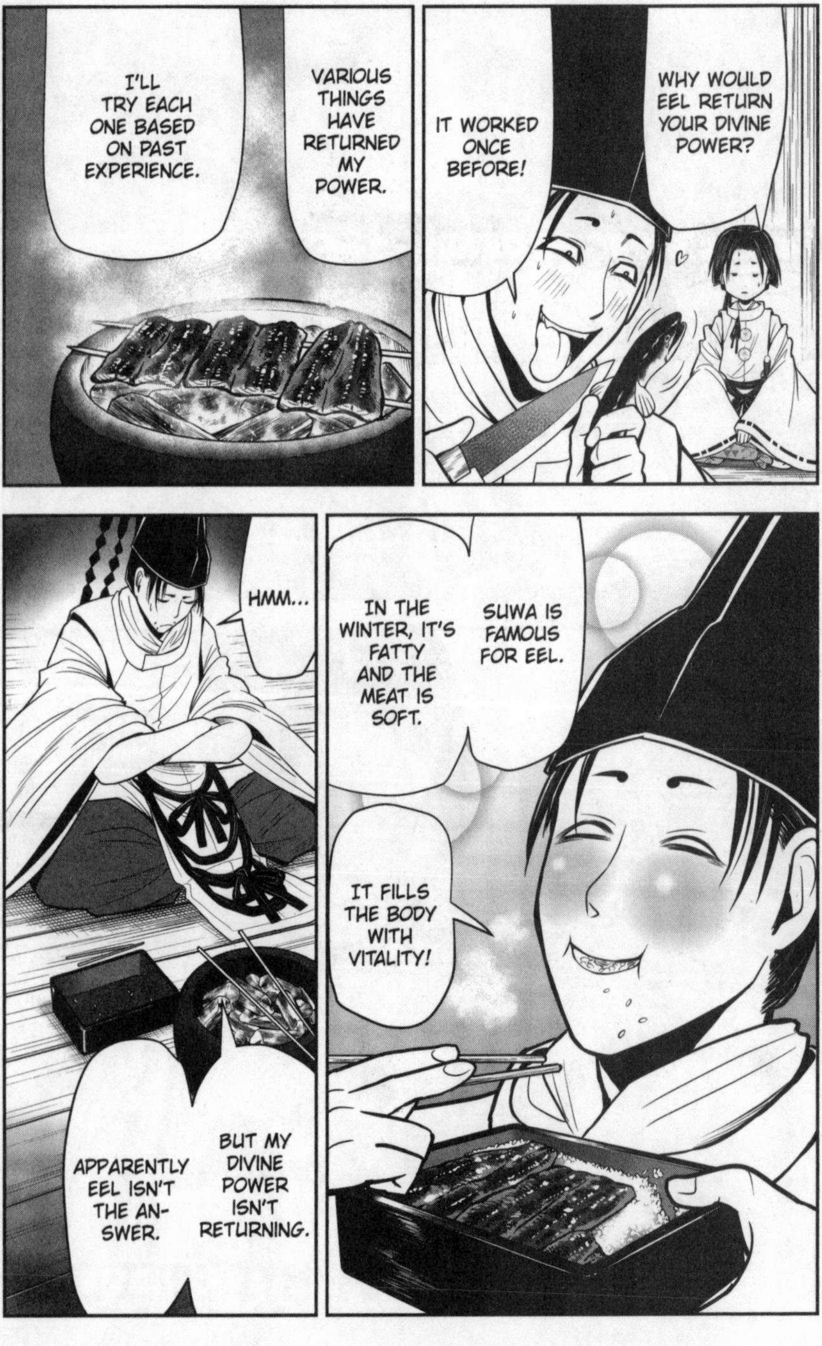
WHY WOULD EEL RETURN YOUR DIVINE POWER?
IT WORKED ONCE BEFORE!
VARIOUS THINGS HAVE RETURNED MY POWER.
I'LL TRY EACH ONE BASED ON PAST EXPERIENCE.
SUWA IS FAMOUS FOR EEL.
IN THE WINTER, IT'S FATTY AND THE MEAT IS SOFT.
IT FILLS THE BODY WITH VITALITY!
HMM...
BUT MY DIVINE POWER ISN'T RETURNING.
APPARENTLY EEL ISN'T THE AN-SWER.

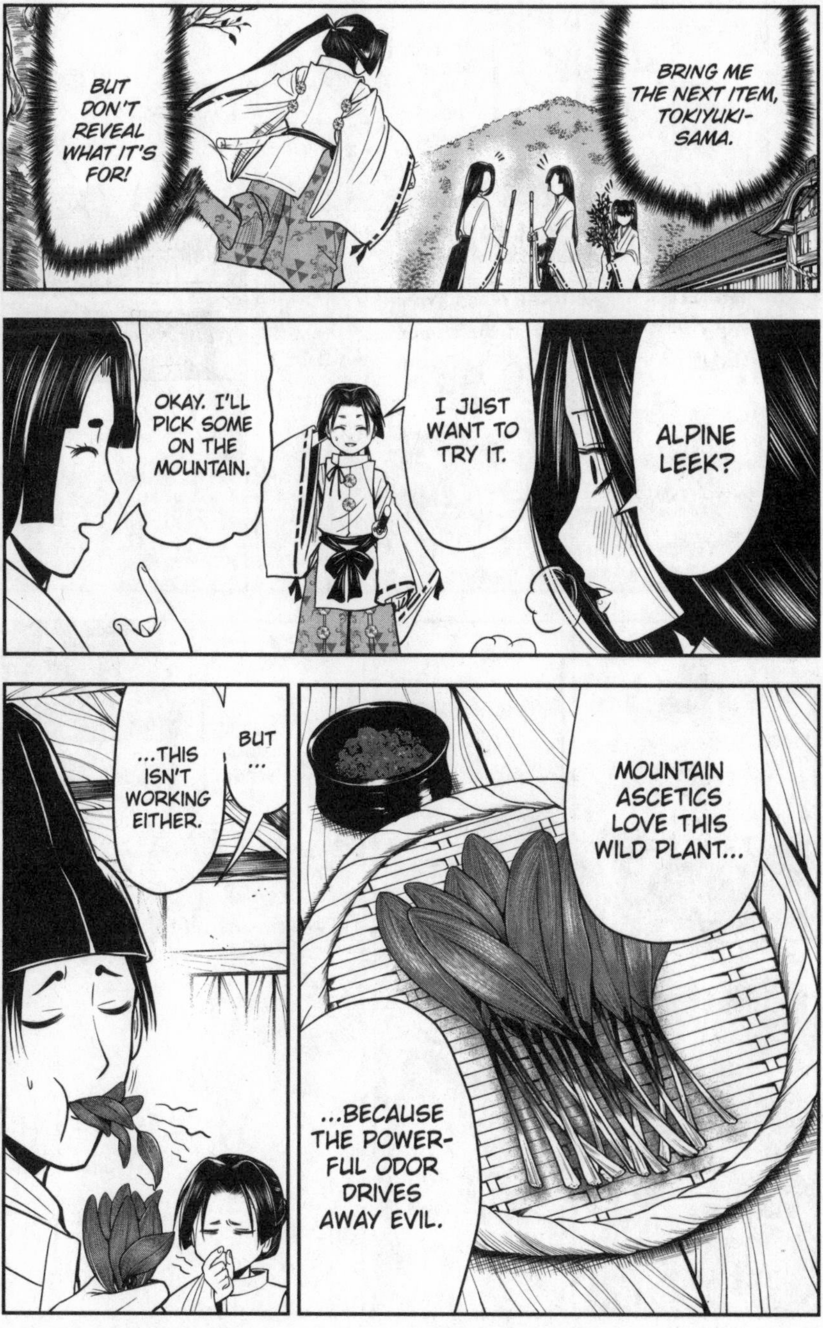
BRING ME THE NEXT ITEM, TOKIYUKI-SAMA.
BUT DON'T REVEAL WHAT IT'S FOR!
ALPINE LEEK?
I JUST WANT TO TRY IT.
OKAY. I'LL PICK SOME ON THE MOUNTAIN.
MOUNTAIN ASCETICS LOVE THIS WILD PLANT...
...BECAUSE THE POWER-FUL ODOR DRIVES AWAY EVIL.
BUT...
...THIS ISN'T WORKING EITHER.

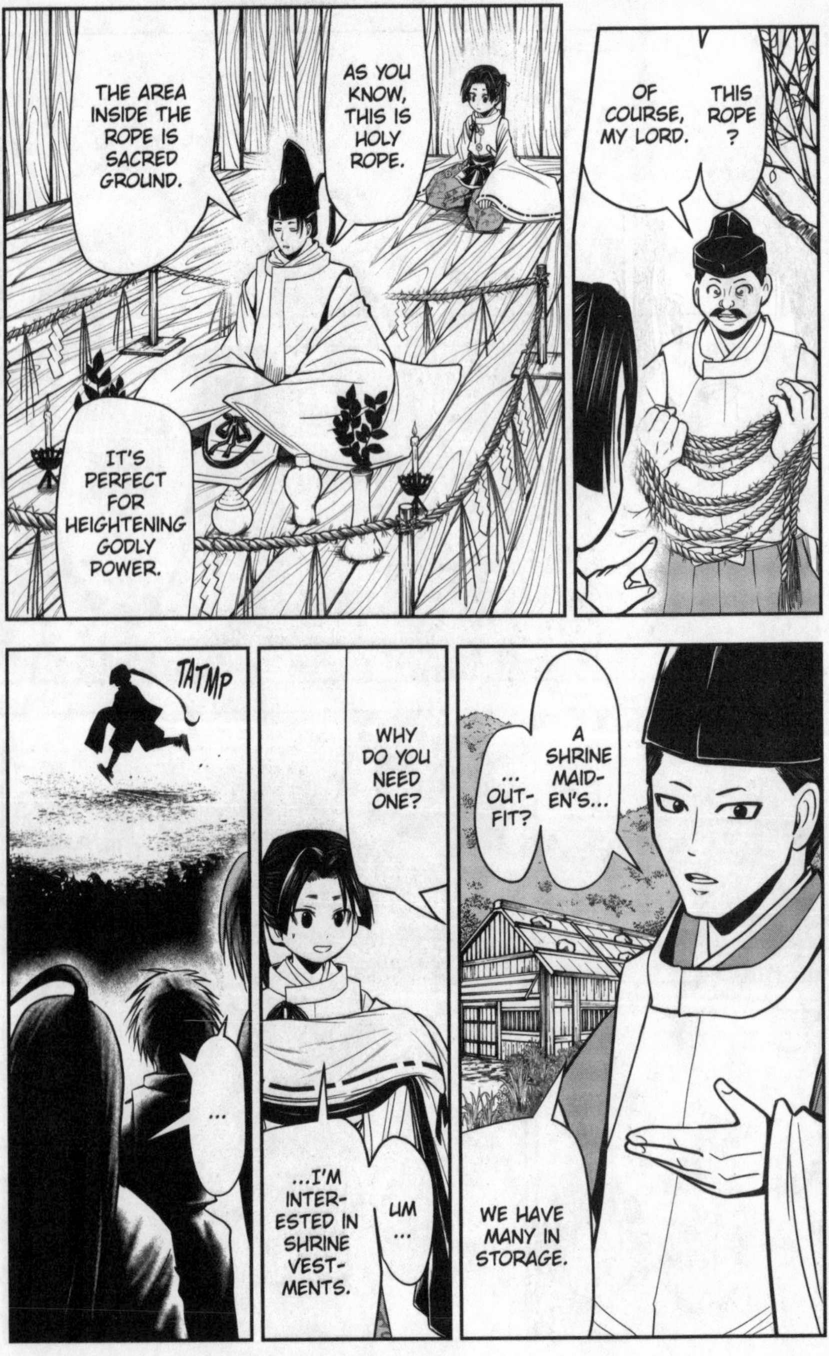
THIS ROPE?
OF COURSE, MY LORD.
AS YOU KNOW, THIS IS HOLY ROPE.
THE AREA INSIDE THE ROPE IS SACRED GROUND.
IT'S PERFECT FOR HEIGHTENING GODLY POWER.
A SHRINE MAIDEN'S...
...OUTFIT?
WE HAVE MANY IN STORAGE.
WHY DO YOU NEED ONE?
UM...
...I'M INTERESTED IN SHRINE VESTMENTS.
TATMP
...

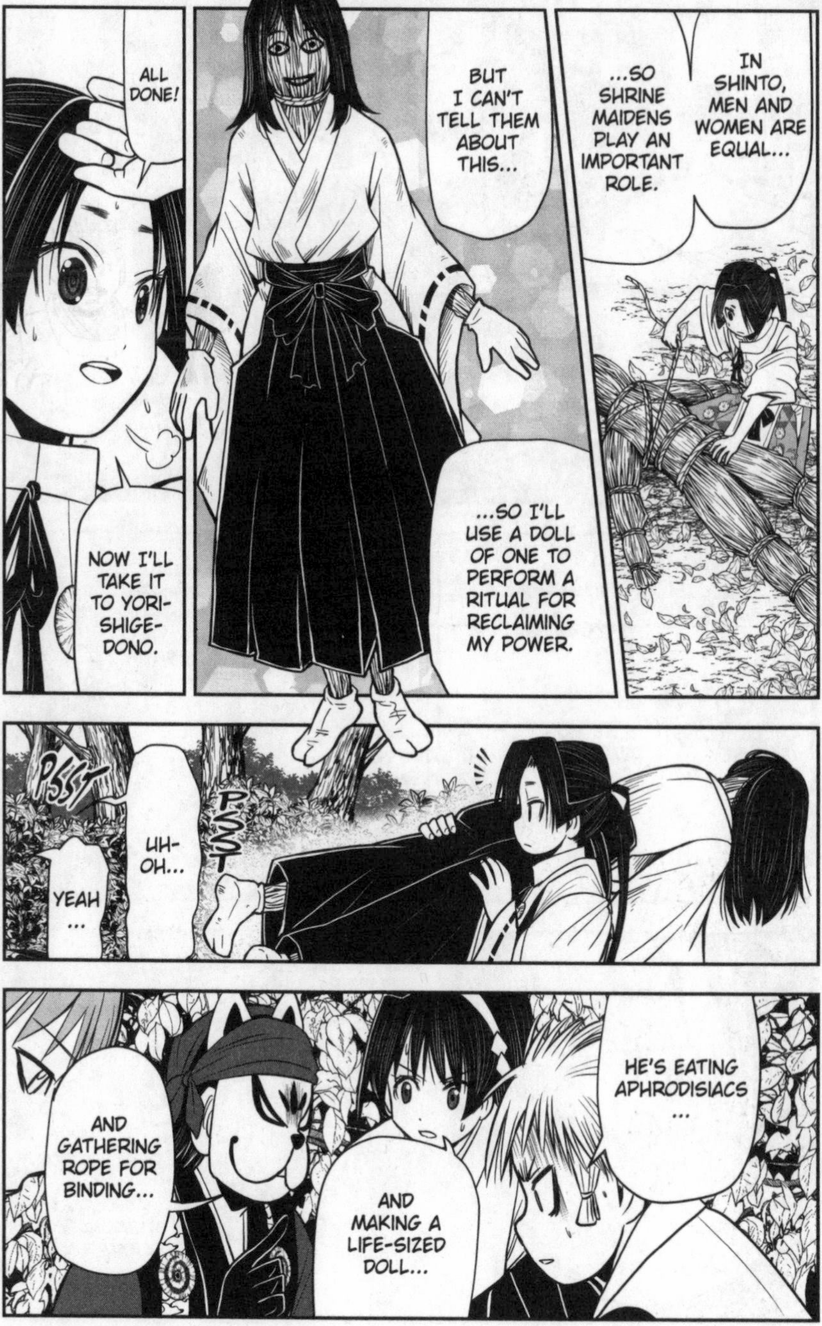
IN SHINTO, MEN AND WOMEN ARE EQUAL...
...SO SHRINE MAIDENS PLAY AN IMPORTANT ROLE.
BUT I CAN'T TELL THEM ABOUT THIS...
...SO I'LL USE A DOLL OF ONE TO PERFORM A RITUAL FOR RECLAIMING MY POWER.
ALL DONE!
NOW I'LL TAKE IT TO YORI-SHIGE-DONO.
PSST
UH-OH...
PSST
YEAH ...
HE'S EATING APHRODISIACS ...
AND MAKING A LIFE-SIZED DOLL...
AND GATHERING ROPE FOR BINDING...

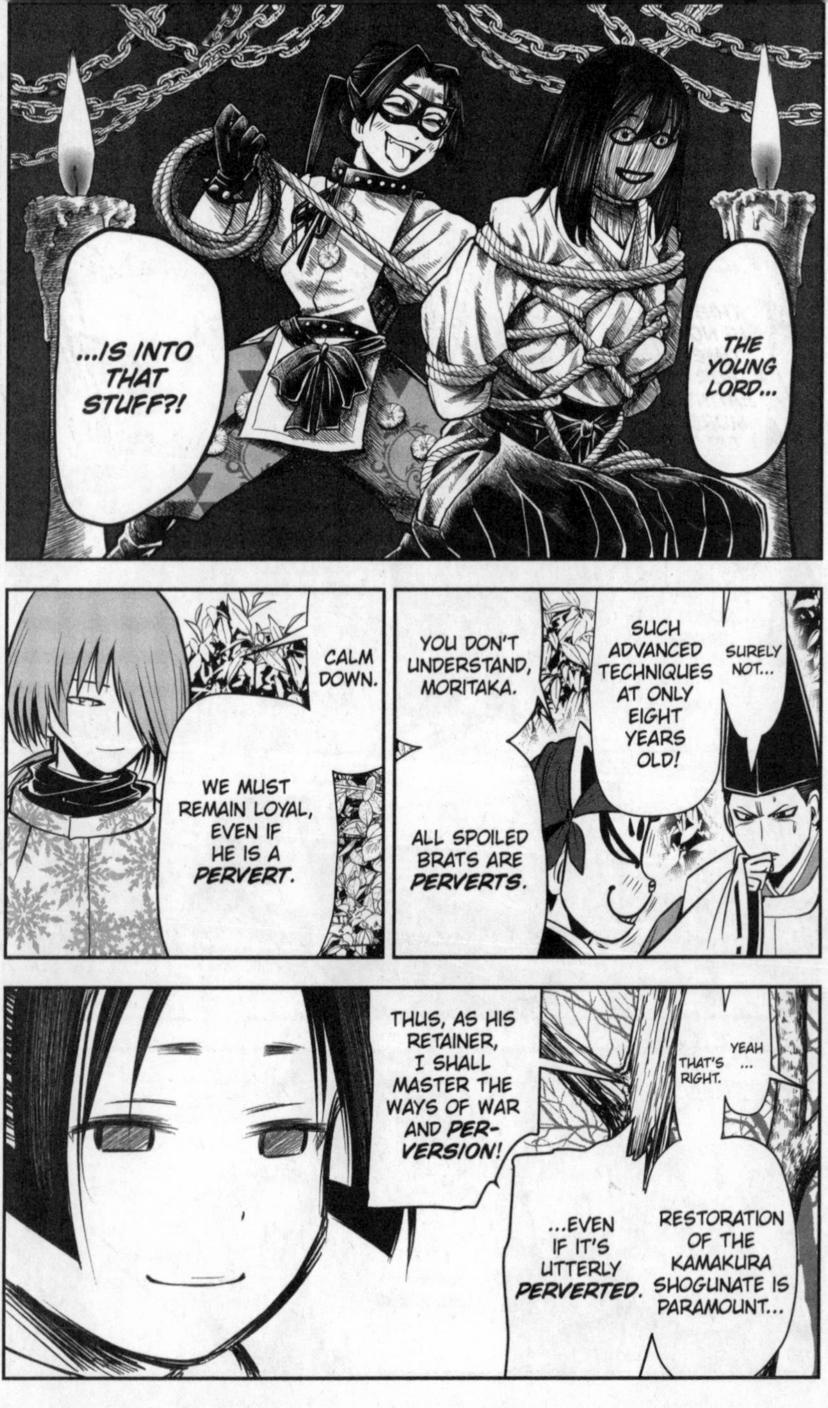
THE YOUNG LORD...
...IS INTO THAT STUFF?!
SURELY NOT...
SUCH ADVANCED TECHNIQUES AT ONLY EIGHT YEARS OLD!
YOU DON'T UNDERSTAND, MORITAKA.
ALL SPOILED BRATS ARE *PERVERTS*.
CALM DOWN.
WE MUST REMAIN LOYAL, EVEN IF HE IS A *PERVERT*.
YEAH ...
THAT'S RIGHT.
THUS, AS HIS RETAINER, I SHALL MASTER THE WAYS OF WAR AND *PER-VERSION*!
RESTORATION OF THE KAMAKURA SHOGUNATE IS PARAMOUNT...
...EVEN IF IT'S UTTERLY *PERVERTED*.

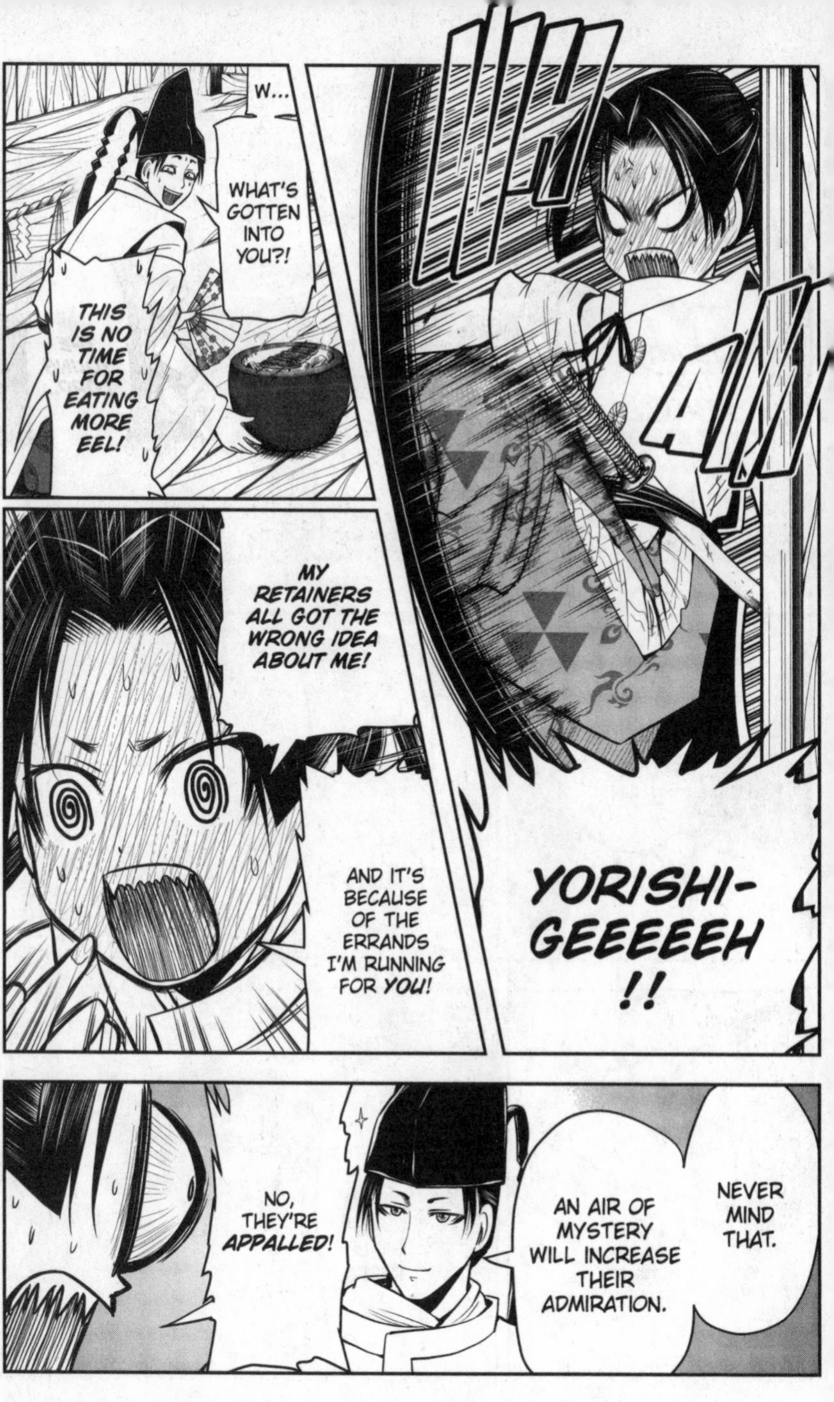
YORISHI-GEEEEEH!!
W...
WHAT'S GOTTEN INTO YOU?!
THIS IS NO TIME FOR EATING MORE EEL!
MY RETAINERS ALL GOT THE WRONG IDEA ABOUT ME!
AND IT'S BECAUSE OF THE ERRANDS I'M RUNNING FOR YOU!
NEVER MIND THAT.
AN AIR OF MYSTERY WILL INCREASE THEIR ADMIRATION.
NO, THEY'RE APPALLED!

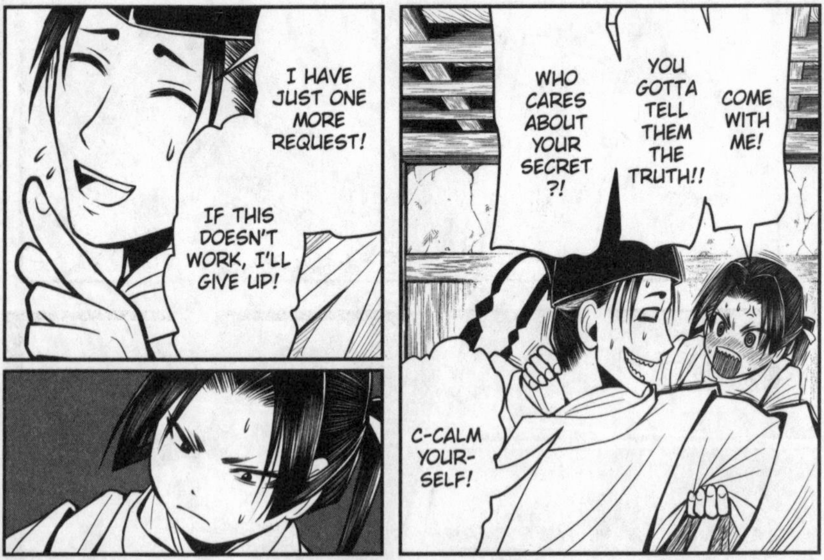
COME WITH ME!
YOU GOTTA TELL THEM THE TRUTH!!
WHO CARES ABOUT YOUR SECRET?!
C-CALM YOURSELF!
I HAVE JUST ONE MORE REQUEST!
IF THIS DOESN'T WORK, I'LL GIVE UP!

*AN ANCIENT UNIT OF MEASUREMENT, ABOUT 2.4 MILES

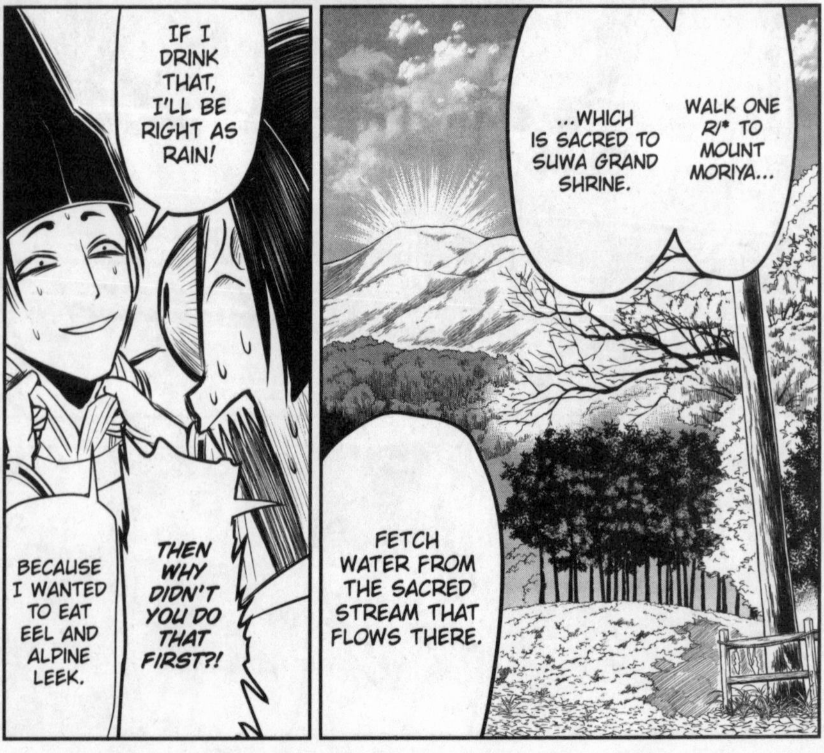
WALK ONE *RI** TO MOUNT MORIYA...
...WHICH IS SACRED TO SUWA GRAND SHRINE.
FETCH WATER FROM THE SACRED STREAM THAT FLOWS THERE.
IF I DRINK THAT, I'LL BE RIGHT AS RAIN!
THEN WHY DIDN'T YOU DO THAT FIRST?!
BECAUSE I WANTED TO EAT EEL AND ALPINE LEEK.

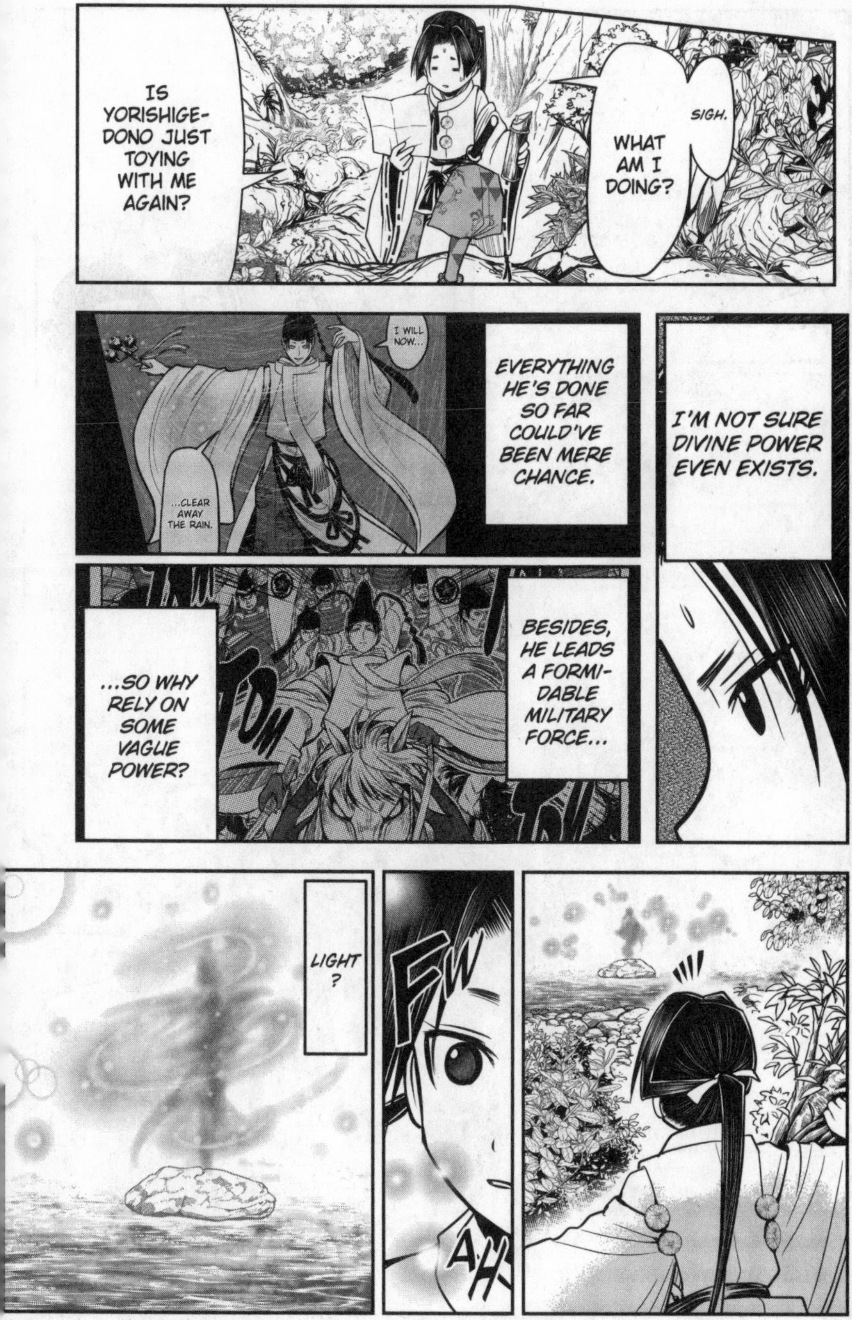
SIGH.
WHAT AM I DOING?
IS YORISHIGE-DONO JUST TOYING WITH ME AGAIN?
I'M NOT SURE DIVINE POWER EVEN EXISTS.
EVERYTHING HE'S DONE SO FAR COULD'VE BEEN MERE CHANCE.
I WILL NOW...
...CLEAR AWAY THE RAIN.
BESIDES, HE LEADS A FORMIDABLE MILITARY FORCE...
...SO WHY RELY ON SOME VAGUE POWER?
FW
AH
LIGHT?

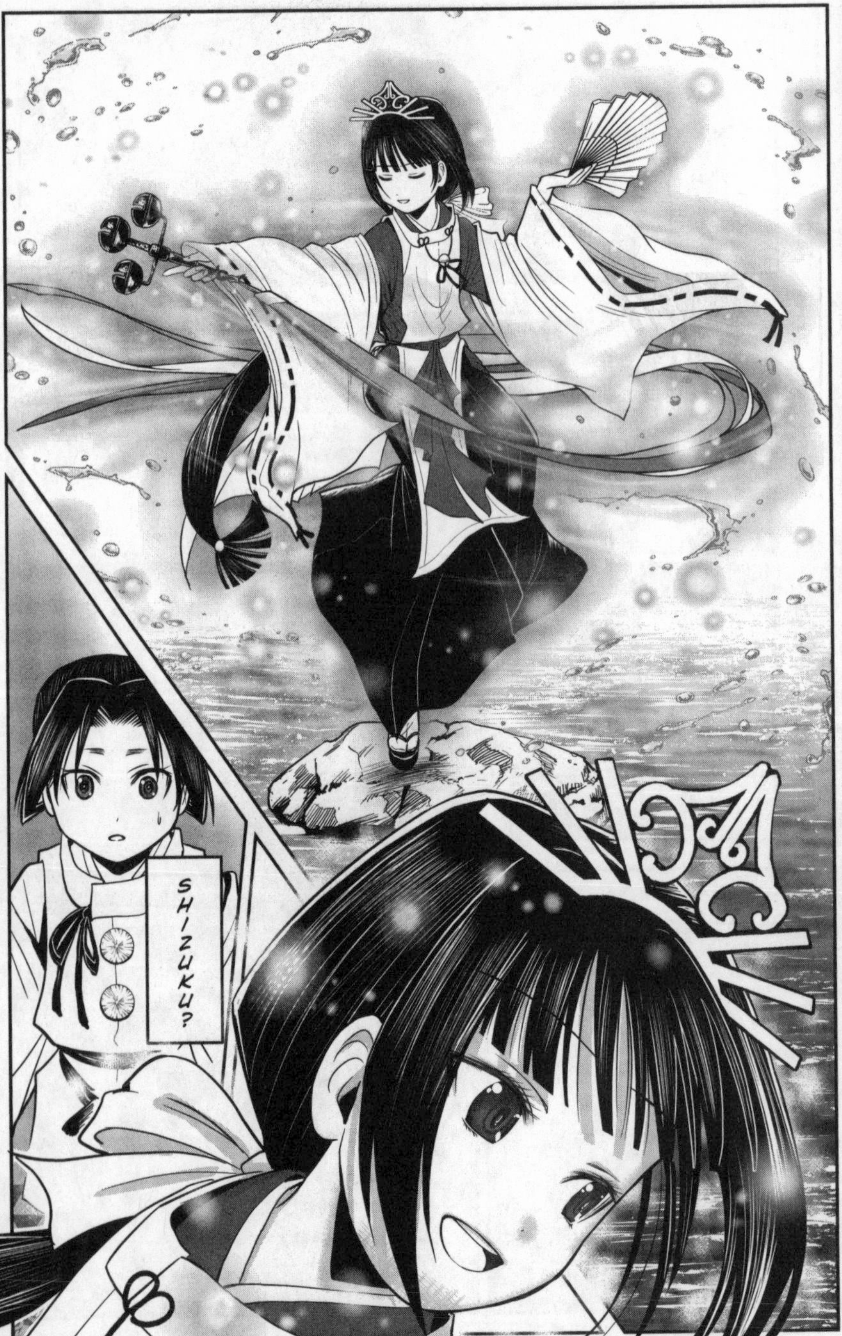
SHIZUKU?

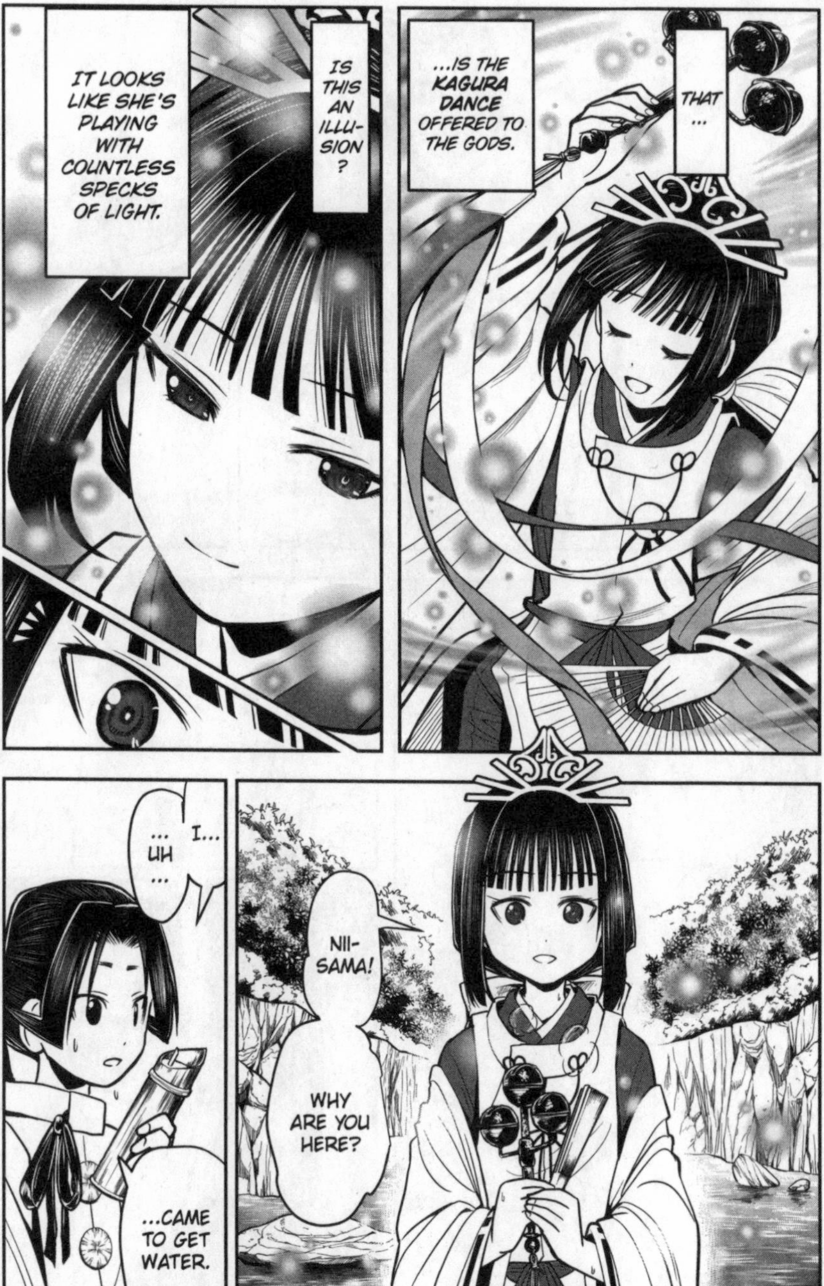
THAT...
...IS THE KAGURA DANCE OFFERED TO THE GODS.
IS THIS AN ILLUSION?
IT LOOKS LIKE SHE'S PLAYING WITH COUNTLESS SPECKS OF LIGHT.
NII-SAMA!
WHY ARE YOU HERE?
I...
...UH...
...CAME TO GET WATER.

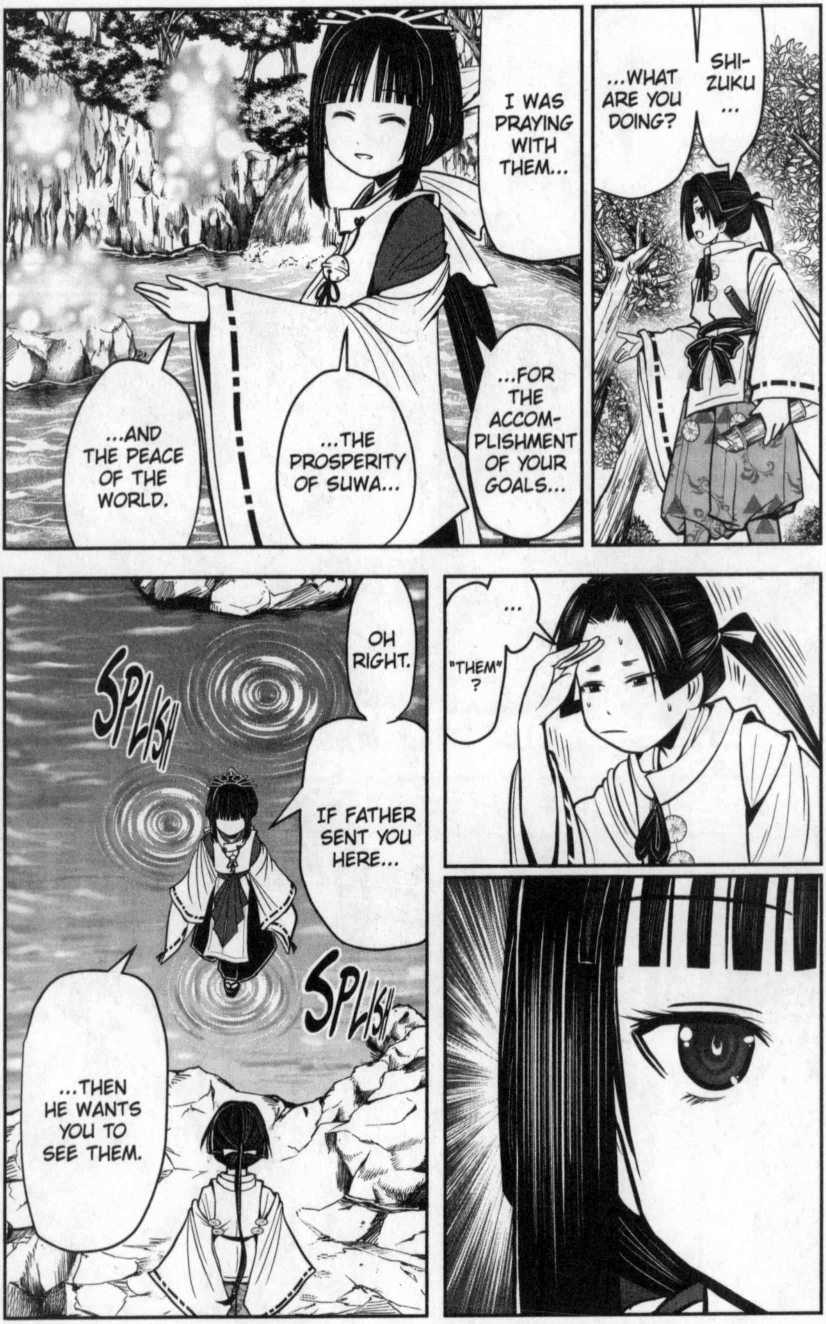
SHI-ZUKU...
...WHAT ARE YOU DOING?
I WAS PRAYING WITH THEM...
...FOR THE ACCOMPLISHMENT OF YOUR GOALS...
...THE PROSPERITY OF SUWA...
...AND THE PEACE OF THE WORLD.
...
"THEM"?
OH RIGHT.
SPLISH
IF FATHER SENT YOU HERE...
SPLISH
...THEN HE WANTS YOU TO SEE THEM.

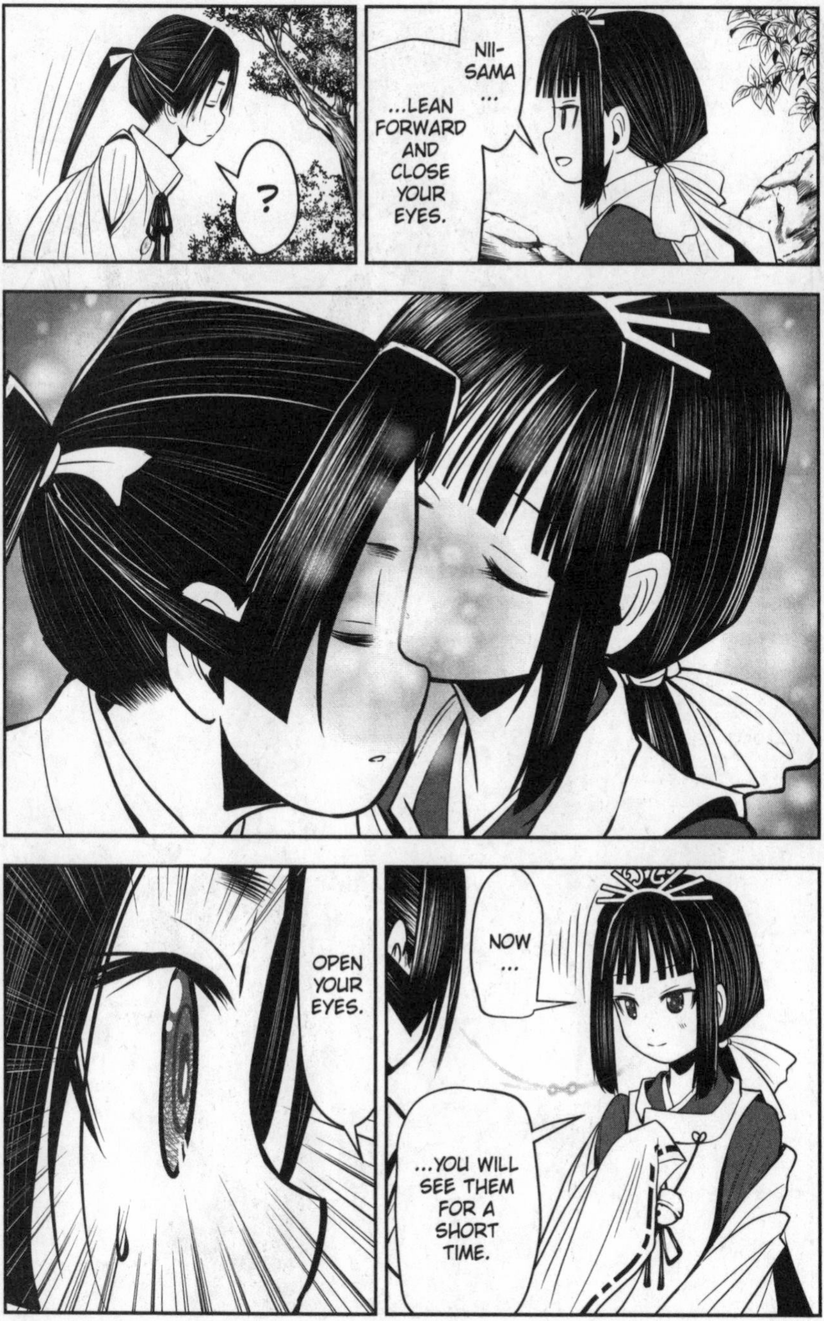
NII-SAMA ...
...LEAN FORWARD AND CLOSE YOUR EYES.
?
NOW ...
...YOU WILL SEE THEM FOR A SHORT TIME.
OPEN YOUR EYES.

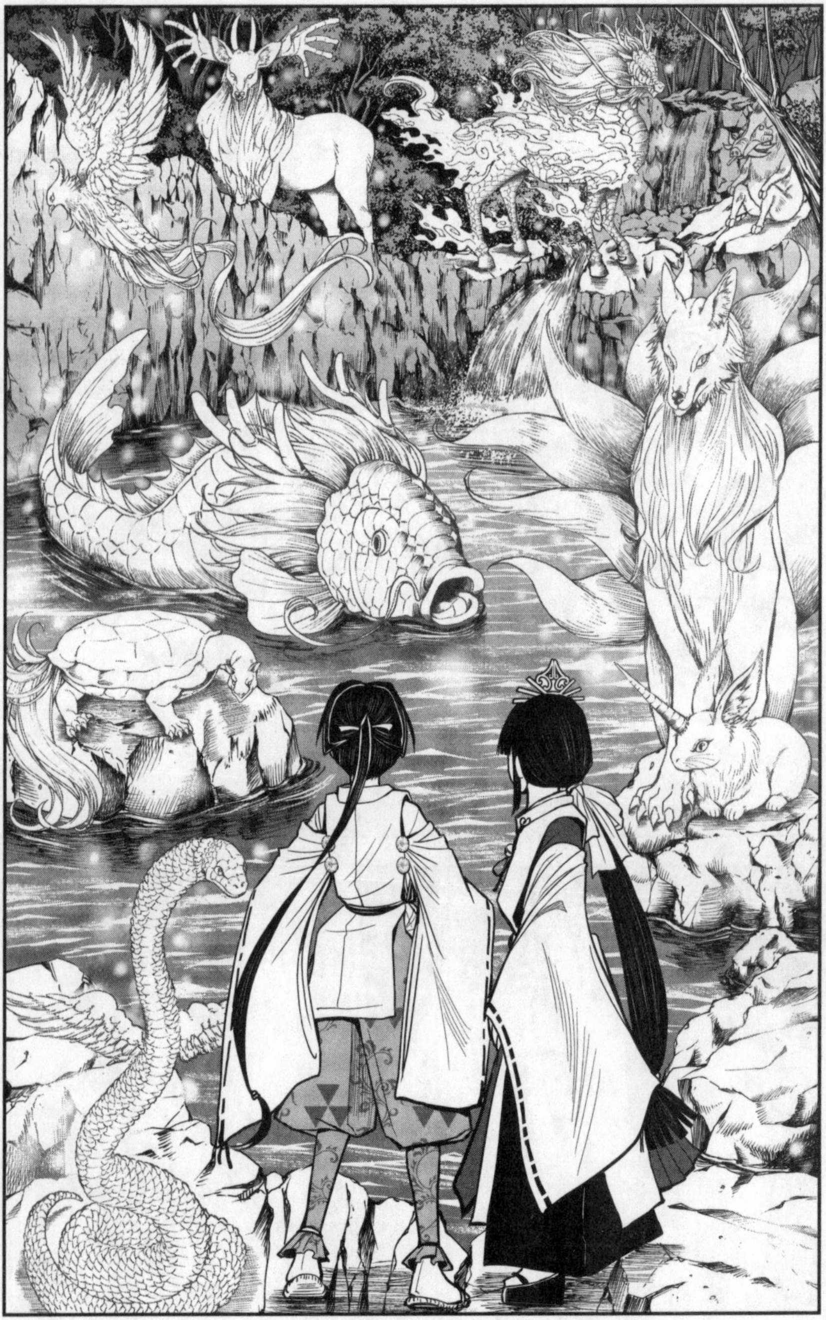

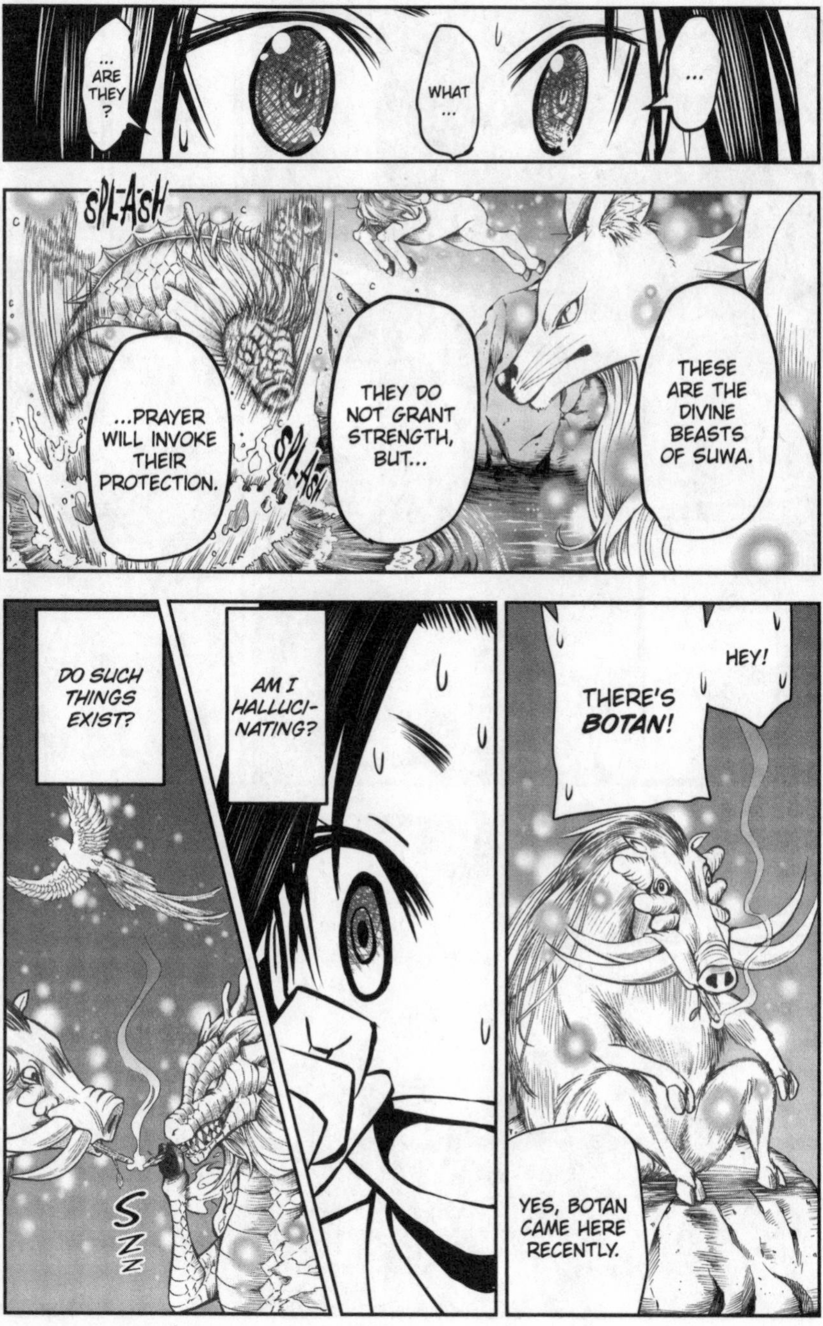
...
WHAT ...
... ARE THEY ?
SPLASH
THESE ARE THE DIVINE BEASTS OF SUWA.
THEY DO NOT GRANT STRENGTH, BUT...
SPLASH
...PRAYER WILL INVOKE THEIR PROTECTION.
HEY!
THERE'S ***BOTAN!***
YES, BOTAN CAME HERE RECENTLY.
AM I HALLUCINATING?
DO SUCH THINGS EXIST?
SZZ

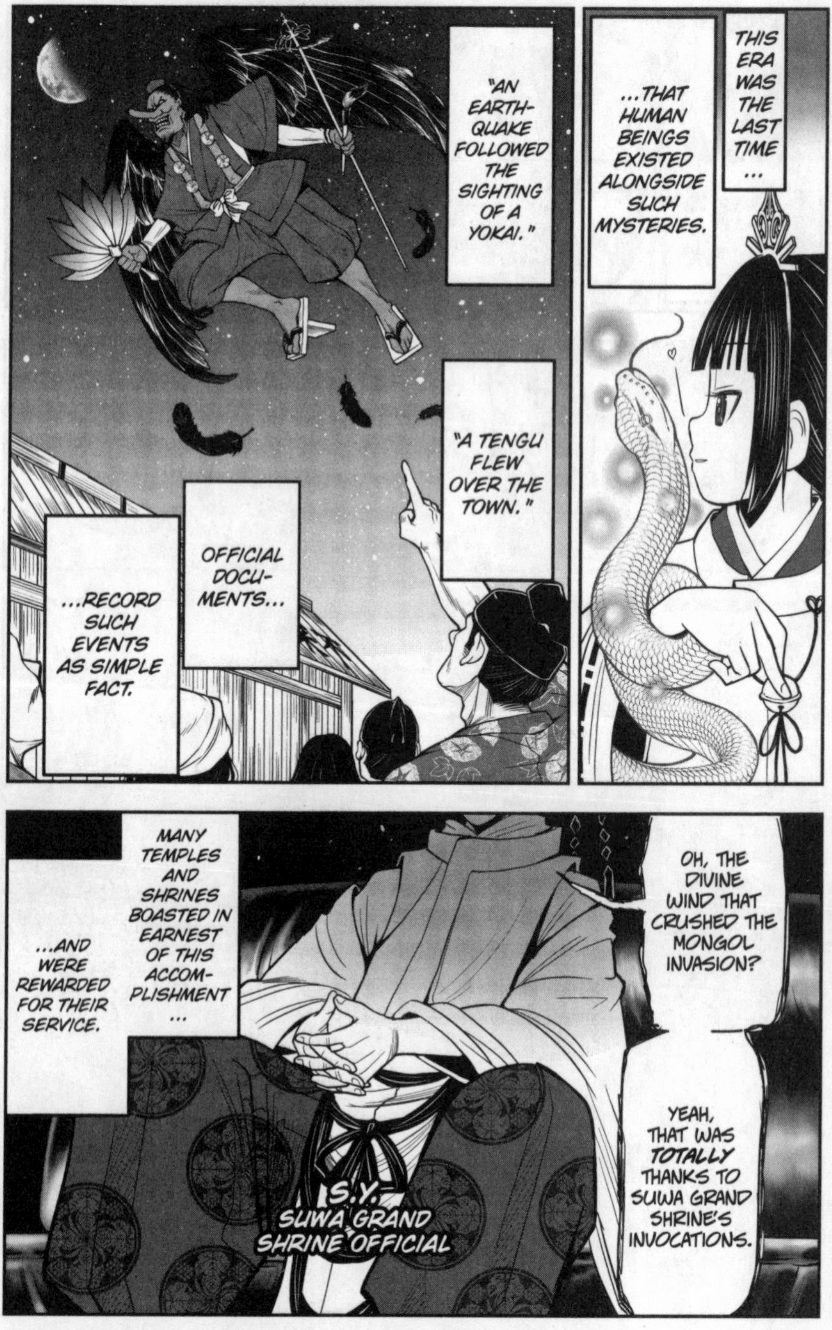
THIS ERA WAS THE LAST TIME...
...THAT HUMAN BEINGS EXISTED ALONGSIDE SUCH MYSTERIES.
"AN EARTH-QUAKE FOLLOWED THE SIGHTING OF A YOKAI."
"A TENGU FLEW OVER THE TOWN."
OFFICIAL DOCU-MENTS...
...RECORD SUCH EVENTS AS SIMPLE FACT.
OH, THE DIVINE WIND THAT CRUSHED THE MONGOL INVASION?
MANY TEMPLES AND SHRINES BOASTED IN EARNEST OF THIS ACCOM-PLISHMENT...
...AND WERE REWARDED FOR THEIR SERVICE.
YEAH, THAT WAS *TOTALLY* THANKS TO SUWA GRAND SHRINE'S INVOCATIONS.
S.Y. SUWA GRAND SHRINE OFFICIAL

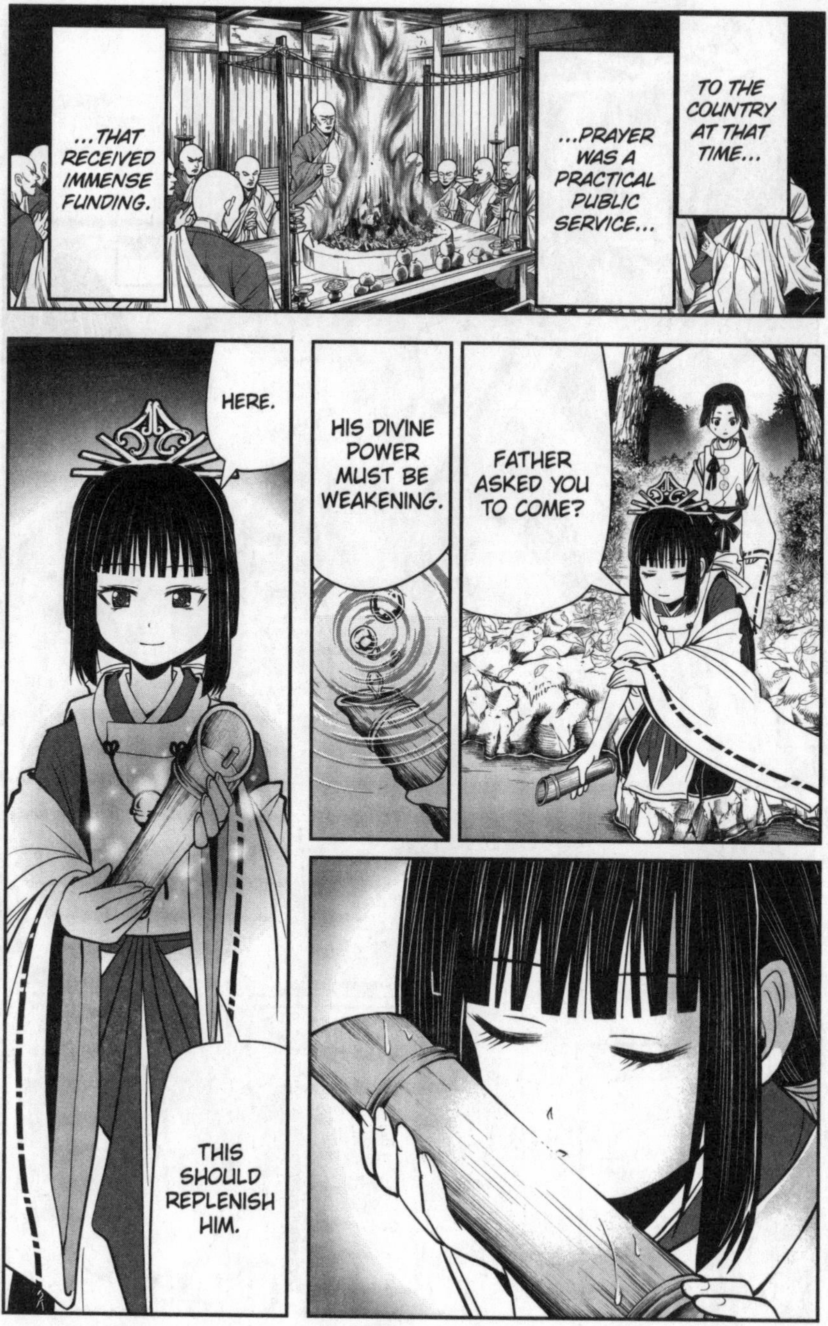
TO THE COUNTRY AT THAT TIME...
...PRAYER WAS A PRACTICAL PUBLIC SERVICE...
...THAT RECEIVED IMMENSE FUNDING.
FATHER ASKED YOU TO COME?
HIS DIVINE POWER MUST BE WEAKENING.
HERE.
THIS SHOULD REPLENISH HIM.

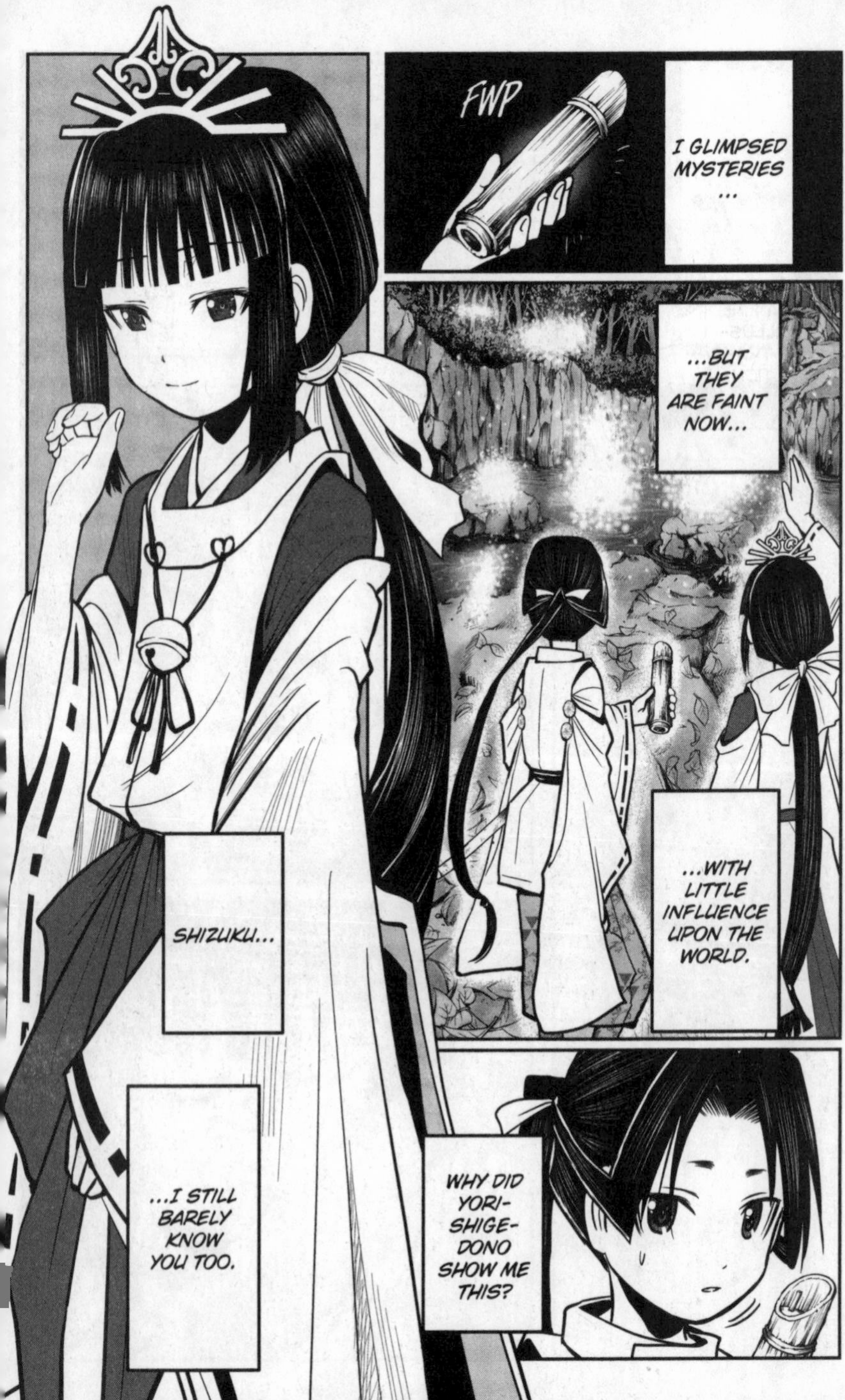

I GLIMPSED MYSTERIES ...
FWP
...BUT THEY ARE FAINT NOW...
...WITH LITTLE INFLUENCE UPON THE WORLD.
WHY DID YORI-SHIGE-DONO SHOW ME THIS?
SHIZUKU...
...I STILL BARELY KNOW YOU TOO.

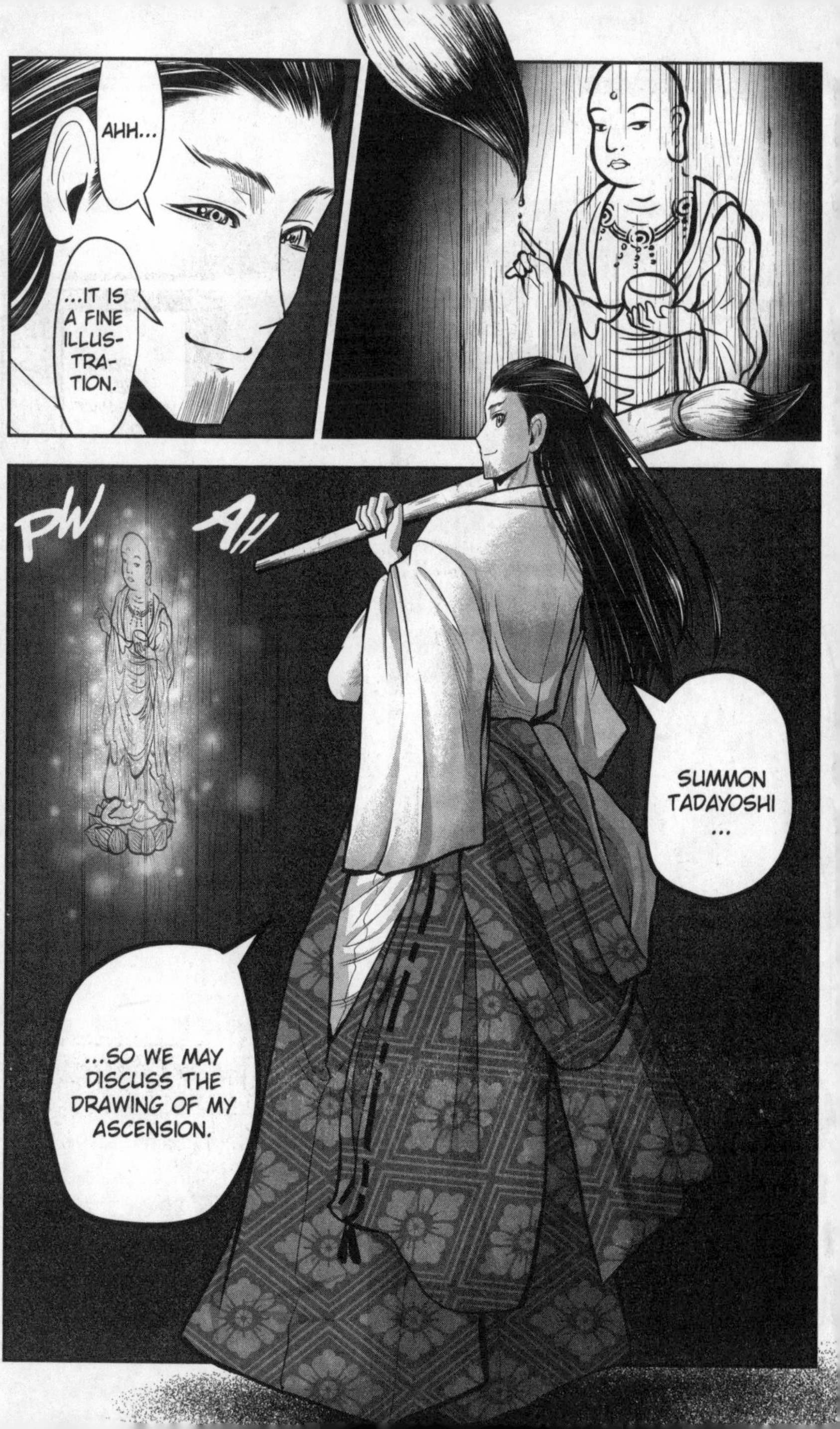
AHH...
...IT IS A FINE ILLUS-TRA-TION.
PW AH
SUMMON TADAYOSHI ...
...SO WE MAY DISCUSS THE DRAWING OF MY ASCENSION.

SHIZUKU

★ ★ R

ABILITIES		NANBOKU-CHO COMPATIBILITY	
MARTIAL ARTS	2	SAVAGERY	5
INTELLIGENCE	45	LOYALTY	95
POLITICS	38	CHAOS	26
LEADERSHIP	49	INGENUITY	41
CHARM	62	RUNNING AND HIDING	27

CREST

PAPER MULBERRY LEAF

SKILL	STEWARDSHIP: ABILITY TO COMBINE ARITHMETICS, NEGOTIATION, AND CHARISMA
SKILL	KAGURA DANCE: TEMPORARILY GAINS DIVINE POWER
CHARACTERISTIC	OTHERWORLDLINESS: 10 PERCENT DECREASE TO POLITICS AND LEADERSHIP

WEAKNESS

IF YOU TREAT HER
LIKE FAMILY, SHE BLUSHES
AND TOTALLY MELTS.

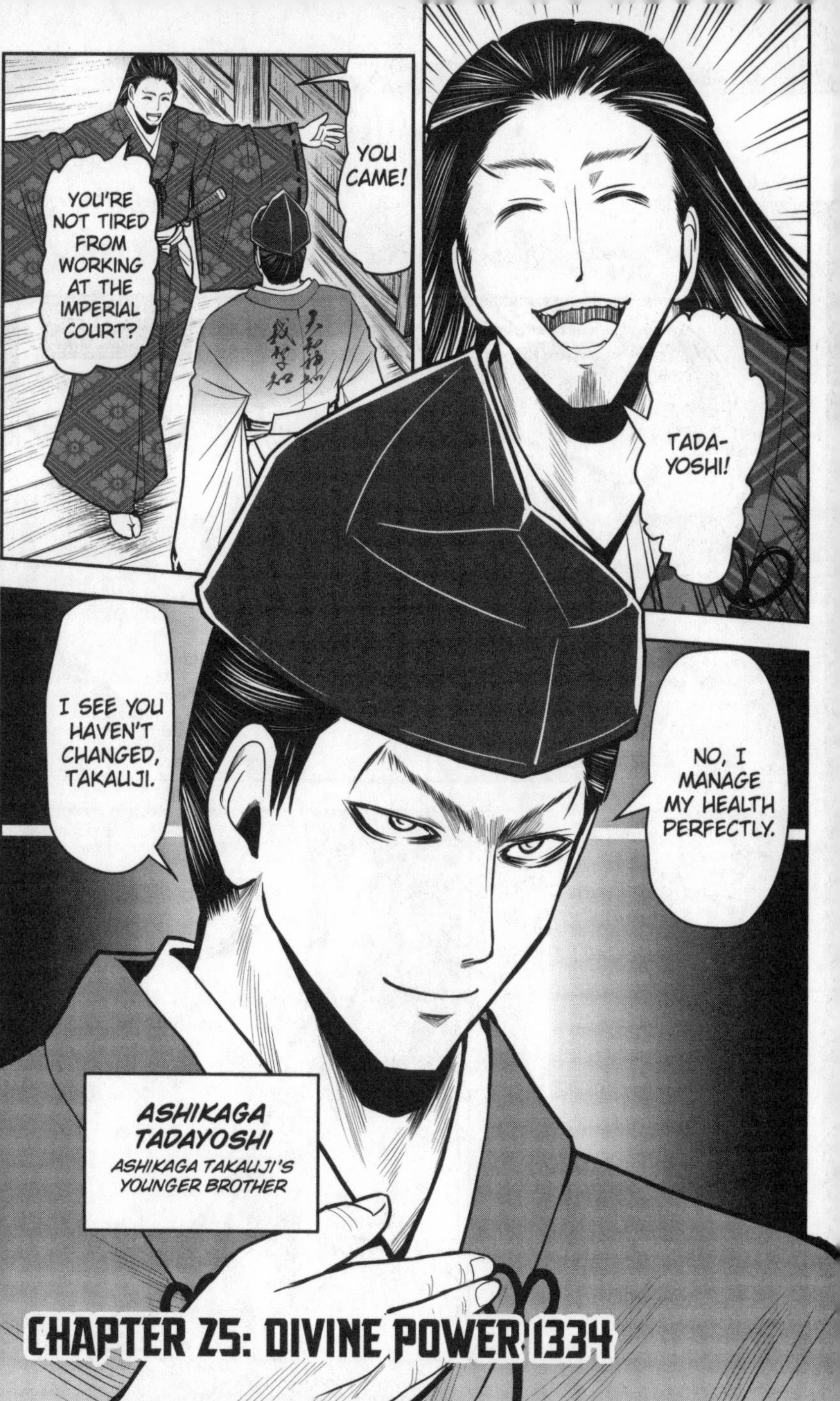
TADA-YOSHI!
YOU CAME!
YOU'RE NOT TIRED FROM WORKING AT THE IMPERIAL COURT?
NO, I MANAGE MY HEALTH PERFECTLY.
I SEE YOU HAVEN'T CHANGED, TAKAUJI.
ASHIKAGA TADAYOSHI
ASHIKAGA TAKAUJI'S YOUNGER BROTHER
CHAPTER 25: DIVINE POWER 1334

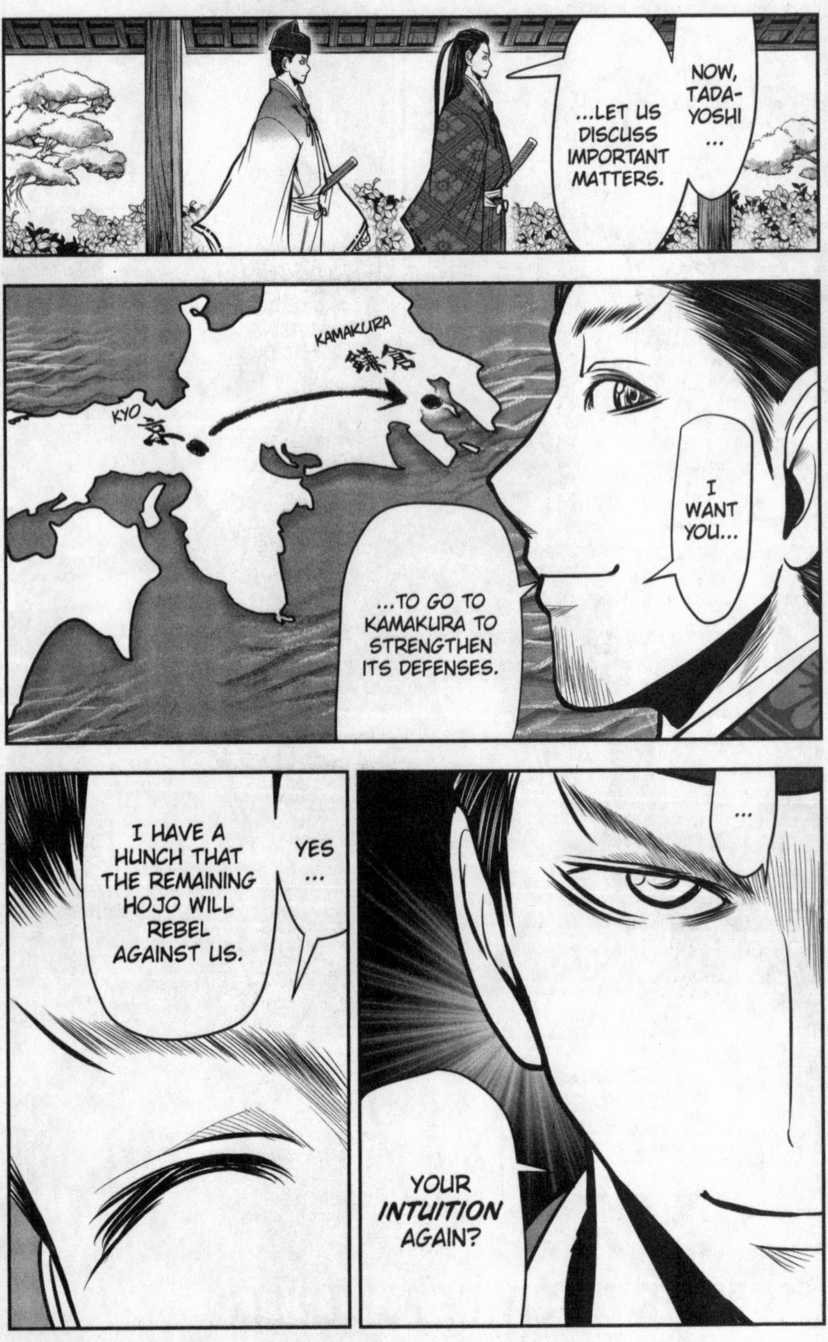
NOW, TADA-YOSHI ...
...LET US DISCUSS IMPORTANT MATTERS.
KAMAKURA
鎌倉
KYO
京
I WANT YOU...
...TO GO TO KAMAKURA TO STRENGTHEN ITS DEFENSES.
...
YOUR INTUITION AGAIN?
YES ...
I HAVE A HUNCH THAT THE REMAINING HOJO WILL REBEL AGAINST US.

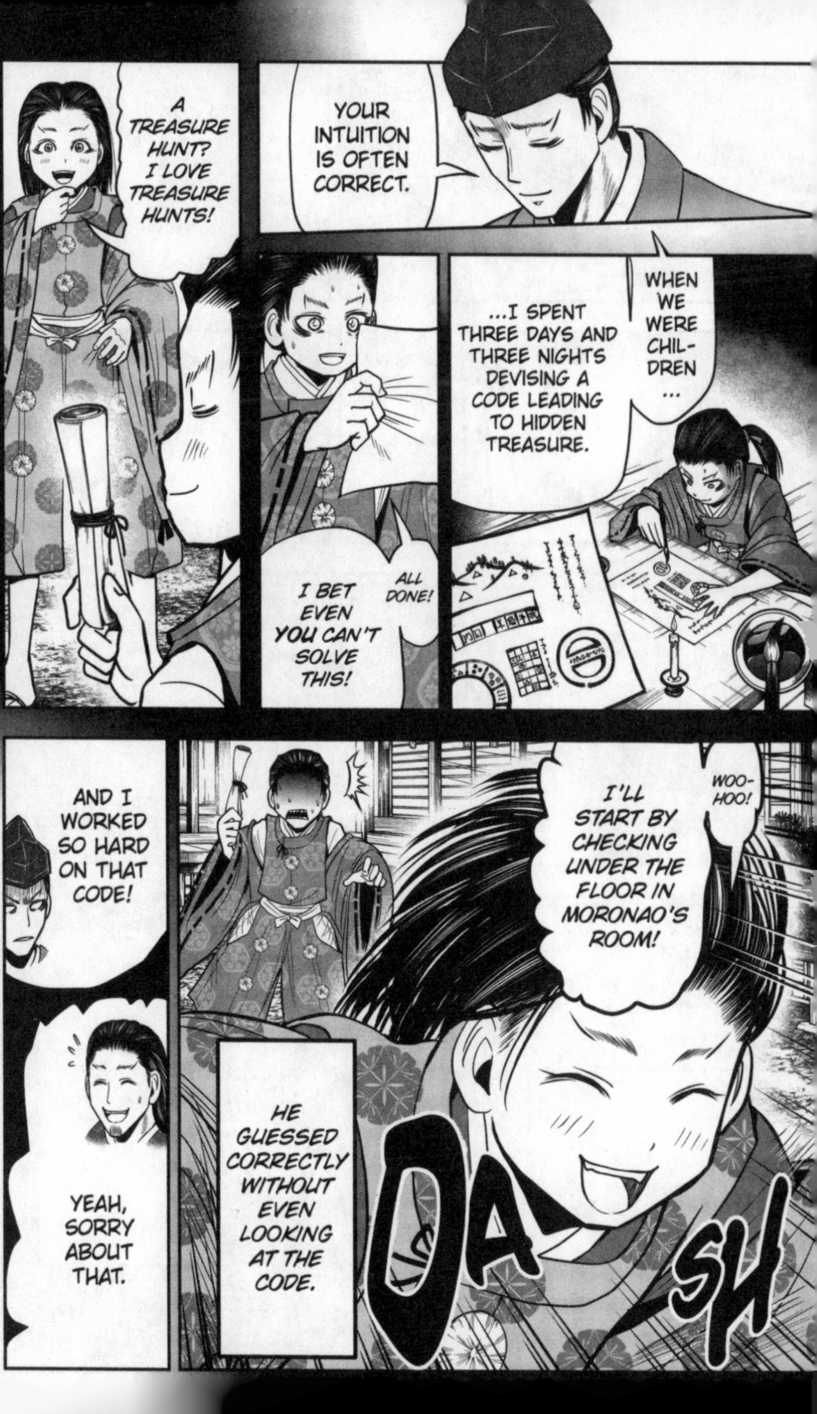
YOUR INTUITION IS OFTEN CORRECT.
WHEN WE WERE CHIL-DREN ...
...I SPENT THREE DAYS AND THREE NIGHTS DEVISING A CODE LEADING TO HIDDEN TREASURE.
ALL DONE!
I BET EVEN YOU CAN'T SOLVE THIS!
A TREASURE HUNT? I LOVE TREASURE HUNTS!
WOO-HOO!
I'LL START BY CHECKING UNDER THE FLOOR IN MORONAO'S ROOM!
DASH
HE GUESSED CORRECTLY WITHOUT EVEN LOOKING AT THE CODE.
AND I WORKED SO HARD ON THAT CODE!
YEAH, SORRY ABOUT THAT.

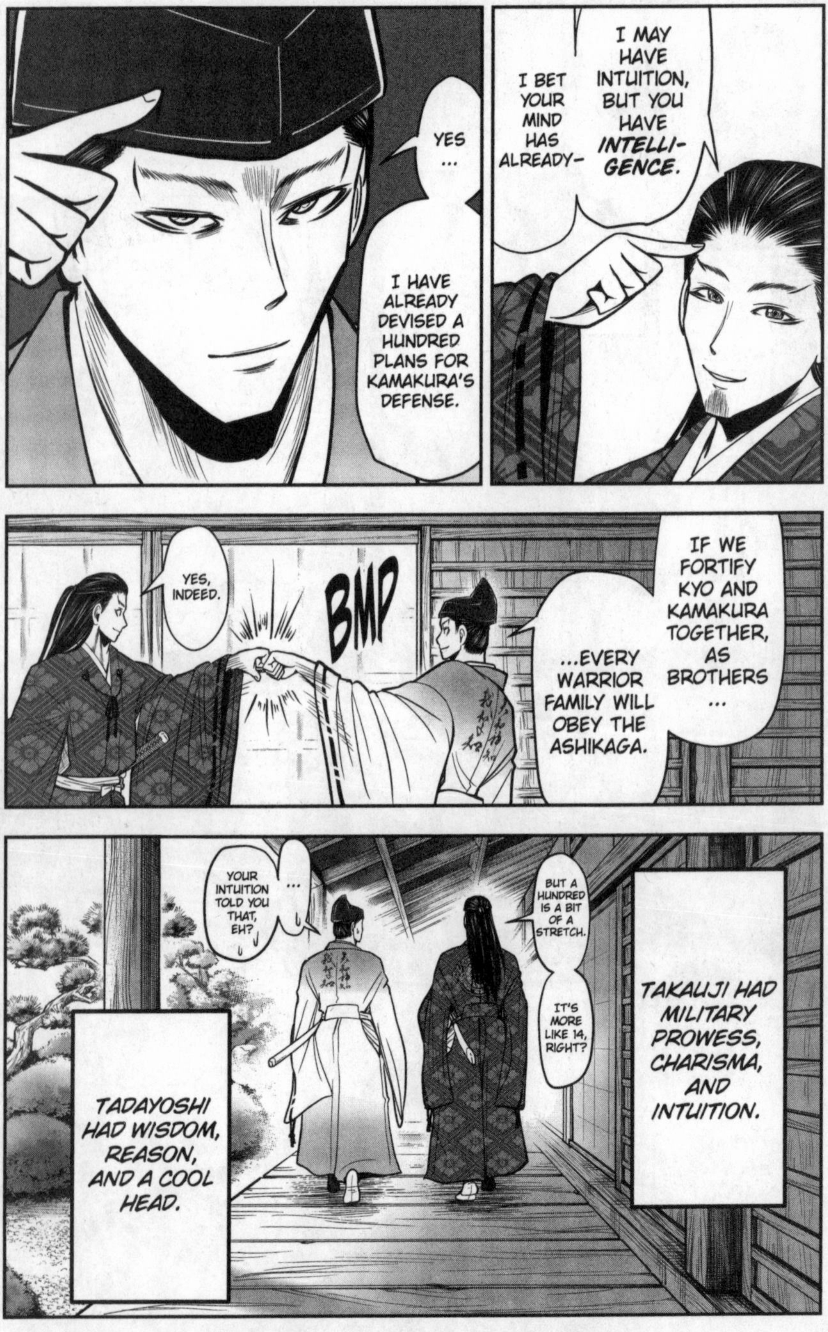
I MAY HAVE INTUITION, BUT YOU HAVE INTELLIGENCE.
I BET YOUR MIND HAS ALREADY-
YES ...
I HAVE ALREADY DEVISED A HUNDRED PLANS FOR KAMAKURA'S DEFENSE.
IF WE FORTIFY KYO AND KAMAKURA TOGETHER, AS BROTHERS ...
...EVERY WARRIOR FAMILY WILL OBEY THE ASHIKAGA.
BMP
YES, INDEED.
TAKAUJI HAD MILITARY PROWESS, CHARISMA, AND INTUITION.
BUT A HUNDRED IS A BIT OF A STRETCH.
IT'S MORE LIKE 14, RIGHT?
...
YOUR INTUITION TOLD YOU THAT, EH?
TADAYOSHI HAD WISDOM, REASON, AND A COOL HEAD.

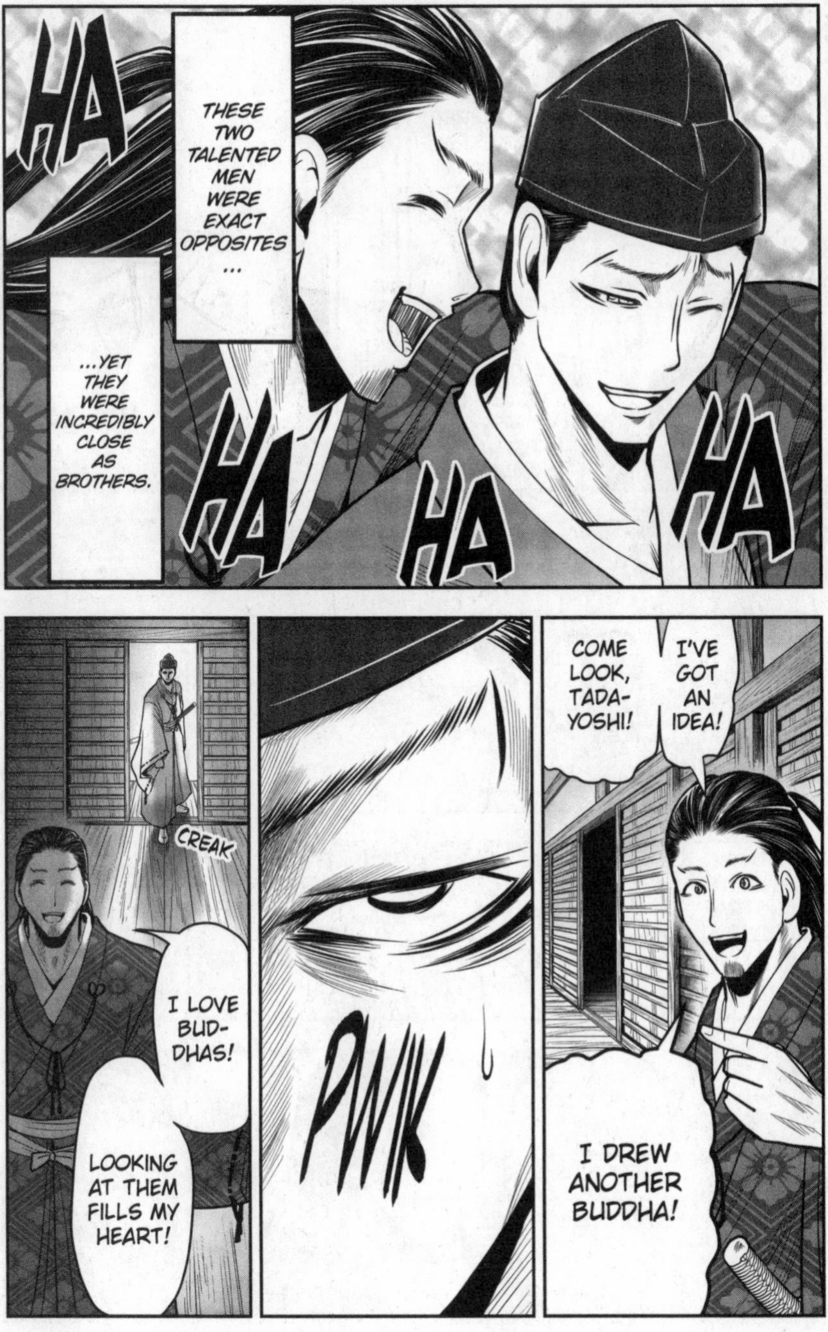
THESE TWO TALENTED MEN WERE EXACT OPPOSITES...
...YET THEY WERE INCREDIBLY CLOSE AS BROTHERS.
HA
HA
HA
HA
I'VE GOT AN IDEA!
COME LOOK, TADA-YOSHI!
I DREW ANOTHER BUDDHA!
PWIK
CREAK
I LOVE BUD-DHAS!
LOOKING AT THEM FILLS MY HEART!

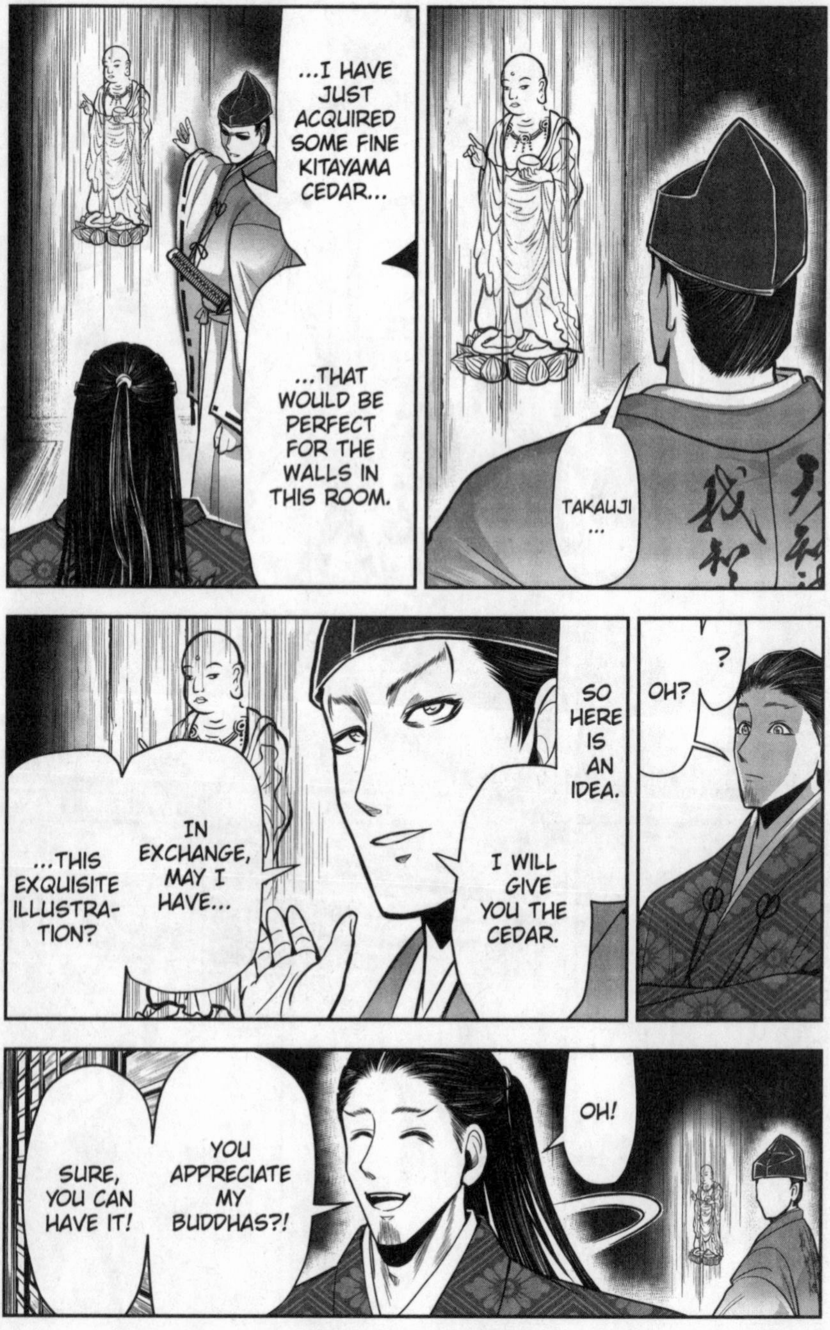
TAKAUJI ...
...I HAVE JUST ACQUIRED SOME FINE KITAYAMA CEDAR...
...THAT WOULD BE PERFECT FOR THE WALLS IN THIS ROOM.
?
OH?
SO HERE IS AN IDEA.
I WILL GIVE YOU THE CEDAR.
IN EXCHANGE, MAY I HAVE...
...THIS EXQUISITE ILLUSTRATION?
OH!
YOU APPRECIATE MY BUDDHAS?!
SURE, YOU CAN HAVE IT!

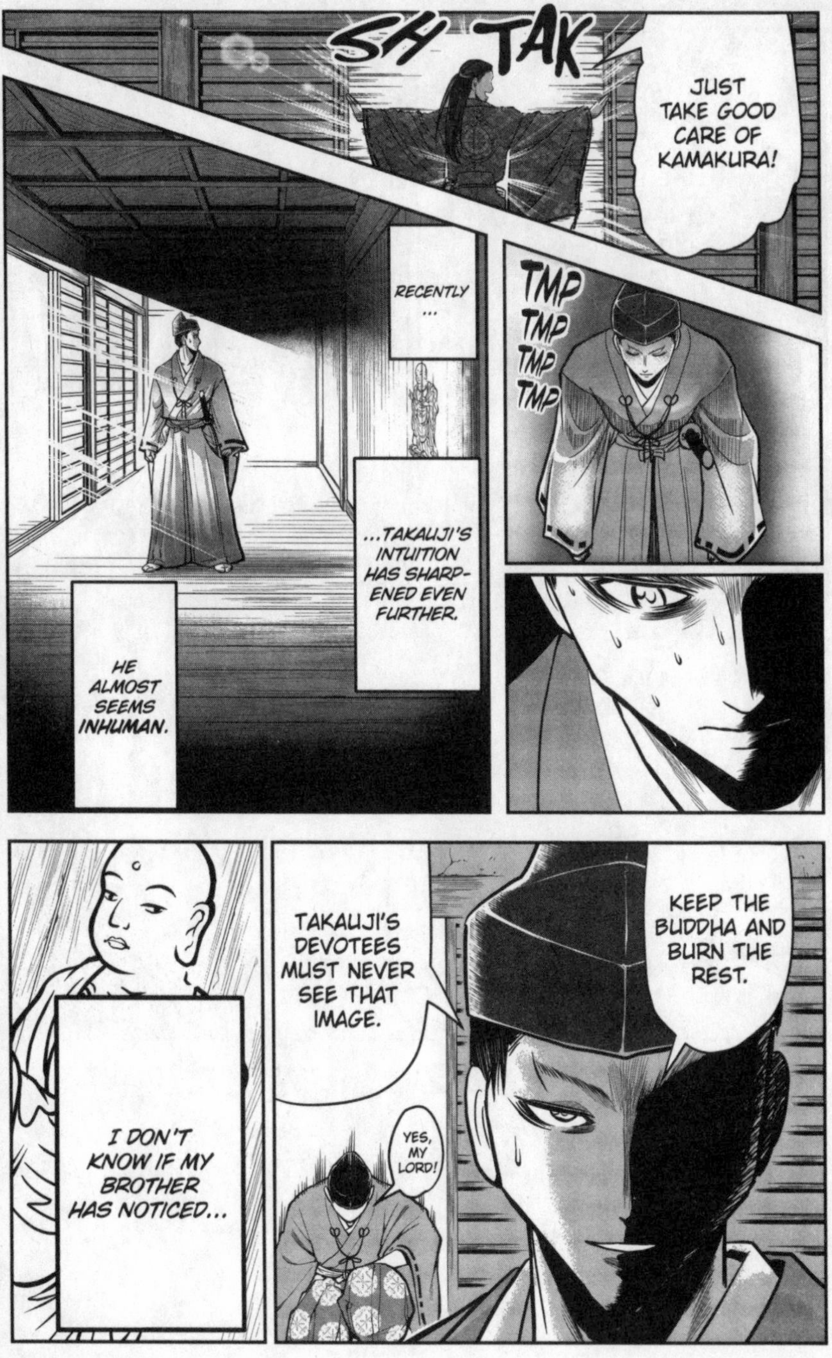
SH
TAK
JUST TAKE GOOD CARE OF KAMAKURA!
TMP TMP TMP TMP
RECENTLY...
...TAKAUJI'S INTUITION HAS SHARPENED EVEN FURTHER.
HE ALMOST SEEMS INHUMAN.
KEEP THE BUDDHA AND BURN THE REST.
TAKAUJI'S DEVOTEES MUST NEVER SEE THAT IMAGE.
YES, MY LORD!
I DON'T KNOW IF MY BROTHER HAS NOTICED...

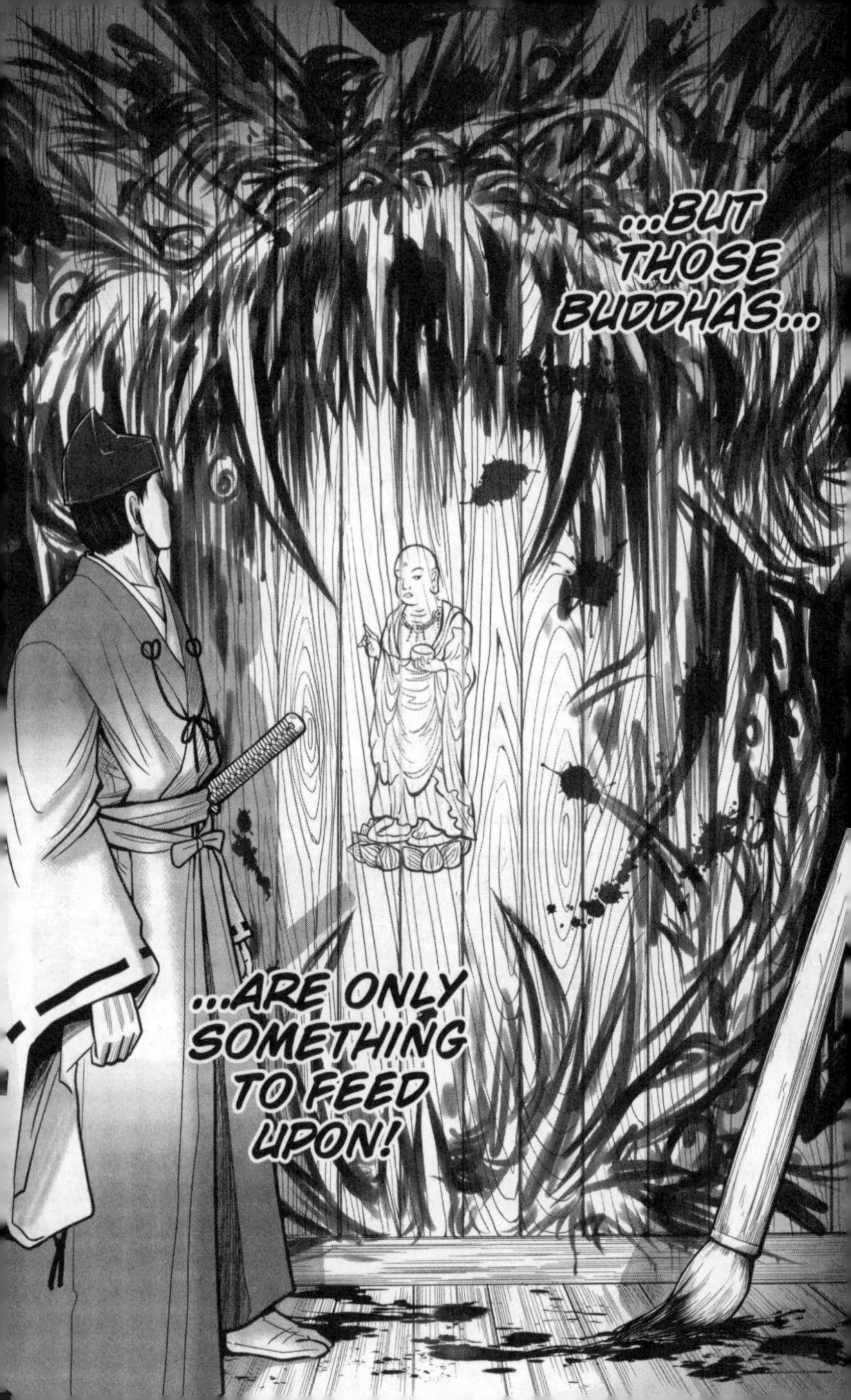
...BUT THOSE BUDDHAS...
...ARE ONLY SOMETHING TO FEED UPON!

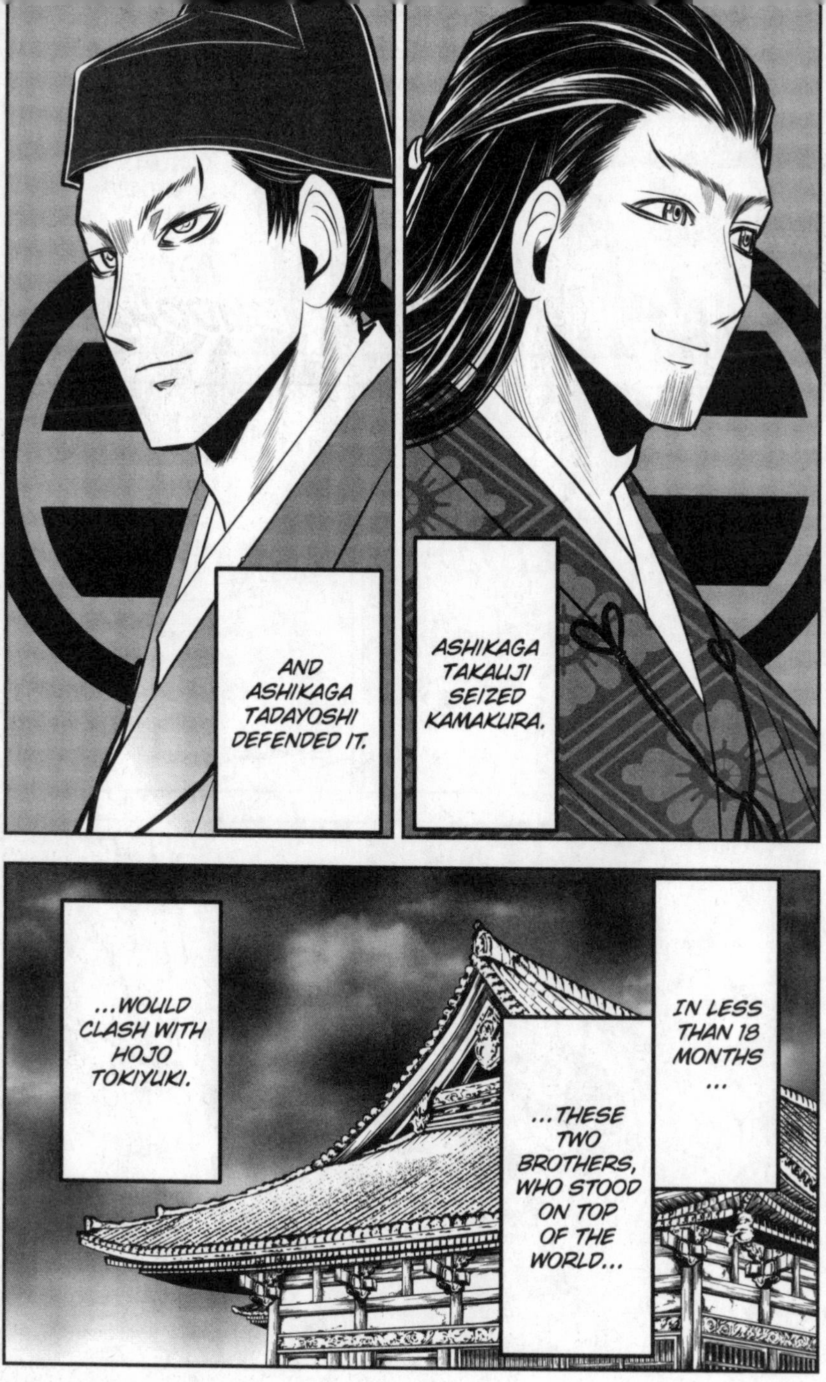
ASHIKAGA TAKAUJI SEIZED KAMAKURA.
AND ASHIKAGA TADAYOSHI DEFENDED IT.
IN LESS THAN 18 MONTHS ...
...THESE TWO BROTHERS, WHO STOOD ON TOP OF THE WORLD...
...WOULD CLASH WITH HOJO TOKIYUKI.

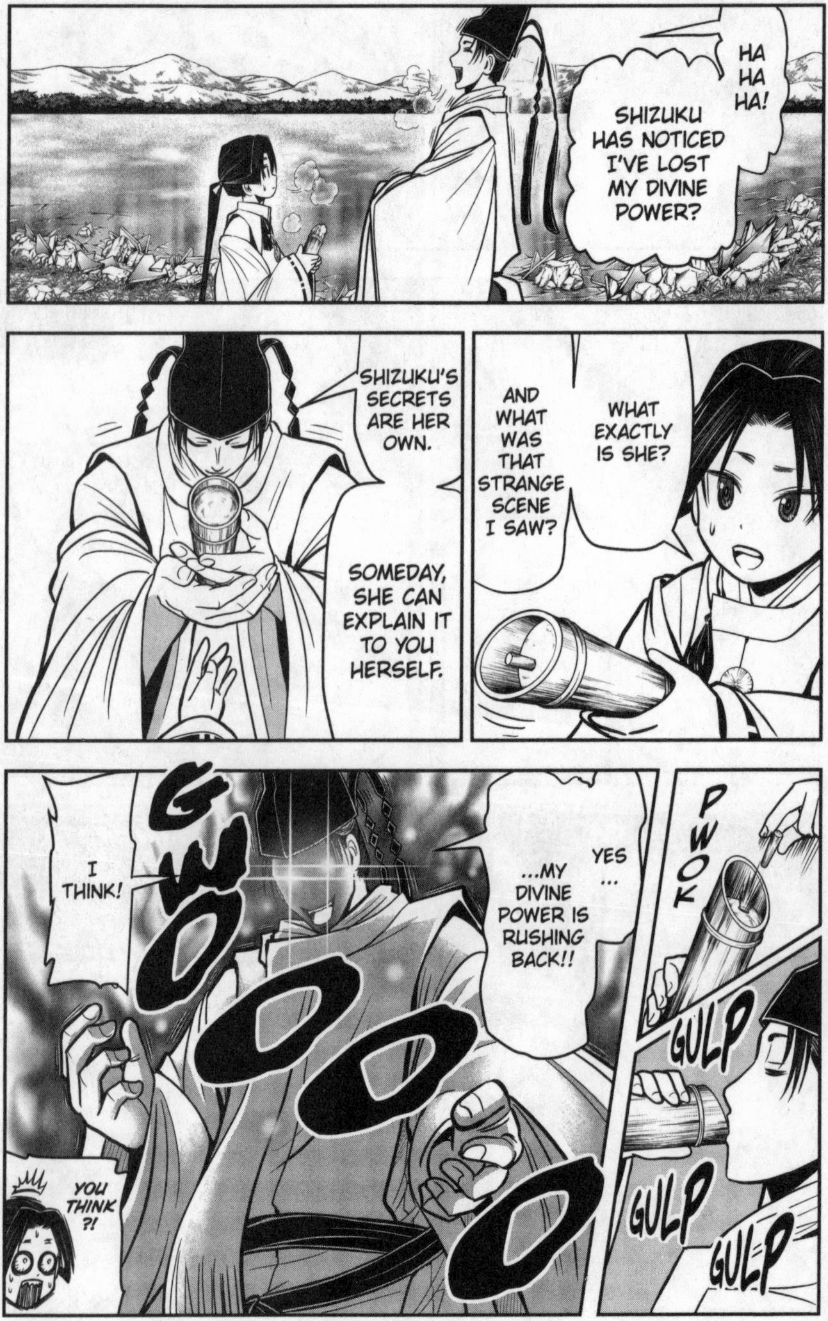
HA HA HA!
SHIZUKU HAS NOTICED I'VE LOST MY DIVINE POWER?
WHAT EXACTLY IS SHE?
AND WHAT WAS THAT STRANGE SCENE I SAW?
SHIZUKU'S SECRETS ARE HER OWN.
SOMEDAY, SHE CAN EXPLAIN IT TO YOU HERSELF.
PWOK
GULP
GULP
GULP
YES...
...MY DIVINE POWER IS RUSHING BACK!!
GWOOOOOO
I THINK!
YOU THINK?!

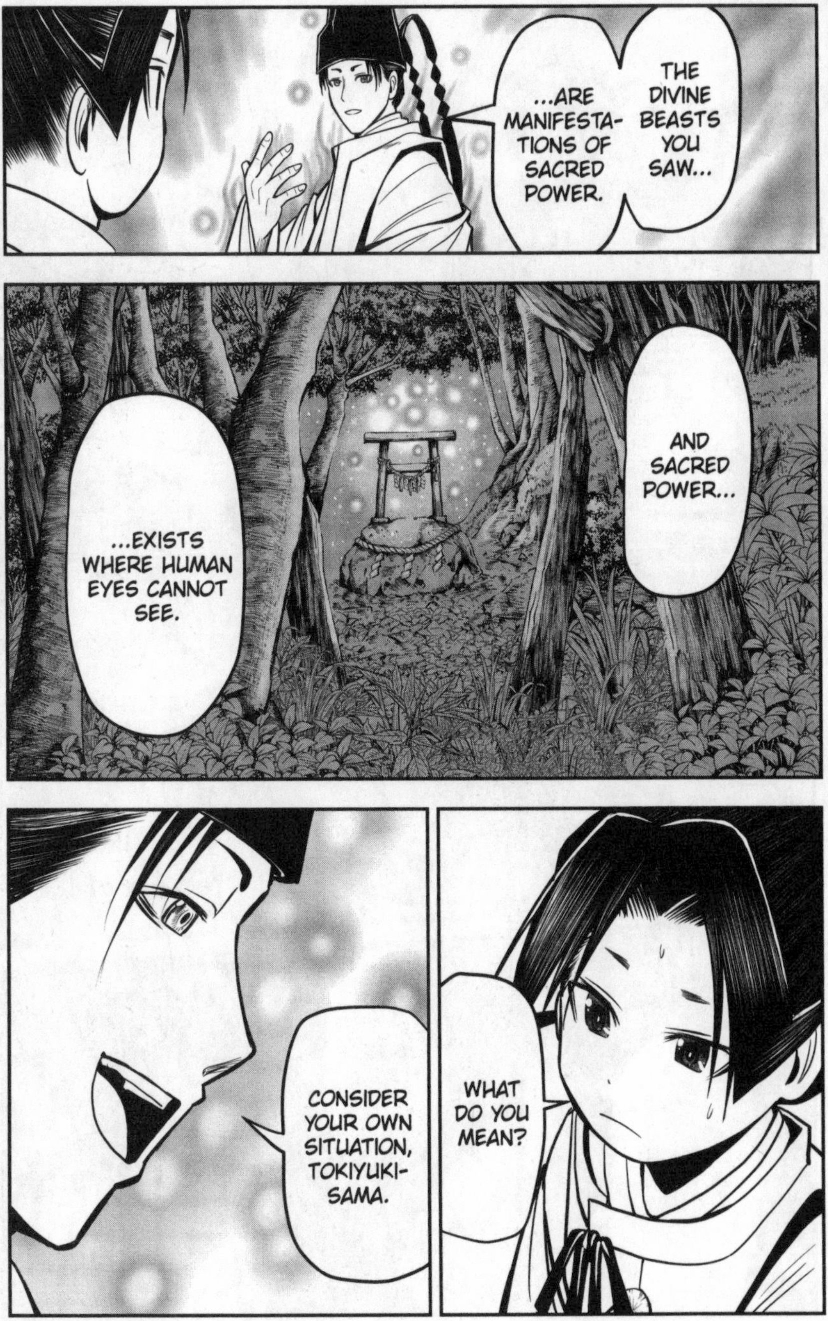
THE DIVINE BEASTS YOU SAW...
...ARE MANIFESTATIONS OF SACRED POWER.
AND SACRED POWER...
...EXISTS WHERE HUMAN EYES CANNOT SEE.
WHAT DO YOU MEAN?
CONSIDER YOUR OWN SITUATION, TOKIYUKI-SAMA.

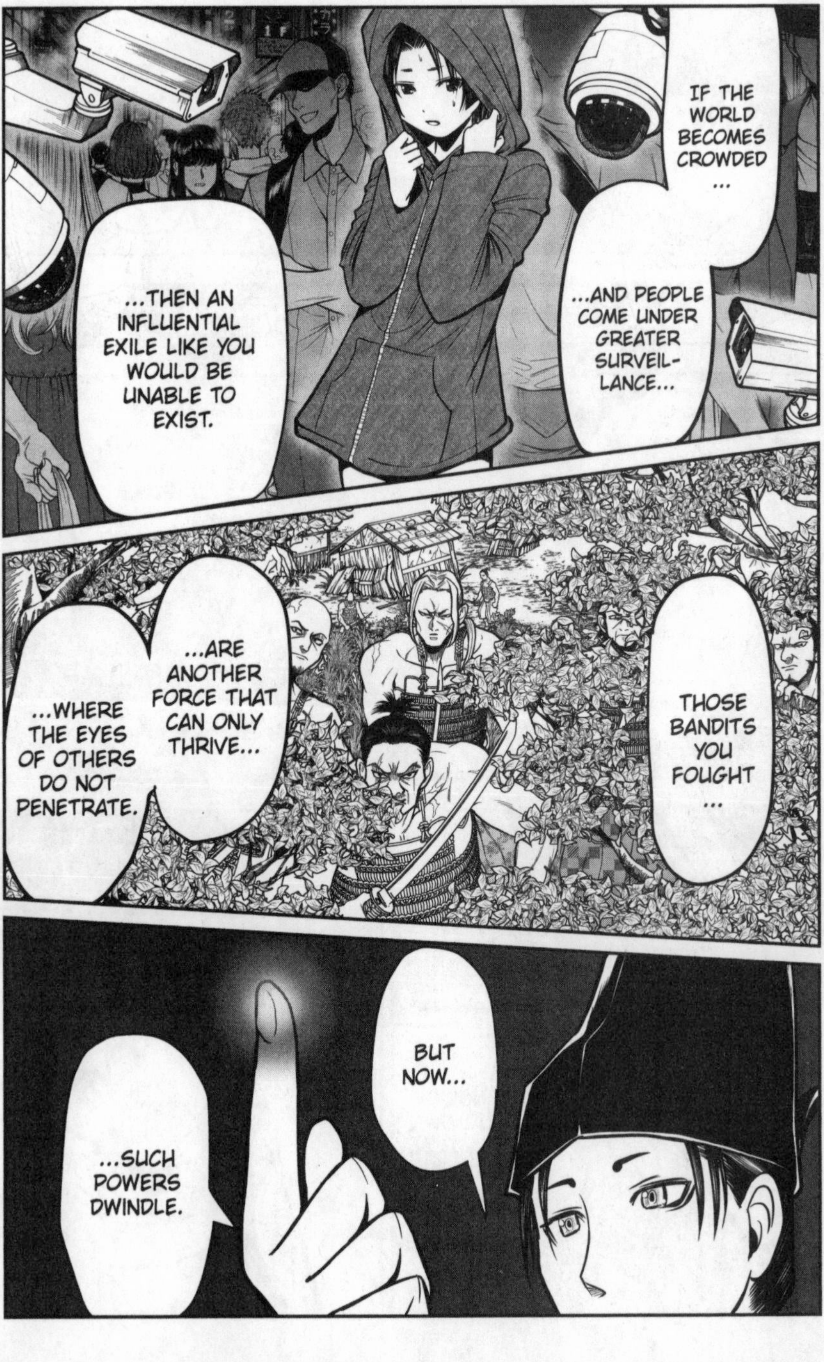
IF THE WORLD BECOMES CROWDED ...
...AND PEOPLE COME UNDER GREATER SURVEIL-LANCE...
...THEN AN INFLUENTIAL EXILE LIKE YOU WOULD BE UNABLE TO EXIST.
THOSE BANDITS YOU FOUGHT ...
...ARE ANOTHER FORCE THAT CAN ONLY THRIVE...
...WHERE THE EYES OF OTHERS DO NOT PENETRATE.
BUT NOW...
...SUCH POWERS DWINDLE.

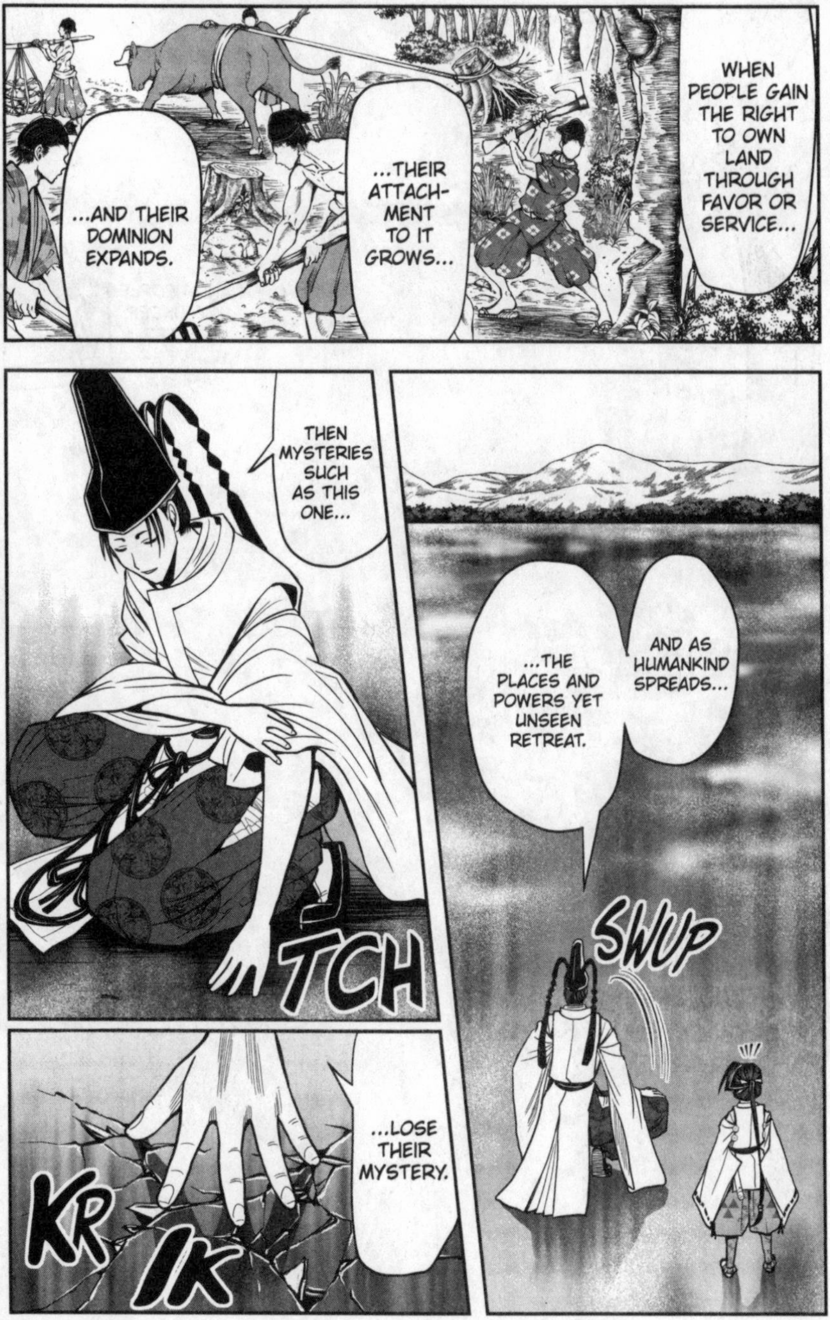
WHEN PEOPLE GAIN THE RIGHT TO OWN LAND THROUGH FAVOR OR SERVICE...
...THEIR ATTACHMENT TO IT GROWS...
...AND THEIR DOMINION EXPANDS.
AND AS HUMANKIND SPREADS...
...THE PLACES AND POWERS YET UNSEEN RETREAT.
SWUP
THEN MYSTERIES SUCH AS THIS ONE...
TCH
...LOSE THEIR MYSTERY.
KRIK

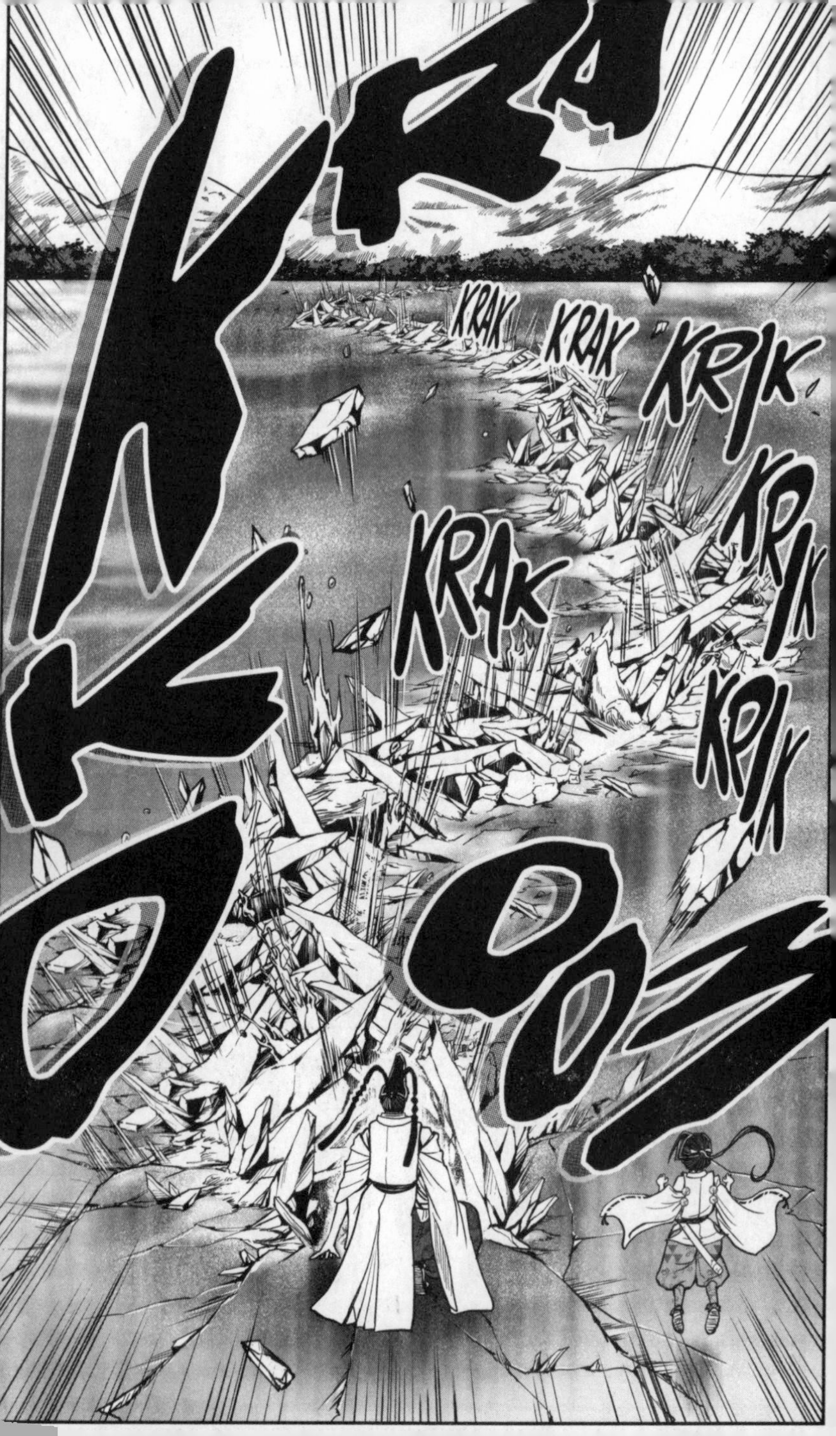
KRIK
KRAK
KRAK
KRIK
KRAK
KRIK

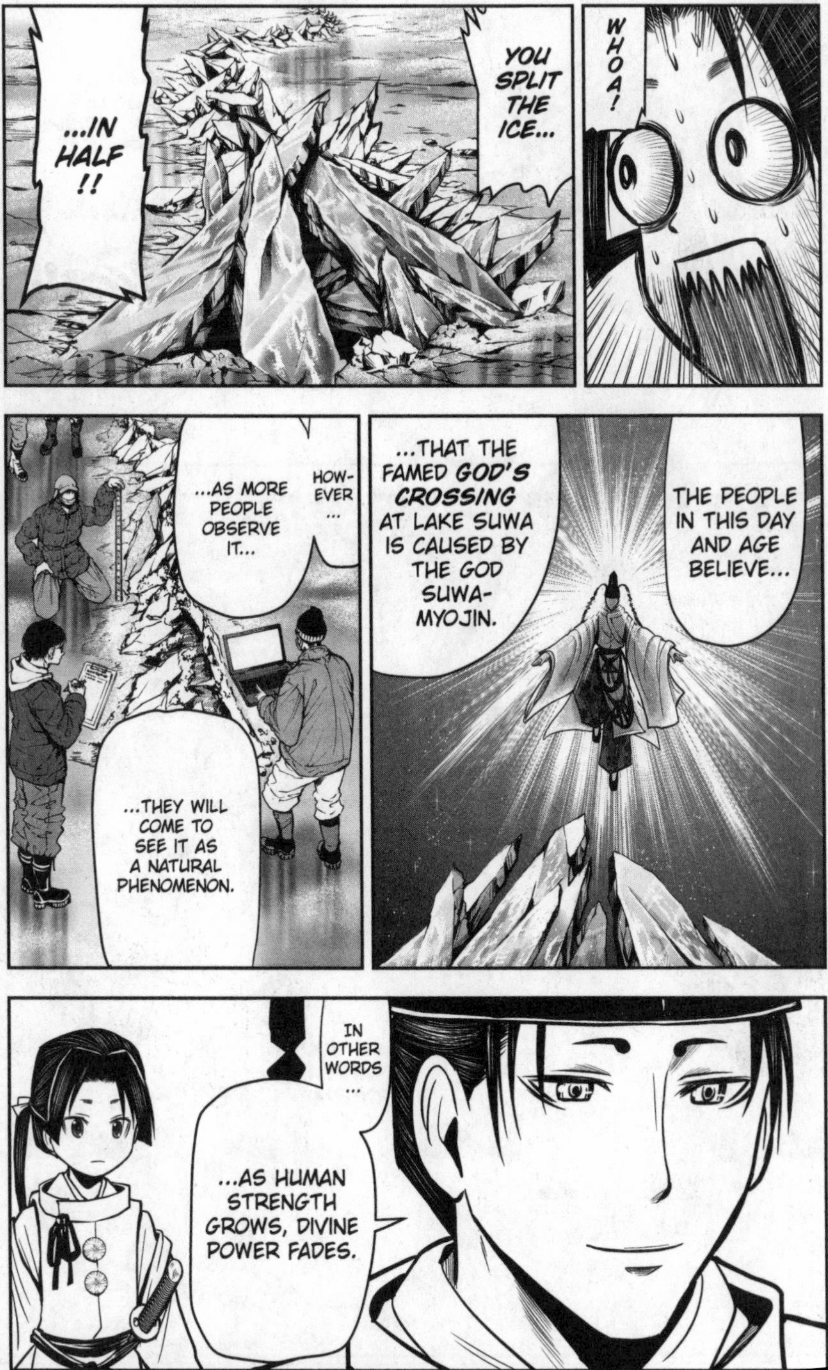
WHOA!
YOU SPLIT THE ICE...
...IN HALF!!
THE PEOPLE IN THIS DAY AND AGE BELIEVE...
...THAT THE FAMED GOD'S CROSSING AT LAKE SUWA IS CAUSED BY THE GOD SUWA-MYOJIN.
HOW-EVER...
...AS MORE PEOPLE OBSERVE IT...
...THEY WILL COME TO SEE IT AS A NATURAL PHENOMENON.
IN OTHER WORDS...
...AS HUMAN STRENGTH GROWS, DIVINE POWER FADES.

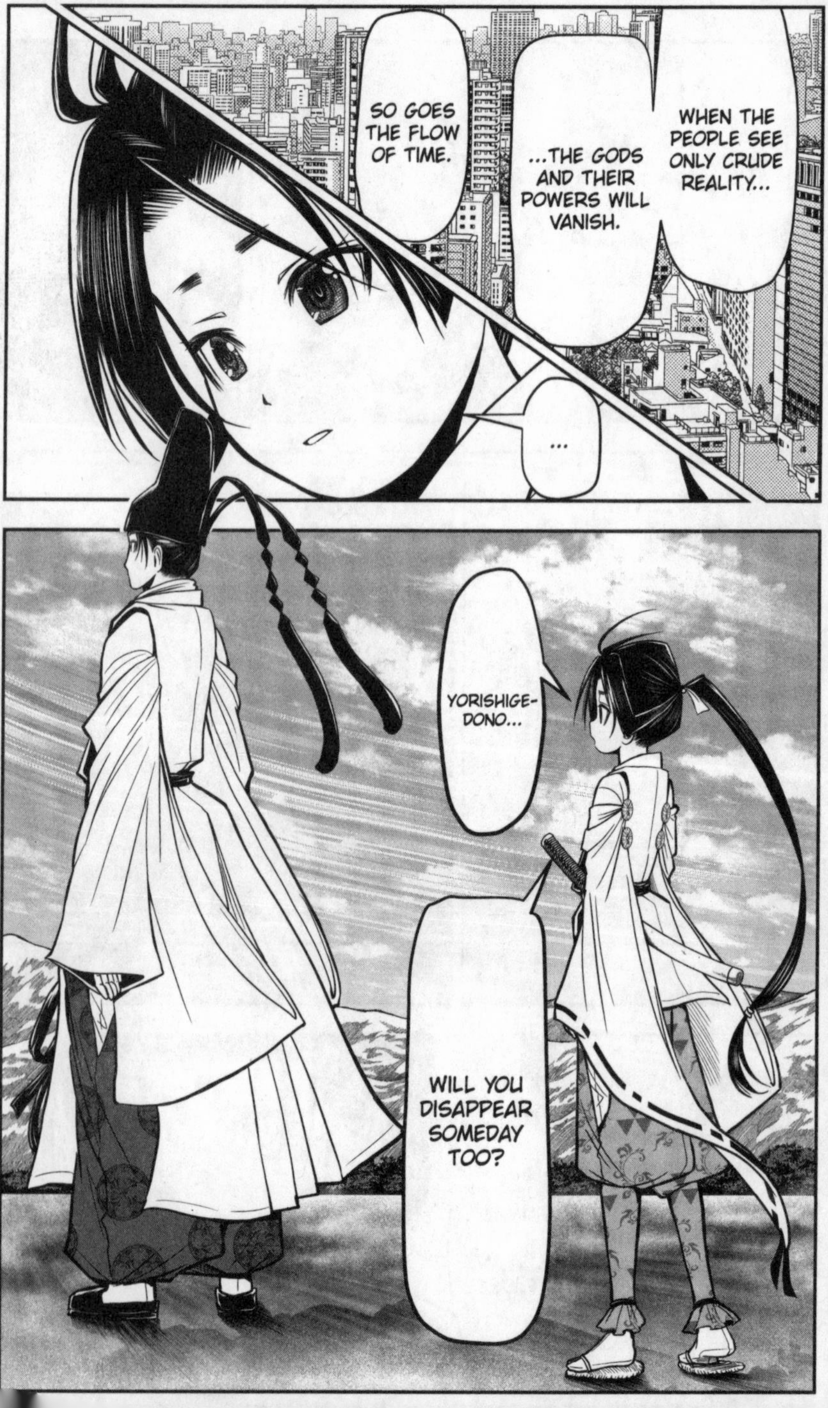
WHEN THE PEOPLE SEE ONLY CRUDE REALITY...
...THE GODS AND THEIR POWERS WILL VANISH.
SO GOES THE FLOW OF TIME.
...
YORISHIGE-DONO...
WILL YOU DISAPPEAR SOMEDAY TOO?

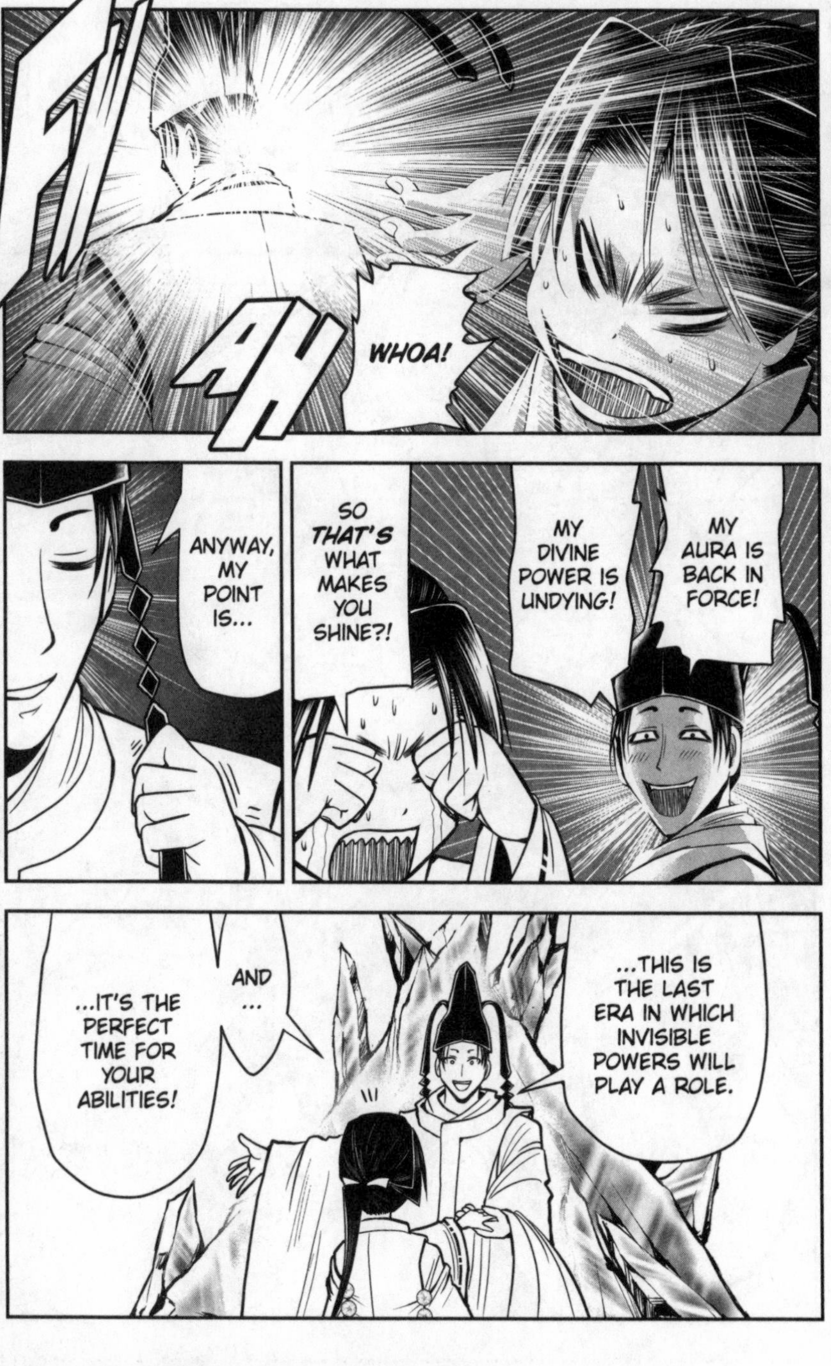
WHOA!
AH
MY AURA IS BACK IN FORCE!
MY DIVINE POWER IS UNDYING!
SO *THAT'S* WHAT MAKES YOU SHINE?!
ANYWAY, MY POINT IS...
...THIS IS THE LAST ERA IN WHICH INVISIBLE POWERS WILL PLAY A ROLE.
AND ...
...IT'S THE PERFECT TIME FOR YOUR ABILITIES!

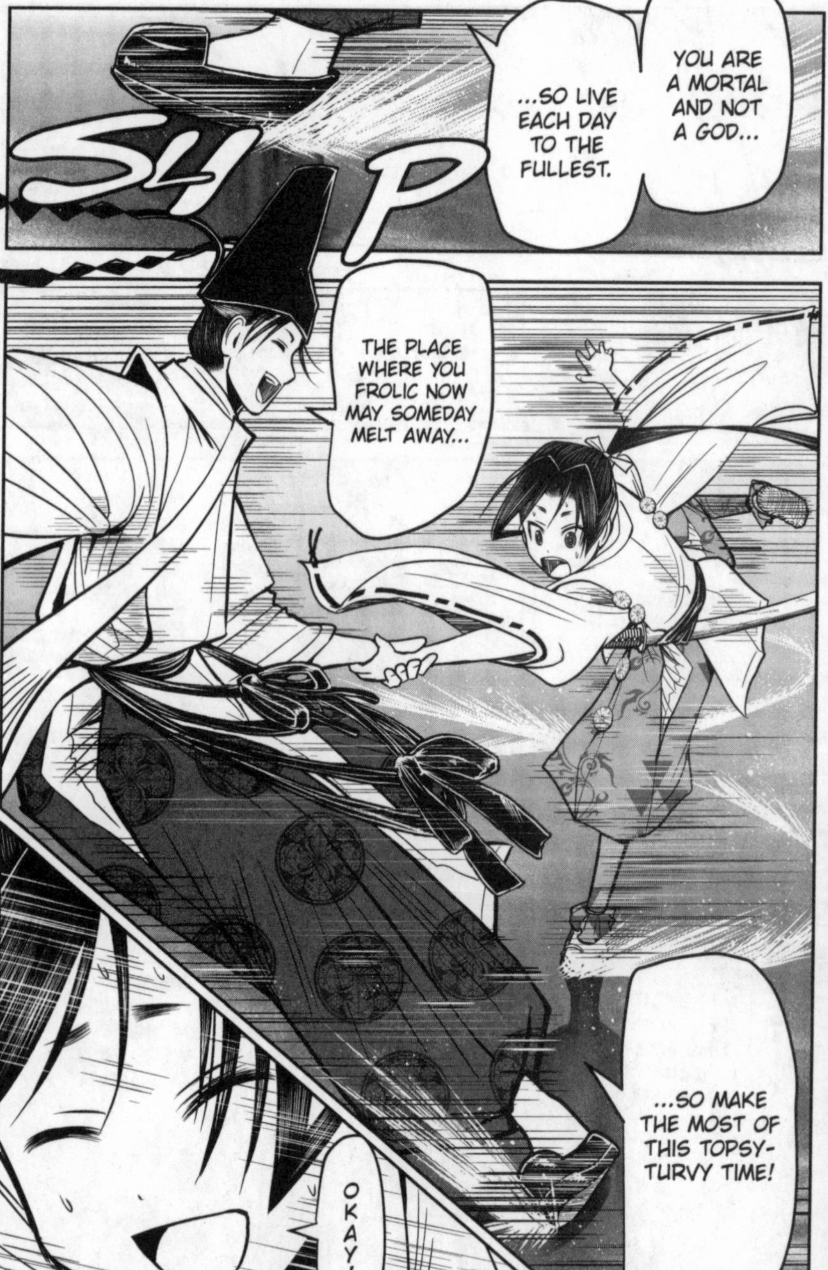
YOU ARE A MORTAL AND NOT A GOD...
...SO LIVE EACH DAY TO THE FULLEST.
SH P
THE PLACE WHERE YOU FROLIC NOW MAY SOMEDAY MELT AWAY...
...SO MAKE THE MOST OF THIS TOPSY-TURVY TIME!
OKAY!

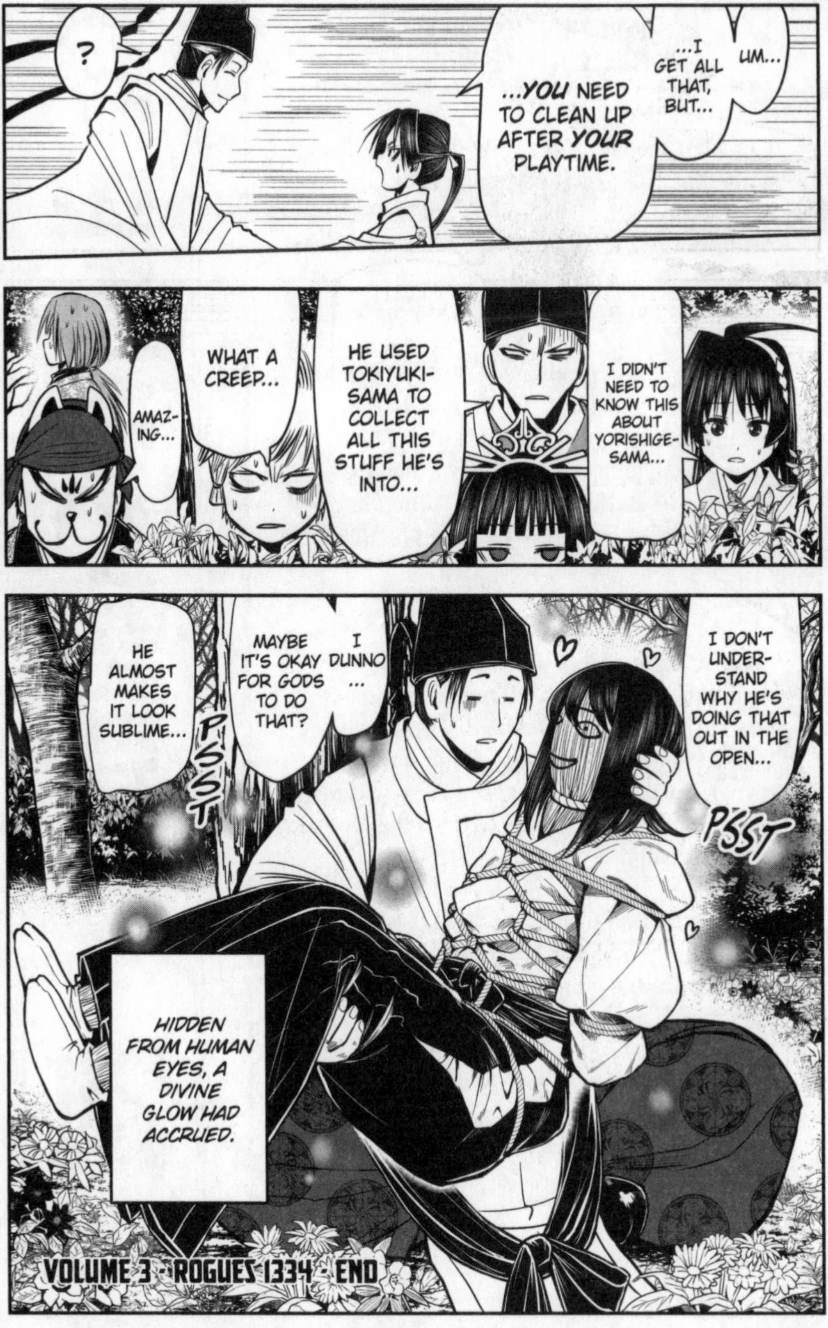
UM...
...I GET ALL THAT, BUT...
...YOU NEED TO CLEAN UP AFTER YOUR PLAYTIME.
?
I DIDN'T NEED TO KNOW THIS ABOUT YORISHIGE-SAMA...
HE USED TOKIYUKI-SAMA TO COLLECT ALL THIS STUFF HE'S INTO...
WHAT A CREEP...
AMAZ-ING...
I DON'T UNDER-STAND WHY HE'S DOING THAT OUT IN THE OPEN...
PSST
I DUNNO...
MAYBE IT'S OKAY FOR GODS TO DO THAT?
HE ALMOST MAKES IT LOOK SUBLIME...
PSST
HIDDEN FROM HUMAN EYES, A DIVINE GLOW HAD ACCRUED.
VOLUME 3 · ROGUES 1334 · END

duplicate

WERE THERE ANY RULES IN FIGHTS OVER TERRITORY?

Consider the word *tochigyō*. Today, it means something like "that particular time," "at one time," and "about that time," but in the Middle Ages, it meant "now." *Chigyō* means "ruling land." Thus, *tochigyō* means "currently ruling that land." Okay so far?

Now, suppose a problem arose with regard to a certain piece of land. Party A had documentation proving rights to the land dating back generations. Party B had driven out Party A and was currently ruling the land. That's *tochigyō*. Which do you think the shogunate would recognize as the owner?

Party A because it had documentation? No. It would recognize Party B, because Party B was currently ruling the land. The shogunate would say that made Party B the rightful owner. Furthermore, once someone had ruled a place for 20 years, their right to the land was rock-solid.

That's why Bandit Party C (like the Seigi Party) might take land by force. It would use violence to rule continuously and gain recognition as the rightful owner of the land. If it held it for 20 years, who could complain? But how would that work without it having any history, lineage, or proof? People could fake that stuff. In the Middle Ages, actions spoke louder than words.

THE ELUSIVE SAMURAI

INCREASE YOUR ENJOYMENT OF THIS MANGA BY LEARNING THE REAL HISTORY BEHIND IT!!

ANALYSIS
KAZUTO HONGO

WHAT WERE ROGUES [AKUTŌ] REALLY LIKE?

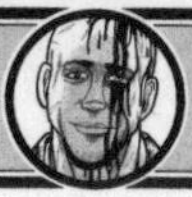

The *aku* in *akutō* means "bad." Of course, it had that meaning in the Kamakura period too, but it also meant "strong." For example, Minamoto no Yoritomo's older brother Minamoto no Yoshihira was called Akugenta. The brave man Ito Kagekiyo who served the Heike also had the name Akushichi Byoe. The bands of rogues who appeared across the land at the end of the Kamakura period weren't merely bad guys. They were both bad and strong.

The *bushi* affiliated with the shogunate were vassals to the shogun and called *gokenin*, which was a term of respect. Some bushi, however, did not belong to the shogunate. If you compare the early and late years of the Kamakura period, you can see that the effects of a monetary economy spread throughout Japan in the middle years, making the end of the period more prosperous. For that reason, there was more room in society for the rise of bushi who were not gokenin.

Some of them quickly adapted to economic circumstances, gathered wealth, turned violent, and attacked gokenin and their villages to steal even more wealth. The shogunate called such bushi *akutō* because they were troublesome and wouldn't obey. Some researchers believe the failure of the shogunate to quickly suppress the activities of the more active akutō was one factor leading to the government's collapse.

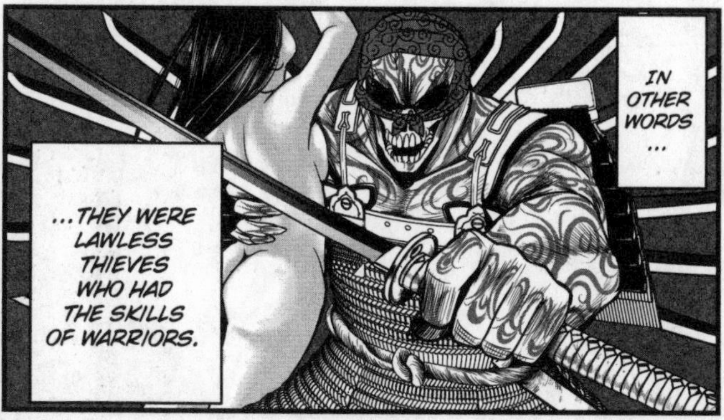
IN OTHER WORDS...
...THEY WERE LAWLESS THIEVES WHO HAD THE SKILLS OF WARRIORS.

*Adapted from material appearing in *Weekly Shonen Jump* issues 25 and 27–33/34

DID BUYING AND SELLING OF PEOPLE ACTUALLY HAPPEN?

In the Middle Ages, paper was highly valuable because it wasn't as easy to produce as it is now. That's why if you received a letter from someone, you didn't throw it away after reading it. You saved it and wrote on the white space on the back. So if you research sutras, you'll find letters about something completely different on the back.

Of course, people wouldn't reuse documents that were important evidence. They would keep documents about land forever and treat them as particularly important. But they would throw away documents about things that had broken or been used up, or they would write in the blank space on the back.

They actually included human beings among those things that broke or were used up, so no proof of buying and selling people remains on the fronts of documents. Researchers have found documentation of this by chance on the backs of sutras, however.

That's how we know for certain that the buying and selling of human beings occurred in the Kamakura period. The families on the losing side in war would be sold, and people would sell themselves if they couldn't pay back debts. The people sold would then save money to buy their freedom, but it's doubtful many of them were successful.

No matter how you look at it, anyone who buys and sells other people is a total villain.

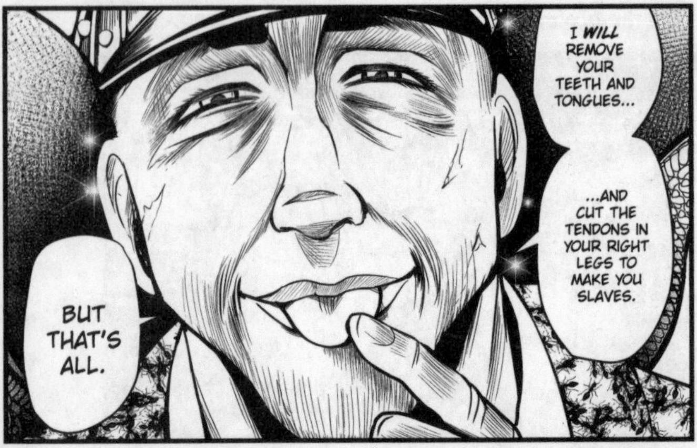
I *WILL* REMOVE YOUR TEETH AND TONGUES...
...AND CUT THE TENDONS IN YOUR RIGHT LEGS TO MAKE YOU SLAVES.
BUT THAT'S ALL.

DID COMMONERS EVER BECOME RETAINERS?

A long time ago, I was involved with a historical television drama titled *Taira no Kiyomori*. Historically, Kiyomori's foremost vassal, a man whose life developed alongside his own, was a bushi named Taira no Morikuni. The show's creators wanted to make him the son of a fisherman and asked me if that was all right. There are various theories about Morikuni's father, but it seems clear that he was a bushi, so at first I thought it might not be good to make him a fisherman. In the end, however, I gave approval because I remembered Sanchōtsubute no Kiheiji.

Chinzei Hachiro Tametomo was Minamoto Yoritomo's grandfather, the greatest archer in the land and a true hero. Someone who faithfully followed him was Sanchōtsubute no Kiheiji. He was Tametomo's confidant and even organized other bushi who were boastful of their skills. However, he may have been a commoner. It's possible that Kiheiji was a fictional creation, but he always shows up in stories of Tametomo, and there is no record of the people in bushi society who read those stories denying his existence. For that reason, I thought it would be interesting to make Morikuni a fisherman.

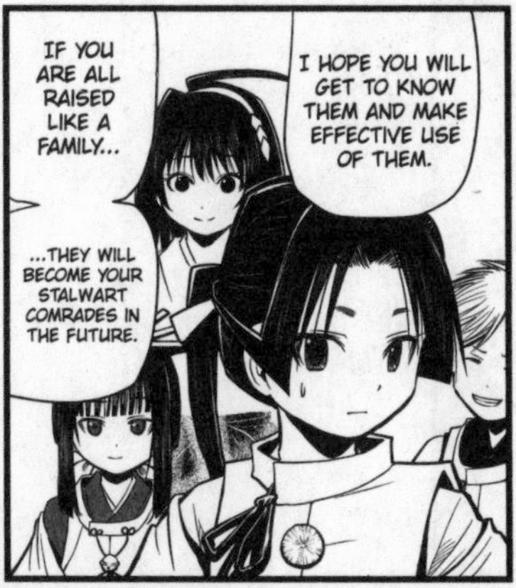
I HOPE YOU WILL GET TO KNOW THEM AND MAKE EFFECTIVE USE OF THEM.
IF YOU ARE ALL RAISED LIKE A FAMILY...
...THEY WILL BECOME YOUR STALWART COMRADES IN THE FUTURE.

In the Kamakura period, the bushi had vassals who would live and die alongside them, as Kiyomori had Morikuni, Tametomo had Kiheiji, and Minamoto no Yoshitomo (Yoritomo's father) had Kamata Masakiyo. They lived alongside each other from the time they were children, polished their combat skills, and grew together. Similarly, such comrades have gathered around Tokiyuki.

DID SOME PEOPLE BORN INTO BUSHI FAMILIES JOIN THE CLERGY?

To the bushi, family was important above all else. People didn't think much about individual rights, so instead of trying to have his children lead fulfilling lives, a father would prioritize the flourishing of the family. That's the first thing to keep in mind.

The second thing is the lack of land. From the Heian period to the Kamakura period, a little land remained that, with some work, could be cultivated. In the middle of the Kamakura period, however, that land disappeared.

For instance, suppose a certain bushi family had three sons. Until the early Kamakura period, it was possible to give land to each one. But as land grew scarce, that was no longer possible. If the father divided his land among all three, they would all be poor and fall to ruin. Considering this, a father would give most of his land to the eldest son and make the second eldest the first's vassal. That was for the good of the family. He would have the youngest leave home and join the clergy and venerate the family ancestors.

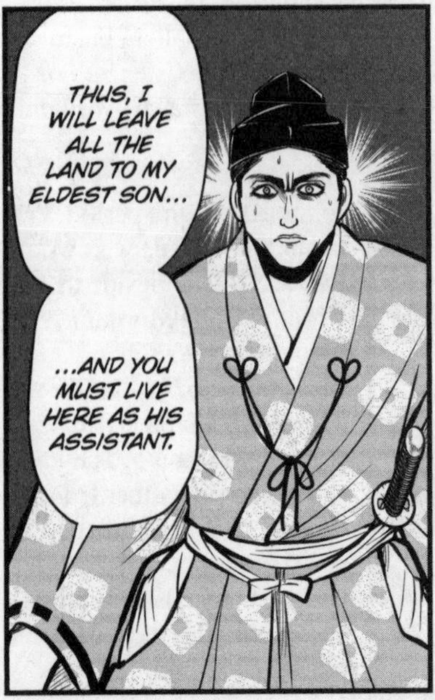
THUS, I WILL LEAVE ALL THE LAND TO MY ELDEST SON...
...AND YOU MUST LIVE HERE AS HIS ASSISTANT.

Thus, many who were born into bushi families had to join the ranks of the clergy.

HOW MUCH RICE DID PEOPLE EAT?

What were people's rice-eating habits like? There isn't much documentation about it. However, it's certain that the bushi generally didn't have much to eat. Side dishes were incredibly scarce—so scarce that they might even serve vinegar.

Tokiyuki's grandfather's grandfather was a wise ruler named Hojo Tokiyori. He summoned his vassals in the middle of the night to drink and talk but noticed he didn't have any snacks. A vassal, having searched the kitchen, brought some miso paste. That was just fine, so everyone was overjoyed. The *Tsurezuregusa* contains that story.

That's how it was for a top guy in the shogunate. The highest vassals were also probably able to eat rice, but it must have been a treat. Thus, the custom was to eat white rice on the side, and to really stuff themselves when they did. One of the three major diseases at the time was beriberi. Eating all that white rice led to vitamin deficiencies and beriberi, which caused the whole body to swell, leading to death. This afflicted both the nobility and the bushi. White rice must have tasted divine.

Judging from that, we can surmise that the common people were rarely able to eat rice. They probably ate other grains, including foxtail millet and Japanese barnyard millet. In the Tsugaru region during the Edo period, when farmers were dying, people would fill a small bag with rice and shake it beside the dying person's ears as a kind of symbolic feast. But the dying didn't get to eat it! The people around their deathbed just made noise with it. That was the most farmers could do. It's doubtful that agrarian villages were any different in the Kamakura period.

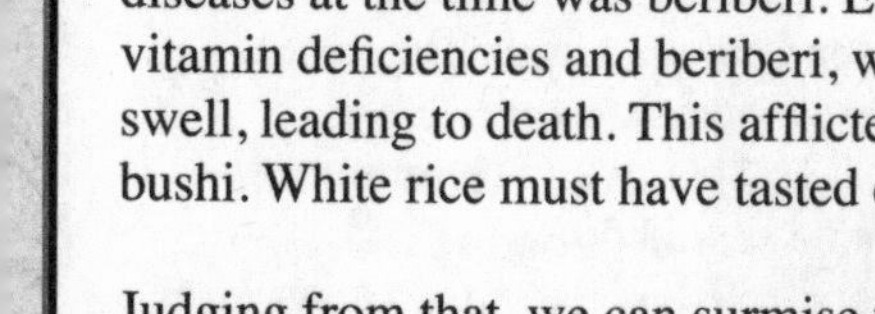

DID PEOPLE TREAT THE SUPERNATURAL AS REAL?

In the Heian era, the upper crust of society believed in Shingon Esoteric Buddhism. This religious sect believed that participating in certain rituals (called *kaji-kitō*) could allow followers to witness many mysterious phenomena. People believed that if good gods existed, then bad demons must also exist.

However, the words of an *imayō* (folk song) toward the end of the Heian period contain the following: "Hotoke wa tsune ni imasedomo utsutsu naranuzo awarenaru." This translates to "The Buddha is always present but is not visible in this world, which is of immense value." Think about this song... Don't you think it sounds like people were beginning to doubt the existence of Buddha?

Some very logical people appeared among the intellectual nobility of the Kamakura period. One example was grand minister Tokudaiji Sanemoto. The story goes that the retired emperor was informed that when land was cleared to erect a separate residence for the retired emperor, everyone was surprised to discover a mass of serpents. When the retired emperor asked Sanemoto what he should do, Sanemoto replied, "Creatures living on land ruled by the emperor would not curse the emperor, so catch them and dispose of them." Thus, no harm resulted.

A skilled noble named Hino Suketomo attended Emperor Go-Daigo. Upon seeing an old clergyman with a bent back, minister of the interior Saionji said, "Aw, how venerable," with a show of emotion, to which Hino replied, "He's just old." Later, however, Hino sent the Saionji residence a feeble, shaggy dog, saying, "Indeed, it appears venerable."

In any case, some dedicated realists were appearing in the Kamakura period, leaving no room for the appearance of monsters. Thus, tales of supernatural creatures dwindled in the Muromachi period.

HOW FAST WERE PEOPLE DEVELOPING THE LAND?

There aren't any records directly pertaining to this, so I don't know. That's the honest truth, but it's kind of boring, so I'll scrape together information from other documentation to work something out.

Noto Peninsula was once called Noto Province. Its crop yield was approximately 200,000 *koku* (approx. 30 million kg) at the beginning and end of the Edo period. In other words, at the beginning of the Edo period, development had stalled. Thanks to a document titled *Shūkaishō*, we know that the total number of fields at the end of the Heian period was 8,500 *chō* (approx. 84 million m^2).

Now looking at agricultural data from the Edo period, it appears that cultivating a 1-*tan* (approx. 992 m^2) field produced 1 koku (approx. 150 kg) of rice. Relying on that data, we can estimate that if 1 chō (approx. 9,915 m^2) was approximately 10 tan (9,920 m^2), then 1 chō produced 10 koku (1,500 kg). Thus, the 200,000 koku at the beginning of the Edo period signifies a number of fields equaling 20,000 chō (198 million m^2). The Heian period ended at about the year 1200 and the Edo period started at about 1600, with the Kamakura period ending at about 1300. If we assume that development proceeded at a steady pace for the 400 years from the Heian period to the Edo period and assign the end point (full development in the year 1600) a value of 10, then the end of the Heian period has a value of 4.25, and the time in question, the end of the Kamakura period, is 5.6. In other words, about half of the land was developed with nearly half left undeveloped. In any case, there's a rough number to go by.

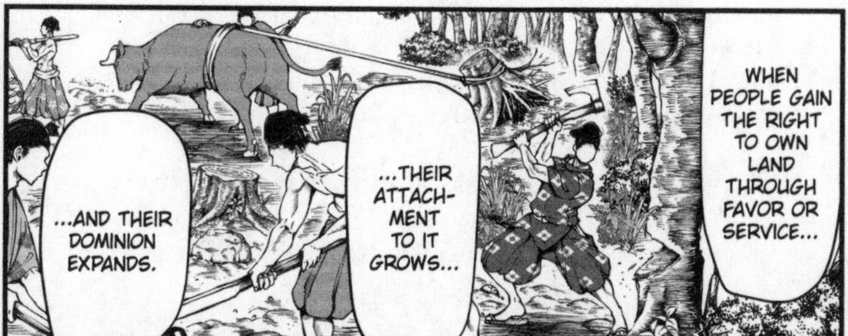
WHEN PEOPLE GAIN THE RIGHT TO OWN LAND THROUGH FAVOR OR SERVICE...
...THEIR ATTACHMENT TO IT GROWS...
...AND THEIR DOMINION EXPANDS.

SPECIAL THANKS

I borrow a lot of people's talents for *The Elusive Samurai*.

PRODUCTION STAFF
TEI ASHIGAKI
His series Make Heroine wo Katasetai!
(I Want to Make the Losing Heroine Win!) began on Jump+ in January 2022!
DAISUKE ENOSHIMA
SAKUJU KOIZUMI
WAHARE KOYOI
KEIJI INOUE
SHINJI WADA

They help me create the art. They're my Kamakura warriors
who're almighty in drawing what I want.

EDITOR
RIKI AZUMA
He's an editor for *Weekly Shonen Jump*. He's from a high-class upbringing,
so he's got a taste for fine food despite being so young.

GRAPHIC NOVEL EDITOR
SATOSHI WATANABE
He handles stuff related to the graphic novel, and he's got really thin legs.

DESIGNER
YUKI MATSUMOTO (BANANA GROVE STUDIO)
She's in charge of the logo and design for the graphic novel.
She's a licensed art curator.